LANDSCAPE AND ENGLISHNESS

'*Landscape and Englishness* is an essential read for anyone interested in why some kinds of interaction with nature are celebrated and others are frowned on. Drawing on a huge diversity of sources – books, films, preservationist tracts, walking guides, novels, music-hall songs, Ministry of Information pamphlets, maps and festival guides – Matless reveals how our assumptions about landscape and national identity were forged in the decades between the Great War and the 1950s, and how deeply they've been shaped by history, class and politics . . . a revelation.'
– Helen Macdonald, *The Guardian*

'cultural history at its best, subtle, multi-layered and full of new ideas and insights . . . this book is a "must".'
– *Contemporary British History*

'creates a convincing portrait of the changing meanings of the English landscape in the twentieth century.'
– *Times Literary Supplement*

'The best book so far on the interpretation of landscape in the middle years of the twentieth century.'
– *The Architects' Journal*, Books of the Year

'a richly informative text for historians of all kinds, especially those concerned with planning and the visual arts in the twentieth century.'
– *Twentieth Century British History*

Titles in the *Oxford Landmark Science* series

'Engrossing and important'
– *Architectural Review*

'absorbing, thorough, detailed and very substantial ... *Landscape and Englishness* is representative of the best of the expanding literature of cultural and historical geography and has much to offer design historians looking at the forces of tradition and modernity, preservation and progress and the city and the countryside.'
– *Journal of Design History*

'This book makes a substantial contribution to current work on the construction and representation of English national identity in the twentieth century ... Matless' great skill [is] the ability to marshal complex, detailed historical sources and weave a compelling narrative from them.'
– *Geographical Journal*

'An extensively illustrated academic study, a thought-provoking guide and reference book.'
– *Landscape and Art*

Landscape and Englishness

SECOND EXPANDED EDITION

David Matless

REAKTION BOOKS

To my parents, Brian and Audrey Matless

Published by Reaktion Books Ltd
Unit 32, Waterside
44–48 Wharf Road
London N1 7UX, UK
www.reaktionbooks.co.uk

First published 1998
Second expanded edition published 2016

Printed and bound in Great Britain by CPI Group (UK) Ltd, Croydon CR0 4YY

A catalogue record for this book is available from the British Library

ISBN 978 1 78023 581 3

Contents

Passport to Plenty:
Preface to the 2016 Edition

Landscape and Englishness was written towards the end of the last century, and published in 1998. This preface to the 2016 edition reflects on things since. The text and images of the original book are unchanged, save for the correction of minor factual and typographical errors, but republication may usefully be framed by consideration of cultural and political developments taking Englishness and landscape into the twenty-first century. This preface offers a guide to the past two decades; there have been continuities, convulsions and surprises.

Passports Green and Pleasant, Politics Feeling Blue

In 2015 I renewed my UK passport, needed in case of travel. The blank pages showed the 2010 redesign, the formerly plain state overtaken by landscape scenes. Pictures of complex grain are there in part to hamper forgers, but also set out a cultural geography. Pages turn to show reedbeds, coasts, canals, mountains, village greens. Here are landscape types, based on identifiable spots around the four constituent parts of the United Kingdom. There is a fishing village, but not a city in sight; nor a factory, an office, a retail park, a motorway. The UK is not short of urban, industrial and commercial icons, which might be made equally unforgeable, but here is what might seem an official statement of, and deliberate revelling in, the mythic qualities of rural landscape, which in all corners of the UK have served to symbolize and refract national identity. The longstanding and complex nature of this work of landscape is the subject of *Landscape and Englishness*.

If my passport's green and pleasant, the twenty-first century has seen heightened state preoccupations with migration, and with eligibility to work and belong. The free movement of labour in an expanded European Union, and Islamist conflict within and beyond the UK, have made 'border control' a political issue to a degree not anticipated in 1998, longstanding questions of Englishness and ethnicity taking another turn. The row of country cottages pictured beneath the passport statement that 'Her Britannic Majesty's Secretary of State Requests and requires' free movement of the bearer is shadowed by state efforts to deny movement to others. Here is the latest hard edge to English pastoral; *Landscape and Englishness* highlighted a number of earlier variants, and one could also revisit Tom Nairn's 1977 analysis of Enoch Powell, English nationalism and race, which draws attention to Powell's pastoral poetry in the mode of A. E. Housman, babbling brooks feeding rivers of blood.[1] In the twenty-first century, immigration became a renewed and newly brutal focal point for national argument, with some attempting movement dying in passage. Freight lorries may bypass the village, with who knows who hidden away. In migration a green and pleasant passport may be the goal, a document of recognition for those seeking, if not to toast the Queen, then to make some better life. Those already resident give a varied response; rejection, open arms, welcome in, wary sympathy.

An officially open UK was offered to the world in 2012, and landscape again shaped national narrative. The opening of the London Olympics broadcast the nation, Danny Boyle and Frank Cottrell Boyce devising a widely acclaimed ceremony. Opening scenes offered a rural country, with a hill evoking part Glastonbury Tor, part J.R.R. Tolkien's Shire; indeed the set bore a striking resemblance to Tolkien's own colour drawings of Hobbiton, a vision of

England itself gone global via Peter Jackson's film trilogy of *The Lord of the Rings* of 2001–3. The ceremony set then transformed to industry, chimneys and furnaces rising, the UK leading the world into one kind of 'revolution' if not others, before progressing to the welfare state, dancing nurses hymning the National Health Service (and leading some commentators on the right to label the ceremony politically left-wing). The industrial Olympic pageantry was informed by documentary film-maker Humphrey Jennings's compilation *Pandaemonium, 1660–1886: The Coming of the Machine as seen by Contemporary Observers*, reissued in 2012 with a foreword by Frank Cottrell Boyce. Jennings's compilation had begun as a series of talks in South Wales, where he had shot *The Silent Village* (1943). Cottrell Boyce commented: 'Who could ever have foretold that a series of talks given in a miners' institute seventy years ago would form the backbone of a massive global media event of the age – watched, tweeted, favourited, streamed by billions of people across the planet?'[2] On a more modest scale, *Landscape and Englishness* (effectively a pre-digital book, in its style and research method) sought in different fashion to make earlier, often forgotten cultural material spark back to the present.

If the organizational structures of Olympic sport demanded a UK ceremony for an event with a UK team, and thus necessitated an inclusive geography across Great Britain and Northern Ireland, English iconography played its prominent part. The 2012 ceremony, like the 2010 passport, negotiated sometimes awkward relationships of Englishness and Britishness, but it is striking how since 1998 a range of works have addressed Englishness directly, as an identity needing attention in its own right. Thus in the early 2000s the UK Labour government commissioned 'Icons: A Portrait of England', via the Department of Culture, Media and Sport's 'Culture Online'.[3] 'Icons' offered symbols for a multicultural, pluralist and open-minded country, proud of many pasts and open to the world, with its dozen opening selections ranging over times, places and people: Stonehenge, 'Jerusalem', Holbein's portrait of Henry VIII, the King

James Bible, ss *Empire Windrush*, Punch and Judy, the Angel of the North, the FA Cup, a cup of tea, Alice in Wonderland, the Spitfire, the Routemaster Bus. The last would make a global appearance at the closing ceremony of the 2008 Olympics in Beijing, with a waving London mayor, Boris Johnson, ushering the world on to 2012. The national flag, despite its wider public appearance following the European Football Championships in England in 1996, did not make the list.

Englishness also became a minor publishing phenomenon, launched by Jeremy Paxman's *The English* in 1999. The too-many-to-mention Englishness books include Robert Colls's *The Identity of England* (2002), Krishan Kumar's *The Making of English National Identity* (2003), and Andy Medhurst's telling study of English comedy, *A National Joke* (2007).[4] Reissues of earlier analyses have followed, including in 2009 Patrick Wright's *On Living in an Old Country* (1985) and *A Journey through Ruins* (1991), and in 2014 Colls and Philip Dodd's edited collection *Englishness: Politics and Culture, 1880–1920* (1986).[5] *Landscape and Englishness* sustains this reissue trend, suggesting that twentieth-century analyses might still gain traction today. A notable twenty-first-century extension of late twentieth-century landscape commentary has also come from the film-maker Patrick Keiller, whose 'Robinson' trilogy, beginning with *London* (1994) and *Robinson in Space* (1997), was completed in 2010 with *Robinson in Ruins*, a cinematic meditation on questions of land, history, property, nature and state through southern Midland English landscape, with Keiller's stated aim 'to promote political and economic change by developing the transformative potential of images of landscape'.[6]

In 2000 I reviewed the upsurge in commentary on Englishness for, appropriately, the *Scottish Geographical Journal*. It was apparent that, politically, Englishness was moving all ways; indeed this seemed in part to define its 'predicament'.[7] From the right it could serve as conservative bulwark against the progressive and/or cosmopolitan, and a cornerstone of Britishness against Europe; or could appear a cultural formation nostalgically holding back the country from an entrepreneurial future. From the left, Englishness could seem a force of conservatism and insularity out of step with a modern global world, or offer a reservoir of subversive outlooks to counter centralizing powers. Reference could be made here to John Fowles's 1964 essay 'On Being English But Not British', with its distinction of a 'Green England' and 'Red-White-and-Blue Britain', setting the subversions of the greenwood against the power of empire, Robin Hood against John Bull, distinctions perhaps too easily missing the complicities of English/British strands.[8] Paxman indeed ended *The English* by musing on a return to 'the green of England' after the 'flags and anthems' of Britishness: 'It is modest, individualistic, ironic, solipsistic, concerned as much with cities and regions as with counties and countries. It is based on values that are so deeply embedded in the culture as to be almost unconscious. In an age of decaying nation states it might be the nationalism of the future.'[9]

Whether England is understood as the dominant cornerstone of Britain-as-world-power, or something modestly standing alone, connects to two matters of neighbourly political geography. Scotland and Europe put England in question in the late twentieth century, and continue to do so. In the 2015 general election the 'nationalism of the future' appeared to be a Scottish one, even if the September 2014 referendum on Scottish independence had returned a 55 per cent 'No' vote for remaining within the United Kingdom. The distinctive nationalism driving the 'Yes' campaign, presenting itself as civic, forward-looking, driven by three decades of cultural invention, and anything but jingoistic and exclusionary, kept its momentum, and the 2015 general election result, returning Scottish National Party MPs for the vast majority of Scottish Westminster seats, sustained this political and cultural shift. The decision of David Cameron as UK prime minister to use the immediate aftermath of the Scottish referendum to foreground questions of English political representation may have helped this along. The Conservative general election campaign was also notable for its appeal to English voters through anxieties over Scottish influence at Westminster, an ostensibly Unionist party playing off intra-Union nationalisms for short-term political advantage. The question of Englishness now rumbles in Westminster. Some itch to assert an English nationalism over the SNP, others see only constitutional confusion and hope for the long grass of a parliamentary commission. If constitutional logic suggests that a full English parliament may be the answer, this may be to presume a political interest in constitutional logic, and the possibilities of a lasting federal settlement in a union of such unequal parts.

If the question of English representation may not easily be resolved, it might provide the spark for a further Scottish referendum. Europe may also speed the process, should the UK vote to leave the European Union in the coming referendum on membership, yet the majority in Scotland vote to remain. The 'No' campaign to leave the EU will be driven in part by the UK Independence Party, whose persona, not least through its dominant figure Nigel Farage, trades on Englishness, indeed on the idea of England as a trading nation needing only to be set free of supra-national bureaucracy, UKIP takes Englishness to the political right, and one reading of the 2015 general election could be that England as a country responds, with Conservative values (and votes) predominant. If the outcome of the subsequent Labour Party leadership election surprised many, it left unresolved the question of how Labour might again speak across England. The English polity is cut across by complex fault-lines of liberalism and conservatism, tolerance and anxiety, individualism and patriotism, and one of the themes of *Landscape and Englishness* is to trace the genealogy of these through landscape, whether through the collectivist politics of war and post-war reconstruction, or the aggressively exclusive versions of Englishness informing some interwar commentary. The complexity of the story suggests however that Englishness has the capacity to migrate across the political spectrum, with the challenge for political imagination, of whatever party, being to articulate an apt language.

To give one example from English socialist history, here is Edward Carpenter in his *Towards Democracy* of 1883. After several pages evoking England's geography ('England spreads like a map below me . . .'), its cities and country, factories and coasts, palaces and cottages, seas and land, Carpenter reflects:

> I see a great land poised as in a dream – waiting for the word by which it may live again.
>
> I see the stretched sleeping figure – waiting for the kiss and the re-awakening.
>
> I hear the bells pealing, and the crash of hammers, and see beautiful parks spread – as in toy show.
>
> I see a great land waiting for its own people to come and take possession of it.[10]

The following hundred years would show the partial realization or continuing frustration of such left-wing landscaped visions, whether Carpenter's nature socialism or a Fabian vision of state planning. *Landscape and Englishness* sought to chart such political landscapes, and they remain open for development, conservation or reclamation.

Attention to Landscape: Modern, Sonic and Green

As Englishness has been reflected upon and reshaped since *Landscape and Englishness* was first published, so new emphases have emerged in work on landscape, notably around the modern and the natural, and in fields of music.

Landscape and Englishness was concerned in part to excavate a conjunction of Englishness and modernism, undercutting assumptions that English landscape necessarily tends towards nostalgia by highlighting the modern in the country as well as the city.[11] At the same time as the book was being prepared, the story of landscape and the modern took a twist with the emergence of modernism *as* heritage. Andrew Saint's 1992 English Heritage publication *A Change of Heart: English Architecture since the War, a Policy for Protection*, registered modernism as a matter of historic concern.[12] This was partly a matter of preserving buildings designed by key architectural figures, as in the National Trust's 1992 purchase of 2 Willow Road, Hampstead, designed in 1939 by Ernö Goldfinger. There was also however a wider social narrative at work. Saint was known for his work on the 'social architecture' of post-war school buildings, questions of style and politics interweaving in architectural commentary.[13] The valuing of modernism could also uphold social democracy.

Gathering modernism into the frame of national heritage challenged conventional understandings of both. As Nigel Whiteley put it in relation to Willow Road: 'Could it be that modernism is now being repositioned as a part of our national heritage? – a move that, one suspects, would not find wide support amongst the majority of the Trust's membership.'[14] The ascription of heritage value to modernism is due in part to the work of the Twentieth Century Society, founded as the Thirties Society in 1979, and renamed in 1992, who have lobbied for the listing of key structures. The Twentieth Century Society fosters a popular appreciation of buildings and designs which in the 1970s and '80s were often labelled as ugly and somehow un-English, with the Prince of Wales reprising language laid down by John Betjeman from the 1960s to damn modernism. *Landscape and Englishness* indeed sought to show the historical complexity of relationships between Englishness and the modern, and to challenge the assumption that those concerned for Englishness had been unconcerned for, or hostile to, modernism. In 2001 the fiftieth anniversary of Nikolaus Pevsner's first county guides to the 'Buildings of England' brought renewed attention to one who sought to make modernism and Englishness converse, with Pevsner himself instrumental in the early listing of modern buildings.[15] A work such as Pevsner's 1945 King Penguin book on *The Leaves of Southwell*, a study of the medieval stone carvings in the

Nottinghamshire Minster chapter house, turns out to tell a story of naturalism and the modern, local craft and international aesthetics, Englishness and the European. A quiet corner of Midland England shelters progressive Europe: 'the leaves of Southwell assume a new significance as one of the purest symbols surviving in Britain of Western thought, our thought, in its loftiest mood.'[16]

A Change of Heart could laud, alongside modern factories, churches and the then quiet Bankside power station (now Tate Modern), the central square of Stevenage new town. In such citation more is conjured than architectural style, and work in a range of fields since the 1990s has evoked post-war modernity as something of fascination and value. The paintings of George Shaw, for example, revisit, sometimes in watercolour, more commonly in Humbrol enamel, the Midland working-class suburban settings of the mid- to late twentieth century; modest semi-detached, lock-up garage, tended garden, marginal wood. Shaw works his own biography, growing up in Tile Hill in Coventry, into an allegorical memorialization of an age, the enamel paints of his childhood rendering an English suburban masculinity in domestic and public landscapes. In a talk in Nottingham in 2010 Shaw evoked a series of iconic Englishmen, writers, comedians and musicians: Tony Hancock, Philip Larkin, The Specials, L. S. Lowry, Thomas Hardy, The Smiths, Les Dawson, John Constable, *The Likely Lads*. Figures from the twentieth century and before are carried forward. Shaw also noted inspiration from the French novelist and essayist Georges Perec, with his attention to 'species of spaces', the mundane and the 'infra-ordinary'. Common sensing and careful thought shape Shaw's extraordinary renditions of everyday landscapes more often demeaned.[17]

The political orientation of commentary on the post-war modern tends to be centre-left, looking back to a social democratic moment from a later twentieth or early twenty-first century overhung by Thatcherite values. There is also nostalgia for a past confidence in the future, for scientific and space-age novelty, and intrigue over an era achieving generational distance yet newly accessible through digital technology. Such sensibilities register in music, with a retro-futurism manifest in enthusiasm for bodies such as the BBC Radiophonic Workshop, and for other early electronica. In the twenty-first century the Ghost Box record label, established in 2004, has been adept at conjuring lost past futures, with, for example, Belbury Poly's 2006 album *The Owl's Map* framed by extracts from a 'Field Guide to British Towns and Villages' on the market town of Belbury, with hill forts and stone circles alongside 'some notable modernist architecture including the Polytechnic College, Public Library and the striking Community Fellowship Church'.[18] The kind of books featured in the later chapters of *Landscape and Englishness* resurface in new music. In May 2008 I was contacted by Antony Harding of July Skies, purveyors of gentle musical experiment, noting that *Landscape and Englishness* had 'assisted with the inspiration' for their album *The Weather Clock*, and its associated EP, compositions invoking a post-war pastoral modernity of school buildings, schools broadcasting and new towns. Indicative titles include 'Broadcasts for Autumn Term', 'See Britain By Train (Pevsner Version)', 'Festival of Britain', 'Distant Showers Sweep Across Norfolk Schools' and 'Harlow'.[19]

Twentieth-century Englands have also registered through the music of British Sea Power. On their 2003 debut album *The Decline of British Sea Power* (reissued in 2015), the coastal themes of songs such as 'Fear of Drowning' and 'Carrion' play on maritime England. Performance warm-up music at that time included John Betjeman's 1970s LPs, with the poet reading over music by Jim Parker. In 2012 British Sea Power provided a soundtrack to Penny Woolcock's film *From the Sea to the Land Beyond*, an evocation of the British coast through archival footage, issued by the British Film Institute, the title a line from the band's 2005 song 'The Land Beyond'. The sleeve of the early nuclear-tinged single 'Childhood Memories' took its font and layout from the Collins series of 'Britain in Pictures' books issued during and after the Second World War. Glancing over the many titles of that series, *Landscape and Englishness* turns out to feature the authors of 21: *British Farm Stock, English Country Houses, British Craftsmen, British Rebels and Reformers, English Farming, British Furniture Makers, English Cities and Small Towns, British Botanists, English Public Schools, The Story of Scotland, The English People, British Photographers, English Cottages and Farmhouses, Wild Life of Britain, English Gardens, The British Theatre, Life Among the English, British Romantic Artists, Wild Flowers in Britain, English Villages, Birds of Britain.* Here are books and authors of varied outlook, from the far-right Earl of Portsmouth (*Farm Stock*) and his fellow organicist Kinship in Husbandry member Edmund Blunden (*Villages*), to progressives James Fisher (*Birds*) and Harry Roberts (*Rebels and Reformers, Gardens*). George Orwell covered *English People*, Betjeman *Cities and Small Towns*. Political cross-currents flow through such cultural references.[20]

How do pasts speak through landscape? Why do things made at one time register in another? The Ghost Box aesthetic is in part, as the name suggests, one of haunting, of spectres from other historical and/or spiritual realms returning, bidden or unbidden, today. As mention of Belbury hill forts and stone circles indicates, there is also an evocation of the ancient and pagan, in keeping with longstanding cultural concerns for what John Lowerson termed 'The Mystical Geography of the English'.[21] Musical mystical geographies have been tracked by Rob Young in *Electric Eden* (2010), where Britain's 'visionary music', classical, popular and unpopular, resurfaces, in part in response to a twenty-first-century upsurge in experimental interest in things folk.[22] Here is the latest redirection of the term 'folk', whether in the efforts of the English Folk Dance and Song Society (EFDSS) to make early twentieth-century folk song collectors' work available online via 'The Full English: Unlocking Hidden Treasures of England's Cultural Heritage', in the resurgence of interest in twentieth-century singers such as Shirley Collins, or in the work of those seeing folk sources as the basis for contemporary experiment.[23] Scotland offers a parallel here, notably in the work of singer Alasdair Roberts, whose diligent regard for traditional song shapes invention. In East Anglia the violin and recorder player Laura Cannell makes equivalent novel play with tradition.[24] One might also look to unlikely folk histories, beyond those registered in 'The Full English'. If the EFDSS provides access to several versions of the song 'Strawberry Fair' ('As I was going to Strawberry Fair / Singing, singing, buttercups and daisies'), including those published by the late nineteenth- and early twentieth-century collector Revd Sabine Baring-Gould, there is no place for perhaps the most heard twentieth-century version, Anthony Newley's No. 3 hit record of 1960, the tune turned to up-tempo pop, the lyrics starting out faithful to folk but gathering current vernacular as they roll along. Newley's London showbiz voice gives folk variety twists: 'I want a girl with a generous heart / Singing, singing, buttercups and oojahs'. In the same year as 'Strawberry Fair', ITV screened Newley's extraordinary television series *The Strange World of Gurney Slade*, subverting televisual conventions almost before they had been established, Newley's title character treating peak-time viewers to park-bench surrealism and, in the third episode, set in the country, hum-duetting 'Greensleeves' with a scarecrow.[25] Another episode includes a performance of 'Strawberry Fair'. A capacious and 'full' tracing of Englishness should embrace such sonic varieties.

In 2015 Robert Macfarlane identified an emergent twenty-first-century English 'eerie counter-culture', taking in music, cinema, photography and drama, such as Jez Butterworth's 2009 play *Jerusalem*, bringing the rough magic of Wiltshire woods to the West End stage.[26] One could also note that longstanding ITV exploration of eerie death, class, sexuality, woodland magic and general rural goings-on *Midsomer Murders*, running through Chiltern settings since 1997, with theme and soundtrack by Betjeman collaborator Jim Parker, and sold for broadcast around the world – Englishness popular in export. Such works reflect and help constitute a cultural braiding of the Green, a theme noted at the conclusion of *Landscape and Englishness*. From the 1970s and '80s natural history writers such as Richard Mabey and organizations such as the environmental charity Common Ground have made concern for nature cultural. Mabey's work continues to be crucial here; as he put it in 1980 in his *The Common Ground* when discussing nature conservation, 'always the argument ends with questions of value and meaning which, like all such questions, can only be answered in a social context by a continuing *cultural* debate.'[27] While Green concerns are often assumed to align the local and the global, Green Englishness has not been neglected. Mabey sets his work in the observational, quizzical tradition of the eighteenth-century naturalist Gilbert White, with virtues found in the close scrutiny of local territory, and scientific understanding and emotional attachment intermingled. Mabey's *Flora Britannica* (1996) inaugurated a genre of books on the cultural place of fauna and flora, while Sue Clifford and Angela King of Common Ground developed their earlier projects for 'Local Distinctiveness' and 'Parish Maps' via the 2006 magnum opus *England in Particular*, an alphabetic 'celebration of the commonplace, the local, the vernacular and the distinctive'.[28] One of Common Ground's early collaborators, on the 'Orchards' project which led to their launch in 1990 of an annual October 'Apple Day', was James Ravilious, who photographed West Country orchards to support their campaign. Ravilious's Devon-based photography was exhibited in 1998 under the heading *An English Eye*, Common Ground's commitment to locality being matched by Ravilious in his 'Beaford Archive', rural documentary photographic work producing 80,000 images of one corner of Devon, a vernacular landscape record.[29]

A full cultural history and geography of such work remains to be written. The 'Green' works most fully considered in *Landscape and Englishness* were those of early organic farming, around the Second World War, and Philip Conford has since produced authoritative accounts of the organic movement's origins and twentieth-century development.[30] Recent Green Englands, like those of the early organic movement, are shaped by particular geographical imaginations concerning nation, region and locality. In 2008 the environmental campaigner and novelist Paul Kingsnorth published *Real England*, a call to cultural authenticity ranging over country and city, orchards and beer, canals and shops, with a plea for 'a new type of patriotism, benign and positive, based on place not race, geography not biology'.[31] Kingsnorth seeks to counter exclusive versions of nationhood based on race with an inclusive and radical sense of place. His 2014 novel *The Wake* may be seen as a parallel working of cultural geography, via a Fenland Norman Conquest tale of Anglo-Saxon resistance to new state power, rendered in Middle English-ish prose.[32] In an essay of 2015 Kingsnorth called for the political left to rediscover an 'ecological Englishness', and identified 'a tentative sense of a renewed cultural Englishness beginning to creep into the light': 'If a nation is a relationship between people and place, then a cultural identity that comes from a careful relationship with that place might be a new story worth telling.'[33]

If Englishness has offered publishers a niche theme for the twenty-first century, nature has become a richer seam. Natural history, nature memoir and topographic cultural history have found popular readership, with authors such as Mabey, Helen Macdonald, Robert Macfarlane and Mark Cocker renewing what was assumed to be a dormant literary field.[34] Such nature voices vary in their literary models, their understanding of the natural world and their authorial self-styling, but all follow Mabey's injunction that the natural be cultural, and examine the enfolding of nature and identity. What emerges is close attention to the nonhuman world, and to the ways in which humans shape themselves through it. Place is also emphasized, writers such as Cocker and Tim Dee examining specific regions of nature in East Anglia.[35] Nature writing here becomes a story of regional cultural landscape, connecting with other strands of regional topographic work such as Nick Papadimitriou's 2012 exploration of the Middlesex–Hertfordshire border upland, *Scarp*, where a form of 'Deep Topography' is shaped through geographic entities such as escarpment and county, or Ken Worpole and Jason Orton's study of Essex, *The New English Landscape*: 'Lofty statements on the true and the beautiful are increasingly resisted as the particularities and historical complexities of local and regional topographies . . . are evaluated anew.'[36] *Landscape and Englishness* offers a genealogy of such topographic and natural historic themes, not least in the way in which different geographic scales – local, regional, global, parochial – fashion national stories. Twenty-first-century works, whether on the natural, the Green, the folk or the modern, continue to play out such cultural geographies.

Plenty to Mine

In 1976, at the University of California, Berkeley, the Irish poet Seamus Heaney reflected on 'Englands of the Mind', finding in the poetry of W. H. Auden, Geoffrey Hill and Philip Larkin a mid-twentieth-century looking 'in, rather than up to, England'. In Heaney's appreciation, 'The loss of imperial power, the failure of economic nerve, the diminished influence of Britain inside Europe, all this has led to a new sense of the shires, a new valuing of the native English experience.'[37] Heaney's 1970s diagnosis chimes with aspects of twenty-first-century England, as does that of the Scottish writer Tom Nairn, whose 1977 *The Break-Up of Britain*, written alongside earlier devolutionary debates, suggested: 'the English need to rediscover who and what they are, to re-invent an identity of some sort better than the battered cliché-ridden hulk which the retreating tide of imperialism has left them.'[38] Rediscovery creeps on, and the works discussed here might perhaps accelerate a response. Is there a grain of material here to parallel thirty years of Scottish cultural work, following Alasdair Gray's 1984 call: 'Work as if you live in the early days of a better nation'?[39] This may be a fanciful thought, with no parallel political project of independence from a dominant power; although UKIP might see the EU referendum that way. There are at least however cultural complexities to quarry, richer than sometimes allowed, which might variously appeal and appal; treasure chests, cans of worms, orchards and murders, strawberries and cream, buttercups and oojahs. *Landscape and Englishness* explored such complexities in 1998, and these have not diminished since. If something must be made of Englishness, there is plenty to mine.

Introduction: Versions of Landscape and Englishness

We should not be deceived into thinking that this heritage is an acquisition, a possession that grows and solidifies; rather, it is an unstable assemblage of faults, fissures and heterogeneous layers that threaten the fragile inheritor from within or underneath ... The search for descent is not the erecting of foundations: on the contrary, it disturbs what was previously considered immobile; it fragments what was thought unified; it shows the heterogeneity of what was imagined consistent with itself. What convictions and, far more decisively, what knowledge can resist it?
MICHEL FOUCAULT, 'Nietzsche, Genealogy, History', 1971[1]

Norfolk is the most suspicious county in England.
H. V. MORTON, *In Search of England*, 1927[2]

A Norfolk Story

Visitors to Potter Heigham always come across something interesting: gifts, boats for hire, books of local interest, multicoloured rock with the place-name through it, pleasant activities. Here, on the lower reaches of the River Thurne on the Norfolk Broads, can be found 'inns, hotels, shops, boatyards and every facility for the holiday-maker',[3] or indeed the casual day visitor. A medieval stone bridge humps over the river, narrow enough to demand lights to marshal the road traffic, and low enough to stop larger boats passing beneath it if the water is high from rain or tide. Morris dancers disport on the staithe on summer weekends. The Thurne churns on changeover day in high season.

Not everyone likes Potter Heigham though:

What has gone wrong? . . . Ugly buildings with no Broads character, kiosks and amusement arcades have sprung up and poorly-designed chalets and houseboats now line some stretches of river bank. In the past, some holiday companies have marketed Broads holidays with scant regard for the unique character and fragile nature of the area, encouraging visitors to come to the Broads *for the wrong reasons.*[4]

The Broads Authority, which holds statutory authority over the region (now given National Park status), find Potter Heigham the wrong kind of landscape for their vision of a 'Last Enchanted Land'. Potter Heigham was the main site of interwar riverside chalet and shack development on the Broads, and new and replacement structures have been added since. Walking east along the north bank of the Thurne from the old bridge you pick up a dirt path behind the shacks, catching glimpses of the water between the structures (illus. 1–3). On one side grazing marshes, on the other bits of twentieth-century Broadland vernacular: a bungalow with verandah, a shed-cum-Nissen hut extension, a 'Sunny Side', a 'Maisonette'. Some plots are vacant, growing over with long grass, perhaps destined to be reclaimed under the Broads Plan as '"green"bank'.[5] In spring a few years ago one chalet had been burnt out during the winter; all that was left was rusted metal, a dead mattress, the black remains of a dartboard. On the far bank, towards Martham, a mock-Tudor bungalow and a cubic houseboat leant alarmingly. But not so alarmingly as a half-submerged Mississippi paddle steamer, waiting for rescue.

This Norfolk story contains within it many of the tensions of landscape and culture explored in this book. From a local example

1–3 Potter Heigham,
Norfolk.

we can draw out arguments of social and aesthetic value, of relations between culture and nature. Considerations of the 'wrong' and 'right' reasons to visit the Broads, of the 'character' of the place and the social and architectural conduct of the people within it – sailing, shacking, motor cruising, birdwatching, Mississippi pleasure-steaming – have been central to definitions of Broadland since the area was appropriated for commercial leisure activities in the late nineteenth century.[6] The Broads Authority purports to offer a multi-faceted vision of the district, reconciling interests of commerce, conservation, residence and pleasure, but the Potter Heigham riverbank marks a limit of conservationist environmental tolerance. The post-war Broads Conference took a similar view: 'a most unsightly and insanitary growth of bungalows along the river banks ... Potter Heigham is a lesson in what not to do on the banks of the Broads.'[7] Consideration of this cultural limit illuminates values running throughout the conservationist vision. If landscape is a site of value, it is also a site of anger; at buildings, against authorities, developers, different pleasures. Statements which might at first appear to be taken-for-granted as to the architectural character of a place rest upon cultural judgements as to what and who belongs there.

Some approaches would regard such social and aesthetic judgements to be mere projections or reflections of more fundamental political-economic disputes. Thus arguments over the look of a shack might be regarded as ultimately grounded in and explained by competing claims to valuable land. I would argue, though, that the power of landscape resides in it being simultaneously a site of economic, social, political and aesthetic value, with each embedded within and not preceding the other. In the Potter Heigham case, land values are certainly crucial; what might be marginal land to a farmer may be a prime site for a leisure scheme or a conservationist desire for open landscape. The economic interests of conservation bodies and holiday companies are evidently central to the Broads story, but I would suggest that economic discourse is here (as elsewhere) constituted through considerations of moral and aesthetic as well as monetary value, just as morality and aesthetics never float free of economy. Landscape can be considered a term which, of necessity, migrates through regimes of value sometimes held apart. Such an argument resonates with W.J.T. Mitchell's suggestion that we approach landscape as a verb rather than a noun, 'a process by which social and subjective identities are formed', considering 'not just what landscape "is" or "means" but what it does, how it works as a cultural practice'.[8] Indeed, the question of what landscape 'is' or 'means' can always be subsumed in the question of how it works; as a vehicle of social and self identity, as a site for the claiming of a cultural authority, as a generator of profit, as a space for different kinds of living. As Stephen Daniels has argued, it is the 'duplicity' of landscape, as a cultural term carrying meanings of depth and surface, solid earth and superficial scenery, the ontological and the ideological, that gives it its analytical potential: 'not despite its difficulty as a comprehensive or reliable concept, but because of it'.[9] What to do with some shacks by a river may at first appear a rather pragmatic and routine matter of everyday land-use regulation, warranting assessment by the relevant environmental expert, but begin to examine the assumptions governing such an assessment and you quickly enter an enormous and complex philosophical and political minefield concerning rights to land, definitions of pleasure and beauty, claims to authority over the content and form of public and private space. Landscape seems the appropriate term through which to explore this area, indeed one could argue that the relational hybridity of the term, which is already both natural and cultural, deep and superficial, makes it an inherently deconstructive force. In Bruno Latour's terminology, landscape might be regarded as a classic 'quasi-object', impossible to place on either side of a dualism of nature and culture, shuttling between fields of reference. Discussing recent environmental debates, Latour asks: 'Can anyone imagine a study that would treat the ozone hole as simultaneously naturalized, sociologized and deconstructed?' Landscape might be one formulation of what Latour terms a 'delicate shuttle', weaving together such matters: 'In the eyes of our critics the ozone hole above our heads, the moral law in our hearts, the autonomous text, may each be of interest, but only separately. That a delicate shuttle should have woven together the heavens, industry, texts, souls and moral law – this remains uncanny, unthinkable, unseemly.'[10]

If landscape carries an unseemly spatiality, it also shuttles through temporal processes of history and memory. Judgements over present value work in relation to narratives of past landscape. Returning to Potter Heigham we find a new 'Museum of the Broads', currently housed in a former boatshed. The area lacks a museum specifically dedicated to life on and around the water, and the new institution will serve as a refracting device for Broadland past and present. It is doubtful, though, that the adjacent riverbank landscape will be commemorated; such structures are seldom considered historic. Likewise the gifts and souvenirs to be found in the nearby stores may not feature as items of cultural value: rude mugs and postcards, the souvenir teatowel showing beer, transistors and accidents galore, and the slogan 'We Survived The Norfolk Broads', the *Spotters Book of Broads Hire Cruisers* listing 1,400 boats with their registration numbers and yards of origin.[11] Such material could itself, of course, be styled as a different kind of heritage, a set of future relics of popular pleasures. As Raphael Samuel shows in *Theatres of Memory*, an extraordinary range of objects has become open to heritage celebration,[12] and indeed one finds the occasional cherishing of such things in Broadland, the vulgar-popular creeping out from under the conservationist net. One of Broadland's more famous visitors was the ukelele-playing variety and film star George Formby, who from 1947 spent part of every summer cruising with his wife. In 1951, anonymous under dark glasses, Formby piloted yachts under Potter Heigham's awkward bridge.[13] The presence of an entertainer more often associated with nearby Great Yarmouth's summer shows ill-fits the conservationist vision of a 'Last Enchanted Land'. When, however, Norfolk County Council sought to demolish Formby's former Broadland home in 1991 to build a bypass, protesting George Formby Society members 'took along their ukeleles and sang Formby classics on the riverside'.[14] Heritage protest can take many forms. I have no particular brief here for shacks, boatspotters or George Formby, but such examples show how attempts to define a landscape necessitate judgements of cultural value, and throw up the issues of power, authority and pleasure which run through this book.

THE BOOK CONSIDERS a period, stretching roughly from 1918 to the 1950s, when many of the contemporary assumptions regarding landscape took shape and yet which also shows striking differences to today.[15] The prevailing theme is the intertwining of landscape and senses of Englishness. Both are seen to be constituted through problematics of class, gender and race, and formulations of environmental conduct and citizenship working through each of these. In general the book does not put forward its arguments through studies of particular sites. While attending to the symbolic meaning of places and the locational *foci* of arguments, the narrative is organized in terms of the versions of landscape and Englishness produced by more or less influential cultural movements. The book is in three main parts, each part containing one chapter addressing visions of landscape and another discussing their connection to questions of citizenship and the body. In the latter respect the book acts as a study of the processes of subjectification effected through landscape, the ways in which different versions of what might be termed a 'geographical self' are central to competing visions of landscape and Englishness.[16]

Part I traces the emergence in the 1920s and 1930s of a movement for the planning and preservation of landscape which sought to ally preservation and progress, tradition and modernity, city and country in order to define Englishness as orderly and modern. The common identification of preservation with nostalgia and anti-modernity does not hold here. This movement posited the view that modern expertise should command cultural and political authority, that the planner-preservationist should be placed in a position of governance in relation to the transformation of landscape. Chapter One shows how this vision of landscape and Englishness was formed through a sense of crisis in landscape and politics in the late 1920s, and details its visions of city, suburb and country. The chapter argues that this desire for preservation must be understood as expressing a particular modernism, committed to order and design, whether in country or city, indoors or out. Chapter Two develops these themes around issues of landscape and citizenship, considering what was termed a preservationist 'art of right living'. Moral geographies of landscape emerge whereby particular modes of conduct in the country are considered to be the basis for citizenship, while others – litter, noise, etc. – are held to denote an anti-citizenship, an immoral geography of leisure.[17] The chapter addresses the general growth of leisure in the interwar countryside, focusing on the formation of an open-air movement through such bodies as the Youth Hostels Association and the Ramblers' Association. By thinking in terms of different *cultures of landscape* – intellectual, spiritual, physical – we can place such leisure within a broader cultural field; indeed this landscaped citizenship at times finds itself uneasily adjacent to bodily practices – nudism, cults of physical form – which could worry planner-preservationists concerned to uphold moral order.

Part II is devoted to a counter-current of Englishness, which far from seeking a modern form of progress in city and country set an organic sense of rural life against modern city living and upheld traditional authority against progressive expertise.[18] Chapter Three shows how this vision of an organic England, cultivated by a small group of ruralist writers, organic farmers and self-styled dissident scientists, can be understood in terms of a series of English ecologies focused upon soil and authority. An organic relationship to land is presented as dependent on and necessary for an organic social order. As in Part I, the historic and foreign inspirations for this Englishness are emphasized; these are hardly insular 'little' versions of Englishness. The chapter also addresses the uneasy links between organicism and fascism, and shows how organicism worked through a regionalism very different to that found in schemes of modern regional planning. Chapter Four shows how organicism envisaged an organic English body at odds with the planner-preservationist ideal of modern citizenship. A stress on the physical over the cerebral, an ethic of craft labour and pure folk culture, went to make up an organic art of living. A holistic concern for the body encompassed issues of consumption, with organicists promoting national health via the consumption of organic food, the recycling of wastes and the cultivation of genetic vigour.

Part III takes up the themes of Part I in the context of war and reconstruction. The general argument is that the Second World War allowed the planner-preservationist Englishness outlined in Part I to achieve a position of considerable cultural and political power. Chapter Five shows how particular events of the War, such as the transformation of agriculture, the evacuation of children and the bombing of cities, opened up literal and metaphorical spaces, thus ensuring that a planner-preservationist discourse of reconstruction could occupy a moral and political high ground. However, we always find tensions, and indeed these run throughout the book, as to whether planned order and Englishness are mutually exclusive. Chapter Six outlines the planner-preservationist geographies of reconstruction from the rebuilding of cities through the replanning of the country to the preservation of nature. Chapter Seven returns to the theme of citizenship to examine formulations of community and domesticity in reconstruction, to show how the open-air citizenship of the interwar years is carried through in the establishment of National Parks, and to highlight the cultivation of an educated 'citizen-scientist' through a new kind of naturalism. In its plans for new environments and its attention to the mind, body and spirit of the citizen, planner-preservationism constitutes a design for life. The book's concluding chapter shows how such arguments have been overtaken by cultures of landscape less enamoured of the modern; the 1951 'Festival of Britain' acts as a starting-point for a discussion of the unravelling of the landscapes of modern Englishness.

General Concerns

Landscape, the Rural and the Modern

Recent years have brought excellent detailed studies of issues of landscape and Englishness in relation to painting, literature, photography and the country house;[19] such material is drawn on where relevant in subsequent chapters, and it is not my intention to review it here. Some general comment is necessary, however, regarding the ongoing debate on the cultural effects of ruralism, nostalgia and a concern for heritage. For some these are symptoms of cultural health, denoting a continuing concern for nature, for place, for roots; for others they signal only cultural decline, a country unable to face up to the modern world.[20] Such arguments tend to assume, on both sides, that the rural, the natural and the historical are at odds with the modern.[21] This book seeks less to arbitrate between these positions, which emerge from radically different assumptions concerning the definition and relative importance of the cultural, the economic and the political, than to examine the genealogy of the terms of debate in a way which puts into question the alignment of nature, country, history and the anti-modern. Much of the book finds instead a powerful historical connection between landscape, Englishness and the modern. When I began working on this material, I did not expect to find this connection and I have been continually surprised at how, with few exceptions,[22] those studying the period have missed the modernity in these influential visions of landscape. Perhaps a feeling that planning and topography was a rather boring, non-cultural, non-aesthetic arena served to place this material effectively out of sight.

Such oversights may also relate to a tendency to lump all cultural expressions of ruralism together as representing a simple, nostalgic and conservative longing for a 'rural idyll'. While there are undoubt-edly a range of cultural phenomena which warrant this label, I am suspicious of its value as an analytical category.[23] The ruralist mater-ial considered in this book, even that which seems most obviously nostalgic and conservative, turns out to have a complexity, either through exhibiting non-nostalgic/conservative traits, or because neither nostalgia nor conservatism are simple phenomena.[24] The use of 'rural idyll' as a category of understanding seems often to reproduce that ease and slackness which it purports to diagnose. It might also be argued that ruralism has not been well served by more celebratory attempts to uphold a coherent and discrete 'rural tradition'. The argument of this book is that the rural needs always to be understood in terms relative to those of the city and suburb, and approached as a heterogeneous field.

Englishness in Variation

Some might regard a preoccupation with Englishness, however critical, as rather insular, denoting a cultural myopia, and this may indeed be the aim of some studies. This book is happy to delve into obscure corners of English life, but it proceeds from the assump-tion that a definition of Englishness as insular or unitary would not only be undesirable but also impossible to sustain. National identity is regarded as a relative concept always constituted through definitions of Self and Other and always subject to internal differ-entiation.[25] To take first internal variations on Englishness. As many have argued, evocations of English landscape are often specifically regional, projecting a Southern Englishness in the name of the whole. Martin Wiener highlights Donald Horne's analysis of the 'Southern' and 'Northern' metaphors of Britishness/Englishness, with the Southern standing for 'order and tradition' and defined as 'romantic, illogical, muddled, divinely lucky, Anglican, aristocratic, traditional, frivolous', and the Northern projecting a nation which is 'pragmatic, empirical, calculating, Puritan, bourgeois, enterprising, adventurous, scientific, serious' and believes in 'struggle'.[26] For Wiener, writing in 1980 with a view to a Thatcherite economic and cultural programme, the Southern metaphor had acted to frustrate an 'industrial spirit', and thus had helped drive Britain into decline. Alun Howkins, in a politically more complex analysis, shows convincingly the cultural force of the 'south country' ideal across the political spectrum in the late Victorian and Edwardian period,[27] but as we move into the interwar period and beyond I would suggest we find a more complex metaphoric situation among those promoting Englishness through landscape. In part, this reflects the continuing operation of longstanding alternative metaphors for Englishness and Britishness. Such metaphors run on East–West rather than North–South lines, with the West associated with the spiritual, the mysterious and the Celtic, and the East with down-to-earth reason and the Anglo-Saxon.[28] Thus we find organicists emphasizing the West Country within a general promotion of Southern Englishness, aiming not least to achieve some cultural distance from an expanding south-eastern metropolis. Westernness, as much as Southernness, structures the symbolic geography of organicism.

The south country metaphor also breaks down in relation to planner-preservationist ideals, but here the situation is more complex. Firstly, we find another form of regionalism cutting across an oppositional North–South divide. Landscape is differentiated in terms of upland and lowland in a manner which, while generally fitting a northwest-southeast geographical arrangement, does not put forward different locations as symbolic of different modes of Englishness. Instead, upland National Parks and preserved lowland scenery are allied in a general scheme for generating English citizenship. Class differences between open-air leisure in North and South may indeed disrupt the unity of this vision, but the preservationists' sense of a multi-faceted Englishness echoes Cosgrove's more recent analysis of the 'iconic landscape structure of Britain', with lowland 'garden' and upland 'wildness' signifying not opposing values but variations within an overarching national landscape.[29]

Secondly, preservationist argument undercuts the south country motif with self-consciousness. The ideal southern landscape is certainly highlighted as a mythic ideal contrasting with 'disfigured' contemporary landscapes, but it is also presented as a picturesque myth, deluding the observer and generating an unhelpful nostalgia. This anti-picturesque line also runs through organicism, and denotes a reflexivity regarding landscape and Englishness which belies the image of idiotically sentimental commentators leading the country into a state of cultural and economic inertia. Ironically, the arguments of Wiener and Robert Hewison regarding nostalgia and cultural decline turn out to have been anticipated by those campaigning for the preservation of rural England. We return to this point in later chapters. The situation is further complicated by the functionalism of preservationist Englishness, which aligns order and tradition with planned modernity rather than illogical muddle. Horne's Northern and Southern terminology is jumbled in this influential vision of the nation. The implication is that, while the Southern and Northern metaphors undoubtedly have considerable cultural power, we should be wary of reaching for them as a general mode of cultural analysis.

If Englishness goes into variation internally, then it is also defined through something outside itself. One might talk, as with landscape, of a duplicity of Englishness, in that an Englishness attempting to isolate itself would find its internal and external historical geographies leading it to self-destruct. Most obviously there is the common conflation of English and British interest and identity, with the term British used in effect as an English surrogate. In terms of the material considered here, though, this conflation works differently according to the geographical reference point. With few exceptions, when these writers discuss English landscape they generally mean England and not Britain. Parts of Wales are occasionally incorporated, with topographic guides to England unconsciously straying into Snowdonia, but Scotland, Wales and a newly independent Ireland are recognized as carrying distinct identities. When national preservationist bodies are established, there are separate Councils and Associations formed for the Preservation of Rural England, Wales and Scotland. Similarly, when H. V. Morton sets off to write his bestselling interwar *In Search Of* travelogues, he goes not in search of Britain but of England, Scotland, Wales and Ireland, looking for national cultural identities. Morton is often regarded as the quintessential exponent of an insular Englishness, but some sense of his cultural complexity can be gathered from a passage in his 1936 Mediterranean travel book, *In the Steps of St Paul*, in which he seeks a language to praise the secularization and modernization of Turkey: 'Kemal Ataturk is not unlike Alfred the Great. He has driven the Danes out of his kingdom and now, his sword cast aside, he is making new laws for his people. The soul of Kemalist Turkey is a Sinn Fein movement.'[30] We return to Morton in a later chapter.

None of this is meant to suggest any necessary humility in Englishness in this period, some newly modest national identity, but it is meant to indicate a specificity. When, however, discussion moves abroad, Englishness and Britishness become almost interchangeable, especially when the subject is the Empire. England is assumed to be the heart and head of the British Empire. Thus when organicists look to experimental work carried out in India, they harness an imperial Britishness for their Englishness without registering any contradiction, even when the work admired is being carried out by Scottish scientists. In terms of the international constitution of Englishness, the material here echoes post-colonial analyses which recast Englishness from a native product nurtured behind white cliffs to, as Simon Gikandi puts it, a 'phenomenon produced in the ambivalent space that separated, but also conjoined, metropole and colony',[31] a phenomenon produced relationally through contested senses of white, as well as black, ethnicity. As the work of Paul Gilroy, Julian Agyeman and Ingrid Pollard, among others, has shown, such questions, whether relating to events within England or without, are central rather than marginal to the politics and aesthetics of Englishness.[32] Colonial and post-colonial formations of Englishness should not, however, lead us to neglect other examples of Englishness found elsewhere. In this book we will encounter versions of England constituted in relation to German motorway construction, Chinese philosophy, American regionalism, Danish health regimes, ancient Egyptian civilization, German organic farming. In the first half of this century European and American reference points were crucial for those asking what modern Englishness might look like and how one might devise the political structures necessary for its development. Europe could also provide inspiration for those seeking to equate England with a particular ethnicity.

Historicity, Spatiality, Genealogy

If Englishness is created through relations with elsewhere and through internal differentiation, then it is also a subject for change. This book can be regarded as a contribution to a historical geography of landscape and Englishness, although with some qualifications regarding the relationship of material and context implied by that term. The aim here is not to explain and thereby confine arguments by placing them within a determining historical and spatial context, but to draw out their *historicity* and *spatiality*, the ways in which practices, discursive or otherwise, constitute senses of time and space in relation to other events and practices, potentially generating contradictions. So, for example, when addressing preservationist attitudes to the past, the question becomes not whether heritage is valued but how specific narratives of history are constructed which posit a particular relationship between past, present and future. What is the historicity of different versions of preservation? Similarly, when a spirit of locality or nation is appealed to, the question is how one scale is constituted in harmonious or antagonistic relation to others; local, regional, national, imperial, global, universal. What are the spatialities of Englishness?

An examination of the assumptions which are normally taken for granted regarding space, time, place, nature, land, etc. should enable this to be more than simply a detailed study of a particular moment in English cultural history.

In the extract at the head of this Introduction Michel Foucault indicates some of the aims of his historical method of genealogy, or '"effective" history':[33] 'a form of history which can account for the constitution of knowledges, discourses, domains of objects etc., without having to make reference to a subject which is either transcendental in relation to the field of events or runs in its empty sameness throughout the course of history'.[34] This is not the place to attempt to summarize Foucault's work, and there is an enormous critical literature which does not agree on that work's implications,[35] but in relation to its approach to history, its discussion of the body and the citizen, its concern to draw out questions of authority and governmentality regarding landscape, this book is informed by Foucauldian studies. It seeks to offer a genealogy, an effective history, of landscape and Englishness. Neither landscape nor Englishness run in any transcendental empty sameness through the book; rather we find an unstable heterogeneity in both. Foucault presents genealogy as having a dual aesthetic and ethical strategy, on the one hand 'grey, meticulous, and patiently documentary', operating 'on a field of entangled and confused parchments, on documents that have been scratched over and recopied many times',[36] on the other approaching history as a masquerade, which the genealogist is not too serious to enjoy: 'Taking up these masks, revitalizing the buffoonery of history, we adopt an identity whose unreality surpasses that of God, who started the whole charade ... Genealogy is history in the form of a concerted carnival.'[37] Attending to the detail of material, I have also been concerned to draw out, where appropriate, its humorous substance, and Foucault's dual genealogical strategy is present throughout the book.[38] Theory does not, however, have a strong explicit presence in the remainder of the text. The book is theoretical less in terms of its evident language than in an angle of approach which permeates its material. Were it not for the historical and philosophical issues indicated in this Introduction, the book would not have been written in this way; indeed would not have been written at all.

PART I

Landscape for a New Englishness

1914. MR. WILLIAM SMITH ANSWERS THE CALL TO PRESERVE
HIS NATIVE SOIL INVIOLATE.

1919. MR. WILLIAM SMITH COMES BACK AGAIN TO SEE HOW
WELL HE HAS DONE IT.

4 Mr William Smith, 1914/1919. *Punch* cartoon reproduced in C. Williams-Ellis, *England and the Octopus* (London, 1928).

Ordering England

A Crisis of English Landscape

At the front of his 1928 book *England and the Octopus* Clough Williams-Ellis reproduced a *Punch* cartoon of war and its aftermath (illus. 4),[1] which showed the betrayal of ordinary Mr William Smith and his green and pleasant land. In 1914 he left behind a village world with church and fields and birds, and now he returns to a town of wires and roads and mess. If, as Paul Fussell and others have argued, a sense of Englishness as being essentially rural was the basis for many formulations of national identity in the 1914–18 war,[2] the message given here is that the patriot and his landscape have been betrayed by vested interest.

Williams-Ellis diagnosed a crisis in the post-war English landscape: 'There are such things as "Dangerous Ages", and the most dangerous ages are those at which the normal rate of change is most abnormally accelerated . . . we are surely living more dangerously now than at any time.'[3] *England and the Octopus* promoted the message of the Council for the Preservation of Rural England, set up in 1926 largely through the initiative of planner Patrick Abercrombie. The book was recently republished by the CPRE in celebration of their seventieth anniversary. Concern for the English landscape was not new in 1926; the National Trust had been campaigning since 1895, the Commons Preservation Society since 1865, the Society for the Protection of Ancient Buildings since 1877, the Society for Checking the Abuses of Public Advertising since 1893. The CPRE was distinctive, though, in seeking a complete coverage of rural landscape through the co-ordination of the efforts of groups concerned with specific issues of architecture, planning, landowning, leisure, local government and wildlife. At first sight, the kind of William Smith imagery used by Williams-Ellis might suggest a movement for the old against the new, for country against city, for tradition against the modern. However, while the CPRE was not averse to rural elegy, the argument of this chapter is that this movement for preservation entailed not a conservative protection of the old against the new but an attempt to plan a landscape simultaneously modern and traditional under the guidance of an expert public authority. We will consider in turn the modes of authority and government cultivated by this movement, the order of settlement it envisaged, and the modern content of its English landscapes.[4]

A sense of the preservationists' self-belief and presumed authority can be gained from considering the typical form of their arguments, namely binary contrasts of good and evil, order and chaos, beauty and horror, which are routinely deployed so as to make preservation appear a matter of national fundamentals. This language is not simply polemical excess. Preservationists use binary absolutes in their statements both to raise the stakes and claim a clear and absolute authority over landscape. Preservationist discourse becomes locked in dichotomy, with a diagnosis of disorder and a will to order feeding off one another. This binary rhetoric was most clearly expressed in photographs contrasting before and after, of what is with what might be. Publications and exhibitions sought to encourage anger. A 'Save the Countryside' exhibition, initially set up alongside the first Countryside and Footpaths Preservation National Conference in Leicester in October 1928, travelled around the country and later went to Belgium and America: 'The show brings home to people in the most vivid manner the desecration that is taking place, and contrasts the debasement of rural scenery with unspoilt examples.'[5] The exhibition was set up by Harry Peach, head of the CPRE's Exhibitions Committee. Peach owned the successful

Leicester-based Dryad Handicrafts firm, and was prominent in the Design and Industries Association (DIA), producers of 'Cautionary Guide' books on town disfigurement for St Albans, Oxford and Carlisle. Their 1929–30 yearbook, *The Face of the Land*, edited by Peach and Noel Carrington, drew heavily on CPRE exhibition material.[6] Display boards in the show contrasted good and bad, before and after, beautiful and ugly, good and evil, order and disorder, basic oppositions suggesting the unquestioning authority of the preservationist. We shall see below how this way of thinking mirrored the aesthetic of clarity and harmony on display; minds, as well as landscapes, should be tidy. Accompanying postcards reiterated a fundamental patriotic authority. 'Saint George for Rural England' (illus. 5) set the patron saint against a dragon of *laissez-faire* commercial culture: motoring, garages, smoke, advertisements, litter. On one side the dragon, on the other Saint George, riding over a foreground of natural rather than human litter, defending the nucleated village and the nuclear family. Precise, composed and triumphant, Saint George stands for a certain England, for a gentle force of order, for the preservationists' sure categories of judgement.

5 'Save the Countryside: Saint George for Rural England'. Postcard issued by the Council for the Preservation of Rural England, 1928.

My argument is that this judgement is a distinctly modern one. That is not to deny that within the broad preservation movement there were archly anti-modern, traditionalist voices, but I would suggest that the dominant voices were those committed to planning and designing a new England. In his 1938 Penguin Special on *Design*, Anthony Bertram asserted the modernity of this preservation: 'there is a grossly unfair tendency to mix up the CPRE with the sort of arid conservatism which tries to mummify the countryside, which automatically opposes all innovations, all new design, all demolition and reconstruction. If any such people hide under the cloak of the CPRE, they have certainly no right to be there.'[7] It was this openness to modern design and reconstruction which enabled preservationist planning to achieve a position of cultural and political power during and after the Second World War; we will now consider the ways in which the interwar preservationist movement was formed through particular assumptions regarding the role of the state and the possibilities of the plan.

Englishness and Government

If a future England was to be planned, the question was, who would plan, and how? Preservation was a call for government which appeared to question prevailing modes of governance for their lack of control over the country. Discussions of preservation have tended to focus on the detail of what was to be preserved rather than setting the argument within the broader field of authority and governance. Here we highlight how the preservation movement constituted itself by connecting Englishness and government in such a way as to challenge private rights and restyle public authority.

Preservationists argued that in the nineteenth century an attitude of *laissez faire* had destroyed the town, and in the twentieth century was destroying the country. In Williams-Ellis's collection *Britain and the Beast* J. M. Keynes described the Victorian 'utilitarian and economic . . . ideal' as the 'most dreadful heresy, perhaps, which has ever gained the ear of a civilised people'.[8] For Williams-Ellis it was a matter of 'Laissez Faire or Government': 'the choice lies between the end of laissez faire and the end of rural England.'[9] In questioning the rights of private property – 'we have definitely begun to realize that to go as you please is no way to arrive at what is pleasant, and that private rights are no longer defensible when they result in public wrongs'[10] – Williams-Ellis claimed the voice of the nation:

> Discipline! How unwilling we English are to submit to even a little of it . . . But we do in the end submit; we did in the War and we shall do so yet again in this matter of preserving England . . . In this matter, I say, we are petitioning to be governed; we ask for control, for discipline. We have tried freedom and, under present conditions, we see that it leads to waste, inefficiency, and chaos.[11]

Preservationists offered their expertise as a means to national preservation.

There were tensions, however, in asserting the public over the private. Preservationists trusted neither the general public (as we shall see in Chapter Two) nor their elected officials: 'What constructive contribution can the average town-councillor . . . make? It is obviously unfair to ask him to make any. This is no routine matter like cleaning streets or erecting urinals. What hope can there be here of enlightened authority?'[12] Wary of the current constitution of public authority, preservationists were cautious of proposing control via public ownership of land. A delicate balancing act occurs whereby 'responsible' private ownership is upheld and a role for the state fashioned which follows landowning etiquette through the metaphor of the nation estate. Abercrombie lamented 'rural disintegration':

> If the country had remained in the hands of the same families who have done so much to create its typical English beauty in

the past ... the greater use of the country ... might have been directed into more defined areas ..., the bulk of the normal country remaining unchanged ... The former guardians of the country are no longer in possession.

Preservationists map distinctions of good and bad ownership onto distinctions of old and new money, the former supposedly willing to submit to regulation out of love of the land and a sense of national duty,[13] the latter likely to be in cahoots with 'a new trade ... the land butcher – a personage entirely ruthless and untrammeled by traditions' and developing land 'in the most brutal manner ... daring a feeble authority to control his efforts'.[14] Yet, however fond the regard for old owners, property is held to be unable to guarantee the landscape any longer; the general trajectory of history is seen as heading towards public authority: 'the landlords are disappearing and the practical problem is, how to order and regulate the break-up of their estates.'[15] The solution might be to manage England as one nation estate:

The government of a country has this essential continuity, and with it power and authority delegated to it by the governed. When the property in trust is a Kingdom, and the beneficiaries a whole people, the proper trustee would seem to be the State, the conservation of a nation's assets and their protection from a spendthrift squandering in our present time being surely matters within the proper function of a Government.[16]

Preservationist geographer Vaughan Cornish mused that 'if England were one man's freehold', regulation 'would be a simple matter'.[17] The estate analogy visualized an ordered future against a crazy present, Williams-Ellis suggesting that: 'If any private estate were managed anything like as inefficiently as England is mishandled and maladministered as a whole, there would be no difficulty whatever in getting the proprietor locked up as a dangerous lunatic.'[18] Proposed government action ranged from upland National Parks through a lowland 'Government Board of Scenery' to a central 'Board of Planning'.[19] Two regulatory options were resisted, however. These were on the one hand land nationalization, an option very much on the political agenda of both Labour and Liberal parties, and on the other the investiture of land in the National Trust. Though a constituent body of the CPRE, the Trust was not regarded as a force for future planning. When historian G. M. Trevelyan argued that the National Trust offered the only sure means of preservation, prominent voices in the CPRE put down his suggestion as a 'counsel of despair',[20] Williams-Ellis suggesting that large-scale Trust holdings would only turn the country into 'a museum in which are preserved here and there carefully ticketed specimens of what England was. The National Trust is England's executor.'[21]

It is important to place the emergence of preservationist argument in the 1920s and 1930s within a widespread interrogation of existing modes of government at a time of economic and political crisis. Across the political spectrum planning, whether via public works, state planning boards or a fully fledged corporate state, was upheld as offering a new basis for social and political organization at a time when *laissez-faire* capitalism was in crisis. Foreign examples were called up, not without some nervousness; Italian fascist corporatism, Soviet central planning (admired by Williams-Ellis), Swedish social democratic welfarism, and later the New Deal of Roosevelt's USA and the transformation of Nazi Germany.[22] If preservationists upheld landscape as an object deserving of and requiring public authority, then the preservationist argument of necessity moved into a wider political field. Individual preservationists varied in political allegiance; Williams-Ellis and Peach were members of the radical Independent Labour Party, the CPRE President, Lord Crawford, was a Tory, Trevelyan and Abercrombie Liberal. It was, however, with the advent of a Labour Government supported by the Liberals in 1929 that the preservationists saw their chance for action. They submitted a Memorandum to Prime

Minister Ramsey MacDonald, a friend of Peach and fellow open-air enthusiast. The resulting Town and Country Planning Bill fell with the administration. Labour Government and preservationist planning would again come into alliance in 1945.

If there is any political philosophy out of tune with preservationist planning, it is Baldwinite Conservatism. At first sight this may seem odd. Stanley Baldwin, Prime Minister from 1924 to 1929 and 1935 to 1937, and dominant in the National Government from 1931 to 1937, was known for his rural eulogies: 'To me, England is the country, and the country is England. And when I ask myself what I mean by England, ... England comes to me through my various senses.' Baldwin called up the sounds of hammer on anvil (it was the smithy and not the iron foundry from which his wealth derived), corncrakes and scythes, the sight of a plough-team, the smell of wood smoke: 'These things strike down into the very depths of our nature.'[23] The CPRE were only too happy to use such statements in their publicity; Baldwin and MacDonald both sent messages of support to the October 1928 conference. While, however, Baldwin's bucolic dreamings could be echoed in some preservationist writing, there is a crucial difference. Baldwin's Conservative Englishness of social harmony, constitutional caution, organic culture and pastoral community is a site for neither anger nor action.[24] A politics of control, regulation and dramatic planning could not belong here. Baldwin's landscape accommodated a quiet, ordinary, evasive little England, not the assertive English future envisioned in preservationist argument. Different political aesthetics work through different senses of order in landscape. Preservationists offered a scene of leadership and action, with the expert rather than the ordinary person the key shaper of the land: 'we shall be an educated people, the leaders of thought will lead all classes, not merely an educated minority.'[25] Concluding his influential 1932 book, *Town and Countryside*, with the question 'Is There Any Hope?', Thomas Sharp compared the aesthetic results of 'Autocracy and Democracy' before settling on a solution of 'Enlightened Control', distinct from the 'pitifully unenlightened' current policy: 'fresh control is needed'.[26] Williams-Ellis similarly went to controlled extremes in discussing the remedy for speculators:

> if we wait for their enlightenment and reform we shall be brought to bankruptcy ... only a strong and far-seeing directorate can by any means save us from that catastrophe.
>
> We need direction and leadership now as never before, because now, in this generation, a new England is being made, its form is being hastily cast in a mould that no one has considered as a whole ... If there is no master-founder, no co-related plan, we may well live to be aghast at what we have made – a hash of our civilisation and a desert of our country.
>
> What then must we do to be saved from this future state of chaos, ugliness and inefficiency?[27]

This was a language more suited to Oswald Mosley than Baldwin. Indeed Williams-Ellis was a friend of the Mosley family. In the late 1920s and early 1930s Mosley was the most prominent voice seeking to combine economic and political reform around a planning philosophy, first from the Left of the Labour Party, then from March 1931 with his corporatist New Party, and from 1932 with the British Union of Fascists.[28] Preservationist C.E.M. (Cyril) Joad was Director of Propaganda for the New Party until summer 1931. The connection with a Mosleyite rhetoric and policy which could shift into fascism is indicative of a tension which will run through this book; visions of dramatic landscape change could trigger yearnings towards authority in those committed to planning and order. We will find, in this and other chapters, uneasy connections with German and Italian schemes of planning and preservation, affinities with what Herf describes in the context of the German Right as a 'reactionary modernism' turning a 'romantic anticapitalism ... away from backward-looking pastoralism, pointing instead to the outlines of a beautiful new order replacing the formless chaos due to capitalism in a united, technologically advanced nation'.[29] It should be noted, however, that there is no evidence of preservationist support for the BUF, who appear in the CPRE's archive only in a polite 1935 exchange regarding fascist graffiti on a Sussex bridge. The BUF insisted that they told members not to 'chalk' if in breach of byelaws, and the CPRE replied with thanks: 'I was quite satisfied that the disfigurement could not have been done by the order of your Organisation; and I now make an appeal to you on behalf of the CPRE to do all in your power to prevent the disfigurement of bridges.'[30]

By 1934 Joad and Williams-Ellis featured in the equally action-oriented *Manifesto* of the anti-fascist Federation of Progressive Societies and Individuals,[31] a document which perhaps most clearly brings home the potential distance of this preservation from vague conservative rustic nostalgia. Introduced by H. G. Wells, *Manifesto* featured essays on world citizenship and reform of the 'sex laws'. Allan Young, a former New Party activist but now secretary to the progressive Conservative Harold Macmillan, wrote on 'The Economics of Planning'. Here was the appropriate context for two essays on town and country planning and preservation by Williams-Ellis and Geoffrey Boumphrey; the assumption was that such a *Manifesto* would be incomplete without attention to 'Our Physical Environment'. Landscape and Englishness could concern the most self-consciously progressive people.

English Settlement

City and Country: Against Hermaphrodites

> The essence of the aesthetic of Town and Country Planning consists in the frank recognition of these two opposites ... Let Urbanism prevail and preponderate in the Town and let the Country remain rural. Keep the distinction clear.[32]

The new preservationist England was to be constituted through a morality of settlement. We shall see later how built structures are judged by preservationists through a moral language of fitness, honesty, harmony; a parallel language is mobilized for places. Settlements are to have a form fit for their function; a town should be clearly and distinctly a town, a village a village. A normative geography of distinct urbanity and rurality is asserted over an England-in-between of suburb, plotland and ribbon development. Such sites become anti-settlements, places not fit for any purpose, lacking visual and social composition. The aim is to produce a proper English settlement.

Here is an interwar preservationist vision of the city:

> In dealing with our cities we need vision. The city of tomorrow will hardly resemble at all the city of the last century. We have come to the machine age. We need to accept the machine and to get the best out of it, and we shall find that our cities if rightly planned for their purpose will be as beautiful as the motor car or the aeroplane.[33]

The detail of urban visions will be considered in a later chapter in relation to wartime plans for reconstruction; the key point to register here is that campaigns for modern rurality go in tandem with campaigns for modern urbanity. That most banal of phrases, 'Town and Country Planning', turns out to embody a framework for living. Green Belts, first introduced around London in 1938 to 'restore to London a unity which it lost once the walls of the Roman lines ceased to enclose the city',[34] would mark out town and country. For Geoffrey Boumphrey such a bounding of the town would foster a 'revival of English corporate life': 'Gone will be the spattering of nasty, pseudo-hygienic little houses, each weakly proclaiming its semi-detachment, and their places will be taken by groups of dwellings, not ashamed to stand together for the attainment of beauty, symbols of that co-operation by which man has conquered Nature.'[35]

Town and country are set up as settlement fundamentals under threat from urban decentralization and rural disintegration. Planner Thomas Sharp connected the waning of authority and settlement:

> Tradition has broken down. Taste is utterly debased. There is no enlightened guidance or correction from authority. The town, long since degraded, is now being annihilated by a flabby, shoddy, romantic nature-worship. That romantic nature-worship is destroying also the object of its adoration, the countryside ... The one age-long certainty, the antithesis of town and country, is already breaking down. Two diametrically opposed, dramatically contrasting, inevitable types of beauty are being displaced by one drab, revolting neutrality ... The strong, masculine virility of the town; the softer beauty, the richness, the fruitfulness of that mother of men, the countryside, will be debased into one sterile, hermaphroditic beastliness.
>
> The crying need of the moment is the re-establishment of the ancient antithesis. The town is town: the country is country: black and white: male and female.[36]

The very certainty of such arguments can, however, confuse. Sharp is here arguing in part against the Garden City as a viable urban form; others, notably the Garden Cities and Town Planning Association, argued for it as *the* urban planning solution. For Abercrombie garden cities, being 'distinct and definite entities standing in the midst of agricultural belts ... which are to remain for ever inviolate', did not violate the town-country polarity.[37] For both sides an urban-rural polarity is desired, and the urbanity or otherwise of the Garden City is the point of contention. The term 'Garden City' could indeed migrate beyond the strict Letchworth-Welwyn template. Thus Cornish proposed London as a high-rise garden city of 'steel-framed buildings on one-third of the space' with greenery between: 'Thus would London town become a garden city.'[38] Boumphrey's Corbusierian green London went further, with 85 per cent open space:

> One can imagine the effect of seeing such a city – the acres of green, broken here and there by sheets of water or playing-fields, the great trees rising to their full country heights, and here and there among them lovely buildings in white and crystal, shining in the clear air.
>
> Rebuilt like this, London would sink to a third of its size … yet increase its capacity. The country could be brought back to within something like reasonable reach of even this hypertrophied city.[39]

Architectural modernism is to serve the maintenance of town and country.

Indeterminate Landscapes: Englishness and Suburbia

For Sharp the problem with Garden Cities was that they were less urban than suburban, and it is the suburb which appears as the chief neutral hermaphroditic villain within such arguments. Over four million houses were built in Britain between the wars, over one third of the total stock, with a peak of private building in 1934–5 when 293,000 units were built. Between 1927–8 and 1933–4 an average 38,000 acres of land were developed each year for housing, rising to 50,000 between 1934–5 and 1938–9.[40] The key site of growth was the suburb, not an entirely novel settlement form but one moving down the class structure and growing on an unprecedented scale, built around new domestic technologies. Suburban growth was most dramatic in the South East and the Midlands as the regional geography of manufacturing shifted and labour migrated, often to produce consumer products for the new suburban home. The suburb becomes a contentious English landscape, valued by some as essentially English in its modest scale, domestic values and humdrum life, and castigated by others for the same characteristics.[41] For preservationists the suburb becomes an English predicament, a site not of pleasant town-and-country blend but an indeterminate place; visually, socially, sexually.

In *Britain and the Beast*, Williams-Ellis's collection of preservationist angry writing, John Gloag tried to look with sympathy on 'The Suburban Scene', finding a potentially romantic English landscape resistant to a 'continental' and abstract modernism; Gloag was less of a fan of Le Corbusier than Boumphrey. Gloag quickly stressed, though, that he was 'not becoming tolerant of muddle and disorder', and 'not making a plea for the retention of those repellent, jerry-built, sham-Tudor houses that disfigure England'. Such structures would, he hoped, have 'fallen into ruin' by the time of 'the Golden Machine Age that is just round the corner'.[42] Just as there were good and bad landowners so there could be good and bad suburbs, with the distinction again often falling on class lines. Gloag's was an unusually sympathetic voice. Preservationist argument in general straightforwardly follows John Carey's analysis of disdain for suburbia: '"suburban" is distinctive in combining topographical with intellectual disdain. It relates human worth to habitat.'[43] Preservationists seize upon three forms of suburban indeterminacy, in land use, class and gender. With land use arguments veer between criticizing the monotonous and the randomly variable. Sharp found in suburbs 'a disorder and vagueness, a violent individualism, that is a direct negation of all that the civic spirit has implied for hundreds of years'.[44] Slough, growing around the new industries of the Bath Road, became the archetype of anti-settlement. Peach and Carrington commented: 'One can imagine that in a few years' time that the local wits will reply to the question, "Do you live in the town or in the country?" "Neither, I live in Slough."'[45] For John Betjeman in his 1937 poem 'Slough', this 'mess they call a town' was of a different class to the leafy suburbia he would elsewhere hymn. Here food was tinned, nature expelled and futures mortgaged, and wives dyed their hair peroxide. Slough 'isn't fit for humans now', but still people live there, lulled into insensitivity by their sham of a settlement.[46]

Betjeman's Slough is also indeterminate in terms of class, or rather holds a class whose status is unclear. How could anyone know their place in such a place? Here was found the new working-class consumer identified by J. B. Priestley in his 1934 *English Journey* as inhabiting a 'Third England' which was neither old country nor industrial town, a place American in orientation and 'essentially democratic in its cheapness': 'the England of arterial and by-pass roads, of filling stations and factories that look like exhibition buildings, of giant cinemas and dance-halls and cafés, bungalows with tiny garages ... factory girls that look like actresses'.[47] Priestley, a frequent contributor to preservationist argument, can be ambivalently sympathetic to this landscape; others were straightforwardly hostile, especially when viewing suburbia as a site of emasculation, a domestic realm constraining the English man. Alison Light has argued that interwar suburbia fostered a private and domestic 'conservative modernity', a feminized Englishness retreating from expansive and imperial masculinities.[48] Suburb and empire were not necessarily antagonistic realms, and yet imperial culture itself became domesticated, the axis of England and empire working more through a dialogue of domesticities across the world than a model of exploration from centre to periphery. I would suggest that two modes of conservative modernity clashed over the suburb. Preservationists set one mode of Englishness – exploratory, wide-ranging, expert, topographic, masculine – over another – suburban, domestic, little, humdrum, feminine and feminizing. While preservationists could set models of community and domesticity in harness, as in the family village of the Saint George postcard, the suburb offended by being a privatized space supposedly without communal function or spirit, where home overwhelmed the kind of restricted 'little' masculinity captured in Strube's *Daily Express* cartoons of the 'Little Man', a modest garden-concerned and common-sensical suburban male.[49]

A sense of suburbia as a site of emasculation is common in English male explorations of the time. In 'Nottingham and the Mining Country-side' D. H. Lawrence anticipated his admirer Thomas Sharp's ideal settlement diagrams: 'Do away with it all, then . . . Plan a nucleus. Fix the focus. Make a handsome gesture of radiation from the focus. And then put up big buildings, handsome, that sweep to a civic centre. And furnish them with beauty. And make an absolute clean start. Do it place by place. Make a new England. Away with little homes!'[50] Rearrangements of domesticity also fuel George Orwell's suburban male George Bowling, *Coming Up For Air* from a mortgaged suburbia worshipping a 'bisexual' god: 'The top half would be a managing director and the bottom half would be a wife in the family way.'[51] Escaping asphyxiation, Bowling drives to the village of his youth: 'I got to the top of the hill. Another minute and Lower Binfield would be in sight. Lower Binfield! . . . Yes, here we are! I declutched, trod on the foot-brake, and – Jesus! . . . The first question was, where *was* Lower Binfield?'[52] Bowling sees suburbs, new factories, Lancastrians, a 'swallowed' place: 'I had the feeling of an enemy invasion having happened behind my back.'[53] An ideal of English settlement is swamped, and so George drinks heavily, but even the beer's not what it was, no longer local and lacking the Thames Valley 'chalky water' taste.[54] Orwell is anticipated ten years earlier in H. V. Morton's bestselling *In Search of England*, which sets off on a similar trajectory, hurrying through 'The Place Where London Ends' on the way to proper country: 'In a field some way off the high road were scared-looking, pink and white villas . . . Wives as new as the gardens and the houses busied about their work . . . London is . . . moving on . . . another mile along the road; more pink and white houses; more shops; more wives; more babies.'[55]

An Octopus in Ribbons

While the suburb in general might be presented as a site of stifling stability, in one form it could signify a misguided and uncontrolled energy. Priestley considered the processes of urban growth: 'very soon the road that was specially made to escape the town has now become a sort of town itself . . . This is called *Ribbon Development*, and it is going on all over England. It is no good to anybody.'[56] Ribbon development made the city an 'octopus', growing in a 'Natural' rather than 'Controlled' style;[57] nature is here a problem rather than the solution. The octopus image was popularized by Williams-Ellis's *England and the Octopus*, but had been originally deployed in 1915 by Abercrombie in an essay on the Belgian modernist poet Emile Verhaeren's *Les Villes Tentaculaires*. Again, English ruralism shows a strange orbit. Abercrombie found in Verhaeren's poem 'Les Idées' 'the motto of town-planners': 'Over the town whose deadly terrors flame / reign, though unseen of man, / The shining plans of thought'.[58] Abercrombie proclaimed 'the power of great ideas, fearlessly advocated, in order to lead the energies of the city into the right channels . . . all the energy is there – it only lacks direction'.[59] The octopus image captured this sense of expansive vigour, ribbon development being presented as an appallingly lively town-country hybrid; 'a vigorous hybrid growth', a 'hectic Saturnalia of ugliness'.[60] Boumphrey admitted that the vulgar might lead active lives:

the great majority, the speculative builder and those who buy his wares, may have shocking taste – they *have* shocking taste; but they are at least vital, alive. They make up the England of to-day, watching bad films, listening to bad music, reading bad literature . . . There is more health in them, for all their bad taste, than in those who would model the future on the past.[61]

Combating the octopus thus demanded not nostalgia or escapism but 'a live, growing sense of order, decency and beauty',[62] with the sense of a necessarily modern response heightened by the aerial nature of the octopus image. Here was a plan view, a mappable disorder. The ability to take a literal and metaphorical overview was

City of Nottingham Housing Department.   "Wirral Countryside Guide" (C.P.R.E.)

Controlled, grouped development, away from the main road. Compact and orderly in itself, this method of development does not injure the surrounding countryside.

Aerofilms Ltd.

Uncontrolled ribbon development.

Straggling, monotonous, and uneconomic, it destroys the country without conferring the advantages of the town.

6 'Grouped Development and Scattered Development'. From Peak District Advisory Panel, *Housing in the Peak* (Sheffield, 1934).

central to preservationists' self-styled authority. Maps and aerial photographs are routinely deployed as a familiar expert currency, signifying a position of advanced technology and expert author-ity.[63] Thus in a CPRE housing guide 'compact and orderly' public housing at Wollaton in Nottingham won out against a tentacle of 'Uncontrolled ribbon development. Straggling, monotonous, and uneconomic, it destroys the country without conferring the advantages of the town'[64] (illus. 6). Such images establish the pres-ervationist as an enlightened overseer; passionate yet detached, expert and mobile, distinct from the supposedly closed-in, narrow, near-sighted developer on the ground. In *Britain and the Beast* John Moore recounted a flight over the Cotswolds:

> you can walk for miles in a straight line over our hills and see nothing that is not lovely, nothing that offends you. But if you take a bird's-eye view of the district as a whole you get a very different impression ... one can see the tracks of the beast very clearly from the air ... I could see the towns and even some of the villages nibbling their way outwards, not wisely and orderly, but as haphazard and casually as caterpillars nibbling at a leaf; I could see the mess creeping along the sides of all the roads that radiated from the towns.[65]

Shacks, Plans and Freedom

From his hired Tiger Moth Moore spotted that even beyond the ribbons, beyond any possible Green Belt, there were outliers of the octopus. The preservationists' country ideal was the nucleated English village; but instead of this they documented a spreading reality of dispersal, of 'pepperpot development', with dwellings shaken at random over the land in an 'indiscriminate scattering'.[66] Dispersal could also proceed through disorganized groupings. Denis Hardy and Colin Ward have documented the conflicts arising from the grouping of 'shacks' on 'plotlands', pieces of land divided and sold to individuals who self-built homes, often with few services laid on.[67] Winifred Holtby's 1936 novel *South Riding: An English Landscape* featured shacks on the Holderness coast of Yorkshire's East Riding, and it is worth quoting her description at length:

> Two miles south of Kiplington, between the cliffs and the road to Maythorpe, stood a group of dwellings known locally as The Shacks. They consisted of two railway coaches, three caravans, one converted omnibus, and five huts of varying sizes and designs. Around these human habitations leaned, drooped and squatted other minor structures . . . A war raged between Kiplington Urban District Council and the South Riding County Council over the tolerated existence of The Shacks.
>
> In winter the adjacent ground was trampled mud . . . In summer the worn and shabby turf was littered with paper, stale bread, orange skins, chicken food, empty bottles, and the droppings of three goats, four dogs, one donkey, three motor-bicycles, thirty-six hens and two babies. In summer The Shacks hummed with exuberant human life. Young men rattled down at week-ends on motor-bicycles from Kingsport. Young women tumbled, laughing and giggling and clutching parcels, from the buses. Urban youths with pimpled faces and curvature of the spine exposed their blotches and blisters to the sun, turning limp somersaults over the creaking gate . . . Gramophones blared, loud-speakers uttered extracts of disquieting information about world politics or unemployment in cultured voices, . . . revellers returned late from Kiplington bars; the lighted tents glowed like luminous convolvulus flowers in the dark humid nights.[68]

South Riding is a complex story of love and local government, new orders of planning and dying squirearchies, whose 168-charactered detail is beyond this study. Holtby is notable, though, in presenting both positive and negative visions of shack life, giving space to a social and aesthetic complexity missing from either the promotion of plots as paradise or the condemnation of them as evil. For Holtby's socialist councillor and planner Astell, the Shacks are 'a public eyesore and a scandal', a 'rural slum' symbolizing a stagnant and reactionary countryside.[69] For summer visitors, they are a site of social freedom. For one of the two year-round resident families, the poor but respectable Mitchells, dreams of property mix with social shame: 'To Nancy Mitchell, keeping herself to herself in Bella Vista, this halcyon life added insult to life's injury. The girls in bathing suits, the boys sunning themselves naked to the waist, the braying of jazz from portable wireless sets . . . the vagabond company of the Shacks destroyed her edifice of respectability.'[70] For the other resident family, the Hollys, with 'no such pretensions', the Shacks are last resort rather than country property. Daughter Lydia Holly seeks escape through education, and Holtby's progressive heroine headmistress Sarah Burton sees planning as a vehicle for improvement: 'The projected road from Kingsport, the subsequent development of the town, were steps towards the education of Lydia Holly.'[71]

Holtby's treatment of the plotlands is complex and relatively generous. For preservationists this world of gramophones, unmade roads, railway coaches and exuberant shack life was simply and nationally disgraceful. Williams-Ellis told of a speculative building 'Archfiend': 'You found five thousand acres of Downland pasture – the immemorial resort of peaceful wanderers from the adjacent towns: you left it a forlorn and struggling camp of slatternly shacks and gimcrack bungalows, unfinished roads and weatherbeaten advertisements . . . You brought chaos out of order.'[72] Plotlands become symbols of speculation, deprivation, visual disorder and social marginality, transgressing the preservationists' morality of settlement, hardly a place and beyond public authority. Preservationists attacked the lack of design in shacks, their improvised construction out of old railway carriages or kit houses. Williams-Ellis picked out the 'Cottabunga' (illus. 7), a kit bungalow with mock-Tudor 'artistic' pretensions which was said to be 'dotted all over the countryside,

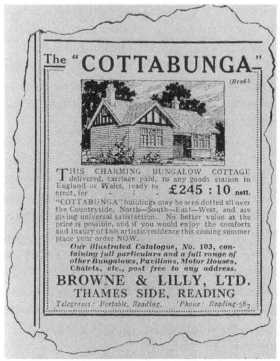

7 The 'Cottabunga'. From Williams-Ellis, *England and the Octopus*, endpapers.

North-South-East-West'. For Abercrombie the danger was that instant buildings might linger:

> It is optimistic to count upon the temporariness of many shacks, caravans-on-posts, old railway coaches, and static omnibuses ... These objects, seedy on their first appearances (as they are seldom new), do not mellow with time, but have a knack of lingering on, patched and botched, into a decrepit and disreputable old age which becomes their perished soul as hoary mouldiness does rotten fruit.[73]

Plotlands also offended as marginal social spaces, although the offence is here accentuated by their echoing elements of preservationist philosophy. Many sites were established in the context of post-war housing shortages and the desire and/or physical necessity for ex-servicemen to live outside an urban atmosphere. While Abercrombie could admire a pioneer spirit in 'the younger people who returned from a life of open-air hardship during the war, and who were determined not to be cribbed in the respectable rows of suburban houses built the sanitary by-laws', he could not admire the resultant immoral geography: 'Hence, egged on by housing shortage, that sudden springing up of congeries of shacks, bungalows and caravans-grown-stationary, which soon become insanitary and have had a certain reputation for lawlessness of life. Many a Medical Officer and, indeed, certain officials from the Ministry of Health have been puzzled how to deal with them and they still remain today.'[74] As Hardy and Ward suggest, a sense of marginality and on occasion Bohemianism was central to the appeal of plotlands since they were places which combined property and freedom in an egalitarian space beyond external authority.[75] Here was a fringe geography beyond planning control, yet one whose ideals, derivative of Morris, Kropotkin and especially Thoreau, echoed the preservationists' own pastoral ideal. However, while preservationists could welcome a Thoreauian engagement with nature, plotlands were illegitimate descendants, 'a travesty of the hut in the wilderness'.[76] Two pastorals clashed; the ordered and systematic preservationist rural Englishness and the ragged, irregular, marginal pastoral of escape, not overly concerned about its setting in a national order of settlement. A Thames Valley shack resident remembered: 'we wanted a place which was primitive, where the children could do what they liked. They could play pirates, build rafts, fall in the river and get covered in mud, and nobody minded.'[77] But some did mind. The CPRE's Thames Valley Survey of 1929 warned against anything other than 'orderly camps of tents':

> *Huts, Shacks and Disused Railway-carriages, etc.*
> The hut or shack built of temporary materials and often patched together should not be allowed on the Thames anywhere …

There is a well-marked tendency for sheds to grow up in an insidious manner. At first a simple hut is erected behind the tents for cooking and other purposes; the next stage is for the family to take their meals in the shed in wet weather; a dining-room follows ... This tendency should be carefully watched and no temporary or semi-permanent buildings allowed by the Local Authorities.[78]

The geographical marginality of plotlands, occupying sold-off strips along rivers and coasts, could paradoxically serve to place them on sites of symbolic importance. The cliffs and marshes of the east coast received rather less preservationist attention than the Thames Valley and south-east coast, where plots pricked the sacred geographies of Englishness:

pollution has infected practically the whole stretch of the coasts of Sussex and Kent ... a bungaloid growth has sprung up of quite unspeakable ugliness and vulgarity. Shacks and old tram cars have appeared on the beach ... all around the coast the same destruction of the elementary amenities of privacy and beauty is going on. Consider Shoreham, for instance, or Peacehaven![79]

Peacehaven, on the Sussex cliffs between Brighton and Newhaven, was the coastal symbolic equivalent of Slough, its name playing on preservationist visions of rural harmony. Here for Howard Marshall was 'a monstrous blot on the national conscience', for Thomas Sharp 'a national laughing-stock';[80] and for Graham Greene in *Brighton Rock* a shabby and exposed overworld counterpart to the urban underworld of Brighton, a cliff-top 'scarred and shabby side of England'.[81] This local site became a national symbol, and thus a suitable climax for one of Williams-Ellis's extended rants on 'the intrusive impertinence of the bungalow': 'they care no more for the country they are billetted on than barbarian invaders are wont to do

...they constitute England's most disfiguring disease...Peacehaven may be cited as the classic example of the ravages of this distressing and almost universal development.'[82]

The Pattern of a Good Country

What then is the nature of the English country which needs to be saved from such atrocity? The preservationist language of violation, disease, rash, disfigurement, feeds off a sense of the country as a body, specifically female, requiring defence by chivalrous Saint Georgic preservationists.[83] This is not the defence of a 'virgin' countryside, rather the country is regarded as a mature and respectable woman; Abercrombie found 'not a Vestal but a Ceres, a well-cultivated matron!'[84] An imagery of sexual chaos and confusion applies here as much as it did in Sharp's hermaphrodite suburb, since architects and builders, 'the chief criminals in England's rape', are accused of having 'prostituted themselves to snobbery' with disfigurements which 'violate every canon of seemliness and order and make a slattern of a countryside once serenely gracious'.[85]

This immoral geography makes sense only in relation to an ideal of good grouping and community, an order of settlement which excludes any visual and social disorder. Abercrombie claimed that England had 'invented the village'.[86] Cornish called lowland village England the British 'Arcadia' and said that, 'whereas every feature of wild landscape in Britain can be matched or excelled in other countries, the unspoilt parts of agricultural England have a beauty which is unique in the scenery of civilization.'[87] Preservationists mix a nostalgic evocation of past village order with an imagery of modern settlement networks, geometries which have no place for shacks. Cornish's account of his peaceful Suffolk childhood mixes bucolic memory with a geometry of settlement form and function: 'The parish boundary was about the limit of the daily trudge from the village street ... Few things that mattered much in our daily life were beyond the horizon of the parish, and everything within that horizon entered into our life.'[88] Driving through Suffolk for his CPRE travel book *The Scenery of England*, Cornish still detected a bucolic geometry: 'Passing quickly, in the modern way, through parish after parish, each successive encirclement of the undulating landscape was seen subordinate to an ancient church with lofty tower for which a slight eminence of land was the pediment.'[89] Parish topography fits communal function, with central buildings giving the community a focus.

The modern secular church-equivalent was the village hall, promoted as a means to centre rural communities which were moving away from an older church- and manor-centred society. The preservation of rural England was seen to entail a revitalization of rural life, with groups such as Women's Institutes and Rural Community Councils offering ways to a new sense of community. Peach and Carrington suggested that it was: 'all to the good that village life is no longer so dull. Women's Institutes, wireless, gramophones and even cinemas have done much to enliven the agricultural worker's leisure. It is all to the good that villagers are demanding better homes, for many of the picturesque old cottages were as unhealthy as they could be.'[90] The distinctiveness of rural life is sustained via its transformation, with voluntary movements seeking to cultivate a new rural social order. In 1939 Mary Kelly, founder of the Village Drama Society, looked back to 1918: 'When a wood is cut down, the seeds of innumerable plants, which have been lying dormant in the shade, feel the sun and the air, and spring into life and flower; and in just such a way all kinds of social forces broke through to the surface after the devastation of the Great War ... we awoke, after the war, to find that we were living in a different world.'[91]

In the event, voluntary action tended less to usurp than to become intertwined with older structures of authority. Such arguments for social change, though, formed part of a general argument in interwar Britain that, after several decades of agricultural depression (the wartime revival having been followed by a further 'betrayal' of farming with the removal of price support

8 'Power Potentials'. From F. G. Thomas, *The Changing Village* (London, 1939).

in 1921[92]), preservation of the country would be pointless without economic revival. With the picturesqueness of the country taken as an expression of decay, the preservationist aesthetic embraced economic liveliness. F. G. Thomas's Devon-based 'essay on rural reconstruction', *The Changing Village*, argued for economic, social and political change to harness the 'Power Potentials' of people and technology (illus. 8), symbolized by a young man posed against a pylon on a modern, wire, concrete-posted fence.[93] The footloose power of electricity might transform the country and so reroot the youth. While in Thomas's account there is a suspicion of the possible restrictive implication of words such as 'preservation' and 'amenity', the discourse of preservation as outlined above shared this taste for tapping new energy. We discuss the preservationist reaction to the pylon below, but in terms of economy the preservationist argument follows that for community; maintain rural distinctiveness through transformation. Abercrombie criticized planning schemes which by excluding agriculture debased it as 'a motive force' and reduced it to a feature 'providing effects for the painter or colouring the views from suburban or weekend windows'.[94] For Williams-Ellis, 'the very notion that "development" excludes agriculture shows how our national outlook has become urbanized, or rather suburbanized'.[95] Geographer-preservationist Dudley Stamp's national Land Utilisation Survey, undertaken with voluntary labour from 1931, sought to provide the basis for a planning which gave priority to the maintenance of good quality agricultural land.[96] In Stamp's work, and elsewhere, an aesthetic of agricultural improvement is based on the assumption that if landscape is not natural but humanly shaped, then it is in the nature of the countryside to be planned and functionally designed. Abercrombie found support in history – 'the pioneer spirit has been planning the English countryside for some two thousand years ... Those who suggest that country planning is a new and repugnant idea are indeed ignorant of the elements of our history'[97] – and suggested that if the 'scientific planning and development' of agriculture entailed removing some 'precious history in greenery' then so be it. Hedge removal might even improve the landscape:

> there are certainly parts of England whose landscape will be improved by a greater display of sweeps of open, highly cropped fields: a new scale may be added to what in some places is a monotonous iteration of hedge and hedgerow tree. Everywhere, where this agricultural change occurs, the quality of landscape fitness and beauty is to be super-added.[98]

It is in this context of a landscaped progress that we should interpret preservationist attempts to formulate aesthetic principles of landscape design. Without an established, expert, disciplinary language of landscape design to turn to, preservationists developed a rhetoric of aesthetic science whereby values and disinterestedness were able to coexist, and detached judgements on beauty could be made. Aesthetic science, like a ride in an aeroplane, enabled the expression of a passionate detachment. Cornish built his own 'aesthetic geography' around 'harmonies of scenery': 'as far as concerns Scenery and Climate I can now formulate a general aesthetic of geography which can be applied ad infinitum in the description of localities'.[99] CPRE President Lord Crawford introduced Cornish's *The Scenery of England*, subtitled *A Study of Harmonious Grouping in Town and Country*, as providing 'a philosophic basis for the aesthetics of scenery, built upon the ultimate foundation of our geology and geography'.[100] The journal *Nature*, for whom Cornish went on to review art exhibitions, devoted an editorial to his 'Science of Scenery': 'The laws of scenery may be compared with those of music. They are the laws of harmony.'[101] While Cornish made his own aesthetic way, Abercrombie sought inspiration for *The Preservation of Rural England* in China: 'It is no use turning to other European countries for guidance . . . their genius in design has been almost entirely confined to their towns . . . But China for a thousand years or more has been devoting its unrivalled artistic genius to this very question.'[102] Abercrombie offered readers the philosophy of Feng Shui, 'the science of "adapting the residence of the living and the dead so as to co-operate and harmonize with the local currents of the cosmic Breath". The veneration for natural science combined with the necessity of humanly using it and modifying it are thus given a spiritual setting. But the aim is equally practical.'[103] Feng Shui appealed as a doctrine of intervention which vested authority in the planner as composer of landscape:

The professor of Feng Shui . . . is placed in a position of extreme power. We can hardly anticipate a practice based upon such esoteric principles . . . But it should be possible to evolve a system of landscape design which will be authoritative enough to prevent brutal outrage on the one hand and a misguided attempt at a bogus naturalism or faked antiquity on the other.[104]

Abercrombie considered the Chinese landscape 'probably the most elaborately composed that has ever existed';[105] parallel compositional principles might be useful in England's Dangerous Age: 'There is no anomaly about the artificial handling of the country . . . the countryside . . . has already been artificialized humanly but unconsciously; it is no crude step to substitute a conscious treatment during a period of sudden change.'[106] The preservation of the country demanded planned action; England wanted designing.

Moral Landscapes

We now consider in more detail the preservationist criteria of praise and abuse. A moral landscape emerges wherein structures are to embody moral principles and offenders are to be cleared out. Loudness, vulgarity, impertinence on the one side, dignity, composure and fitness on the other, provide a lexicon of architectural (and human) conduct for English landscape.

Languages of Abuse

Preservationists delighted in listing offending articles; in *England and the Octopus* Williams-Ellis offered a 'Devil's Dictionary' of 23 mostly offensive categories from advertisements to water, while for Abercrombie there were 'seventeen headings, with some minor subdivisions' covering actual and potential disfigurement.[107] Four key terms of abuse run through such lists: loudness, impertinence, alienness and shamness.

An unsigned account of a visit to the Leicester 'Save the Countryside' exhibition tells of a loud surprise:

As one entered the quaint and restful garden which surrounds the pleasant University building, two large hoardings on the lawns shouted at one. These consisted of the usual enamelled petrol and cigarette signs with their hard, brutal colouring; and how incongruous they seemed here! Over each was written: – 'You don't like these here. Why do you have them on the streets and countryside?' This was one of the notes of the Exhibition.[108]

Advertisements, especially enamel signs, were held to be loudly offensive in both country and town. Signs were found guilty of 'the "hogging" of the English village',[109] with the only solution being removal so that the cultural signs of landscape and built heritage could be open to view: 'Building, road widening, petrol stations, cry out for control; the hoarding, in a loud and rancorous voice, for extermination.'[110] The CPRE responded to roadside symbols of *laissez-faire* by trying to present preservationism as commercial sense, hailing Shell's decision to remove signs from open country and use lorry hoardings instead as a gesture of environmental responsibility and a selling point: 'Shell's Ways are Different.'[111] If in the country extermination was the only solution, in the city some tidy displays might be allowed. The tidy signs of the Empire Marketing Board and the neat hoardings of Zurich, 'city of tidiness',[112] were applauded as standing out from a general chaos. Civic affront was most acute at the entrance to the towns, Williams-Ellis declaring that, 'many of our larger towns have allowed their main approaches to be devastated . . . tatterdemalion and slattern'.[113] A Bovril sign welcomed visitors to London: 'After meeting this . . . one is not surprised to find London as it is.'[114] Hoardings were a sign of a deeper malaise which helped decline along.

Signs were not only loud but 'impertinent', lurking and unpredictable country monsters, appearing 'like mushrooms in the night'.[115] This schoolmasterly tone runs through Peach's December 1929 address to the Royal Society of Arts in which he denounced 'the vulgar shouting signs which spring up behind hedges'.[116] Advertisers and their signs needed to be taught a lesson; in such accounts it is as if the sign itself takes on a life of its own, popping up here and there and making a visual racket. Also impertinent were bungalows, especially those with loud pink asbestos roofs. These spoilt Cyril Joad's country pleasures: 'You may have been walking for an hour in a secluded valley . . . you feel at peace with a world which, in becoming remote, becomes innocuous. You top a rise and immediately there breaks upon the view some shouting pink horror.'[117] Such things were not only seen as loud and impertinent but as alien, although here there was debate over what exactly made for alienness. Colour? Form? Texture? Preservationists argued especially over whether a building made out of non-local material could harmonize with the landscape. Historically it was agreed that the use of local building materials had produced a harmony of architecture, geology and scenery; the Cotswolds were upheld as the archetypal example. Debate arose over whether contemporary buildings should harmonize through material and stylistic imitation or contrast. On one side, some preservationists effectively played up to a regressive image. L. Dudley Buxton considered the:

> appalling tendency to put wrong things in the wrong places. Economic reasons no doubt must in the end carry the day, and we cannot all build Cotswold manor houses, but I am assured that, within reason; it does not cost more to build a house suited to its environment, provided we know the type that really is suited. If we shoot partridges at all, we do not shoot them in May, so why should we be less particular in our habits when we start out to make a new road, a new house or a new suburb?[118]

On the other side were those like A. R. Powys, Secretary of the Society for the Protection of Ancient Buildings, who like Bertram criticized 'the group which *echoes, without digesting them*, the words and phrases that the leaders of the Council for the Preservation of Rural England movement, or of the Society for the Protection of Ancient Buildings movement, have used in relation to some special case'. For Powys localism for its own sake was a barrier to preservationist progress: 'They demand the use of local materials, a use which has become a burden to the man who needs to build; they demand that England shall live in accord with the catchwords of a few men who do not know that what was once good is now bad.'[119] The argument turned on the question of what belonged, on the appropriate geography of building, with the general solution offered as a principle of ordered variety according to function. For some purposes standardization was appropriate; the pylons for the new National Grid and Sir Giles Gilbert Scott's new red telephone boxes which for Williams-Ellis disproved the notion that 'standardization means ugliness'.[120] In all cases, though, diversity in design would only imply variation within rather than fragmentation of a national order. Bertram echoed Powys: 'Uniformity is better than chaos. But what the town-planner wants . . . is order. That is not at all the same thing as uniformity. No, we want variety, but ordered variety, not everybody following their own sweet will, which seems usually nowadays to be not at all sweet.'[121]

'Shamness' was the final term of abuse; an object should harmonize historically as well as geographically by expressing its own time. Peach and Carrington contrasted a 'genuine old half-timbered English house', whose construction methods were equivalent to today's 'modern steel', with 'the silly sham which a cult of "old-world" atmosphere has given us. Creosoted planks are usually nailed on the front of ordinary brick construction.'[122] Such dishonest buildings were held to nurture sham people. Bertram echoed Osbert Lancaster's caricatures of 'Stockbrokers Tudor' and 'By-Pass Variegated' in condemning the 'Tudoristic' or 'bijou baronial' of the 'average bungalow': 'If the owner were logical he would wear cheap tin armour or hodden grey. In fact he wears a cap and a reach-me-down and maybe a bowler hat and gent's suiting on

9 'The Last (Or Museum) Stage of the English Country!' From C.E.M. Joad, *A Charter for Ramblers* (London, 1934); drawing by William Kermode.

Sundays, because he is neither a knight nor a villein, but Mr Smith of "Osocosy".[123] Bertram casts himself as a design physician for the suburban self: 'we must kill by ridicule the absurd "ye olde worlde" cult that has infected English design with dishonesty'.[124] Such attacks on the sham anticipate more recent caricatures of the 'heritage industry'. William Kermode's frontispiece to Joad's *A Charter for Ramblers* showed 'The Last (Or Museum) Stage of the English Country' (illus. 9):

> Its beauty may be embalmed and preserved as an exhibit in the form of beauty spots, with price of admission at so much per head. A meadow, a clump of elms, a water wheel, a thatched cottage, featuring roses round the doorway and an old lady spinning in the porch, with rustic fauna . . . gathered around her skirts, and rustic apparatus . . . thrown in to taste, would do very well as an exhibit.[125]

Preservationists posited a different relationship between tradition and modernity, with the truly traditional being true to its own age. The CPRE's Peak District Advisory Panel, identifying a local tradition of 'Harmony with the Landscape' and 'Fitness for Purpose', proposed 'Difference Without Discordance', with new materials such as concrete deployed in forms 'of necessity different from the old'.[126] Fearful that 'it would not be surprising if future ages called this one the Bogus Age',[127] and suggesting that 'those of us who advocate twentieth-century houses for twentieth-century people are the real traditionalists',[128] Bertram saw the DIA and CPRE leading the way into a new age of design: 'I am convinced that the tide has turned. I am convinced that out of the chaos of a hundred years, in all its aspects from towns to teapots, a way is being found towards a new and better era of rational and beautiful twentieth-century design.'[129] We now consider the detail of preservation's modernity.

Towards a New England: Moral Modernities

Terming this preservation 'modern' or 'modernist' begs a series of questions. The term can signify rather more than a general subscription to 'progress', and I suggest here that preservation needs to be understood in relation to a particular form of modernism which was seeking to produce what might be termed a moral modernity. Preservationists subscribe to a modernism of orderly progress driven by planning; this is hardly the modernity of flux and transition embraced by some forms of literary and artistic modernism. Order and fitness are the key terms as preservationists mix a functionalist tradition deriving from the DIA with elements of the Modern Movement in architecture and design.[130] 'Fitness for purpose' is the key slogan as an orderly, serious and concrete modernism is embraced as opposed to a 'jazz' modern which is put down as frivolous, even ornamental.

Modernism wrote itself up as it went along as the dominant strand in twentieth-century architecture and design, placing itself on the leading edge of a history told in terms of progress. The careers of key CPRE figures such as Abercrombie and Peach indeed follow the movement from the Arts and Crafts pioneers to the machine-age modernists. This path would be mapped out by Pevsner and others as the key trajectory in design history.[131] Peach followed the 'fitness for purpose' philosophy of W. R. Lethaby, later presented by Lewis Mumford as the original modernist: 'no one ever put the case for functionalism better than Lethaby did long before Le Corbusier's manifestoes appeared: all the better because he saw that it was an ordering principle in all aspects of life.'[132] Peach looked to Germany for examples of advanced design and social philosophy, promoting the work of the Deutsche Werkbund, founded in 1907 to connect design and industry, and visiting the Bauhaus in 1927. English preservation and German modernism also connected through Frank Pick, involved in the DIA from its foundation in 1915, head of the London Passenger Transport Board and the key figure in promoting modern design on the London Underground. Pick was also a CPRE Executive member from 1926 until his death in 1941. When Walter Gropius's *The New Architecture and the Bauhaus* was translated into English in 1935, Pick provided the Introduction, hailing the book as connecting architecture and everyday design in order to 'restore grace and order to society', with 'spatial harmonies' and 'functional qualities' making for 'a new architectonic arising out of a collective understanding of design in industry'.[133]

Concern for English landscape could therefore embrace the foreign as well as the modern, although here the question is begged of the relationship between national preservation and the international. Preservationists seldom embrace an internationalist language of the modern. On the one hand, preservation plays off different 'national moderns', upholding, say, German and Scandinavian modern order against the American associations of the 'jazz' style. On the other hand, elements of the international modern could be repatriated into Englishness. Whether via affinities of the modern and the Arts and Crafts, or the modern and the Georgian (of which more below), England could be presented as the historic and contemporary home of a modern spirit, thereby able to accommodate the international modern and shape it through its own modern tradition.

Preservationists were not shy of exhibiting the modern. *The Face of the Land* mixes pastoral imagery with strikingly modern locomotives, bridges and factories. Pick's London Underground is upheld for its 'efficient', 'tidy', 'fine' modern station design.[134] Preservation and the most-modern meet in what Bill Luckin has termed a 'techno-Arcadian' response to the National Grid constructed in the late 1920s and 1930s,[135] with the pylon part of a preserved, modern, rural England. The Grid, if laid with care, carried aesthetic as well as social Power Potential. Abercrombie weighed up the possibilities of modern harmony:

It is possible to consider that the two lofty steel standards which are placed on either side of the Severn and are seen from the cliff at Nuneham give a fine vertical note to a somewhat flat scene ... Or again, the series of pylons seen striding across the bare and rather dull hills of Palestine may possess some of the impressive qualities of the aqueducts on the Campagna; but carry that same hard line across the South Downs and a scene of exquisite balanced beauty is mechanized and marred.[136]

The Face of the Land similarly suggested that special areas like the South Downs should not be pyloned for 'the sake of uniformity',[137] but its response to the pylon as an object was unambiguously positive (illus. 10). While ungrouped wooden transmission poles were found 'disquieting', pylons stood out as fit for their purpose and in harmony with the landscape, shot in perspective to convey a composed march of power over the land: 'No one can deny a real beauty in the standards of the upper picture.' These are not the preservationist standards one might expect.[138]

Behind this valuation of the contemporary is a particular narrative of English landscape history. The general temporal principle of modern tradition is underpinned by a specific story of historic highs and lows, with England presented as falling from pre-Victorian grace into present chaos. A display board in the *Save the Countryside* exhibition juxtaposed a reproduction of the 'Hay Wain: England as John Constable saw it', with Strube's *Daily Express* cartoon vision of 'England as we are beginning to see it: Had John Constable Lived To-Day', also issued as a CPRE postcard. Willy Lott's cottage is reduced to a teashop, the haywain carries coals, a garage is by the pool, a vaporous trail of 'Soap' is left across the sky by a skywriting plane.[139] The preservationist history of beauty climaxes in the late eighteenth and early nineteenth centuries: 'A hundred years ago, just before the railway age, this island was almost all beautiful, even more beautiful, perhaps, than it had been a thousand years further back . . . not least the improvements that had been made in the eighteenth century, harmonizing with the older parts in which they were set.'[140] Sharp contrasted the 'bareness and patchiness' of the 'Unconsciously Humanized Landscape' of 1600 with the 'Consciously Humanized Landscape' of 1800: 'New knowledge demanded new forms for its expression . . . It was a wonderful opportunity and it was wonderfully utilized.'[141] The eighteenth century is evoked as an era of

[Photo. Arch. Review

[Photo. C.P.R.E.

The vexed questions of electric pylons can only be touched on. No one can deny a real beauty in the standards of the upper picture, but the lower is disquieting.

10 Pylons. From H. H. Peach and N. Carrington (eds), *The Face of the Land* (London, 1930).

improvement and design whose spirit was lost in Victorian times but might be renewed in modern form today. Preservationist planning becomes the latest manifestation of an English tradition of progress. John Gloag applauded 'the modern movement' and looked back:

> A new world is being prepared and it will be ready when we acknowledge the Machine Age instead of running away from it; and that promised world of open cities and rich countryside, healed of industrial scars, would have perplexed and worried my father, whose world was the nineteenth-century world of disguise and façade, although it would have been perfectly appreciated and understood and enjoyed by my grandfather, who was born in the last golden age of design.[142]

Father was born in 1835, grandfather in 1798. The Georgian and the Modern stand apart like town and country with a Victorian mess in between; the preservationist task was to sweep away the clutter and connect to an earlier age of English design.

Roads

We conclude this chapter by taking the road as a landscape which brought together modern disorder, orderly response, national plans, foreign models, futures and pasts.

E. H. Fryer of the Automobile Association spoke for the CPRE at a 'Beautiful England Conference' on 'Beautiful England as seen by the Motorist on the Road':

> Visualize please a modern, post-war arterial road . . . in a year or two bungalows (cheap and nasty perhaps); allotments; muddy chicken runs; pig styes; filling stations; advertisement hoardings; news bills; flagrant stores . . . a modern highway cursed by . . . ribbon development – or 'go as you please' – It is offensive, objectionable, unnecessary and wasteful.[143]

Similarly angry at the traffic and signs and cafés of a new commercial roadscape, Williams-Ellis commented: 'If that is "modern landscape", I would have none of it.'[144] As we have seen, though, Williams-Ellis was not averse to the modern. Vaughan Cornish envisaged another modern roadscape:

> now we have to cut out new roads which, being for free-wheel traffic at railway speed, must be as straight as possible. They will sometimes obliterate beauties, but if adapted to their various environments will bring in new harmonies. Some should be planted as league-long avenues, vistas of delight, others may run unfenced through the wide prospect of the moor, but never should the great trunk road degenerate into a street of houses.[145]

In this version of the modern road, construction harmonizes. Williams-Ellis saw 'something rather noble about the broad white concrete ribbons laid in sweeping curves and easy gradients across the country – something satisfying in their clean-planed cuttings and embankments'.[146] In *The Face of the Land* a camera set up the view to vanishing point of 'A new road conceived with real vision' (illus. 11), undegenerate, delightful, a contrast to the aerial views shown elsewhere in preservationist literature of 'Our new Great West Road and what has become of it'; running in splendid isolation in 1924, suburban by 1931.[147] In his account of *British Roads* Boumphrey stressed that: 'the Road is the thing – and on that all the accent should be laid … let it bear plain the evidence of our pride rather than of any wish to disguise or hide it.'[148] Boumphrey envisaged a new motorway aesthetic, with novel 'trumpet', 'clover-leaf' and 'double-sided side access' junctions: 'the creation of a new beauty to accord with their purpose, the service of speed and of modern life. Thatched petrol-pumps and suchlike idiocies have no place beside them.'[149]

From 1928 Government concerned itself with road aesthetics through the Ministry of Transport's Roads Beautifying Association.

A new road conceived with real vision. The entrance to Birmingham from Bristol.

11 New roads. From Peach and Carrington (eds), *The Face of the Land.*

Advice on *Roadside Planting* suggested silver birches on outer bends to show up in headlights and poplars planted to signal crossroads. Vegetation would mix function and beauty: 'at the moment we have a glorious opportunity, which will not recur in the future as far as we can see, of planting the roads of England on a comprehensive scale.'[150] Preservationists were, however, suspicious of the RBA as a front 'hiding the misdeeds' of the Ministry,[151] reflecting a divorce of beauty and use, hiding modernity under a bush rather than embracing a modern functional aesthetic. The CPRE promoted an anti-picturesque roadside, with fallen 'Roadside Stones and Monuments' re-erected into 'a firm and upright position',[152] and simple and standard new signs: 'Beauty proceeds from order; disorder makes for danger. The claims of both beauty and safety require that we tidy up our roadsides.'[153] The *Architectural Review*, urging that signs follow 'a modern aesthetic' rather than be 'compromised by added ornament',[154] told a fable of 'Chaos at the Crossroads', with a quiet country junction developing into chaotic jumble: 'signs and accessories everywhere, on the road surface as well . . . their multiplicity by now quite defeats their purpose. Chaos and, inevitable arrival, the ambulance.' The journal totted up the 'remarkable collection' at Tibbett's Corner on Putney Heath: '11 Belisha beacons, 11 lamp standards, . . . 13 "Keep Left" signs, . . . 8 direction signs of different sorts, 4 assorted notice-boards, 1 large "roundabout" island with a decorative pole in the centre and 6 small islands, 1 telephone box, 1 police box, 1 milestone, 1 seat, numerous small posts and trees and the remains of a horse-trough.'[155]

Roadside argument was dominated by the petrol station. J. B. Priestley took the bus from Leicester to Nottingham:

> The two small boys who sat behind me were only interested in filling stations. 'Oo, there's a petrol shop', they cried every time. 'I'n't it pretty?' They are lucky, these lads, for if their taste does not improve, they will be able to travel on all the main roads of England in an ecstasy of aesthetic appreciation.

Perhaps many of their elders think the petrol stations pretty.
Perhaps the confounded things *are* pretty, and we are all wrong
about them.[156]

Preservationists regretted 'impertinent' and 'Wild West' garages
with 'violent' colours and 'slatternly' advertisements generating 'the
most reverberating discord'.[157] The DIA's *The Village Pump* offered
a 'Guide to Better Garages', with Pick and Peach photographing
functional pumps in Europe and the USA: 'The petrol station need
not be ashamed of itself if it is properly fit for its purpose.'[158] A
garage at Beckenham in Kent, 'a style falling between a pagoda and
a half-timbered manor', lost out to a Dorchester station which 'imitates nothing' in 'Fitness for purpose versus the picturesque' (illus.
12). National preservationists were embarrassed when county groups
in Somerset and Oxfordshire organized good garage contests and
handed awards to thatched stations. While *The Service Station*
magazine, sponsors of the Oxfordshire contest, hailed 'A Group
of Picturesque Service Stations', the *Birmingham Sunday Mercury*
poked fun at 'a beauty contest for petrol pumps'.[159] National CPRE
Secretary Herbert Griffin was gloomy: 'thatch and petrol do not
somehow seem to harmonize when it comes to fitness for use.'[160]

Preservationists argued that appropriately bordered roads should
network the nation in modern style, with old lanes preserved by
moving traffic onto a 'first-rate National system'.[161] When the 1937
Trunk Roads Act transferred control of 4,500 miles of road from
county councils to the Ministry and proposed a nationally planned,
constructed and numbered network, the CPRE approved: 'In the
history of nations, roads stand out as lasting memorials of man's
constructive ability, and the progress and prosperity of a people can
be grasped by the quality and efficiency of their lines of communication.'[162] Boumphrey presented roads as arteries of the national
body: 'it is precisely because Britain is so highly developed and
densely populated that she needs a progressive transport system
capable of fulfilling her exacting requirements. The athlete has need

[*National Gardens Guild*

[*National Gardens Guild*

Fitness for purpose versus the picturesque. The upper (at Dorchester, Dorset) imitates nothing yet achieves real beauty of line. The lower (Beckenham, Kent) a style falling between a pagoda and a half-timbered manor, only detracts from an excellent lay-out.

12 'Fitness for purpose versus the picturesque'. From Peach and Carrington (eds), *The Face of the Land*.

of a better circulation than the sedentary worker.'[163] Spatial grading would preserve old local 'Lanes' and speed new traffic along 'Trunk' roads and high-speed 'Race-Track' motorways:[164] 'we may build great double roads linking the country from sea to sea ... we can do these things and bring order out of chaos to our through roads, peace after turmoil to our homely service roads and little country lanes.'[165]

History again showed progressive precedents. For Abercrombie, Telford's eighteenth-century Menai-Holyhead road anticipated modern zoning: 'Under modern conditions Telford would have eliminated all cross-roads or direct access to his new road, except perhaps three or four in the 25 miles; it would then, used in conjunction with the old road, have met local as well as through needs in a truly modern way.'[166] Further back the Romans had been 'the first to plan the country consciously on a national scale'.[167] Interwar road histories consistently posit a contemporary rediscovery of Roman 'road sense': 'We have in our Roman roads a magnificent heritage which has been of incalculable service to us in the past as well as an inspiration to generations of road-makers. Surely it is a mistake not to use it to the utmost.'[168] Still further back some seized upon the 'Old Straight Track' system of ley lines, 'discovered' in the 1920s by Alfred Watkins (and to which we return in Chapter Two), as an advanced ancient system.[169]

Roads also demonstrated the preservationists' tendency to construct their modern Englishness in relation to elsewhere. Robert Moses's U.S. 'parkway' model showed the potential of State roadside regulation: 'one feels that one is traversing a drive threading a far-flung national park, which is indeed the case.'[170] Griffin corresponded with Moses, then Commissioner for Parks in New York, who sent the CPRE some policy reports;[171] a future demon of environmental destruction makes common ground with English rural preservationists. In Europe fascist Italy's autostrada also offered hoarding-free road design,[172] but the key model for the English motorway was the German autobahn.[173] For a 1937 delegation

13 'Plan and Afterthought', showing auto-bahns and arterial roads. From N. Carrington, *The Shape of Things* (London, 1939); drawings by 'Lehlak'.

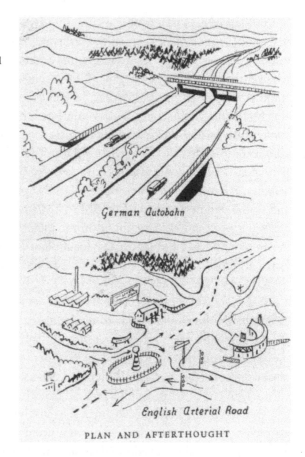

German Autobahn

English Arterial Road

PLAN AND AFTERTHOUGHT

of British MPs here was 'sheer clean beauty', 'vigorous sweeping curves', 'bold and severe design' in harmony with landscape.[174] The *Architectural Review* felt that: 'To form an idea of the way in which such roads can be made to merge into the countryside, we can hardly do better than to consider . . . the Reichsautobahnen.'[175] In *The Shape of Things* Noel Carrington contrasted 'Plan and Afterthought' (illus. 13), the autobahn moving through and with the landscape, the English Arterial Road a wobbly cluttered form unsure of its aims.[176] On the autobahn network a *Landschaftsanwalt*, a counsel for the landscape, supervised landscape harmonies in each district.

The borders were to be model ecological landscapes, symbolic land-scapes of German plant geography. Preservationists suggested the same for England, with 'virgin soil and turf ... set aside and re-used to cover the scars'.[177] In January 1937 Griffin sought advice not only from Moses but also from Walther Schoenichen, Director of the Reichstelle für Naturschuss, with whom Peach had corresponded some years earlier over questions of litter and citizenship, and who recommended the General Inspector of German Highways periodical *The Road*, and Erich Heinicke's *The Unity of Road and Landscape*. A translated article on the 'Landscaping of Highways and Autobahns in Germany' (from *Die Reichsautobahnen. Principles of Design and Construction*), found in the CPRE Archive, stressed harmonies of road and landscape, local planting, 'Principles of Form' and the 'rhythm and change' of landscape in the 'adventure of movement' which was high-speed travel.[178]

Nazi Germany promoted the autobahn as a distinctly Nazi achievement, showing off roads to foreign delegations, and praise for the autobahn again raises suggestions of authority in English preservationism. Boumphrey thought that there was 'little enough reason to concede over-much merit to Nazi Germany for the encouragement of art or culture generally; but for the design and construction of the Reichsautobahnen she must be given the high-est praise. These great roads ... are magnificent and inspiring.'[179] The *Architectural Review* admired more than design: 'impossible not to admire the boldness and comprehensiveness of thought with which the Germans are constructing these roads. In England ... we get no further than talking of preservation; in Germany, realizing man's creative abilities, they set out to create amenity.'[180] James Shand has argued that: 'Given the conditions of the 1930s, only a dictatorship like Hitler's could mobilize the nation for the con-struction of such a highway system so far ahead of the needs of its time.'[181] While it would be absurd to equate autobahn admiration with fascism, it would be equally absurd to ignore the intimations of cultural and political authority present in these road discussions.

If preservationists argued that the state of the landscape was a reflection of the state of the nation, if they stressed ordered progress under new authority, if they sought to make a moral landscape through national planning, then they could not view the autobahn as a non-political road. For fascist enthusiasts the message was simple: the autobahn was a symbol of good fascist order. For most preservationists things were less straightforward; English order meant something different and authority would take a different route. The autobahn was an awkward inspiration for the shape of things in England; confusingly clear.

2

Arts of Living: Landscape and Citizenship, 1918–39

> if our belief ... in the permanent importance of right leisure using ... has any content and meaning, then we shall see in the English countryside not only a possession of beauty which, having inherited from the past we are morally bound to hand down undefiled to posterity, but an instrument, the most important we possess, for the training of the citizens of the future in the art of right living.
> CYRIL JOAD, 1934[1]

Between 1918 and 1939 open-air leisure in England took on a new scale and scope. This chapter traces how the vision of a new, ordered Englishness extended to matters of landscape and citizenship.[2] Arguments over conduct in the country formed part of a broad culture of landscape; we will encounter here communist ramblers, scouts and guides, saucy satirists, health campaigners, charabancers, modern dancers, youth hostellers and nature mystics. For preservationists walking, cycling, camping and map-reading made up an 'art of right living' whereby individual and nation might give form to itself environmentally, generating intellectual, moral, physical and spiritual health.[3] However, arguments for citizenship always worked in relation to a sense of 'anti-citizenship'. While a landscaped citizenship is set up as potentially open to all and nationally inclusive, it depends for its self-definition on a vulgar other, an anti-citizen whose conduct, if not open to re-education, makes exclusion necessary. If the landscape was to be a public space, what kind of public should it permit and cultivate? Statements on landscape are again bound up with claims to cultural authority over its value and purpose.

Distinctions of citizenship and anti-citizenship turned on questions of appropriate conduct and aesthetic ability. Landscaped citizenship worked through a mutual constitution of the aesthetic and the social, the eye and the body. The aim of extending visual pleasure to the people was tempered by a desire to control potentially disruptive bodily effects. The education of the eye was to be accompanied by a self-control in the body. Eagleton has argued that the aesthetic as a category has consistently been torn between an abstracted elevated beauty and a grounding in sensual bodily pleasure, and that such a dialectic of embodiment and elevation generates a power in the aesthetic to disrupt and disturb.[4] The purpose here was to extend the social power of beauty, yet maintain it as a discrete category for controlled reflection and definition. Dialectical tensions of eyes and bodies, the visceral and the cerebral, pleasure and citizenship, ecstasy and organization, run through these landscapes of leisure. Indeed they are inherent in any attempts to legislate for enjoyment, always there to be negotiated, stretched, stumbled over, inhabited.

Motoring Pastoral

In the interwar period the spaces of rural leisure were transformed in terms of technology, social movement and literary accompaniment. Urban excursions into the country were not new; people of all classes had made their way before by rail and cycle. The railway, focusing passengers into the area around a station, still played a key role, with companies issuing walking guides and organizing excursions. Joad described a Manchester escape scene: 'The Central Station at Manchester early on a Sunday morning is an unforgettable sight; with its crowds of ramblers, complete with rucksacks, shorts, and hob-nailed boots ... this generation has replaced beer by "hiking" as the shortest cut out of Manchester.'[5] The railway was by this time a familiar part of the landscape;[6] the car and bus were something new. As car ownership extended into the middle classes, and bus travel and communal charabanc trips were offered for the urban working class, new rural spaces for urban leisure emerged. For Joad the 'motor's capacity for ubiquitous penetration' had 'created a new situation'.[7]

Readers of Kenneth Grahame's *The Wind in the Willows* will recall that the pre-1914 car could be a symbol of reckless modernity and abuse of social standing on the part of necessarily wealthy, Mr Toadish owners.[8] Between the wars the car moved into the symbolically safe hands of the middle classes. Arguments continued to rage over road safety and speed, with the Pedestrians Association exercised by judgements such as that exonerating a motorist who had hit an 86-year-old: 'Old ladies who go about like this may cause any amount of danger to other people. In trying to avoid them, motorists and cyclists may find themselves in difficulties.'[9] While car ownership varied regionally from 23 per 1,000 population in 1927 in Cambridgeshire to 5.8 in Durham, a general increase in numbers, from 78,000 in 1918 to over two million in 1939, reflecting falling prices and a trend to smaller vehicles, allowed the car to establish a middle-class right of way on the road. With the bus and charabanc facilitating working-class motor movement, rural leisure became restyled around the petrol engine, and a motoring pastoral developed, in terms of both the object and style of movement. In 1934 Joad noted a change 'in the last dozen years' in 'the habits of motorists', with 'speed' no longer the purpose but instead a diversion from main highways 'in search of beauty'.[10] The Automobile Association transformed itself from a vigilante anti-speed trap group before the War to a respectable club, tour guide and hotel inspector, aiming 'to establish the fact that motorists were good citizens'.[11] AA Secretary Stenson Cooke told the Association's story in *This Motoring*: 'The thruster is nuisance enough on foot. On a horse he can be dealt with. On wheels he became a menace. Fortunately he was rare. The question was how to diminish the species."[12] AA Handbooks opened with a call for politeness:

> With road manners, particularly, as with life itself, it's the little things that count. Every unimportant moment we concede to fellow travellers is an investment in the Bank of Good Nature, returning interest a hundredfold.
>
> We must school ourselves readily to concede that unimportant moment – to allow others their right and proper share of the Road.
>
> Courtesy begets Courtesy.

Motoring became styled as a modern practice in pursuit of an older England, serviced by the AA and a wide illustrated literature. The petrol engine allowed a nostalgic passage to an old country, its landscape and rustic inhabitants fitting through photography and prose into pictorial pastoral conventions.[13] Publishers such as Odhams and Batsford established a distinct mode of country reproduction, while the BBC gave the traditional countryside extensive airspace. It is perhaps too easy, though, to assume that such work was all of a nostalgic piece. If the argument of this book is that ruralism is heterogeneous, then even within self-consciously nostalgic literature we find variation. For example, the Shell County Guides published from the late 1930s under the editorship of John Betjeman and John Piper sought to mark themselves out as more cultivated and aesthetically open than more 'conventional' guides.[14] Brian Cook's distinctive cover wrappings for the Batsford series could shelter dramatic variation within, from H. J. Massingham's *Cotswold Country* ruralist organicism to Edmund Vale's *North Country* landscapes of manufacturing.[15] If one book can be credited as establishing a motoring pastoral genre it is H. V. Morton's 1927 *In Search of England* (illus. 14), which was into its twenty-sixth edition by 1939.[16] Morton suggested that to find England one should go

IN SEARCH OF
ENGLAND

by H·V·MORTON

14 H. V. Morton, *In Search of England*, 32nd edn (London, 1944), dust-jacket; illustration by Alfred Taylor.

into the country; photographs highlighted the old and quiet – 'A Lane in England', 'Wells Cathedral', 'The Pedlar's Way', 'The Avon at Stratford'. Morton ends up with a vicar after harvest festival: '"Well," smiled the vicar, as he walked towards me between the yew trees, "that, I am afraid, is all we have." "You have England," I said.'[17] Even in Morton's text, though, we find a complexity which belies the image of nostalgia as simple. Morton's search had a harder racial edge:

> The 'Back to the Land' cry is a perfectly sound instinct of racial survival ... If those men and women who, as my letter-bag so clearly proves, are starting out in their thousands to discover rural England will see it not merely as a pretty picture ... but as a living thing ... we may be a step nearer that ideal national life: on the one hand the wealthy industrial cities; on the other a happy country-side, ready to give its new blood to the towns, guarding the traditions of the race, ready always to open its arms to that third generation from the city in need of resurrection.[18]

Morton also did not always travel away from the modern. In *In Search of Wales* he lingered over the industrial culture of the coal-fields in a far from idyllic fashion.[19] In *In the Steps of St Paul*, besides finding admirable modernization in Turkey, he presented Paul as 'one of the few men in ancient literature who is absolutely modern', and wondered at the 'magnificent standardization' of ancient Roman communications.[20] Morton's rival nostalgist S.P.B. Mais could similarly turn his hand to the modern, moving from pleasant lanes to marvellous autobahns in his story of 'The English Highway'.[21] And even in Morton's English Cornish 'Eden' of St Anthony-in-Roseland there were machines: 'I turned and saw, framed in the yellow window, the new picture of rural England: old heads bent over the wireless set in the light of a paraffin lamp. London coming to them out of space.'[22]

Morton also sought to mark his guide out from those which gave only a 'pretty picture', thereby identifying his readers as reflective and intelligent travellers, unlike certain others: 'I have seen charabanc parties from the large manufacturing towns ... playing cornets on village greens and behaving with a barbaric lack of manners which might have been outrageous had it not been unconscious, and therefore only pathetic.'[23] The search for England is based on social and aesthetic distinctions concerning how to look and who could see the country. The searchers did not include barbaric charabancers or sheep-like tourists such as Joad's frontispiece museum-gazers, or Americans at Stratford: 'I suppose the old religious shrines also received thousands of sheep-like pilgrims who had no idea why they were pilgrims beyond the fact that it was the right thing to do. How I detest the word "pilgrim" in its modern sense. Also the word "shrine."'[24]

One further complication makes Morton and those like him difficult to dismiss as straightforward nostalgists. This searching is highly reflexive regarding its own conventions. Morton distances himself from his own youthful, rural belief in making England happy 'by teaching it to morris-dance and to sing folk-songs ... by hand-looms and young women in Liberty gowns who played the harpsichord',[25] and indulges in serious and ironic play with travelling roles of pilgrim and romancing knight. Always prominent in his own story, Morton asks the reader to follow not his route but his self-conscious way of experiencing a country. His England is a highly theatrical place, a land consisting of what MacCannell in his analysis of more recent tourism terms 'staged authenticity'.[26] Here is Morton in an Exmoor pub: '"Here," I thought, "is the typical old man for whom I have been looking since I struck Exmoor!" He accepted a tankard of ale with a merry twinkle; and I settled down to hear the simple story of his life.'[27] At Kenilworth Castle, where a guide brings 'an emotional Boston woman' to tears with his history, Morton congratulates him on his oratory: '"I am glad you feel like that. I was an actor once ...".'[28] As in Urry's analysis of the 'tourist gaze', in Morton's England everything is to be consumed as a sign of itself; the village as village Englishness, the pub as typical village pub.[29] Sites become archetypes, and if they are not archetypes they are not proper sites. Morton is hardly the first to do this; as Taylor shows, earlier guides searched for Englishness region by region.[30] His distinction, though, is in carrying out this way of seeing on a national scale. Searching for England becomes a national movement, with an equivalence of travel, literary format and scale of meaning.

Morton's themes of social distinction and the self-conscious cultivation of ways of seeing and being in landscape will recur throughout this chapter. Onto this complex scene of motoring pastoral the preservationists projected their own sense of modern Englishness and modern citizenship. We now consider how they, like Morton, held to particular country manners.

Cultural Trespass: Conduct Unbecoming

While country leisure could be welcomed by preservationists as the means to right living, it could also mark pollution. If Morton warned of cornets, Mais suggested that, 'man has to go through a vigorous training before he can see the country at all'.[31] Country movement could be an act of cultural trespass. Landscaped citizenship is counterpointed by a vision of 'anti-citizens', male or female, and most often belonging to the 'vulgar' working class. As Greta Jones has shown, the progressive planning ideal of good citizenship distinguished between those for whom a better environment would act as a useful habitat, and those irredeemably confined, as progressive social scientist Richard Titmuss put it, to 'the Social Problem Group . . . the source from which all too many of our criminals, paupers, degenerates, unemployables and defectives are recruited'.[32] An inclusive nation rested upon exclusion. A social and anti-social geography comes into play, with bad conduct presumed to emanate from the interior of the city. Behaviour appropriate to a particular urban habitat is out of place in the English rural landscape. The anti-citizen is labelled 'Cockney', regardless of his or her precise sound-of-Bow-Bells geographical origin. Harry Batsford advised on *How to See the Country*, and how to not see:

> We have most of us enough city-dreading Anglo-Saxon blood to feel a rejuvenating transformation at cutting adrift from the huddle of human habitations. But by contrast, take the case of the large party, presumably from the East End, who, a friend of mine said, disgorged themselves from motor-coaches under the Duke of Bridgwater's column on Berkhamsted Common above Aldbury. They produced a gramophone, and started foxtrotting on the turf. 'Why couldn't they have done that at home, Daddy?' said my friend's little boy.[33]

The Cockney acts as a cultural grotesque, signifying a commercial rather than industrial working class whose leisure is centred around consumption and display.[34] Landscape is promoted as a public cultural space through rules of conduct excluding certain members of the public. An ecology of pleasures maps people and their practices onto environments. Cockneys in the country denote cultural transgression, although it is never conversely suggested that a rambler might be an offensive presence in a seaside resort. The encouragement of meaningful access to the country assumes an unbridgeable and hierarchical cultural geographical divide, whereby if one enjoyed, for example, loud music and saucy seaside humour, one could not and would not want to connect spiritually to a hill.

Specific activities signified the anti-citizenship of working-class charabancers and middle-class motor-picnickers: litter, noise, flower-picking and the euphemistic 'disobedient bathing'. Peach's *Let Us Tidy Up* detected a 'flagrant breach of national good form': 'The problem of litter ... has grown out of our laissez faire of the nineteenth century ... We have temporarily lost that sense of fitness and order which helps to make the beauty of the remaining unspoilt bits of eighteenth century England ... This lack of order applies to all sides of our life.'³⁵ For Joad litter was 'a grimy visiting-card which democracy, now on calling terms with the country, insists on leaving after each visit'.³⁶ The CPRE promoted its 'Anti-Litter Campaign' through a postcard showing picnickers gormlessly poking through their mess (illus. 15). Peach contrasted such conduct to 'The Native Indian's Consideration For His Countryside', and to the anti-litter initiatives of Zurich, New York and Germany, corresponding in 1931 and 1932 with Walther Schoenichen of the Prussian Department for the Protection of Nature Reserves on well-designed German bins with rhyming notices. At home there were only the efforts of Girl Guides, local 'Anti-Litter Societies' and the valiant Mrs Bryant Salmon of Braemar, who had 'been trying to help cure the litter plague by "amusing litter rhymes" for three years past'.³⁷

As with buildings, fitness is hailed and alien loudness condemned. Abercrombie detected 'a special ... tone in different countrysides ... the honk of the motor-car, the sound of the gramophone ... do not

ANTI-LITTER CAMPAIGN

Member of Picnic Party (just leaving) "Better have a look round among our litter and see we haven't left anything be'ind."
—By kind permission of " Passing Show."

15 'Anti-Litter Campaign'. Postcard issued by the Council for the Preservation of Rural England, 1928.

enter into the chord: their dissonance is seriously felt and of singular pervasiveness'.[38] Gramophones disturbed the music of place, Joad singling out Black and American alien noises in the Lake District: 'the atmosphere vibrates to the sounds of negroid music. Girls with men are jazzing to gramophones in meadows.'[39] The Anti-Noise League, seeking the 'conservation of nervous energy', encouraged 'the well-mannered citizen to become noise-conscious', and urged prosecution of the loud.[40] Worse still was excrement. The CPRE reported on the dangers of reservoir pollution:

> excretal matter, decaying organic matter from vegetables, fruit, food; and other waste matters etc lying about ... Plus disobe-dient bathing; the swimming of dogs in the reservoir ... and fouling of places where in either small or large numbers one cannot be allowed to relieve nature. These are the temporary but might be serious evils, at the start of a huge, salutary, unanticipated movement.[41]

To guide the giant movement, an informal Country Code was proposed, seen as emerging from walkers' good practice. Joad found a 'special code of townsman's manners in the country': 'they have a passion for the closing of gates, hunt litter like sleuths ... They even appoint voluntary officers ... to see that other walkers obey these ordinances which they have imposed upon themselves.'[42] Cornish evoked the educational importance of being 'taught better', with its inherent threat:

> It cannot be said that the squalid crowding of Haytor Rocks and Becky Falls, with the legacy of filthy litter, is an improve-ment in the recreation of the people. The people who do these things should, in their own interests, be taught better, and when they have been taught they will derive more pleasure from their visits, for some enjoyment of natural beauty will be added to that of mere jollification.[43]

Movement

THE O-A.M. [open-air movement] IS QUITE UNSTOPPABLE. NOR
CAN IT BE BEST GUIDED OR CONTROLLED BY HOSTILE FORCE – FOR
THE VERY LIFE AND SOUL OF THIS O-A.M. IS A NEW DIS-IMPRISON-
MENT: AND THE ETERNAL RECURRENT RIGHT TO A NEW FREEDOM
AND EXPANSION – THE PRINCIPAL INHERENT ATTRIBUTE OF THE
BRITISH. It is indeed and has from its inception already been ruling
itself, educating itself quickly, admirably, and remarkably; but great
numbers in its ever wider national embrace are still quite ignorant.
E. P. RICHARDS, 1935 [44]

People walking in the country, solo or en masse, were seen as part
of a movement comparable in self-definition to modern movements of architecture. The material and metaphorical merge in this
movement, invariably presented as moving morally, spiritually and
physically upwards. Political tensions arose, though, regarding the
freedom to roam over country owned by others.

The year 1930 saw the formation of the Youth Hostels Association
(YHA) and the initial moves towards a National Council of Ramblers'
Federations, which became the Ramblers' Association in 1935.
Cornish welcomed 'a new development of great promise . . . the
formation of clubs and associations for touring the countryside
under definite rules of conduct'.[45] E. P. Richards reflected in 1935
that: 'Only four years ago if one wore a rucksack while walking on
the moors or in the English countryside one drew much attention
and facetious remarks – but today nobody takes any notice.'[46] Some
rambling bodies, however, asserted modes of conduct which did not
fit easily into the preservationist vision of England. A landscape
culture of mass rally and action emerged, ranging from the benign,
as when in 1932 Mais led 16,000 to see the sun rise at Chanctonbury
Ring in Sussex (it was cloudy), to the militant.[47] Movements of this
number inevitably began, especially in the north of England, to
come up against property. Tensions of property and propriety arose

when access was denied, and trespass was the response. In the face of distinctive mass mobilization normally bombastic preservationists, wary of offending landed interests, became reticent, except for Joad.

Joad addressed several mass outdoor rallies: 'It would be difficult to exaggerate the difference between these gatherings of ramblers ... and the ordinary indoor meeting, held in some stuffy hall, where the speaker's voice is punctuated by the coughs of the ailing audience.'[48] Joad spoke of alert and increasingly 'militant' ramblers, 'ready to take the law into their own hands',[49] and recounted the most public example of militancy, the first Mass Trespass on the Derbyshire moorland of Kinder Scout in April 1932. Here was a popular, politicized walking, representing a different country to the England desired by most preservationists, and organized by members of the communist British Workers' Sports Federation. The media were unsympathetic and spoke of political manipulation, as if politics and the open air were mutually exclusive. Trespass organizer Benny Rothman recalls a land reclamation by the people, an assertion of a right to walk on moors closed by owners for shooting,[50] a weekend movement from below, socially and topographically.

Such political walking troubled preservationists and 'respectable' rambling leaders. It is important, though, to stress that preservationists and political ramblers offered parallel arguments for walking: a physical and spiritual escape from the city, a morally beneficial leisure activity taking the working class out of the pub and cinema. This was moral practice for all sides. A Sheffield socialist Clarion Club booklet cover declared how 'A rambler made is a man improved.'[51] Even those engaged in mass trespass would insist on their own good conduct in the country, practising, as Howard Hill puts it, 'an ethic of nice trespassing'.[52] Phil Barnes ended his trespassing photographic survey, 'Views of the Forbidden Moorlands of the Peak District', by criticizing 'the behaviour of a small section of the public', and presenting a code to be followed in the country.[53]

Differences, however, remained, with often wealthy preservationists tracing problems to the abuse rather than to the possession of landed wealth. Hill and Stephenson point to the role of preservation bodies, especially the Commons and Open Spaces Society, in diluting rights of access in the 1939 Access to Mountains Act. Initially supported but eventually opposed by the Ramblers' Association, this act included a 'trespass clause' which made trespass a potentially criminal offence.[54] And when hundreds strode up Kinder, the preservationists' mix of elitism and populism hesitated. The political actions of others trampled any expert middle ground underfoot. Here they were faced not by meek individuals seeking regulated education but by bolshie groups who marched to the urban folk songs written by the young communist Ewan MacColl:

> I'm a rambler, I'm a rambler from Manchester way
> I get all my pleasure the hard, moorland way
> I may be a wage slave on Monday
> But I am a free man on Sunday[55]

While not a vulgar 'jazzing' of the moors, this was a dangerously political walking tune. Did such a song 'enter into the chord' of the country? The preservationists found a more easily landscaped citizenship in the youth hostel.

The YHA offered a less militant open air, their motto being 'To help all, especially young people of limited means, to a greater knowledge, love and care of countryside, particularly by providing hostels or other simple accommodation for them in their travels.' G. M. Trevelyan acted as President until 1950,[56] Abercrombie was a Vice-President. Here was a different cultural space; the bolshie mass rambler hardly belonged in a youth hostel. The movement began in Germany before 1914, the British movement emerging from a joint initiative of the CPRE, rambling clubs and the National Council for Social Service. This was a particular moral environment, with pleasure to be taken in simplicity. Annual Handbooks outlined the rules of single-sex dormitories, no dormitory smoking, no intoxicants, no gambling, lights out and silence after 10.30, beds to be made on arrival, maintenance chores to be divided between hostellers, with the Warden able 'to retain the card of any member whose conduct is open to objection'. A proto-Country Code appeared alongside lists of necessary and sensible equipment and clothing. Rules were presented not as moral clamp-down, but as devices to foster a new morality; indeed the YHA ran up against the self-declared 'guardians of public morality'.[57] Here males and females mixed, except in dormitories, and often in shorts; Lowerson notes the YHA's 'achievement' in creating 'a sense of institutionalized respectability for activities all too readily seen as subversive'.[58]

The doctrine of simplicity extended to hostel design. Country houses inherited by the YHA from private owners might infringe the principle, but new hostels were conspicuously lacking in ornament, whether built in local vernacular or modern functionalist form. Among them were Abercrombie and Williams-Ellis's functional hut at Maeshafn in Flintshire and Howard Lobb's modern cubic National Demonstration Hostel at Holmbury in Surrey. Inside, undecadent beauty was the order. National Executive member W. H. Perkins stated in 1939: 'I would define my standard of simplicity as daily life lived . . . on a principle of self-service, a minimum of privacy, and absence of all kinds of upholstery, physical and mental . . . Subject to that, I do not think it can be made too beautiful.'[59] The arrangement of the hostels into regional and national networks also suggested modern order. Regional Groups sought to colonize their own areas and link into adjoining networks, aiming 'to cover England with a chain of hostels, each within a day's walking distance of the next'.[60] YHA posters showed hostels as red triangles on a large contoured map, stepping stones across the land. By 1939, 280 hostels formed simple chains for a holiday.

Cultures of Landscape

Country leisure was set up as mental, spiritual and physical exercise, three cultures of landscape linked in what Joad termed 'The Making of Whole Men and Women'.[61] We first consider the intellectual culture of landscape around issues of observation, orientation and mapping, including connections to popular academic practices of geography and archaeology, then address some alternative cartographies of the country produced at the time, before discussing the spiritual and physical cultures of landscape. The term 'culture of landscape' suggests the ways in which particular sets of practices are seen to generate particular ways of being in the landscape, which thereby becomes the occasion for an intellectual, spiritual and physical citizenship.

Orientation

To avoid a future of dancing 'over glazed floors to the strains of negroid music' Joad suggested that people be 'educated in the right use of their leisure':[62] 'I would have every child . . . pass an examination in country lore and country manners before he left school . . . There is much to be said for requiring every townsman who had not succeeded . . . to wear an "L" upon his back when he walked abroad in the country.'[63] However, while 'Good Manners' were 'not Instinctive, but Acquired'[64] and could thus be easily taught, aesthetic education demanded a different approach. A sense of beauty was exposed in the child but buried in the adult, the task of education being, as planner Frederic Osborn put it, 'to regain something of the direct appreciation of the child'.[65] Peach suggested that: 'Children do not really love ugliness; on the contrary, they have a natural love for beautiful things.'[66]

The preservationist open-air ethos connects to youth movements and youth literatures, especially those nurturing open-air boys. Arthur Ransome's adventure tales pitted open-air children against the ignorant or malicious. In *Coot Club* good children defend the birdlife of the Norfolk Broads against ignorant 'Hullabaloos' charging around in their motor cruiser, gramophone blaring: 'A very loud loudspeaker was asking all the world never to leave him, always to love him, tinkle, tinkle, tinkle, bang, bang, bang.'[67] Heroes Tom and Dick act as vigilantes for the local wildlife, while heroine Dorothea goes into romantic feminine reverie over nature. Such literature echoes the youth movements which drew on a 'native' and 'primitive' knowledge of nature, from the conservative Scouts to the socialist Woodcraft Folk founded by former Scout leader Leslie Paul: 'we were socialists ... of the Edward Carpenter stamp, in love with a mystical vision of England.'[68] Youth movements formed part of a broad popular culture of the open air, the 'Gilcraft' scouting booklet on *Exploring* listing the 'Useful Addresses' of various preservation bodies: 'If we can get our Scouts to enjoy the unspoilt country-side, they will be missionaries for its protection, for no man destroys what he loves.'[69] 'Hiking' was 'the explorer's method above all others';[70] an 'Explorer's Chart' (illus. 16) suggested a diagrammatic processing of the Scout into a citizen: insert boy at top, hike and observe, remove citizen at bottom.

In scouting and non-scouting literature a dibdobbery of observant walking emerges: 'Remember that it is a disgrace to a Scout if, when he is with other people, they see anything big or little, near or

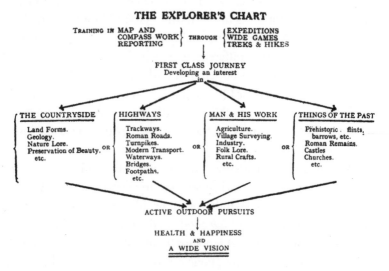

16 'The Explorer's Chart'. From 'Gilcraft', *Exploring*, 2nd edn (London, 1942).

far, high or low, that he has not already seen for himself.'[71] Books instructed youth and adult on 'How to See'; how to get around, how to use your eyes, how to be other than a dancing Cockney.[72] Tom Stephenson advised on best touring practice: 'On a tour one gains a broad view of the ground covered. It is possible to build up a mental map of the route followed, to see the country in proper perspective, and learn the main features of the land, and what we might call their geographical relativity.'[73] The car could complement the walk: 'The car can be most useful ... in a first general survey of the area, enabling us to visualise the lie of the land, to note to what extent certain features are common or how others vary.' Stephenson warned, though, that disorganized touring might produce 'hazy confused impressions ... topographical indigestion'.[74]

The key document of educational movement was the map. Stephenson advised 'Making the Most of the Map', instructing through diagrams of orientation, traverse and triangulation, and suggesting a walker's 'Good Companions' of rucksack, boots and map (illus. 17–20).[75] Batsford thought that you could learn 'more of a patch of country from an Inch Ordnance map in half an hour than by poking around it aimlessly for days'. Map-sense could also mark you out: 'Country folk are generally not map-conscious ... You can astound the company of the village bar by telling them the message of the map for ... the surrounding landscape, and if you produce a map measurer you are likely to be suspected of black magic. They are ... unknown in country circles.'[76] C. E. Montague's influential essay 'When the Map is in Tune' presented a harmonic cartographic magic for those in the know:

> The notation once learnt, the map conveys its own import with an immediateness and vivacity comparable with those of the score or the poem. Convexities and concavities of ground, the bluff, the defile, the long mounting bulge of a grassy ridge ... – all come directly into your presence and offer you the spectacle of their high or low relief with a vivid sensuous sharpness.[77]

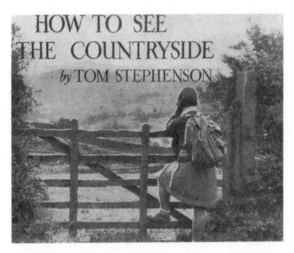

17–20 Seeing the country. From T. Stephenson (ed.), *The Countryside Companion* (London, 1939).

21 J. W. Tucker, *Hiking*, 1936. Tempera on panel, 51 x 60 cm.

Magic comes not from vague dreaming but from an alert mind trained to see. The map and its readers were shown in action, most notably on Ellis Martin's covers for the new Popular and Tourist Edition Ordnance Survey maps.[78] Invariably the map-user is stationed on a hill overlooking a valley. A church-focused nucleated village nestles below. Unfolding the map unfolds the country. A sense of survey satisfies. Martin's standard covers evoked non-militant exertion in a southern landscape. J. W. Tucker's 1936 *Hiking*, painted at Avening in Gloucestershire, similarly showed a composed English movement (illus. 21). Three young women walk in the landscape, kitted out for freedom with packs, shorts and accessories, moving over the country, finding localities within the National Grid, coming upon things over hills, fixing their place by the symbol for a church with a tower, fully equipped for their mission of discovery. Sun shines on the map, indeed the scene's light almost beams from the map, casting its message over the country.

The stress on observation and orientation indicates the making of a 'geographer-citizen'. Leisure meets fieldwork, and overlaps with the emerging field of academic geography.[79] Both aimed to produce observant citizens through survey. *Exploring* and *The Countryside Companion* read like handbooks for elementary geographical education. Montague sought to raise geography 'from the dead' to 'the sensuous imagination': 'Geography, in such a guise, is quite a different muse from the pedantic harridan who used to plague the spirit of youth with lists of chief towns, rivers and lakes, and statistics of leather, hardware and jute.'[80] For geographer Cornish it was 'the duty of the academic world to educate the nation in the appreciation of its heritage of scenery. When the benefits of scenic beauty are thus extended from the few to the many, the people themselves will guard the goodly heritage.'[81] Geography and open-air titles are interchangeable: *Observation, Exploration, Discovery*. Charlotte Simpson's *Rediscovering England* set geography within a wider context of landscape discovery in 'holiday-making, or home life, or education': 'Many schools are trying to interest children in "citizenship"... and from these points of view (especially if they are considered in relation to the topographical background) any district is full of interest for adults as well as for children, even if it has none of the features which usually attract visitors.'[82]

Geography and open-air leisure share a literal viewpoint, an 'outlook geography' whereby knowledge comes through observation from a high point. The pamphlet *Discovery* began: 'BIRD'S EYE VIEW – Climb to the top of a hill, tower or high building to get a bird's eye view of your district.'[83] Anyone with experience of a geography field trip will recall a teacher pointing at things from a hill, perhaps around the kind of metallic 'orientation chart' proposed by Fagg and Hutchings in their guide to regional surveying: 'there is something peculiarly stimulating to the imagination in the contemplation of one of these charts.'[84] In *Observation* Victor Branford described 'A View of Hastings': 'Reaching the flat-topped summit, we look around and see the rolling ups and downs of the land and the gleaming expanse of sea. This panorama *is* Geography.'[85] Such survey work connected empirical and conceptual overviews, inspired by geographer-sociologist-biologist-educationalist Patrick Geddes's insistence that: 'our view be truly synoptic . . . Large views in the abstract . . . depend upon large views in the concrete.'[86] Geographical citizenship worked through a certain topography.

Open-air orientation connects also to the culture of field archaeology, which emerged in self-consciously modern form in the 1920s through the journal *Antiquity*, edited by Ordnance Survey employee and trained geographer O.G.S. Crawford and with a cover designed by Ellis Martin. With marmalade millionaire Alexander Keiller, Crawford revealed *Wessex from the Air* through the new medium of aerial photography.[87] If aerial views paralleled preservationist planning, so too did Keiller's impeccably modern preservationist restoration of the Avebury stone circles and avenues from 1934, with buried and fallen stones re-erected and a small concrete plinth set up to mark empty stone holes. Bushes were cleared, fences repaired, access gates provided: 'A number of unsightly structures were removed.'[88] The decayed piece of prehistory photographed by Paul Nash a few years earlier was landscaped into a modern monument to prehistory: 'the stones of Avebury are beginning to regain their former dignity.'[89] Field archaeology also stressed observation and orientation, and sought to popularize its way of seeing. For Crawford the countryside, 'a palimpsest, a document that has been written on and erased over and over again',[90] was 'an admirable training ground' for distinctly English observations: 'Field archaeology is an essentially English form of sport.'[91] Crawford described his own cycling trips, luggage and maps dangling from bags on the handlebars (illus. 22). One day he did 72 miles fully laden, 'one stretch of fourteen miles being accomplished without dismounting'.[92] Crawford produced prehistoric os maps including *Roman Britain* (1924), *Neolithic Wessex* (1933) and *Celtic Fields of*

22 O.G.S. Crawford. From O.G.S. Crawford, *Said and Done: The Autobiography of an Archaeologist* (London, 1955).

Salisbury Plain (1937), again with Ellis Martin covers. The *Daily Mail* heralded *Roman Britain* as 'opening up a new era in motor touring'.[93] Contemporary guides such as L. V. Grinsell's *The Ancient Burial Mounds of England* offered 'Practical Hints':

In the first place the prospective barrow-hunter should make up his mind to go 'hiking'. Incidentally, barrow-hunting is strongly recommended as an outdoor hobby for hikers, and the writer knows several who have taken it up already. The walker should set out armed with a reel-tape, preferably 66 or 100 feet long, with which he will be able to measure the earthworks he finds.[94]

Pegs, map, camera and notebook were the good companions of popular archaeology.

Other Cartographies

If a culture of oriented observation offered one way of seeing landscape, there were other cartographies, directing vision to different ends, or criticizing its power. We here consider two, one querying the gendering of vision, the other directing the eye to less established objects.

Discussing his failure to date female students at Oxford, Crawford suggested that perhaps women 'do not as a rule take readily to the geographical way of thinking'.[95] Such a statement chimes with recent feminist analyses suggesting that outlook geography has been a classically masculine way of seeing landscape, feminizing an object of study as an object of distanced desire, and priding itself on a masculine self-control and reason which has resulted in a cultural exclusion of women from a 'male gaze' on the landscape.[96] Such arguments have made important connections between vision and masculine power, but have been criticized for an ahistorical psychoanalytic-based schema of masculine and feminine desire which effectively excludes women from the possibilities of taking pleasure in landscape.[97] If Crawford's geographical frustrations seem to fit such arguments, Tucker's self-controlled hiking women cut across them. The open air could be presented as a space of equality and freedom for women and men, offering a direct and democratic contact with landscape which did not respect conservative conventions of gender. Such variation does not undercut a gendering of landscape, but rather suggests that different senses of landscape have been produced through versions of masculinity and femininity as much as through assumptions of class and race.

The identification of a 'male gaze' over landscape itself has a complex history. In Sylvia Townsend Warner's 1926 novel *Lolly Willowes* Laura Willowes moves to the Chilterns from London by buying a guidebook:[98]

> It was just what she wanted, for it was extremely plain and unperturbed. Beginning as early as possible with Geology, it passed to Flora and Fauna, Watersheds, Ecclesiastical Foundations and Local Government ... now at last she was simplifying life for herself. She unfolded the map. The woods were coloured green and the main roads red.[99]

Laura moves to Great Mop, population 227, with Norman church and windmill. Once settled, however, she rejects formal geography:

> About this time she did an odd thing. In her wanderings she had found a disused well ... Here, one evening, she brought her guide-book and her map ... The time had come. She took the guide-book and the map and threw them in.
>
> ... She scarcely knew what she had done, but she knew that she had done rightly, whether it was that she had sacrificed herself to the place, or had cast herself upon its mercies – content henceforth to know no more of it than did its own children.[100]

Tom Stephenson is inverted; Laura makes the least of the map. By contrast her nephew Titus, who 'burgeoned with projects' to improve village life, brings a different, more Batsfordian eye to Great Mop, which unnerves Laura as they walk together: 'It was comfortable, it was portable, it was a reasonable appreciative appetite, a possessive and masculine love. It almost estranged her from Great Mop that he should be able to love it so well, and express his love so easily. He loved the countryside as though it were a body.'[101] When Titus leaves, Laura moves towards another knowledge of country, that of witchcraft: 'When I think of witches, I seem to see all over England, all over Europe, women living and growing old, as common as blackberries, and as unregarded . . . In places like Bedfordshire, the sort of country one sees from the train.'[102] The journey out of London is presented as an approach to her secret self: 'If it were attainable she would run it to earth here, sooner or later. Great Mop was the likeliest place to find it.'[103] It turns out that all the villagers, even the vicar, are involved in witchcraft, and Laura finds herself at the village Sabbath after a bite from a cat familiar: 'She, Laura Willowes, in England, in the year 1922, had entered into a compact with the Devil.'[104] She meets Satan as a gamekeeper on the downs, and he leaves her falling asleep outdoors. Satan has a rather different view of landscape to Titus: 'A closer darkness upon her slumber, a deeper voice in the murmuring leaves overhead – that would be all she would know of his undesiring and unjudging gaze, his satisfied but profoundly indifferent ownership.'[105]

Townsend Warner's 'other cartography' works in part through an opposition of reason and magic. At the same time as she was writing *Lolly Willowes*, the Herefordshire businessman, naturalist, photographer and antiquarian Alfred Watkins was discovering ley lines (illus. 23).[106] Just as Crawford doubted the ability of women to read landscape, so he doubted the wisdom of Watkins's *Old Straight Track*: 'one of the craziest books ever written about British archaeology'.[107] Watkins's ley theories have in recent decades been revised into a mystical doctrine of earth energy lines, but mysticism is a minor theme in the original formulation. Leys were primarily roads: 'Utility was the primary object. Later on, magic, religion, and superstition blended with the system.'[108] I would suggest that Crawford's dismissal of leys as 'Crankeries' reflects the fact that Watkins is less his anti-rationalist opposite than an eccentric mirror-image of field archaeology, and indeed of the preservationist outlook in general. The ley idea came to Watkins while he was contemplating an os

23 Alignment sights. Frontispiece of A. Watkins, *Early British Trackways, Moats, Mounds, Camps, and Sites* (Hereford and London, 1922).

map on the Bredwardine hills. Watkins saw in the landscape a network of straight lines, ancient trackways or 'leys' aligned through objects such as stones, mounds, ponds, trees, camps, hillside notches and place names containing the words 'cole' or 'clod': 'All these works exactly on the sighting line.'[109] Here was 'a geometric aspect of topography', a communication system 'brought to efficiency by Neolithic man' such that the Romans 'found Britain a network of cleverly planned straight tracks, although perhaps in a state of partial decay'. Experts in seeing planned this land: 'the surveyor was the first professional man, with that primitive instinct for power which keeps skilled methods secret.'[110] Watkins suggested that the chalk figure of the Long Man of Wilmington in Sussex represented a surveyor with staffs. In Watkins's writing early British everyday life becomes populated by ideal Ellis Martin cover-stars: 'Trained sight (in air not polluted by smoke) easily picks out a distant hill peak 60 miles away, and dropping the eye in line it falls upon many intermediate hill ridges; hence the mounds or marking points in alignment on these ridges.'[111]

If the original ley was a sight-line, careful observation was needed for its rediscovery: 'Both indoor map and outdoor field exploration are necessary. Field work is essential.'[112] Watkins illustrated his books with photographs of mark stones, and shots across country implying significance, the ley running through the lens out over whatever is shown. Citing Crawford's aerial photography, Watkins predicted future take-off: 'The method in the future is an aeroplane flight along the ley.'[113] 'Ley hunting' could also detain the hiker: 'The outdoor man, away on a cross-country tramp, taking in the uplands, lingering over his midday sandwich on the earthwork of some hill-top camp, will look all round "to get the lay of the land". He will first pick out the hill points.'[114] Youth could also hunt the ley: 'I have a mental vision of a Scout Master of the future, out ley hunting with the elder boys of his troop, instructing them as they look out from a high sighting point.'[115] In 1933 Watkins spoke to 500 Woodcraft Folk camped around the Queen Stone by the Wye.

Watkins had written about its possible sacrificial role; as he spoke two boys sat in a sacrificial wicker cage on top of the stone.

Some ridiculed all this:

> Reflecting on the instinct of the unregenerate walker to make for the nearest pub, the reviewer took the same one-inch map and, selecting inns as his sight-marks, obtained similar results to Mr. Watkins. His first, and best, effort, produced six inns in line; another, four inns and the significant place name Two Pots House. Four lines of four inns can be drawn, each terminating on one of the Noon Follies (associated with Watkins' midday sighting lines); and considering the original meaning of noon – about 3 o'clock – and the impossibility of obtaining a drink at that hour, the result is no doubt significant and our English road system is to be attributed to Mr. Watkins' sight-walker, gradually developing into Mr. Chesterton's reeling English drunkard.[116]

Others, though, took up the ley. Citing the network at the start of their road histories, Boumphrey and Anderson declared that, 'the evidence he produces and illustrates with many photographs puts the general truth of his theory beyond all argument.'[117] Ley hunting crossed into popular leisure, the *Birmingham Gazette* commenting that: 'It is given to few people to create, even on a small scale, a new out-door hobby.'[118] Amateurs circulated discoveries and met on picnic expeditions through the 'strictly private' Old Straight Track Club, founded in 1926 and disbanded in the mid-1940s. Watkins wrote *The Ley Hunter's Manual* giving 'Working Instructions' and suggesting 'local Ley Ramblers' Clubs'.[119] Popular topographer Donald Maxwell proposed ley hunting in *A Detective in Surrey: Landscape Clues to Invisible Roads*, suggesting it as an 'out-door game for topographical detectives' who could search out 'invisible lines over hill and dale'.[120] A 'Watkinsian' gives Maxwell *The Ley Hunter's Manual* and a box containing a snail, colloquially known as the 'dodman', carrying the equivalents for sighting staves on its head.[121] Finding his first ley in ten minutes, Maxwell comments: 'In the field of archaeology and topography the most wonderful discovery concerning prehistoric England – a discovery which has received singularly little attention from archaeologists – was made by a man who was going for a walk and had a good eye for scenic effects.'[122] Old England is reclaimed from professional oversight.

Pilgrims of Scenery

Country movement also touches on the spiritual, in terms of both the general conduct of leisure and specific provisions for recreation. Preservationists presented nature as both a universal and a national spiritual resource, Trevelyan coining an often-quoted phrase: 'Without vision the people perish, and without natural beauty the English people will perish in the spiritual sense.'[123] The spiritual culture of landscape was to focus on the National Park, for which the CPRE campaigned from the late 1920s, with Cornish playing a leading role;[124] the Parks were eventually established in 1949. In this socio-spiritual space the mystical rubbed shoulders with the legislative. For Cornish the Divine was transcendent and immanent in nature; in National Parks 'the urban population, the majority of our people', could 'recover that close touch with Nature which is needful for the spiritual welfare of a nation'.[125] Parks were proposed in areas of 'wild scenery' accessible from major cities, with their establishment seen as both an educational process and an assertion of preservationist cultural authority:

The National Parks which we constitute now will, it is reasonable to suppose, endure as such for centuries. The present careless indifference of the town tripper in his charabanc will, I believe, be replaced by a different mood in the succeeding generations. The faculty of appreciating beauty is latent in the generality and merely requires educating . . . Within a time which will be short compared with the secular life of the National Park we shall be an educated people, the leaders of thought will lead all classes, not merely an educated minority, and signs are not wanting that the aesthetic contemplation of nature will shortly attain the status of a cult.[126]

In such areas recreation would be 'only of a kind which will be consistent with the maintenance of the natural scene . . . it will not include the provision of playing fields'. Cornish also hoped to control the use of the surrounding land so that 'we may not be obliged to run the gauntlet of discordant vulgarities in order to reach the beauty of wild nature'.[127] Abercrombie dreamt of a more dramatic kind of arrival: 'In many ways, aeroplane approach, landing the visitor in the midst of wildness through which he must find his way on his primitive feet would be the ideal; but this might be considered too heroic a measure.'[128]

Cornish's nature mysticism, like his 'aesthetic geography', was geared around principles of latency and direct perception; spiritual, aesthetic and social judgements are intertwined. The argument that sensory perception rather than intellectual reflection was a means to achieving the mystical state made it potentially open to all through Wordsworthian principles of wandering 'until the tumult of busy thought dies down and the faculties of direct perception obtain their opportunity'.[129] The trained eye was a revelatory organ:

When . . . no association of ideas can be found to account for the ecstatic mood this is often attributed to some spiritual faculty higher than ordinary thought and thus further removed from the mere senses. I have found however, by personal experience that even the mystic state is often due to sense perception. In my view this does not imply that such mystic experiences are illusory; on the contrary I regard the refined action of the senses as revelational.[130]

While everyone might have such an experience – 'The notion that such moments are the sole privilege of the world's great prophets is, I believe, entirely erroneous'[131] – the current state of common ignorance despite common latency meant that the 'educated' needed to take a leading role, advising on contemplative methods and regulating land use: 'the quietness of the scene is essential, for only in quietude can Man hear the voice of Nature and receive its message of eternal truth.'[132] A methodological mix of elitism and populism follows. Cornish suggested that 'as the matter has to do with senses common to us all' he could draw on his 'individual experiences',[133] having checked the 'normality' of these with 'an educated audience'.[134] Cornish's claims to authority become circular, with his own class and self defined as exceptionally normal. In the uneducated present, many were not yet able to find, or were disturbing, beauty and the mystical due to their too-common senses. Popular mysticism demanded elite guidance.

While National Parks might be special areas of mystic potential, any area of the country was a possible spiritual space. Country leisure is regularly presented as pilgrimage, giving a religious air to the purpose and style of leisure. Morton denigrated Stratford's 'sheep-like pilgrims' only to counter with his own 'real pilgrimage' to the woods by the Avon which he was sure had inspired *A Midsummer Night's Dream*.[135] Cornish termed himself, and anyone who might follow him, a 'Pilgrim of Scenery',[136] revering both nature and nation. His book *The Scenery of England* gave an iconographic gallery of English (and occasionally Welsh) environments; mystical experiences are recounted at Stonehenge and Ullswater. It is important to stress how mysticism is not presented here as an anti-modern practice of spiritual escapism, rather nature worship is held to be at one with modern scientific conceptions of matter: 'The nature worship of . . . primitive times, apart from the cruel practices then associated with religion, has a strong appeal to the Modern Man of culture, by whom Nature is no longer regarded as mere mechanism, as was the fashion of mid-Victorian times.'[137]

The complexity of this landscaped theology, centred on a Christian evolutionary vitalism, is beyond the present discussion,[138] but again questions of cultural authority are central. Cornish stressed principles of transcendence as well as immanence, wary of the tendency in some nature-mystical work to dispense with a focused deity. At that time the most prominent example of English nature-mysticism was the late-nineteenth-century writing of Richard Jefferies. While Jefferies's general naturalism could fit well with a preservationist ethic of country observation, the uncentred spiritual landscape of his autobiographical *The Story of My Heart* had a less easy appeal: 'There is no god in nature, nor in matter anywhere, either in the clods on the earth or in the composition of the stars.'[139] For preservationists such a position, with no allowance for transcendence, threatened to dissolve authority; pilgrimage by contrast entailed some degree of submission. In his most mystical passages Cornish always retains composure, immersed within yet always looking up to one God. Such a landscaped theology of immanence and transcendence would ensure that 'our people' retained a measured sense of 'the true proportion between civilisation and the cosmos which is essential to the religious welfare of a Nation'.[140]

Bodies of England: Landscape's Physical Culture
i. *Discipline, Exposure, Regularity, Choreography*
The walking body, equipped for its purpose with distinctive clothing and accessories, moved in a broader body culture. One can identify four key dimensions of the open-air body; discipline, exposure, healthy regularity and choreography.

For Cornish there were three 'disciplines' in the 'cult of Scenery': for the spirit the 'cultivation of the state of receptive contemplation', for the mind the 'acquisition of the scientific faculty ... often the hardest of all for people of emotional temperament', and for the body the 'athletic' discipline. Cornish lamented that beauty was often 'suspect on account of the opinion that the aesthetic life often leads towards sybaritic luxury rather than spiritual exaltation. But the Pilgrim of Scenery is beset by no such snare, for a Spartan habit is needed for the enjoyment of Nature in her sterner moods.' Cornish looked to mountaineering, 'where the supreme satisfaction of seeing the world spread out at one's feet is attained only by those who keep the body in fine discipline'.[141] Scout leader Robert Baden-Powell also prescribed a climb: 'the best possible physical developer of nerve and muscle and endurance. A good rock climber cannot be a c3 man. And it is ripping good sport.'[142] Attending a 1931 International Rover Moot in Switzerland Baden-Powell admired 2,500 Rover Scouts, 'storm-troops of the larger army': 'Their arms are alpen-stocks, their discipline that of good will from within … one saw the endless succession of these splendid specimens of the young manhood of all nations setting out in comradeship together with heavy packs on their backs and ice-axe in hand to tackle the neighbouring mountains.'[143]

The Spartan model also implied exposure, an elemental physicality of more-than-observation. Joad held that in the making of whole people, 'the culture of the body as well as of the mind must play its part … Whence can we derive … an education alike of body, of mind and of spirit, so happily as from Nature? The feeling of the air upon the skin, of the sun upon the face; the tautening of the muscles as we climb … these things have their influence upon every side of our being.'[144] Walking provided communion with earth; Stephenson suggested that 'He who travels on his feet has the feel of the earth beneath him, and a sense of being at one with the land, an experience denied to the cyclist insulated by his tyres.'[145] Other elements too would register with the open-air human. Cornish felt that:

The wind made all Nature one, for, above, the sky was a procession of sailing clouds, below, the boughs bent obedient to the common impulse, and all around was the sound of a going on in the upturned leaves. Neither was this unity external only, for man himself showed the response to the great invisible agent, his breathing deepened, muscles braced and skin aglow with the fanning of the breeze.[146]

The key exposure text was Trevelyan's 'Walking': 'The fight against fierce wind and snowstorm is among the higher joys of Walking, and produces in the shortest time the state of ecstasy.'[147] Tensions arise, though, in relation to the individual approaches to such practices, evident in Trevelyan's definition of the desired conditions for 'really *walking*': 'Whether I am alone or with one fit companion, then most is the quiet soul awake; for then the body, drugged with health, is felt only as a part of the physical nature that surrounds it and to which it is indeed akin, while the mind's sole function is to be conscious of calm delight.'[148] Trevelyan is conspicuously not in a mass rambling party. This classically romantic language, full of Wordsworth and George Meredith (subject of a Trevelyan biography), has somehow to translate to popular walking. Class contradictions arise in translation, leading writers such as Joad to make further distinctions between proper ramblers and regimented walkers who stride in line and walk in time across the country to clock up miles regardless. Even within the open-air movement preservationists find it necessary to register fault lines between physical culture and mass practice, and political models which offered to resolve the class contradictions of mass romanticism could themselves generate tension in preservationist argument, of which more below.

Open-air movement also offered regularity, in terms of general physical health and specific bodily function. E. P. Richards found in the open air 'a coming chief antidote in Great Britain to city, office, shop and factory confinement; to cancer and constipation, nerves and tuberculosis . . . to "THREE C-ISM" in all its senses – physical, mental and higher'.[149] Body and landscape are to move in functional harmony, with open-air body culture connecting to a wider wholefood dietary culture:

The extent to which they breathe uncontaminated air, the extent to which they eat unprocessed foods, and, for example, the chances open to them of getting a wet shirt in either their work or their play. It is a depressing thought to contemplate that there must be millions of people in England to-day who have never experienced the exhilaration of a thorough good drenching, and whose individual coefficient of rurality must be practically nil.[150]

While preservationist argument does not concern itself with organic food production schemes, which we address in later chapters, it can be regarded as evoking a wholefood Englishness, aligning natural and national values.

The final dimension of the open-air body appears in a choreography of physical movement. The breadth of this body culture is evident in Harry Roberts's *The Practical Way to Keep Fit*, where open-air movement and healthy diet go alongside 'sensible' clothing and posture, sports and holidays, medicine, town planning for air and gardens and emotional education (see illus. 30).[151] Posture and movement indicate how this body culture entailed a choreography of citizenship. In Stallybrass and White's terms we find an opposition between the 'grotesque' and the 'classical' body.[152] Whereas awkward Cockneys blare, hikers and hostellers move in composed formation, echoing the movements of such groups as the Women's League of Health and Beauty, set up in 1930, with the motto 'Movement is Life': 'Movement is Life. Stillness is the attribute of death. The stagnant pond collects the weeds which will finally choke it, but the moving river clears itself.'[153] The WLHB was known for demonstrations of 'mass physical culture', one League photograph being captioned: 'They Lifted 4,000 Legs To A Ceiling That Must Have Been Mildly Astonished.'[154] The League prided itself on non-regimented bodily coordination: 'There is a complete absence of discipline, no rules are imposed, and the members come and go as they please. These classes have given happy recreation to hundreds of women who had never known the joy of movement before.'[155] Distinctions of mass trooping and voluntary coordination again apply. The WLHB produced a 'Health Chart for Ladies' in association with the brown-bread producers Hovis, makers of 'the National Health Bread': 'Wake up and begin to Live! . . . Do you seek health, fitness, ability to get more out of life? . . . Ask your Baker definitely for Hovis.'[156]

The outdoor choreography of the WLHB is echoed too in Modern Dance, with figures such as Rudolf Laban and Mary Wigman reacting against theatrical ballet and expressing themselves through a modernist outdoor 'eurhythmics'.[157] At first sight such practices might seem far from rural rambling, but if landscape is to enable a relational way of thinking then one can connect, though not equate, such a philosophy with Harry Roberts's call for more open-air dances: 'There is a pleasing, and not unintelligent, abandon, which provides exactly the ideal condition for the efficient working of those unconscious processes of metabolism which make up the whole basis of healthy life.'[158] Tucker's hiking women might be seen as performing a folk-modernist dance around the map, their bodies in trim with the rhetoric of preservation. Moving to England after his expulsion from Germany in the late 1930s, Laban was the originator of the 'Basic Classification of Movement Analysis' which was adopted by the Ministry of Education. He later co-authored the Laban-Lawrence Industrial Rhythm, assessing the kinetic quality of labour: 'it might be permissible to call "Modern Dance" the movement-expression of industrial man.'[159] Through considering the migration of choreography through different zones of culture and economy, we can begin to trace the alignment of open-air movement with a broader modern philosophy of bodily education. In *Modern Educational Dance* Laban noted that: 'modern working habits frequently create detrimental states of mind from which our whole civilisation is bound to suffer if no compensation can be found. The most obvious compensations are, of course, those movements which are able to counterbalance the disastrous influence of the lopsided movement-habits.'[160] Whether in the open air, the factory, the gym or the dance hall, the assumption is that the modern body must be balanced, composed and harmonious. Hikers were never lopsided.

ii. National Fitness

Reporting on *British Health Services* in 1937 the progressive Political and Economic Planning group suggested that: 'it is only necessary to look at any group of British citizens of any age, and social or income class and any geographical origin, to see at a glance that only a small minority either know or care how to hold themselves, how to keep themselves reasonably fit, or how to develop their bodies.'[161] The PEP report was made at a time of increasing state concern for individual fitness; we here consider the connection between open-air culture and state schemes regarding the governance of individual bodily health, and indicate some of the tensions of authority arising from the translation of body culture into state policy.

In 1939, in a Nottinghamshire village, thirteen men, aided by a trestle table, balanced themselves into a curious human pyramid (illus. 24). What possessed them? Had they eaten too much Hovis?: '"The Nottinghamshire Countryside!" What an inspiring title, and how well it links up with the National Fitness Movement!', exclaimed Lord Aberdare, Chair of the National Fitness Council (NFC), in the Notts. Rural Community Council journal.[162] The village thirteen, consciously or not, were balancing in a national movement. The NFC was set up under the 1937 Physical Training and Recreation Act to instigate a National Fitness Campaign:

> The aim of the Government is not to secure that between certain ages every boy and girl practises certain physical exercises ...but to inculcate a wider realisation that physical fitness has a vital part to play in promoting a healthy mind and human happiness. It is a way of life and an attitude of mind, the importance of which is continuous and not limited to certain years in early youth.[163]

24 Keep Fit in a Notts. Village. From *The Nottinghamshire Countryside* (Notts. Rural Community Council), III/1 (1939).

The Council made films, organized 'mass physical culture' demonstrations, gave grants to gymnasia, swimming baths, campsites and youth hostels, all modern sites for modern bodies. John Gloag opened the Council's March 1938 'Health, Sport and Fitness Exhibition' by stressing 'love of the open air' and praising the Scouts: 'the finest fitness movement the world has ever seen'.[164] NFC publications showed people striding outdoors and doing synchronized exercises indoors (illus. 25–8); bending and stretching in the village hall, lifting arms for the WLHB, racing round tracks, 'training leaders' in the gym, camping and walking in the country: 'I have two doctors, my left leg and my right.' On the campaign booklet cover a boy in shorts stretched an arm down a leg: 'It is everybody's duty as a citizen to be as fit as possible.'[165]

Debates over an 'AI' or 'c3' nation went back to the eugenic 'National Efficiency' drive which followed the revelation of poor physical capacity in Boer War recruits.[166] Outdoor citizen and anti-citizen mapped onto AI and c3 respectively. While in part a response to continuing military concern, the NFC also reflected a wider ethos of fitness as a positive social force. As *The Countryside Companion* put it: 'camping helps him to become a good citizen, and the health-giving powers of recreation ... are widely recognised as being of great assistance in the creation of an AI nation.'[167] Former Chief Medical Officer Sir George Newman's 1939 book *The Building of a Nation's Health* noted that 'the English people themselves are beginning to reap substantial benefit by living, working, eating and playing more in the open air', and commended the 'Open-air School' movement: 'nature study, open-air geography, gardening and manual work, happily conjoined with games and physical training, sunbathing, dancing and singing'.[168] State action seemed able to generate an art of right living: 'Bands of youth, young men and maidens, are thus being enlisted into a new kingdom of health ... the Art of Living shall be taught. The Government has provided the means and the method. It has ensured that all the children in the State schools shall be trained in hygiene and body culture ... it is for the people to build thereon.'[169]

Like other fitness fans Newman looked to Germany, which had offered a model of body culture before the Nazi accession to power. The German Movement was self-consciously socially progressive and was expressed from the 1900s in the 'Wandervogel' youth who toured the country in minimal dress, and later in youth hostelling, sunbathing and nudism. In 1931 Anthony Bertram found a 'physical culture' of bodily modernity in Germany:

The bodies of young Germany are slim and golden-brown and muscular: they are fine machines, and well cared for. In

THE NATIONAL
FITNESS
CAMPAIGN

25–8 Illustrations from National Fitness Council, *The National Fitness Campaign* (London, 1939).

the baths and stadiums of the cities, over all natural lakes and rivers, you may see them. And when you see them beside the bodies of old Germany, you realize what Germany has won. These beautiful bodies are the soldiers of modernism.

In England, too, I think, the new soldiers are stirring . . .[170]

Of the old bodies Bertram, having wondered 'if there were fat Greeks', noted: 'it is the mission of physical culture to make such bodies impossible. Let us forget them.'[171] By the time he wrote up his tour in 1933 Bertram was worried, fearing that while Nazism was 'certainly not "unmodern"'[172] it might be destructive of modernism and its bodies. It is not hard to see, though, how, for all his concern, Bertram's cult of beauty and the useless fat could itself be channelled into state schemes of national and racial health. The Nazis took over and extended the German hostelling movement, building grand, purpose-built hostels such as the 5,000-bed Josef Goebbels hostel in Düsseldorf.[173] Modern Dance was restyled as 'German Dance', with Laban entrusted with the dance component of the Berlin Olympics before Goebbels's disapproval led to his exile.[174] Supporters and critics of fitness in England registered the German parallel. The WLHB's use of mass spectacle, uniform and 'Racial Health' rhetoric brought associations of fascism, despite the rational dress uniform expressing a feminism more than a fascism and the displays being as much Busby Berkeley as Nuremberg. The NFC was inspired by a parliamentary report on the German *Strength Through Joy* movement, which Newman considered 'a very popular branch of the Labour front, organized in 1934 for encouraging leisure-time occupations, sports, camps, physical exercise, games, folk-dancing, etc.'. All this was 'contributing to the transformation of the German physique'.[175] Yet enthusiasts warned of over-regimentation, Newman stressing that British people should 'come of their own free will and good pleasure, and not by compulsion'.[176] While in Germany there could be 'no doubt about the effect on health and happiness of the whole people', it was 'physical health and not political or military objective' that should be 'the principle and purpose'.[177] Gloag similarly sought a union of fitness and Englishness: 'the lords of propaganda on the troubled continent have made such a song and dance about national fitness that, as usual, we attribute our interest in it to their example, whereas like most other sensible ideas it began here.'[178] The national origins of body culture echo the roots of architectural modernism in English Arts and Crafts.

Harry Roberts also reflected on the German experience: 'The "hygienic" revolution that took place in Germany a few years ago was not particularly Teutonic in its essence. Nothing but organizing zeal is needed to make the movement spread all over Britain.'[179] It is likely that the socialist Roberts here equates the 'Teutonic' and the fascist in order to claim fitness and hygiene for Leftist politics. In isolation, though, his statement could imply that fascist methods might easily move between nations, and in other instances, preservationist citation of Germany certainly raises questions regarding political admiration for Nazism. Looking for 'Lessons from Other Countries' in *Britain and the Beast*, Lord Howard of Penrith quoted as 'characteristic and essentially true' some German legislation on nature: 'The protection of objects of natural interest which has been growing for centuries could be carried out with but partial success, because *the necessary political and cultural conditions were lacking*. It was only *the transformation of the German man* which created the preliminary conditions necessary for an effective system of protection of Natural Beauty.'[180] Which 'lessons' from Germany are implied here? Back in the 'inspiring' Nottinghamshire Countryside we find, opposite Aberdare's fitness piece, an anonymous article headlined 'Strength Through Joy: Suggestion For a Rural Fitness Policy', suggesting a 'national rural fitness festival' in every village, with competitions including No.7 Gymnastic Displays, No.11 Folk Dancing, No.12 Volleyball, No.18 Relay Race for Parish Councillors, No.19 A Series of Purposeful Games: 'Can Notts. villages give us ... just that experience in practice that will enable us to plan a modern "Merrie England" along the lines of Strength Through Joy?' A Nazi ethos could be locally reworked: 'While continental countries achieve fitness by discipline imposed from above, Britain plans to succeed with fitness schemes that appeal because they come from a selfimposed discipline generated in the heart of the individual.'[181] This is half-sinister, half-farce, with Parish Councillors relaying to a higher plane of citizenship through discipline nicer than the nasty continental sort. People are to impose themselves upon themselves. The author tries to detach the slogan from its country of origin, freeing it for Englishness. Why, though, use the slogan?

Beyond the Pale: Arts of Wrong Living?

Dangerous Ground

In its ambitious breadth the preservationists' art of right living courted dangers other than those of political association, straying into territory seen as beyond moral order, and open to ridicule for its bodily and spiritual concerns. The preservationists' self-definition as pioneers of a new art of right living could appear to others as eccentricity, fanaticism, perversion or faddism. In *Coming Up For Air* Orwell, himself not above suggesting health improvement via brown bread, picked on the wealthy open-air lovers of Upper Binfield, including 'Professor Woad, the psychic research worker': 'I knew the type. Vegetarianism, simple life, poetry, nature-worship, roll in the dew before breakfast ... They're always either health-food cranks or else they have something to do with the Boy Scouts – in either case they're great ones for Nature and the open air.'[182]

An everyday English leisure drugged with health and admiring transformed bodies could suggest hedonism and voyeurism; arts of wrong living. Preservationists were on their guard against wrong associations. Cornish highlighted 'the tactile sensation' but immediately went on to warn against decadence: 'Those who intend to get the maximum of pleasure from the world's scenery should cultivate an outdoor habit which will extend the range of pleasureable response to heat and cold. The Spartan not the Sybarite is the epicure of scenery.'[183] Care was taken to insist that mysticism produced spiritual clarity rather than hazy bliss, and proceeded from bodily discipline. Asking 'What is Health?', Roberts cautioned against indulgence: 'happiness and fullness of life must not be confused with that much misunderstood thing, pleasure.'[184] Such a broad field of movement was, however, hard to hedge; outdoor bodies might move beyond the pale. If bodies like the WLHB brought to mass popularity activities which, as Matthews puts it, 'had formerly been relegated to the world of foreigners and health cranks – sunbathing and tanning, hiking, dieting and slimming',[185] dubious associations could remain, with pre-Nazi Germany an awkward reference point. In his autobiography Stephen Spender recalled life in 1920s Berlin: 'Roofless houses, expressionist painting, atonal music, bars for homosexuals, nudism, sun-bathing, camping, all were accepted . . . It was easy to be advanced. You had only to take off your clothes.'[186] Here was a different citizenship. Lights out at 10.30? Unshared beds? Preservationists should perhaps be regarded as moving a Victorian morality into a restrained modernism, self-consciously different and new, but not morally subversive, echoing the WLHB who were, in Matthews's terms: 'conservative progressives on the side of a beauty culture that was winning the struggle to dissociate the cultivation of physical beauty from accusations of narcissistic vanity and sexual abandon'.[187]

Nudism crops up in corners of the open-air movement. Joad, hitting at 'The Power of the Old' to impose a non-progressive morality at the seaside,[188] recommended nude sea bathing on deserted beaches, where 'afterwards you lie on the floor of the cove, naked to the sun',[189] while WLHB founder Mollie Stack advocated private nudism for 'skin-airing'.[190] Roberts gave characteristically careful consideration to the matter:

Perhaps a word should be said about a movement that has recently attained a good deal of notoriety, the nudity movement. It is probably difficult for most people to contemplate this development with an impartial mind. It is doubtful if, in this country, except possibly for a few weeks in the year, nudity is hygienically practicable. On moral and aesthetic grounds this is probably regrettable.[191]

However much it presented itself as 'naturism' or 'gymnosophy' and guarded against sauce by stressing 'The Aesthetics of the Human Body', or 'Gymnosophy and Humanitarian Democracy', or *Health and Efficiency*,[192] nudism remained an easy target for nudge and wink satire. Variety and film star George Formby had a little snapshot album:

I've got a picture of a nudist camp
In my little snapshot album
All very jolly but a trifle damp
In my little snapshot album
There's Uncle Dick without a care
Discarding all his underwear
But his watch and chain still dangles there
In my little snapshot album.[193]

Formby also starred in a 1937 fitness skit, *Keep Fit*, poking fun at 'Biceps, Muscle and Brawn'. Attempting to create a new Englishness through a new bodily morality, the preservationists also lived in an England of Formby songs and seaside postcards.

Those who roared at Uncle Dick's watch and chain might also be tempted to peer, and elements of voyeurism do appear in the promotion of physical culture, especially where youth becomes the thrilling object of the gaze of older, usually male authority. The scouting rhetoric of catching and holding and moulding boys while upholding the daily cleaning of 'the racial organ' and warning against dubious women and 'self-abuse'[194] laid the ground for scoutmaster

29 Bodies up hills: 'The Author Ski-ing in the Alps. Nearing the Summit'. From Lt J. P. Muller, *My Sun-Bathing and Fresh-Air System* (London, *c.* 1930).

jokes and fears; *Scouting for Boys* becoming a ready-made *double entendre*. Upright authority walks straight into mockery. This elevation of the outdoor, active young male forms part of a wider cultural adulation, often emanating from the political Right. Their heroes included such figures as mountaineer George Mallory, aviator Charles Lindbergh, T. E. Lawrence and Edward, Prince of Wales, all seen as physical emblems of a force for change.[195] Fitness literature could often suggest a worship of young physicality. To take one random example from the popular *My System* series by Danish army officer J. P. Muller, *My Sun-Bathing and Fresh-Air System* ('Issued under the patronage of HRH The Prince of Wales') moves between everyday exercise tips, hedonistic action in extreme climates and delight in bodily display, usually male and mostly Muller's own. Alongside arguments for vitamins and town planning we find Muller 'bathing' in snow, skiing up mountains aged 60 in shorts (illus. 29) and performing 'rubbing exercises'. This landscaping of health (illus. 30) begins to pull the open-air ethos into other territory.[196] A final homoerotic image shows 'Young Sunbathers in

30 Bodies up hills: 'Towards a Healthy and Contented Life'. From H. Roberts, *The Practical Way to Keep Fit* (London, 1942).

the Wood', in which two young men in a clearing contemplate each other in minimal yet extended trunks.

Moral danger regarding bodily adulation may, however, have been diffused by an institution through which many preservationists had passed, the English male public school. Sporting worship and homosexual hints appear less 'dangerous' when this safe ground of what Jeffrey Richards terms 'manly love' is recalled.[197] Here was scouting's ancestral turf. Cornish, secure in this class masculinity, could recall without moral risk the thrill of sailors in the Great War: 'In the home country the aspect of Manhood at this period was less exhilarating, but there was a distant haven in home waters, Scapa

Flow, where one could feel the full force that lies pent in the finest specimens of our Race.'[198]

Solution: Citizenship as Channelled Desire

The preservationist emphasis on beauty, mysticism and the body could not help but raise matters of emotion and desire. The response is to advocate a channelling of latent forces. Emotions and desires are conceived of as fluid, and from this derives potential as well as risk. For Roberts 'Educating the Emotions' involved their direction into 'useful channels' such as mountaineering.[199] Keynes, arguing in *Britain and the Beast* for the provision of public festivals and upholding George v's 1935 Jubilee as an example, warned 'western democracies' that they should tend communal feeling: 'These mass emotions can be exceedingly dangerous, none more so; but this is a reason why they should be rightly guided and satisfied, not for ignoring them.'[200]

A concern to channel and mould emotion extends for some to an interest in psychoanalysis. In *England and the Octopus* Williams-Ellis declared that: 'English people need mass psycho-analysis. We know the morbid symptoms – false standards and values, blindnesses and callousnesses and such-like. We need to discover the root causes of these disastrous anomalies, and having discovered them, we may hope to prescribe for a cure.'[201] An intriguing story remains to be written on the links between environmental and psychological theory at this time. While Joad criticized psychoanalysis as a 'cult of unreason',[202] others engaged with Freudian theory. R. G. Stapledon urged contact with nature as the chief psychological need implied by psychoanalytic findings.[203] Arthur Tansley, a key figure in post-war nature conservation, was the leading British proponent of both ecology and *The New Psychology*:

We must now look to a state in which the individual must again be subordinated to the herd, to the national herd in the first place, but ultimately to the universal herd, but in which the herd control is enlightened … The licence of individualism must be curbed, but the instincts and powers of the individual must not be crippled or stunted.[204]

Preservationist geographer C. C. Fagg corresponded with Freud, and published his work on the potential harnessing of psychoanalysis for evolutionary planning. Fagg claimed for Freud that: 'by discovering and fearlessly investigating the Oedipus complex he has given hope that we may someday be able to make a world fit for our children to live in; a family and social environment in which our already abundant super-babies may develop into super-men.'[205] The reaction of the Croydon Natural History and Scientific Society to his 1923 Presidential Address on *The Significance of the Freudian Psychology for the Evolution Theory* is not recorded: 'I do not feel that any apology is needed for my choice of a subject for this evening's address, although I originally intended presenting to you a study of our Regional Survey Area based upon the recently made Surface Utilisation Survey.'[206] Such Freudian eugenic town and country planning was echoed in the work of the Health and Cleanliness Council (motto: 'Where there's dirt there's danger'). George Green, author of its *Healthway Books* for children and *Keep Fit: A Book for Boys*, also provided an early guide to *Psychanalysis* [sic] *in the Class Room*: 'the object of psychanalysis is to investigate the unconscious regions of the mind, and to make possible the removal of the obstructions which dam or divert the stream, so that the freed "libido" may flow singly, as a powerful river, from unconsciousness into consciousness, there to be diverted into interests of value.'[207] For techniques of orderly flow Green looked to youth movements, upholding the Scouts and Guides' use of ritual to impress upon children their position in 'the circles of the family, the school, the country and the empire'.[208]

Whether or not preservationists engaged with psychoanalysis, questions of psychology were integral to their programme of landscape and citizenship. The individual and the collective mind could be remade through environmental practice. This chapter has entailed excursions into litter, noise, country walking, maps, trespass, youth movements, fitness, mysticism, hedonism, voyeurism, fascism and psychoanalysis. Should noise be made in the country? Why is it good to be in the landscape? Which practices and people are fit for the English countryside? Such questions continue to underlie arguments over the uses of the country, and take shape in their modern form in this period. Matters of culture, psychology and geography were at the heart of a highly influential discourse of self and environment whose assumptions often remain taken for granted in everyday life.

PART II

Organic England

3

English Ecologies

This and the following chapter consider a rather different vision of the English landscape, one which is less enamoured of the modern, espousing an anti-urban ruralism and promoting an organic vision of agriculture and society. In contrast to the preservationist vision of a planned, modern Englishness, this organicist vision had little policy or popular impact and yet it is in many ways more familiar today in its resemblances to current Green thinking. Again we find an interconnection of issues which are often held apart elsewhere; soil, politics, culture, health, genetics, regionalism, the body. Discussion of this self-consciously alternative-conservative sense of Englishness serves to further underline the heterogeneity of the rural and to bring out the contested nature of landscape in this period; preservationist-planners were not the only cultural movement to claim authority over the cultural terrain of landscape and Englishness.

This section breaks the chronological pattern of the book. Part I was concerned with the interwar period, while Part III takes up the story of planner-preservationism post-1939. These two chapters, however, draw on material from the 1920s through to the post-war years, showing how a body of organicist ideas and practices was galvanized by war and disappointed in peace. Previous studies of this material have downplayed the impetus given by the War to organicism, even going so far as to suggest that organicism, because of some associations with fascism in the 1930s, became inarticulate in wartime. I would argue, though, that whatever the wartime political tensions for some organicists, it was the transformation of agriculture in war which gave organicism both urgency and coherence; the bulk of organicist literature was indeed issued in wartime. In 1941, reviewing arable farming in the key organicist collection *England and the Farmer*, C. Henry Warren caustically commented, 'War makes agriculturalists of us all.'[1] Before the War much of British agriculture had been both depressed and effectively organic. Investment through state agencies in wartime to safeguard food supplies produced dramatic changes in agricultural prosperity and technique. Organicists opposed both the authority gained by the modern state over the land, and the use of artificial fertilizers to increase yields. As we shall see, both themes are linked in an often angry organicist analysis, mobilizing one version of English ruralism against a state-patriotic mobilization of land in wartime. Far from pushing organicism into the shadows, war brings it out into the open, revealing it to be a complex and fascinating cultural movement whose ideas, if having minor impact at the time, have, in an altered state, both popular and political influence. We return to these contemporary resonances at the end of the book.

Significant Soil

English Earth, Dissident Science

An anonymous labouring hand takes up 'English Earth' (illus. 31). Fork, foot, arm, veins, hand and soil have equal emphasis. The key themes of organic Englishness are projected into this image. The land is a site to be worked, the soil something to be trod, handled, tested for texture. The visible remains of plants mark future humus, an organic cycle of fertility. And the cycle of soil, labour and fertility makes sense in national terms. This is not just any earth, but English earth, held by a strong and healthy arm veined, we are to assume, with English blood. Soil, blood, health, humus, England.

31 'English Earth'. From H. J. Massingham (ed.), *England the Farmer* (London, 1941).

'English Earth' was chosen from the stocks of the Mustograph Agency for H. J. Massingham's 1941 collection *England and the Farmer*, a 'Symposium' bringing together agriculturalists, scientists, doctors and novelists to present a vision of an organic rural economy, polity, society and culture. Most of the contributors became founder members in April 1941 of the 'Kinship in Husbandry',[2] described by leading player Rolf Gardiner as a 'band of Englishmen' seeking to lobby against perceived wartime inorganic short-termism and the approaching post-war 'bureaucratic or managerial Welfare State':

It was deemed better from the start to remain a hidden, unofficial, band of friends and accomplices: *kinsmen in husbandry*.

Such a free association, based on loyalties and affections, had great advantages. It enfolded common thinking and activity whilst avoiding all the paraphernalia of democratic business. Yet we were able to percolate many movements and appear in different guises.

The 'sound views'[3] of the Kinship and its associates run through this chapter.

Earth is the key element of organic England. It is striking how little water and air figure in organicist accounts. While industrial if not agricultural pollution of water and air is a concern at the time,[4] and while organicists seek an holistic, ecological understanding embracing all elements, earth takes priority. Massingham presented earth as the key element in a spiritual materialism:

It is the interaction between man and nature which alone can make the full man at one in his middle status between God and the living dust of earth. There is a kind of music in the order of the universe which penetrates man by and through the earth ... In losing touch with the organic processes of the earth man is fouling the sources of his own being.[5]

A stress on earth lends literal substance to the organicist claims to a physically ground Englishness. G. T. Wrench described *Reconstruction by Way of the Soil* as entailing a search for 'correct terrene being': 'we are first and formost terrene animals.'[6]

Like preservationist-planners, organicists presented themselves as anti-picturesque yet also opposed the call for a functional design aesthetic. In fact, both preservationists and tourists alike were presented as being guilty of picturesque fantasy. Massingham, suggesting that 'the purely aesthetic attitude is not enough ... its weak spot is the peril of the picturesque',[7] set prettiness against a virtuously prosaic and down-to-earth materialism:

The Picturesque
Within this dell's green anodyne
Where drowsy falls the thrush's song,
Where flowery cups spill opiate wine:
There dwells a slug four inches long.[8]

Beauty in organic England would emerge unselfconsciously through labour. Organicists offered a functionalism not of design but of rooted 'husbandry', a term appealing to Massingham in its anti-progressive overtones – 'the word "husbandry" is in itself almost obsolete like the word "coney" for rabbit'[9] – and its suggestion of a masculine care for earth: 'If we look well into the word "husbandry," we can risk a definition of it, namely loving management. It means man the head of nature, but acting towards nature in a family spirit.'[10] Like the preservationists, organicists styled themselves as chivalrous defenders of a feminized England, an *England Herself*, against *The Rape of the Earth*.[11] Massingham offered the craftsman as a male model: 'He did not conquer nature but married her in husbandry.'[12]

Whatever the past appeal of husbandry, though, English tradition was to be supplemented by scientific experiment. A dissident ecological science was seen as confirming the virtues of traditional practice as opposed to contemporary 'progressive' orthodoxy. The developing science of ecology could also, of course, form part of a modernizing vision of landscape and nature, but for organicists ecology denoted a counter-modern form of holistic understanding which resisted an orthodox science in hock to business and state. In such an analysis soil serves as a base element refracting arguments about agriculture, nationhood, health, morality and spirituality. Towards the end of her summary of organicist argument, *The Living Soil*, Eve Balfour argued that 'wherever the ecological balance of the soil is seriously disturbed, disorders in crops, animals, and man follow'.[13] Balfour justified the moral and political range of her discussion by arguing for a discourse mirroring ecological interconnection: 'You may ask, what have all these platitudes to do with humus? The answer is, a lot. Our attitude to the soil is dependent on our attitude to life in general.'[14]

Organicist debate turned on whether humus produced from organic matter was essential to soil fertility, and whether artificial fertilizers were damaging. 'Humus' and 'Artificials' schools were formed in the late 1930s and early 1940s, largely influenced by publications issued by Faber and Faber.[15] *The Living Soil* was effectively the founding document of the Soil Association, set up in 1945 with Balfour as Chair and a Council which included Kinship founders Rolf Gardiner, Lord Portsmouth (formerly Viscount Lymington) and Massingham, alongside compost theorist Maye Bruce and Faber commissioning editor Richard de la Mare.[16] Balfour directed the Haughley Research Trust, set up alongside her Suffolk farm in 1939 as an organic counter-body to the government Rothamsted Experimental Station under Sir John Russell.[17] Balfour and the organicists offered a vitalistic argument of a soil alive: 'Soil is a substance teeming with life. If this life is killed, the soil quite literally dies.'[18] Soil death came from the extension of a manufacturing ethic to the land: 'The vegetable kingdom has for too long been considered as a sort of factory.'[19] Massingham set conventional science, expressing such an ethic, against an alternative holistic understanding: 'But health-wholeness-holiness, only the very rarest man of science is aware of this trinity, a three-in-one. Average science will not stop men from preying on the soil.'[20] A 'rare', non-average science would, by contrast, seek an understanding in terms of holistic flows rather than discrete organic or inorganic units. Northbourne's *Look to the Land* presented life as being constituted through a fluid ecology: 'the mechanism of life is a continuous flow of matter through the architectural forms we know as organisms.'[21] Such argument connects to a post-Darwinian revaluation of nature as a holistic and qualitatively evolving entity, Massingham suggesting that 'the world of animate nature has on the whole emerged into a more qualitative being'.[22] Darwin's revelation of 'one living substance of all the phenomena of life' implied for Massingham a rejection of a social Darwinian anti-spiritual materialism envisaging the 'Cosmical Process' shot as 'a gangster film'; of T. H. Huxley he commented: 'it would undoubtedly have been better for mankind if he had never been born'.[23] While for planner-preservationists a vitalistic and mystical sense of evolutionary holism implied a modern mode of understanding in keeping with a planned evolution of society, for organicists such an understanding was symbolically anti-modern, a dissident form of science countering a progressive orthodoxy, and demanding a return to the soil.

The vital soil substance was humus, defined as 'a product of the decomposition of animal and vegetable residues brought about by the action of micro-organisms'.[24] Humus production schemes were established, most prominently the Indore process of composting devised by Sir Albert Howard when Director of the Institute of Plant Industry at Indore in India between 1924 and 1931. In this process animal and vegetable wastes were mixed in pits or heaps to produce humus. For Massingham this was the 'true but heretical science of earth-culture',[25] and he adopted the process in his garden, producing 'yearly increases both in excellence and mass of fresh food', and finding eternity and heaven in his heap:

> I can sense the mystery – time, the seasons, nature, death and life wheeling like the figures of a dance in the work of transmutation. I can grasp the immensity of Sir Albert Howard's conception of the endless circulation of organic matter through soil, plant and animal and back again in the reverse movement – a continuous chain of interwoven living processes.[26]

Maye Bruce presented her 'Quick Return Method' as similarly amazing: 'Opening a ripe heap never loses its thrill of amazement! The change is so dramatic, the aroma so sweet and satisfying, the soil so clean and vital, one cannot keep one's fingers away from it.

But I am not sure that the results of using the compost in the garden are not even more astounding.'[27]

Composting was part of a general subscription to a 'Rule of Return' (illus. 32), Northbourne arguing that: 'Only by faithfully returning to the soil in due course everything that has come from it can fertility be made permanent.'[28] Here was economy, society, poetry: 'All this question of observing the rule of return is no mere economic question, nor is it a purely scientific one. It is part of the wonder and beauty and poetry of living. There is poetry in the ever-recurring process of the conversion of ordure and decay into utility and beauty.'[29] Northbourne even embraced his own human cast-offs: 'If you burn your old trousers, presumably made largely of wool, you are destroying potential life, committing a sort of murder. Properly composted (for the quality of the life you renew in them is of primary importance) they can give power to a living plant to seize upon hitherto non-living material in the soil and bring it into the living world.'[30] Unlike old trousers, artificials gave no

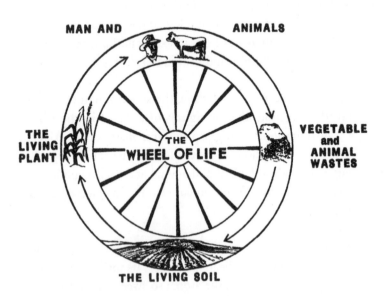

32 'The Wheel of Life'. From L. Picton, *Thoughts on Feeding* (London, 1946).

profound return, breaking the Wheel of Life with its circuit of consumption, dung and growth. Howard worried about the progress of emergency wartime plough-up: 'What sort of account will Mother Earth render for using up the last reserve of soil fertility and for neglecting her great law of return.'[31] For organicists the Rule implied both a local recycling of waste and the use of stock to generate local manure: 'Mixed farming is real farming. Unduly specialized "farming" is something else; it must depend on imported fertility, it cannot be self-sufficient nor an organic whole.'[32] We return to the spatial economy implied by such a schema below.

Howard also worried about a hurried introduction of certain new technologies: 'The practice of artificial insemination for livestock can only be described as a monstrous innovation which can only end in life-erosion.'[33] In general, organicists have an ambivalent relationship with technology. An anti-mechanistic philosophy did not imply being anti-machine *per se*: 'The machine . . . is no more an unqualified "good" than it is an unqualified evil.'[34] Mechanism, however, was not to drive philosophy, Massingham suggesting that: 'The engineer is useless except as an accessory.'[35] At times organicists could certainly show nostalgia for a pre-mechanical past; Massingham preserved old farm implements in a Hermitage in his back garden,[36] finding some still useful for garden jobs. Lymington considered that 'ideally speaking the wooden plough of our ancestors was the proper implement to use on the land rather than the steel machines of to-day. The wooden plough did less harm to the ground.'[37] Yet the machine is generally considered a force for good if embedded within organic husbandry, Jorian Jenks arguing that if the task was to instigate a 'new "Cultural Revolution"' by the 'husband-like cultivation of the native landscape', then 'the machine can be made to aid us'.[38] The clearest organicist embrace of the machine comes in land reclamation, which further demonstrates an anti-picturesque attitude to 'useless' waste. The leading British lobbyist for land reclamation was Stapledon, whose influential 1935 book *The Land* looked to Italy for a lead: 'The integral land improvement policy of Mussolini aims at creating agricultural land and a vigorous agricultural population where before there was nothing or practically nothing. To put through reclamation work of that order . . . cannot fail to have a stimulating influence not only on all who are directly concerned, but also upon the nation as a whole.'[39] Stapledon proposed the reclamation of The Wash for George v's Silver Jubilee as 'a national monument': 'the carrying of it through to success would have far-reaching psychological influences'.[40]

If organicists upheld a dissident science, they also appealed to traditional country knowledge, to 'the countryman's wisdom' over agricultural 'intelligence'.[41] Dissident science and English Tradition are put in harness, in part by styling the countryman as a traditional ecologist. Massingham argued that: 'healthy peasant civilisation is sound ecological doctrine . . . The peasant way is not that of a mathematical problem, nor is it a mere mechanism of production. His is the animate and biological approach . . . He intensifies natural processes and modifies them, but always, if he be a genuine peasant, within ecological bounds.'[42] Such human action cared for and was content to be cradled by the environment: 'The qualitative view . . . allows for both humility and greatness; it accepts man's limited control of his material and environment.'[43] In their appeal to rural tradition organicists called up not some rustic yokel but an ecologist-countryman, who appeared to be in agreement with other 'traditional' practices such as shooting and hunting; this ecological worldview is deep yet unsentimental, embracing death in its sense of harmony. Massingham wrote a column from 1938 for the country sports journal *The Field*; hunting and shooting could be presented as functional elements of rural ecology, denoting an ecological realism at odds with a 'sentimental' and 'picturesque' urban view. Novelist and ruralist Henry Williamson described a harsh mutuality of species: 'A thump on the roof, the noise of claws getting a grip on the ridge-tiles. A hollow quavering, bubbling cry, a squealing outside the walls. A tawny owl has got one of the rats. Good; the harmony of nature.'[44]

Englishness and Elsewhere

Foreign Inspiration

As well as upholding English country wisdom and dissident science, organicists looked to sometimes surprising foreign pasts and presents. In Europe Wrench upheld the historic example of Arab Spain, 'A Kingdom of Agricultural Art in Europe', where advanced science ensured that independent smallholdings followed the rule of return, creating 'a pro-life civilisation'.[45] In contemporary Europe there was the bio-dynamic farming of Ehrenfried Pfeiffer, hailed by Gardiner as a 'far-seeing earth-healer', whose demonstration farms at Walcheren in Holland were visited by Lymington and Howard in the late 1930s.[46] Pfeiffer was a disciple of Rudolf Steiner's anthroposophy, although here organicists could become cautious. While appreciating the 'non-scientific', they resisted connotations of irrationalism. While Pfeiffer might be praised as 'a farmer of scientific distinction who put to the test the mocked-at "muck and mystery" teachings of Rudolf Steiner',[47] Steiner himself could be seen as a victim of 'occult suggestion' and not down-to-earth enough: 'Occult "Forces" radiate through the air, inter-penetrate the soil, quicken the seed, harness the roots to the earth and enable the plant to "defy the Laws of Gravitation."'[48]

However, as Philip Conford has highlighted, organicists looked more to Asia than to Europe, finding an 'alternative' wisdom in Orientalist customs.[49] The key reference point were the Hunza people of north-west India, considered by Wrench and McCarrison to be exemplary in diet, health and physique thanks to a system of terrace farming which obeyed the rule of return: 'Here, then, within the precincts of British-supervised India, was a people who brought quite a marvellous message from the remote past, a past that justifies the tradition of the Golden Age, a past of perfect relations between men and the soil. The Hunzas had created a symphony of nature.'[50] Massingham found echoes of ancient Dorset in Hunza wisdom: 'an agriculture based upon the same principles as that of ancient Abbotsbury and on the same principle of the cycle of death and renewal which the Giant of Cerne symbolises in one way and a modern science beyond science has proved to be the secret of human health and soil-fertility today'.[51] As an example of 'primitive' people succeeding without orthodox science, the Hunza could inspire a dissident Western science. Howard thought that while the Hunza might not understand their own knowledge, the Western farmer could: 'it is his privilege, and here he may claim to be in advance of the Oriental peasant, to be able to understand some of the scientific truths which constitute the laws to which he is working.'[52] The Hunza, 'British-supervised', are one example of a two-way imperial traffic, with the governing group convinced of their superior right to govern, yet taking inspiration from 'native' practice to critique 'advanced' Western life. The imperial agricultural and forestry services provided an appropriate space in which to nurture dissident organic science, distant from central orthodoxy. Japan and China also showed Wrench a 'supreme example of the Wisdom of the East in contrast to the Science of the West'.[53] While Abercrombie had looked East for design principles, organicists found humus and recycling: 'For four thousand years the peasants of China have adopted methods which are equally in harmony with those of Mother Earth. Time has proved the correctness of their agricultural practices.'[54]

Foreign Implication

Englishness was connected with the rest of the world not only through foreign example but via the implications of being caught in global and/or imperial processes. Organicism, while determined to root itself in something called English tradition, was far from being simple little Englishness. We will develop this point in the following section on soil economy, but here address the implications of global soil erosion. While not seen as a dramatically pressing issue in north-west Europe,[55] erosion impacted via its potential effects on global agriculture. The key reference point was Jacks and Whyte's 1939 survey *The Rape of the Earth*, which claimed a quantitative diminishing of land: 'Probably more soil has been lost since 1914 than in the whole previous history of the world.'[56] This global survey indicated a global crisis and offered a moral argument for enlightened control: 'To gain control over the soil is the greatest achievement of which mankind is capable.'[57] Jacks and Whyte argued that erosion was 'solely due to human mismanagement', and made 'a knowledge of the underlying principle of human ecology – the art of living together with animals, insects, and plants – one of the most urgent needs of mankind'.[58] The u.s. Dustbowl of the mid-1930s was the trigger for concern: 'By 1935 the illusion that nations could get rich quick at the expense of a beneficient, unresisting Nature had been finally shattered.'[59] *The Rape*'s frontispiece image showed 'Dust Over Dakota', a man walking through a cloud of blowing ex-soil.

While organicists broadly welcomed the u.s. soil conservation measures, there was unease over the statist reading of these by Jacks and Whyte and others.[60] Was conservation only possible through large-scale state action? Tension generated by the u.s. example runs through the intriguing 1945 UK publication by Faber and Faber of Carey McWilliams's *Ill Fares the Land*, an account of migrant labourers arguing for democratic public control over land use. McWilliams is a hero of Mike Davis and Don Mitchell's recent socialist readings of Californian environmental history, but in this instance his work was highlighted for different reasons. Lymington, by then Earl of Portsmouth, wrote the 1945 preface, and the text was edited by Jorian Jenks, soon to be editor of the Soil Association journal *Mother Earth* but late of Mosley's British Union of Fascists, for whom he was agricultural adviser. *Ill Fares the Land* was commandeered for organicism. Wary of McWilliams's praise for trade unions and a welfare state, Lymington cautioned against 'the Beveridgeization of the farm labourer . . . Mr. McWilliams is constantly calling in the Government'.[61]

Lymington had anticipated *The Rape of the Earth* in his 1938 book *Famine in England*, in which a mini-global survey of erosion picked out the Dustbowl as 'man's handiwork': 'No followers of Jenghiz Khan raped the virgins of Samarkand as thoroughly as the pioneer raped the virgin soil.'[62] An Orientalist barbarism and nomadism is projected onto the USA. For Lymington soil erosion was an urgent problem in its threat to white imperialism: 'It is the greatest danger threatening the security of the white man and the well-being of the coloured man in the tropical and sub-tropical lands of Africa and India.'[63] Jacks and Whyte similarly assumed white soil control as the solution: 'the soil demands a dominant, and if white men will not and black men cannot assume the position, the vegetation will do so, by the process of erosion finally squeezing out the whites.' Whatever the praise for the Hunza elsewhere, there is no sense here that indigenous knowledge might suffice: 'They cannot, in fact, be left to work out their own destiny.'[64] The fear was that in its imperial impact soil erosion might trigger global shifts: 'soil erosion is altering the course of world history more radically than any war or revolution.'[65] Imperial history gave warnings, with decline traced to human-induced environmental change: 'The desert has succeeded to the cities of the past because, being cities, they bred a race which forgot the soil on which it fed. To-day there are well-schooled but poorly educated children in English industrial areas who cannot believe that milk comes from the cow, and not the tin. These children had their counterpart in Rome and Nineveh.'[66]

Soil Economy

Mere money-making and arithmetical abstractions must give way to the need for fresh, unprocessed food, health, stable living, and pride of work. The satisfaction of real and local needs must be substituted for the artificially stimulated exchange of unreal surpluses ... Our aim in a word must be to replace a

mechanistic conception of society by an organic, and man as mere consumer and middleman by man as a producer and craftsman.
ADRIAN BELL, 'Husbandry and Society'[67]

... the writers in this book make no attempt to avoid the economic issue.
MASSINGHAM, *England and the Farmer*[68]

Just as preservationist argument connected to a particular economic discourse, so organicists traced economic implications from their soil-based analysis. Indeed soil becomes the root of economy as well as of everything else. Ecological and economic crises are seen to be intertwined, Northbourne arguing that: 'International debt and soil erosion are twin brother and sister, inseparables ... it is to the lender's advantage that the borrower should not get out of debt.' Interest repayments were leading countries to exploit their soil fertility for exportable cash crops: 'the relation of financial cost to what may be termed "biological cost" has not been considered, still less estimated. Biological cost may be translated "ultimate effect on vitality."'[69] In organicist analyses the transfer of 'soil capital'[70] is held to undermine the exporting country – 'Those of us who sat down to eat our cheap imported food before the war were in fact too often eating ruined homes, ruined lives, and ruined soil'[71] – and to uproot a black and white global racial order: 'So the railways and ships of the world ply to and fro with the products of exploited labour in exchange for the products of exploited land. Sand comes to African grasslands so that niggers can buy bicycles.'[72] Jacks and Whyte, noting that 'capitalism has never seriously concerned itself with its repercussions on the humus content and structure of soils', proposed economic nationalism as a first response, 'enabling the obvious, common-sense measures of soil conservation to be adopted on a scale commensurate with the extent of erosion'.[73] With international trade restricted, non-Western fertility might recover, thus enabling a new era of colonialism: 'No longer will soil fertility be traded across the seas for civilization;

civilization will migrate to build up soil fertility.'[74] Wrench suggested that trade might be reordered through international 'Banks for the Soil', to 'collect all forms of imported soil substances after use, make them into soil-food and return them to the exporting countries'. International exchange was to be literally grounded: 'What the soil needs as payment ... is not, of course, money. It does not want *symbols of reality; it needs reality itself*'.[75] Against a world economy geared around mobile and invisible forces of capital organicists mobilized a model of 'Real Economy',[76] soil economy; harmonious, controllable, solid, embedded in ecology. Ecology became a discourse to root economy, to earth the liquidity of money.

Organicists drew on interwar proposals for monetary reform, ranging from the guild socialism of Kinship member Philip Mairet's *New English Weekly*[77] to the Distributism of Belloc and Chesterton to the Social Credit philosophy of Major C. H. Douglas and Frederick Soddy.[78] Economic problems were traced to 'usury', defined as 'the practice which converts money into a traded commodity'.[79] For Massingham one of the many virtues of the medieval church was its outlawing of usury; Wrench admired Islamic Spain for the same reason. The usurer is presented as 'a human parasite', whose modern form is the private bank, 'accumulating the power of money at the expense of both producer and consumer by acquiring real wealth for less than its true value and selling it for more than that value'.[80] An analysis of the usurer as uprooter of capital could easily slip into a racialization of finance. Bradshaw notes the anti-Semitism of the Social Credit arguments of Douglas, Soddy and T. S. Eliot, of whom more later,[81] and when Lymington looks for an example of international monopoly control he lists the Jewish names of the directors of the Palestine Development Corporation, based not in Palestine or the mandate power Britain but in New York:[82] 'Pogroms in East Europe and measures of marketing in Ireland spring from the same cause, and have a healthy, underlying instinct.'[83]

Whether or not finance capital is racialized, the argument is for control at a national or local level in order to provide a steady environment for private productive capital: 'nationalization of international middlemen interests might be as healthy as nationalization of individual production is unhealthy.'[84] Northbourne traced problems back to the Tonnage Act of 1694, which passed the issuing of money from the Crown to the Bank of England: 'from this small beginning there grew up the gigantic hydra-headed monopoly of banking and credit ... Usury, condemned by the schoolmen as a venial sin, became the basis of trade.'[85] Repeal of the Act would remove the Bank as the cornerstone of a private fictitious economy. Northbourne's loyal Royalism suggested a revived 'real money – King's money – not the present fantastic system of private IOUs which take the place of money'.[86] Organicists characteristically claimed that their values had substance and were based on fact, setting substantive tradition against modern fiction, whether the matter was artificial fertilizer or forms of economic transaction: 'We must have King's money to prevent money being held up against the community's interests. For the same reasons the land must be the King's; that is to say, held by the King in trust for the people, and administered on his behalf by his Government. This is the right "kind" of nationalization.'[87] The monarch, somehow detached from the modern state, is to become a credit to the community, with land taken back by the Crown if the user failed an 'efficiency test' based on fertility. A Court of Privy Council, presumably staffed by organicists, would run the system.[88]

Organicist economic discourse set the nation up as a potentially self-supporting (though not isolated) 'local' zone which was in opposition to rootless global forces.[89] National argument is complemented by a stress on internal local political economies nurturing 'those vital associations which enable the individual to become aware of his place in time and space and so make possible the good life'.[90] The sheltering framework of the nation is to foster a local life working through interest-free credit via Crown loans to 'local communities'.[91] Scaling down the economy, anticipating more recent schemes of local credit, economic relationships are to be stabilized through a spatial order: 'not only the rate of interest but the distance needs fixing'.[92]

Massingham Looks Back and Abroad: Ancient Englishness

> It's a queer thing: everybody in England has heard of the Taj Mahal, Rheims Cathedral, the sky-scrapers of New York, the Great Wall of China, and nobody at all outside the readers of archaeological works and county histories seems to have heard of Maiden Castle.
> MASSINGHAM, *In Praise of England*[93]

We conclude this section with a story which brings together the themes of dissidence and foreignness which feature in an organicist search for English origins. In Chapter Two we saw how prehistory could be a site of cultural dispute, with Crawford's field archaeology meeting Watkins's ley lines. A further counter-cartography of ancient England appeared in the work of Massingham, who saw another significance altogether in ancient soil. Again themes of social order, landscape and dissident knowledge come together in Massingham's promotion of an ancient *Downland Man* as the original organic Englishman.[94] Massingham directed 'A Theory of Peace in Ancient Britain' against present orthodoxy:

> When ... pseudo-Darwinism is the philosophy of the industrial system, the credo of opportunist politics, the justification of the predatory and aggressive elements in modern society ... you are not going to get rid of it by argument, still less by the revolt of the soul against it. There is only one weapon sharp enough to pierce its hide – that of the historical method.[95]

Massingham posited a peaceful, megalithic civilization evolving out of an earlier Golden Age, with Avebury as the 'First Capital of England'. Massingham presented an advanced, ancient society in order to emphasize later decline: 'Such a complex of lines and settlements reminds one of a modern railway system with Avebury as Paddington, Euston, Victoria, and Liverpool Street all fused into one junction.'[96] Camelot becomes 'the Crewe of the west and south-west of ancient England', stone circles are 'a kind of aristocratic Rural District Council and Church combined'.[97] The scale of earthworks indicated that they must have been built in a time of peace and stability rather than war: 'It would, I think, be truer to speak of the earthworks as taverns, letter-boxes, signal boxes, shrines and rest-houses between the mining and agricultural districts, than as fastnesses.'[98]

Like Watkins, Massingham echoes professional archaeology in dissenting from it: 'Trust your eyes, take no books on your journey ... I am certain that if any of my readers were to spend a fortnight's holiday getting his eye in with the greater earthworks (and a grander holiday does not exist) he or she would settle the short-sighted fumbling dubieties of professional archaeology over this problem for ever.'[99] While Crawford combines aerial and ground views, Massingham just walks: 'Certainly the ancients had a marvellous eye for landscape, and my advice to a patriot in the undebased sense of the term would be to make a pilgrimage from earthwork to earthwork, and barrow to barrow, and use his eyes from their tops.'[100] Massingham conducts a visual exchange with Downland Man, assuming that the amateur English eye could cross over history. What Massingham sees, though, is not the traces of an insular national past. In the early 1920s Massingham was on the staff of the UCL anthropology school, working with the Diffusionists Elliot Smith and Perry, whose work posited a common Egyptian origin of archaic civilization: 'The essential features of English civilisation were determined long before the Romans crossed the Straits of Dover ... To interpret the real spirit of England it is necessary to discover how its culture came into being.'[101] In the Diffusionist story cultural monuments turn out to be of imported origin; the Cerne Giant is Hercules, the Long Man of Wilmington Mercury, and

Merlin one of Egypt's 'children of the sun', part of 'an International Board of Thaumaturgy'.[102] Massingham finds 'Egypt in Downland': 'this English poem, English to the tip of every grass-blade, bears the water-mark of Egypt.'[103] Eighteenth-century antiquarian William Stukeley is claimed as a pioneer dissident: 'Silbury then is a pyramid, a royal tomb of a distinctive cult and type. Stukeley the derided came, two centuries ago, to much the same conclusion.'[104] Diffusionism becomes the archaeological equivalent to the Indore process of composting: 'that knowledge is going to burst the safe and studious walls of the archaeological hermitage and throw its beams upon the world as it is to-day'.[105]

Egypt in Downland did not last, and present England was in limbo. In his Batsford book on *English Downland* Massingham reflected that: 'we step upon their springing turf as aliens, or at least with the dim awareness of having strayed and of seeking once more the ancient mother of our race.'[106] And if Avebury remained as a symbol of ancient English peace, Stonehenge symbolized the fall. For Massingham its stones had been the product of an earlier militarism and thus uncannily belonged in the contemporary surroundings of Salisbury Plain: 'Nobody dreams of connecting them with the military hutments that thrust themselves upon the sight in every direction. But, alas, they are connected, and in the relation of father to son, no matter how many centuries separate them, for out of the first, in slow and logical sequence, grew the last.' Counter-history triggers Massingham's visual imagination; if Avebury prompts a happy ancestral memory, at Stonehenge English heritage takes on different meaning: 'Meanwhile, we have arrived at Stonehenge, that in relation to the barbed wire and military encampments hustling it round looks like a super-shell dump.'[107]

Organic Authority

The Politics of Soil

As with preservationist arguments, we must understand organicism in terms of its articulation of particular modes of cultural and political authority. Organicists set themselves against visions of a planned future. Balfour commented on wartime schemes:

> The topic is given a great variety of names, 'The New World Order', 'Reconstruction', 'Post-War Planning', and many more. It is good that we should be thinking of these things. But too often the would-be reformers of society, while planning the visible details of this new world, forget entirely to consider the foundation upon which the edifice must be built.[108]

If society emerged from the soil, then authority was to be similarly grounded. The extension of wartime state authority triggers organicist calls for, as Massingham put it, 'a new orientation of society far more deep-seated than the State socialism that now reigns side by side with the older money-power'.[109]

The story is again more complex than one of simple nostalgia for a supposedly natural social order. Adrian Bell cautioned that while the old England may have harmoniously emerged from 'unconscious growth', things were different now: 'a new order must be conscious and disciplined from its inception. This must occur at a much higher level than any so-called back-to-the-land movement of the past. We must be conscious not dreamily but dynamically.'[110] We find a curious mix of reference points as organicists search for a political order which is neither socialist nor capitalist; High Toryism, guild socialism, imperialism, fascism. In *Disraeli and the New Age* Stapledon, inspired by the historian and Kinship member Arthur Bryant, reinvented High Toryism around soil, and looked from 1943 into the future:

1939–1944

Predominant opinions are generally the opinions of the generation that is vanishing ... and you will witness a development
of the new mind of England which will make up by its rapid
progress for its retarded action.

1944?–1953?

My Politics are described by one word and that word is
England. And my Politics, which I declare to be the politics
of the real England, are:

THE POLITICS OF THE STRAIGHT FURROW.[III]

This is hardly Baldwin's Conservative country idyll. If Stapledon
was, as Waller argues, 'a reactionary Conservative in reaction against
what he had considered had corrupted the Conservative Party, and,
indeed, the mind of the nation',[112] then so too was Lymington.
Conservative MP for Basingstoke from 1929 to 1934, when he found
himself 'unable any longer to breath the polluted atmosphere of the
National Government',[113] Lymington had already in 1931 sought
to rediscover 'The Tory Path' in his book *Ich Dien*: 'Perhaps we are
lost because we have forgotten the way. This book is an attempt to
remember it – by re-discovering our Englishness.'[114]

Organicism looked beyond England for models of authority
through which to rediscover Englishness. Empire offered one
model based on a conviction of superiority rather than democracy. Stapledon argued that: 'The British peoples – and now I
am also thinking about their Empire – have it in them to be
stupendously great. To be stupendously great is our obligation to
the suffering world.'[115] Stapledon was quite clear as to the kind
of power in operation here; imperialism sprang from 'the urge to
dominate; or as it is more usually referred to, the will to power',[116]

and this did not imply it was bad: 'Imperialism has had much to its credit and has been responsible for a not inconsiderable amount of sublimation of the urge to dominate.'[117] If empire offered one model of authority, Europe provided others. For Massingham Denmark's 'co-operative peasant population' indicated 'a true modernism building up from a stable peasant foundation'.[118] More often, though, the model for what Gardiner termed 'conservative revolution, a restoration of the good things',[119] lay in the authoritarian practice of Germany and Italy, especially the former with its strong rhetoric of soil. This is a complex and sensitive historical field, with not all organicists admiring such regimes, and some venturing criticism before the War. In 1936 Adrian Bell criticized fascism as a rigid and mass 'state-worship': 'The fluid essence hardens into a concrete symbol; the springs of individual thought and action are paralysed by the hypnotic passes of propaganda.'[120] However, as with preservationism, we have here a way of thinking so convinced of its minority authority as to be liable to consider authoritarian models for transforming itself into majority practice. Yet when organicists admired Germany it was less for specific features such as the autobahn than for the practice of a seemingly coherent and holistic philosophy of land and life. Josef Craven's analysis of organicism and non-Mosleyite 'Radical Right' politics shows the extent of the admiration for Nazi Germany current in the 1930s and early 1940s. Arthur Bryant continued to issue anti-Semitic eulogies of Nazism up to April 1940.[121] Edmund Blunden, who hosted the founding meeting of the Kinship, reviewed Germany in June 1939 and praised 'a great clearness and freshness of life, a pervading revival of national dignity and personal unselfishness.'[122] Christopher Turnor's 1939 *Yeoman Calling* welcomed Hitler's 'carefully thought-out plan to use the land as a means of regenerating the nation' by settling selected settlers-with-wives on hereditary holdings.[123] Turnor constructed German-style cottages on his Lincolnshire estate (illus. 33): 'those erected since 1933 are invariably pleasing to the eye.'[124]

33 'Cottage built by the Author on his Estate in Lincolnshire'. From Christopher Tumor, *Yeoman Calling* (London, 1939).

One cannot, however, trace a strict divide between Mosleyite corporatist industrial thinking and organic ruralism. The most famous Mosleyite ruralist, Henry Williamson, headed his 1942 account of moving to the land in North Norfolk, *The Story of a Norfolk Farm*, with a Mosley quote on land, and included a chapter on joining the party of a Norfolk aristocrat, 'Lady Sunne', who was campaigning for soil, soul and nation.[125] Williamson's farmyard at Stiffkey was decorated with the BUF symbol. Williamson's ruralism hardly runs counter to organicism. Likewise, Sussex farmer Jorian Jenks also crossed any organicist-Mosleyite divide, writing a weekly column in the BUF paper *Action* from April 1937 until it folded in June 1940: 'In every land where the Fascist banner has been carried to triumph the men on the land have regained the rights stolen from them in an era of national degeneration. It will be the same in Britain.'[126] Jenks moved to an organic farming position, editing the Soil Association journal *Mother Earth* and contributing to Massingham's 1947 collection *The Small Farmer*, even though he was still serving on Mosley's Union Movement Agricultural Council. Massingham introduced him as a farmer who had become 'the critic of modern economics, well known among the small resistance minority to its catastrophic repercussions'.[127]

Of the 'resistance minority' Lymington and Gardiner had the deepest links with Germany. For Lymington in 1938 it was 'a question of re-education and leadership; it has happened in Germany and Italy in a very few years, but not by the compulsion of dictators but by leadership towards the realization of sound values after too much experience of corrupt values'.[128] Lymington lectured in Berlin in spring 1939 from *Famine in England*, meeting Hitler.[129] Anti-Semitic racial theory, fostered through the journal *New Pioneer* and groups such as the English Mistery, the English Array and the British Council Against European Commitments,[130] was turned on the English city:

> in every great city there is a scum of subhuman population willing to take any chance of a breakdown in law and order ... They are the willing tools of the communist ... Some of these are naturally the dregs of English blood. But many are alien ... These immigrants have invaded the slums and the high places as well. It should not be forgotten that those aliens who now appear to have a stake in this country have a stake also in many others.[131]

Lymington discerned a conspiracy of political economy, with Judaism and communism conflated, and called for an alignment with fascist nationhood against the non-national communist: 'the self-sufficiency of sovereign states like Germany and Italy, the service of race and soil, is in his eyes a menace.'[132]

Gardiner offers a more complex case, having been closely connected to German youth movements well before the Nazi accession to power during the 1920s and 1930s.[133] Gardiner happily joined Lymington in the English Mistery, the English Array and the *New Pioneer*, comparing Germany favourably with England – 'the one championing the values of earth and bread, the other cleaving to the advantages of commerce and usury' – and suggesting a return to 'our own English religion which was nurtured in the soil of our land until supplanted by alien, neo-Phoenician ways'.[134] Gardiner visited Germany with Lymington in 1939, meeting the Minister of Agriculture and organic enthusiast Darré, and in 1943 would recall 'the serious extent of constructive example which not only survived Hitler but was released and even extended under his regime'.[135] Like Lymington, Gardiner admired workcamps as 'an instrument of social and political change': 'the national revolution which swept the Nazis to power was being developed in terms of soul and soil'.[136] When in January 1935 Gardiner sought Civil Service funding for his land workcamps for the unemployed at Springhead in Dorset an official noted: 'There was, as is usual in these circles, a little over-emphasis of the realities of folk activities … There was at the same time evidence of energy, probable organising power, self-confidence, good manners, with possibilities of egotism. I have ascertained privately that he is in half-a-dozen movements, including the Nazi in Germany.'[137]

In the 1920s Gardiner had set out a vision of Britain/England and Germany as pillars of a North European culture and polity, with Britain as 'The temple of Europe',[138] although he stressed in 1928 that this did not imply 'any nonsensical racial theory such as a dogmatic belief in the "Nordic race"'.[139] The 1914–18 War hangs over Gardiner's Anglo-German efforts in the 1920s. Thomas Hardy's 1915 poem 'The Pity Of It' fronted his collection *Britain and Germany: A Frank Discussion Instigated by Members of the Younger Generation*:

> I walked in loamy Wessex lanes, afar
> From rail-track and from highway, and I heard
> In field and farmstead many an ancient word
> Of local lineage like 'Thu bist,' 'Er war,'

English and German appear as 'kin folk kin tongued'.[140] Gardiner was close to those German *Bundische* youth and folk movements which connected nature, rural culture and nation, organizing Anglo-German-Dutch-Scandinavian interchanges of folk dancers, musicians, drama groups and youth leaders: 'The camps ... were acts of trust, fidelity and patience; they were essays in the wholeness and polyphony which are the true destiny of Europe.'[141] Furthering his search for '*interlocality*, not *internationalism*' in 'The Younger Generation',[142] Gardiner took sword and Morris dancers to the 1936 Berlin Olympics. At the October 1938 Kassel Music Festival he evoked a profound Anglo-German connection with a symbolic gift from Dorset. As his friend Georg Goetsch, Director of the Musikheim at Frankfurt/Oder, sat on a throne, Gardiner processed towards him, with a man bearing the Springhead flag in front, and women singing the Springhead song behind. Gardiner carried a bowl of earth from Springhead, to be 'taken to the Musikheim where it will be interred on the German Day of remembrance, November 9'. The bowl, with some of the soil, would sit under a scroll: 'English Earth / from Springhead / Fontmell Magna / Dorset'.[143] English Earth with English humus goes abroad to a place of affinity, the ultimate cross-cultural fertilizer.

The Wartime Enemy

For German enthusiasts war proved awkward. Arguments for patriotic English soil on a German model stalled. Gardiner reshaped Germany into a case of: 'misguided idealism. National-Socialist Germany set out to restore the experience of blood and soil to a rapidly urbanized nation. But the experience remained a doctrine and the blood and soil were sacrificed to the Baal of war.'[144] Germany failed to live up to its own ideology. The general wartime organicist argument, extending that made by Bell before the War, was that the Nazi state, far from being an expression of rural values, had revealed itself to be the ultimate manifestation of urban materialism. Gardiner broadcast on the BBC in 1940 attacking Nazi distortions of Darré's organic ideas.[145] Germany became the enemy not only in military terms but in the values to be fought for in peace. Suggesting that a wartime 'bureaucratic' imposition of culture on the countryside was an 'unconscious form of cultural fascism',[146] Gardiner projected that of which he stood accused onto the British state.

In 1945, introducing the Kinship's *The Natural Order*, Massingham gathered up all the organicist critiques of progress, industry and the city and hurled them at a modern, urban Nazi Germany:

> The 'blood' appeared in anti-Semitic racialism, but where is the 'soil'? ... The worst symptoms of German decadence – the mob-credulity, the arts and crafts of propaganda, the cultural mediocrity, the police system, the slogans and shibboleths, the crowd-psychology, the perverted religiosity, the mass-persecutions, the contempt for the individual, the corruption of youth, the cheap generalizations, the regimentation, the pooled emotionalism, the tom-tom Baal-worshipping festival, the debased education, and the rest – were all the sacrifices of the personal life, personal responsibility, and personal freedom, all proletarian vices, all the machinery of State absolutism, all urban in origin.

The population of Nazi Germany emerge as a large and stupid cinema audience marshalled by particularly stern ushers; mass executions and concentration camps are a 'logical extension'.[147] Massingham draws on Hayek's *The Road to Serfdom* to encompass social-democratic state planning in his critique. Ironically, the founding philosopher of the New Right, whose work set up a choice of either the market or state planning,[148] is praised by one who could not bear to see these as the only options. For Massingham Hayek's work implied that Germany could not be considered 'an isolated volcanic eruption'; there was a parallel British threat in the 'mass-psychology' of the 'urban proletariat', in commercialism and the development of 'the same sinister *rapprochement* between the State and the combine that fixed Hitler in his seat'. For Massingham wartime Britain was a 'technocratic Power-State' of 'centralization and large-scale semi-totalitarian planning'. The nation's saving grace was 'the greater depth and rootedness of our rural traditions, . . . of individual and institutional liberties, and our richer cultural inheritance'. Thanks to this, English tradition might just hold out: 'How then can we recover not our former state but ourselves? The answer is by a return to husbandry.'[149]

Even within such an analysis, though, Germany could still hold some positive lessons. Balfour argued that: 'Nazi Germany has taught us what can be achieved when a whole people is imbued with an ardent faith. We believe that faith to be inspired by a conception of life which is essentially evil. But the fact that it is evil does not prevent it having the power to "move mountains."'[150] For Balfour this showed the possibilities of the state if geared around a 'complete mutualism' of state and individual, with citizenship and the franchise to be withdrawn from those refusing to serve: 'A period of service to the community should be the price of entry into the privileges of membership . . . Any national who did not think it worth his while . . . would do the community little good as a citizen.'[151] The state mutates through organic argument, one minute signifying Nazi order, the next Nazi horror, the next an embracing English community. Towards the end of the War organicists set the state as potential communal family against the welfare state of social democracy, Gardiner harnessing Saint George for something far from the preservationist-planning ideal: 'The peasant and the bureaucrat are as alien to one another as the horse is to the reptile. This is the real meaning of Saint George and the Dragon today: Saint George must slay the servile state.'[152] Massingham saw the 1945 election of a Labour Government as 'a bound forward into an arbitrary and despotic rule unknown in England since the dictatorships of Henry VIII, and Cromwell'[153] and reflected in 1951 that 'there is something seriously wrong with the England of the mid-twentieth century':

An old friend of mine who holds a public office of trust and responsibility recently told me that when he saw the cliffs of Dover on his return from a holiday in Western Europe his heart sank. For the first time in his long experience of foreign travel, he did not want to come home again, and the white battlements of 'this blessed plot, this earth, this realm, this England' seemed to frown upon rather than to welcome him.[154]

White cliffs can no longer be celebrated as the edge of freedom. The Channel ferry home takes the road to serfdom. The War has been won. The enemy has triumphed.

Local Authority

Organicists did not only address national authority. While all of their efforts are set within an ideal of national Englishness, the local is highlighted as an inevitable scale of life at which, in contemporary circumstances, experiments in organic authority could be carried out. William Beach Thomas deduced the locality of Englishness from environment: 'Geographically, climatically and, therefore, socially, England is a local country.'[155] Massingham connected culture and economy in urging a 'return to smaller units of social-economic life' which might 'reaffirm the spirit of place and ease away the intolerable burden of living, producing and consuming by the mass. We should cease to be what Lord Lymington calls "slaves of the anonymous", the disease of modernism.'[156]

The archetypal local was the village. Massingham asked: 'Where does man belong? He belongs to his own place which he has almost lost. In his own place he is able to be himself; in his own place he is in touch with what is beyond space and time. The simple Christmas story affirms this to be so. Its tale of the infinite lodged in a village is absolute truth in a nutshell.'[157] The village stood for community and harmonious class coexistence under benevolent authority. Malcolm Chase has pointed to the tension between 'peasant' and

'landlord' models of village order in such arguments,[158] but organicists happily negotiate the two through models of the socially
independent yet culturally deferential peasant, and the responsible
locally embedded landlord. If Massingham could criticize the great
houses of 'the usurping Tudor gentry' as 'local Whitehalls', he was
not against squirearchy: 'I prefer my manor houses, like strawberries,
small.'[159] Organicist estate owners such as Lymington and Gardiner
looked to improving landlords of the eighteenth century not as
preservationist-pioneers of modern landscape design but as figures
connecting soil and technology in harmony, 'pioneers of leadership
on the land'. The implication was that: 'The landlord system in some
form should go on because ... it is the one way of keeping responsible leadership on the land.'[160] Local leadership was a necessary
consequence of Lymington's argument that difference and equality
could not go together: 'All men are not equal. They are different.'[161]

Massingham traced contemporary rural problems to 'functional
disturbance' in the 'Village Bedrock' of peasant, yeoman, craftsman, parson, squire: 'There are three anatomical essentials in every
genuine English parish – the church, the houses, and the fields,
corresponding to the three ultimates – God-Man-Earth ... Every
authentic village recognizes this triune order by its siting.'[162] Village
'folk' appear as happy to be caught in a social and topographical net;
Massingham's 1945 Introduction to Flora Thompson's *Lark Rise to
Candleford* welcomed a 'triple revelation of the hamlet, the village,
and the market town', a picture of 'a local self-acting society living
by a fixed pattern of behaviour and with its roots warmly bedded
in the soil', only to warn of its passing under suburban spread,
'the vanguard of the city blackcoats and proletariat, governed by
the mass-mind'.[163] There is a sense in organicist work of the melancholy pleasure inherent in documenting something doomed, as
when Massingham documents relict farm tools or old craftsmen.
Combined with this is a search for new strategies of renewal against
enormous odds and in the face of what Lymington termed 'The
Anatomy of Rural Melancholy'.[164] The elegist and the pioneer join

hands. For Gardiner renewal demanded a new local authority: 'The question of leadership is vital. The emergence of a new *elite* rooted in the soil is the greatest political need of England. Between now and the year 2000 it must be cultivated and protected.'[165] Although current aristocracy is diagnosed as being largely unrooted, an aristocratic model of authority is embraced: 'Broadly speaking, democracy (political liberalism) is predominantly quantitative, while aristocracy is essentially qualitative.'[166] Gardiner 'stressed the combination between more highly trained individuals and the average community, between cultured talent and a popular rural culture', setting up his Springhead estate as a model 'venture in rural reconstruction': 'The regime of the wealthy country house is over, and the future of these places must be typified by simple living and strenuous work . . . The manors must become the power-stations at which the current of rural vitality is generated and from which it is distributed to the surrounding countryside.'[167] While Gardiner could work through other models of local authority, winning election to Dorset County Council in 1937, local cultivation was the key: 'I believe deeply in the interaction of such effort and the genius loci; I believe a place takes on the memory of noble doings and adds their spell to itself.'[168] Gardiner sought leaders by example, exerting influence through a percolation of rural life: 'they will exert power in the lanes and hamlets of England, and their authority will be as anonymous as the seasons.'[169]

Gardiner put himself at the head of the Springhead Ring, formed in the early 1930s to develop Springhead as a model centre of Summer Schools, festivals, Land Service camps and a planned rural university: 'We knew that we must proceed by the toilsome route of patient example and win others by the suffusing glow of infection. As D. H. Lawrence said to us long ago: "You must have a silent, central flame, a flame of *consciousness* and of warmth which radiates out bit by bit. Keep the core sound, and the rest will look after itself".'[170] Massingham loved the place: 'The whole movement seemed to me a new regional growth arising spontaneously from our native earth, lifting its shoots from the fibres of our national being ... Was it the bud of the England to be?"[171] In *England Herself* Gardiner leads the reader over the downland (symbolic setting of the 1645 meeting of 'Wessex Clubmen' to organize 'armed independence') to a Springhead 'crouching in secrecy', where 'Wessex awaited her resurrection and renewal'.[172] Gardiner marked out his cultural efforts (of which more in the following chapter) from Leonard and Dorothy Elmhirst's Dartington estate in Devon, a rather different cultural model: 'Troupes of dancers and actors from Chelsea, Boston and the more exotic cultural capitals of Europe disported in the numerous theatres and dancing arenas, but endeavours to develop an indigenous artistic tradition satisfying the needs of the countryside petered out.' Against this 'caricature of nearly everything which this chapter has sought to prescribe"[173] Gardiner offered a contrasting image (illus. 34), taken by Miss M. de Bunsen, journalist and later colleague of Gardiner on the Soil Association

34 'A May-Day Procession on a Wessex Estate'. From Massingham (ed.), *England and the Farmer*.

Council, of 'A May-Day Procession on a Wessex Estate', by implication utterly non-exotic to local onlookers: 'In restoring seasonal
festivals Springhead had no antiquarian interest. It realised that
modern men and women must regain their consciousness of the
year's rhythm in a fresh way.'[174]

Organicist local authority also had spiritual content, with the
Cistercians often upheld as a pioneering spiritual agrarian model:
'Just as the monasteries served as the nuclear units of medieval
Christendom, so we shall need a new series of centres.'[175] Gardiner
argued that the rural church should be 'led by parsons who farm their
own glebe and preach by example'. Values of ground and substance
are directed against the church: 'Like every other intellectual body it
is too abstract and needs literally to come down to earth.'[176] Balfour
similarly looked to a 'Christian God of service' with church and land
connected: 'happiness through service is a creative force of unlimited
power for good. In its atmosphere ecology – the most needed of all
the sciences – could flourish, and could in time help us to become
truly aware that everything in Heaven and earth is but part of a single
whole.'[177] There is a specific organicist theology here, working through
themes of obedience and immanence, seeking both to reinvigorate
a focused religious authority and reveal the immanent presence of
spirit in matter. Gardiner's call for 'a great revolt of the laity against
a fusty and academic ecclesiasticism' could go alongside a welcome
for the 'priestly help of the wise'.[178] Organicist theology also presup-
poses a particular religious spatiality, a locally rooted universalism; it
was for this reason rather than because of any specific doctrine that
Massingham embraced Anglo-Catholicism in the 1940s. The model
is of a universal parochial church, attentive to often semi-pagan seasonal ritual, with place itself becoming a church to belong to and
revere. Gardiner called for: 'the subordination of ourselves and our
tools to a larger organic authority, the authority of the Natural Order,
which is based on rhythmic laws. This is no denial of Christianity
but rather its enlargement and fulfilment in the acceptance of the
Holy Spirit.'[179] An emphasis on Divine Immanence subordinates

the believer to place and nature through a collective mystic materialism emergent from and to be nurtured by an organicist rural life. Massingham presented Adrian Bell as an exemplary seer of grounded rural spirituality, reviewing his work as demonstrating: 'the transfiguration of the common appearances of the earth-life. Let us not make the common mistake of confounding mysticism with airiness, volatility and the vagueness of the immaterial ... your true mystic sets profound and wholesome store by material things. He is the living yeast working in the dough.'[180]

Organic Regionalism

Between the local and the national another scale of authority is suggested by organicists as a means to reorient England. If planner-preservationists saw the region as a unit of modern planning, organicists offered a different regionalism, decentralized and ruralized: 'The whole secret of England is her regionalism. She is one but composite in infinite variation.'[181] Organicists build up the region from geology and topography as a counter-modern unit. For Massingham regional symbolism could include the most traditional country squire: 'his values are individual, co-operative and regional ... The regional idea as the nursing ground of the home and family sense is contrary both to individualism and the automatism resulting from it, and the squire is regional both in history and in vocation.'[182] As part of his *Alternative to Death* Lymington proposed a regionalism of 'ecological comity', with 'each ecological region as self-supporting as possible': 'England should be divided into regions which have an ecological and historical background rather than the arbitrary regions evolved for war-time defence ... functional development and self-government should take place within these regions.'[183] Gardiner also searched for a regional political vocabulary in wartime: 'there is a way out. It is to seek real self-government through small-scale regional communities. Philip Mairet's phrase "regional socialism" has much to commend it.'[184]

Organicists never work out a full national-regional scheme, rather certain regions are evoked as exemplary, offering future hope in their distinction from the modern world. Organic regionalism alights on parts of southern England which are beyond the daily orbit of London and outside large cities, especially in the Cotswolds and Wessex. While such sites meet many of the criteria of the 'Southern Metaphor' of Englishness identified by Wiener and others, they cut across any simple north/south distinction in being defined as not part of a south-east metropolitan zone. Massingham can lovingly describe parts of the Chilterns, Sussex, Kent etc., but only as places being rapidly eroded by metropolitan influence. The country in the west, by contrast, retains a rural-regional integrity. Massingham's region of choice was the Cotswolds, which had made him 'a convert to the idea of the region', a place where 'The parts, the units, the cells, are not separable, and the region itself is what binds them together into a living whole.' The Cotswolds were a 'garden of stone', an unconscious 'work of art' at once 'accepting and transcending the limitations of its material . . . man and rock are the end and the beginning of the masterpiece which is the region'.[185] Massingham and Gardiner took a similar delight in Wessex, promoting a 'Wessex regionalism'[186] around a 'Holy Land of England'[187] which was centred on ancient sites such as Cerne Abbas in Dorset, 'subconsciously still a node'. The chalk hill-figure of the Giant with his club and prominent phallus becomes a symbol of organic regionalism: 'In the principle of husbandry that returns to earth what is taken from the earth and feeds new life with old death, chalk Helith comes to mean something again. He sleeps and is not dead, as Wessex sleeps.'[188]

The Cotswolds and Wessex offered an organic regionalism grounded in geology, in an English regional grain documented by Massingham in his trilogy of Batsford books, *English Downland*, *Cotswold Country* and *Chiltern Country*. These were studies in 'comparative regionalism, cultural and topographical',[189] two on chalk and one on Oolitic limestone: 'The rocks of England speak a different language among one another, just as did the men.'[190] Despite being set up as general surveys of English chalk and Oolite, neither *English Downland* nor *Cotswold Country* give much space to areas north and east; instead Wessex and the Cotswolds are the focus. Massingham sets up an English geological parentage of mother chalk and father Oolite: 'Like the goddess, chalk originally rose from the sea, white and gleaming as she.'[191] Chalk has a 'pregnant' and 'billowing'[192] harmony, while Oolitic limestone has a more masculine composure:

> Harmony is the essence of the limestone ... an expression of order and unity. Free as are the giant's limbs, massive as is his frame, spacious his stride from county to county and noble the gesture with which he flings an arm about his valleys and his villages, there is an inborn self-discipline about his every movement. Even his wildness is never a wilderness.[193]

Massingham saw past architecture as having 'its primary fidelity to its particular rock ... the English village is a better handbook of geology than any printed text ... An observant man ... can guess the landscape by looking at the roof.'[194] Alongside extensive photography, *Cotswold Country* is illustrated with paintings by Adrian Allinson and Sydney Jones presenting a place where walls and houses grow out of the ground (illus. 35), a lived-in and functional rockery, walls moving regularly over regular contours, houses and barns made on parallel lines.

If the region is an ideal scale of living, modern administration violates natural boundaries. Imagining his Buckinghamshire garden set within 'the regional body', Massingham drew the boundary line at the watershed of the Chilterns: 'This is a true regionalism, thus to regard the Chilterns as integral with my garden. But it is the very reverse of modern practice which carves out an administrative region pivoting on a great town arbitrarily centred on Whitehall through its satrapy at Reading.'[195] The only example of geological regionalism being violated in *Cotswold Country* is a site more

35 Adrian Allinson, 'Cotswold Cross Road'. From H. J. Massingham, *Cotswold Country* (London, 1937).

commonly seen as an English glory. Massingham's beloved medieval vernacular building is contrasted to Bath, the site of Renaissance 'exhibitionism' by a 'mob of Italian artificers':

> at Bath the tradition with which my journey has been in association, is abruptly severed. It is cut off from the south, which I have called the Holy Land of England, cradled in pagan legend, and it is equally cut off from the Cotswolds on the north, the great centre of the tradition in its building aspect. Bath is the only place throughout my itinerary where the limestone is forced to conform to the classical style of a particular period. Everywhere else, it is the stone that makes the style.[196]

Massingham finds Bath's 'embodied spirit' at Prior Park, which he pictorially contrasts with an earlier home which exhibits wealth more responsibly, in Chipping Campden (illus. 36). Geological

GREVEL'S HOUSE, CHIPPING CAMPDEN. Home of a great wool merchant

55 PRIOR PARK, BATH, SOMERSET. Palace of a City magnate

GOTHIC AND CLASSIC DESIGN IN CONTRAST

36 'Gothic and Classic Design in Contrast'. From Massingham, *Cotswold Country.*

principle is further violated in the 'Conquered Country' of the Bath suburbs. In Twerton, a 'red-brick settlement', Massingham searches for the line of the ancient Wansdyke, and finds mythic England traduced: 'I wanted a glimpse of it crossing the hills like a great dragon. But I could not find it until, losing my way in the brick wilderness, I looked at the name of one of those grimly featureless streets that have struck out every character of the hills except their steepness. It was Wansdyke Road.'[197]

As Massingham's language of submission to geology indicates, this regionalism further demonstrates the organicist tendency to find virtue in formal limitation as a means to focus authority. Gardiner considered the possibilities of political husbandry: 'If we are to be husbandmen in politics we must begin humbly with our immediate polis: the region . . . We must love our region in its very limitations, just as we love the limitations of form in a dance or a madrigal. Only in this way shall we attain to mastery of ourselves and our own affairs.'[198] Besides this discipline of form, the region might also be a scale to ground capital, Gardiner proposing 'self-governing regions raising taxes within their own province and circulating the bulk of the money within the self-same region without incurring the lesion which takes place in the Whitehall arteries'. Economic watersheds would shelter 'the cellular life which is the source of a nation's strength and fertility . . . vitality properly distributed is the outstanding need of England today – vitality of soil and of men in organic conjunction'.[199] Seeking an example of potential regionalism, the organicists looked to the flax industry of the south-west. Massingham found 'An Example of True Husbandry' in Kinship member J. E. Hosking's chain of West Country flax mills: 'It would have meant little to me if I had seen the factory without the fields or the fields without the factory in their neighbourhood. For it is only in and through their organic interrelation that use and beauty can find their union.'[200] Massingham presented wartime bureaucracy as frustrating Hosking's work, and similarly criticized the 'arbitrary' closure of the Slape Flax Mill in Dorset by the Board of Trade in 1946. Gardiner had run this mill until his removal by the Ministry in late 1942 for being, he thought, 'a thorn in the side of the commissar of home flax production'.[201] Gardiner described the process of restoring the mill from its 'melancholy decay' as an entry into 'regional economics'.[202] The flax was grown at Springhead and processed via Fontmell Industries, a vertically integrated regional industry under organicist control. Flax harvest camps and flax festivals with flax songs rounded off a project of organic economy and culture:

And sing: flax, flax,
Stacks of flax,
Here's to the flax
We'll wear on our backs.[203]

We conclude this chapter by noting two other versions of organic regionalism more or less connected to those considered here. Gardiner's flax ditty would not be out of place in a contemporaneous region of Englishness, Tolkien's Middle Earth Shire. There is no evidence of organicist awareness of Tolkien's work, which was written and published during this period, but the organicists might have felt at home in the agricultural and spiritual climate of the Shire, where authority was given rather than elected and tradition was restored to respect. There too a scoured land was remade together with its organic society and was redeemed from industrial pollution by new leaders connected to tradition, a 'well-ordered and well-farmed countryside' turning on machinery no more 'complicated than a forge-bellows, a water-mill, or handloom'.[204] Organicist dreams come true in Middle Earth, and as Veldman has noted both connect to a romantic sensibility which would re-emerge with new cultural force in the 1970s.

If there were no personal organicist links to Tolkien, there were several to T. S. Eliot, whose 1948 *Notes Towards the Definition of Culture* was dedicated 'in gratitude and admiration' to Kinship member Philip Mairet.[205] Massingham, Stapledon, Gardiner, Lymington and Mairet all contributed to Eliot's *Criterion* journal in the 1930s, and Eliot devoted a chapter of *Notes* to 'Unity and Diversity: The Region', set up as a scale for an 'ecology of cultures' whereby 'local loyalties' might be maintained. Mass demographic mobility appears a threat: 'On the whole, it would appear to be for the best that the great majority of human beings should go on living in the place in which they were born. Family, class and local loyalty all support each other; and if one of these decays, the others will suffer also.'[206] Such regional arguments are related to Eliot's 1934 connection of place stability and racial rootedness in *After Strange Gods*, praised by Stapledon:

> It is not necessarily those lands which are the most fertile or most favoured in climate which seem to me to be the happiest, but those in which a long struggle of adaptation between man and his environment has brought out the best qualities of both; in which the landscape has been moulded by numerous generations of one race, and in which the landscape in turn has modified the race to its own character.[207]

Relative demographic homogeneity was therefore for the best: 'reasons of race and religion combine to make any large number of free-thinking Jews undesirable . . . a spirit of excessive tolerance is to be deprecated.'[208]

Eliot's regionalism was also a matter of spiritual authority. His *Idea of a Christian Society* presumed a placed religion: 'I am not presenting any idyllic picture of the rural parish, either present or past, in taking as a norm, the idea of a small and mostly self-contained group attached to the soil and having its interests centred in a particular place.'[209] Suggesting that 'the natural life and the supernatural life have a conformity to each other which neither has with the mechanistic life', Eliot saw mechanistic modernity exemplified in 'the results of "soil-erosion" – the exploitation of the earth, on a vast scale for two generations, for commercial profit: immediate benefits leading to dearth and desert.'[210] All this might suggest that Eliot could be termed an organicist in terms of regionalism, local-ism and spirituality, but one should be cautious of extending such a definition to all of his work. If the *Four Quartets* can be discussed, as Steve Ellis has done, in terms of their refraction of particular forms of English ruralism, it would be glib to simply label them as organicist poetry, not least because they work through a rather different landscaped theology to that outlined above in relation to organicism and spiritual authority. An examination of this differ-ence can illuminate both Eliot and organicism, as varied emphases on immanence and transcendence generate different socio-spiritual visions of place. The 'significant soil' of the churchyard in Eliot's 'The Dry Salvages'[211] may be constituted in part of useful humus from the bodies of the buried, but the *Four Quartets* in general offer a melancholy and empty land. When we are given a glimpse of rural folk, dancing in the early part of 'East Coker', they appear through a shift into self-conscious historic rusticity, with Elizabethan spelling; a picturesque, past language. Live rural culture is only glimpsed as a vision round a bonfire on 'a summer midnight', a vision which only lasts 'If you do not come too close, if you do not come too close'. Such folk-life has passed – 'The dancers are all gone under the hill'.[212] This is not Springhead.

Eliot's melancholy country also departs from a hopeful organi-cism in the spatiality of its theology. An organicist theology of ecological immanence lends itself to omnipresent hope, since every-where is a substance for renewal, and space and time are malleable. Eliot's stress on the presence of the *timeless*, on transcendence over immanence, serves to abstract hope, leaving a melancholy absence at the heart of a place. Spiritual authority has to come from else-where.[213] If the *Four Quartets* have been seen as poems of place – though it is hard to imagine an illustrated edition – they are not seeking to tap an inherent local place spirit. The glimpses of some-thing 'Now and in England' in 'Little Gidding' are only melancholy vibrations; spirit's eternal transcendence makes this 'England and nowhere. Never and always';[214] now-here and no-where, far from that forever-present emergent Englishness conjured by Gardiner through his immanent theology at Springhead.

4

The Organic English Body

Just as preservationist-planners populated their England with improving citizens, so the organicists posited organic English bodies; this chapter thus acts in counterpoint to Chapter Two. While similar themes crop up concerning health and the environment, these organic English bodies are not citizens visiting but residents rooted, and the stress is on the physical before the intellectual and spiritual; on labour, bodily culture, diet and genetics.

A Physical Existence

As the image of 'English Earth' which opened Chapter Three suggests, contact with soil was to be valued primarily as a physical experience. Adrian Bell argued that: 'It is just this physical awareness that life of the radio car-owning standard mesmerizes away. These accessories have become the central, incessant fact. At all costs we must get back to physical experience, and mend the poverty of our resources.'[1] Northbourne likewise upheld the 'spiritual value of contact with reality, of feeling oneself part of nature', as one argument for 'the nation ... having many people on the land'.[2] The spiritual proceeds from the physical, just as in Gardiner's philosophy the corporeal outweighs the intellectual: 'You cannot explain away existence: the secret of the Smile of the Sphinx is her Smile ... to live means to live in the body, in the physical live tangible world of sense, to be part of the sensual rhythm of life, with its birth, marriage, parenthood and death, with spring, summer, autumn and winter: to try and live in pure thought is to live in death.'[3] A thinking through the body embeds the self into larger rhythms, with fulfilment derived from submission and rooting.

Gardiner's framing of the body within the family and the seasons is echoed in organicist wartime accounts of returns to the land by men with families.[4] Kinship associate and pacifist Ronald Duncan's *Journal of a Husbandman* told of his withdrawal 'from the world of letters to seek self-sufficiency by the reclamation of a farm in the West Country'.[5] Much of the *Journal* had appeared as 'Husbandry Notes' in Mairet's *New English Weekly*. Duncan's initial communal experiment dwindled as the 'incentive to acquire' property could not be repressed: 'just as a man cannot share his wife so he cannot share his home or his few acres or even his tools – perhaps they are to him very much the same thing.'[6] Duncan's wife is mentioned in the journal only in connection with the decoration of a cottage. Duncan rejected 'postcards of the Post-War Paradise' where 'the State's the father, the Creche the mother, and the family becomes a matter of paper and allowances'.[7] He tried Howard's composting and Chinese soil management, proposed that local credit banks should challenge international finance – 'Whoever loses this war, the banks are winning it'[8] – supported tidal and water power, and sought spiritual revival through agriculture based not on 'vague pantheism' but 'precise dogma': 'The reality behind words is things. The reality behind things is soil. And in places it is three inches thick and in places the earth is bald or is becoming so,'[9] Duncan's message was that thought needed earthing, and that 'Idea-ots' should be avoided.[10]

Such back-to-the-land accounts vary in detail but share a sense of linked physical and moral purpose. Peter Howard, the former England rugby captain and a leading figure in Frank Buchman's Christian anti-communist, anti-homosexual 'Moral Rearmament' campaign, similarly went 'Back to Earth' in wartime: 'I was groping

37 'A Family in the Harvest Field': Peter Howard and family. From R. Harman (ed.), *Countryside Character* (London, 1946). This is the final image in a photo-essay by Kenneth Belden on 'The Spirit of Britain'.

with my heart for something more permanent in life than the shifting scene of salaries, bonuses and the sack which is Fleet Street.'[11] Farming becomes an exercise in moral rearmament, 'a factory of character – and character is the framework of a nation', with Howard evangelizing the soil and those who happen to live in the vicinity. Land is not simply reclaimed but converted by 'The Spirit of the New Agricultural Pioneers' who live under a 'Farm Charter' of 'sacrificial God-controlled living'.[12] Howard and his family provided the uplifting conclusion to Kenneth Belden's photo-essay 'The Spirit of Britain' (illus. 37),[13] where they are pictured striding over a stubbled field which might almost be alive with the sound of music. As Howard says: 'To be at grips with the earth, to bleed and sweat and be bruised in the battle with it, is an age-old experience which educates men and leaves them different. Their sense of true values alters and is renewed."[14] Howard might be striding to the tune of one of MRA's propaganda records, such as the one on which 'Farmer Jarge' sang 'A Song of Moral Re-Armament':

> What was it the jolly old farmer meant,
> When he talked about Moral Re-Armament?

Literal metaphors carry a jaunty folk tune along to a Christian revivalist conclusion as the moral farmer suggests pulling up weeds, building new barns, looking to roots and putting aside 'funny ideas about money':

> It's moral dry rot our country has got
> And not just housemaid's knee.[15]

However, just as preservationist bodily ideals strayed into areas beyond the pale, so the organicist group could be open to other associations. The organicist equivalent to Formby's skits on fitness and nudism is Stella Gibbons's *Cold Comfort Farm*,[16] which famously targeted a romanticism of beauty and impractical soil-based wisdom when heroine Flora Poste moves to join her rustic Starkadder cousins in Sussex. One could suggest that Gibbons effectively pokes metropolitan satire not just at romanticism but at things rural *per se*. Through Flora, who is initially satirized for her idealism but by the end has become a neat heroine tidying up rustic affairs, Gibbons retains a position of metropolitan judgement over others more straightforwardly ignorant than her. Ruralism may be satirized, but in *Cold Comfort Farm* a cultural gradient is maintained, which descends from London into the sticks. Gibbons's prime target was the sexually charged mystic materialism of novelists such as John Cowper Powys and Llewelyn Powys,[17] who for moralistic organicists could provide the equivalent to dubious nudist association. Thus in Llewelyn Powys's novel *Apples Be Ripe* an intense masculine urge moves through the places and women of Wessex: 'Apples be ripe / And nuts be brown / Petticoats up / And trowzers down.'[18] In J. C. Powys's four Wessex novels we find similar nature-geared males finding ecstasy on hill forts which carry 'terrestrial magnetism'[19] and getting away from a culturally dead city life to a mystic earth connection:

> He asked himself lazily why it was that he found nature, especially this simple pastoral nature that made no attempt to be grandiose or even picturesque, so much more thrilling than any human society he had ever met. He felt as if he enjoyed at that hour some primitive life-feeling that was identical with what these pollarded elms felt, against whose ribbed trunks the gusts of wind were blowing.[20]

If this was uncommon nonsense for the sensible Gibbons, for his supporters Powys's work could 'only appear pseudo-rural to the intellectual town-dweller whose understanding of the country is secondhand and purely objective'.[21] Judgements of Powys, like the judgements of organicists, turned on who could claim to know the country.

Labour

Craft

The fulcrum of this physical, organic England is the act of labour; craft for men, housecraft for women. Warning against 'an ideal which views man as a consumer only, and forgets that he is equally a producer', Bell looked up with disdain to 'the high peak of the consumer's universe: the Riviera *rentier* liverishly sucking in the products of an exploited world while creating and producing nothing, and only able to continue to live at all by constant colonic lavage … while it is true that man works to satisfy his hunger, it is equally true that man satisfies his hunger in order to be able to work'.[22] While old farm labour had been hard, men lacked a sense of reward in their new hard labour: 'If men could begin to realize the rich physical heritage which they have lost, cheated by industrialism of their birthright, then they would turn and seek first and foremost for a new wholeness.'[23] War could here provide an organic opportunity, with adults helping with the harvest and children working in 'Land Service' camps. Bell saw evacuees transformed from 'a pathetic little party . . . Their animal spirits, which would have led them into heaven knows what mischief in the London streets, have been regulated and satisfied'.[24]

Organicism valued work-as-craft, whether on the land or in a workshop. Traditional knowledge, unconsciously applied, is held to generate a productive beauty, a 'rural aesthetics' with no division between beauty and use, embedded within everyday life rather than alienated via a fetishized commodity form.[25] Here is a different kind of functionalism to that of modern design; non-commodified, undesigned. This craft fundamentalism seeks to channel a politically and culturally wide-ranging concern for craft to a conservative end. What David Pepper has termed the 'eco-socialist' strand of craft political philosophy deriving from Morris and Carpenter[26] declines in this period as the Left increasingly focuses on a different kind of Labour as the means to transform society. The guild socialism which influenced Massingham, Mairet and others becomes detached from the socialism of the main Labour Movement, and craft philosophy with its concern for unalienated labour and community takes shelter in spaces away from a modern world. In 1942 Massingham could still use the language of 'mutual aid' coined by the late-nineteenth-century Russian anarchist Kropotkin when describing farming in Lakeland, but he was using it to hail a conservatively 'uncommercialized husbandry': 'They are held together as parts of a regional organism by the interacting and integrating forces of independent ownership and mutual aid.'[27] Mairet worked closely with Eric Gill, who spent the interwar period founding

Springhead-like centres of hope in the country, counter-examples which demanded isolation to nurture their message.[28] In *Chiltern Country* Massingham paused over the site of a Chartist land experiment 'in the heart of Metroland': 'Chesterton who lived at Beaconsfield, Eric Gill who had a printing press at High Wycombe, they might almost be called the last not exactly of the Chartists but of those who have borne on their standard the legend for which the Chartists implicitly fought – "For England, Home and Beauty."'[29]

Admiration for Gill contrasted with a rejection of the general Arts and Crafts movement as sentimental and impure. Tom Rolt found only:

> false and empty sentimentality and nostalgia about the past which was to bear fruit in our own times as an outbreak of Olde Worlde Tea-Barns ... the wholesale exploitation of the things of the past by a people totally ignorant of the principles that informed the way of life of which they were the natural product ... The few remaining countrymen found themselves evicted from their homes into brick-box council houses to make room for weekend rustics.[30]

Arts and Crafts failed two key organicist tests, those of authenticity and local connection. Massingham found in 'Artfulness and Craftiness' the sin of the picturesque: 'The Arts and Crafts movement devoted itself to fostering craftsmanship on the condition that it served no useful purpose and so would not interfere with trade.'[31] Massingham could find true male craft culture only in the pages of texts such as George Sturt's *Change in the Village*,[32] and in those secluded spots which lingered under the nose of progress in the Cotswolds or Chilterns, sites showing 'the true, the timeless England at the moment of its last sigh'.[33] Chiltern craftsmen, who were usually of the same 'Neolithic' racial type,[34] appeared to be symbiotic with both nature – 'The craftsman knows nature *in the grain* and never goes against it'[35] – and family: 'The home, the family

38 'Samuel Rockall and Son'. From H. J. Massingham, *Chiltern Country* (London, 1940); drawing by Thomas Hennell.

and the country – craft embraced all three in one.'[36] This labour acknowledged its place: 'He necessarily subdues his craft to the qualities of natural materials, the grain of the wood, the texture of the stone, the run of the straw, the consistency of the clay.'[37]

Massingham's frequent hero is Samuel Rockall, the Chiltern bodger, who figures in at least five books as 'the flower and excellence in human terms of his particular natural environment'.[38] Samuel is a man absolutely embedded and beyond temporal change: 'The natural scene as particularised at Summer Heath was waiting for its Samuel, its king and servant. He arrived, and there he is, the predestined, the meaning of the place, its human expression, its being made manifest in the man. I do not know how else to put it.' Is this last sentence an admission by Massingham that he is using overblown language such as the vernacular-speaking Samuel would never use? Or is it that the only appropriate language for such a figure is theological?: 'Given those woods and that heath – Samuel's life in them are what theology used to call "the will of God" or "the

39 Fanning out the skirting of some steeples. From H. J. Massingham, 'The Wiltshire Flax-Mill', *Geographical Magazine*, xvi (1943–4); photo by Bill Brandt.

word made flesh".'Massingham doesn't give any address for Samuel, but as the only house on Summer Heath this craft church would not be hard to find. Massingham is caught making an exhibit out of 'the daily humdrum life of Samuel the Bodger'.[39]

Rockall and his co-bodgers also embody Massingham's principles of 'rural aesthetics'. The bodger's workshop exhibits a deep order which crucially is *not* obviously apparent to the outsider: 'The gigantic muddle of modernity, the consequence of losing ends in means, is shamed before this spectacle of creative order emergent from chaos.'[40] Chiltern bodgers are photographed or drawn without clear composition, men twisted around their work, caught up in poles and sticks. The key draughtsman for this aesthetic of labour was Thomas Hennell, a regular organicist illustrator (illus. 38).[41] Rockall, with his apprentice son, hardly stands out from the general flurry of activity.[42] When looking at Hennell's drawings the eye takes a while to work out the labour process. The implication is that while for those working the pattern is obvious, the observer does not deserve an edited clarity.[43] Massingham found parallel scenes of 'true husbandry' in Hosking's flax mill, where he was reminded of a picture by Edward Calvert in which 'the workers are celebrants and the task is a form of worship': 'the girls moving between the aisles in bright tops and dungarees and turning each steeple so that wind and sun can reach the straw. The action has the elements of ritualism and must be performed just so.'[44] Massingham's *Geographical Magazine* essay on flax was illustrated with photographs by Bill Brandt. While there is no indication that the two worked together – neither this text nor Massingham's later reworking of it in *Where Man Belongs* refer to the images – Brandt's pictures (illus. 39), if more theatrically posed than Hennell's drawings, catch the organic sense of rooted labour. In them lines of girls and stooks are shot together, the flax skirting the figures so that both appear to be a local crop, connected to Wiltshire earth by labour.

Housecraft

While single young women in the flax field might form appropriate scenes of labour, the general organicist assumption is that women's destiny is domestic. Lymington declared: 'The first duty in education should be to teach the girls the value of housecraft in every aspect. For this is the foundation of husbandry.'[45] Craft and housecraft support one another. While organicist doctor Lionel Picton admitted that 'an answer must in justice be found to the exceptional woman who demands the male type of education', the 'proper place' for women was the 'higher plane' of motherhood: 'even on materialistic grounds the feminist-materialists were wrong. Their basic notion that, but for the anatomical needs of child-bearing, men and women are identical is simply untrue: the differences are fundamental.'[46] The idea that difference and equality might go together is not entertained; the body is taken to root inequality. Wartime 'Women's Institute Communal Jam-Making in Kent' was praised as the kind of activity which might remedy domestic deficiencies:

'Modern education has deprived women of their instinctive and traditional skill . . . modern industry has often taken her out of the home . . . it is small blame to her to-day if she is both incapable of choosing (among rich and poor alike) wholesome food and of cooking it properly.'[47] Rolt defined a woman's 'education for freedom': 'though freedom of opportunity must remain, the more effectually we restore the craft and associations of the hearth the less will be the tendency of women to pursue vocations which are the more natural functions of men.'[48]

Husbandry indoors and out came together in the family farm. Lymington's *Alternative to Death* was subtitled 'The relationship between soil, family and community'. Indeed he argued that: 'The soil decrees the unit of the family; since, except for the infant, each member fits into his or her place for livelihood.'[49] Bell suggested that war, with 'our civilisation . . . twitching in its death-throes to the combined crash of jazz and bombs', had prompted a search for 'the germ of a new coherence'. The 'Family Farm', as opposed to the 'business' farm, should act as 'a symbol . . . a steadying concept', nurturing 'two sorts of health, social and physical, two loyalties, of kindred and of place, yet combined in a single culture'. Within old farmhouses, Bell recalled, 'the girls learned the arts of life'.[50]

Organic Cultures

Country versus City

Physical experience was the root of the organicist model of culture beyond specific acts of labour. Country is set against city, and the categories of 'true' experience set against 'artificial' modern distinctions of work and leisure. Massingham criticized the efforts of groups such as the Rural Community Councils on the grounds that: 'To fix attention on the countryman's leisure rather than on his labour is the fatal error of an urban philanthropy.'[51] Leisure is labelled as an 'urban' category, with the 'Leisure State' appearing alongside the Welfare State as a modern bogey. Happiness was, for Balfour, 'a by-product of activity, not ease', and it was not to be achieved via 'material comfort, more leisure, more money, more gadgets', and certainly not to be 'confused with pleasure'.[52] Lymington envisaged that in an organic England the content and form of non-work would be different: 'With a full and exuberant country life cinemas and football matches (amusement as looking on and not as acting) will no longer be considered necessities; and the merry England, which knew none of these things, will return.'[53]

Organicists looked to history for a model of an holistic work-rest-and-play society. Massingham saw the medieval period as one of a craft-based economy without meaningful distinctions between work and leisure, art and craft, secular and spiritual. Gothic architecture, religious or otherwise, was its legacy: 'our churches were the picture-galleries and cinema houses of the past. That was one very good reason why the old religion lasted for nine hundred years. But progress insisted on the Little Bethel, and so the lovely playhouses of God mouldered.'[54] Puritanism cuts out pleasure, and so progress leads to the cinema, leaving the church Low and dry. Wandering through *Chiltern Country*, Massingham digresses on R. H. Tawney's *Religion and the Rise of Capitalism*: 'it was the Puritan party which divided ethics from economics and played a decisive part in the change-over from the conception of society as a spiritual organism to that of society as an economic machine'. Puritanism had been 'the bridge in the transition from a rural to an urban England',[55] although one could still cross the bridge back to organic society by considering certain country social rituals: 'The Evening Pint',[56] village green cricket. Ideal country culture just holds out against what Williamson described as the city's 'over-intellectualism, spiciness and hyper-stimulation of feeling: too many cocktails, too-glamorous movies, a rootlessness showing itself in artistic distortion; pavementism'.[57] Massingham, writing in *The Field*, exercised himself over cricket and 'The Emperor Jazz'. In 1948 the ball-by-ball commentary on the Test Match – 'simply a development of village cricket' – had been interrupted by a 'confectionery' of 'light music', and this just when England were recovering: 'it was at this psychological moment that the Light Programme saw fit to reduce the commentaries, and replace them with the crooner wailing for his sex-mate'. Jazz disturbed England's dreaming: 'When Bedser made fourteen in one over, one believed in the impossible.'[58]

If Test cricket was organically English, so too was Shakespeare, who was styled by Massingham as 'William Shakespeare of Warwickshire', with his 'dyed-in-the-wool ruralism': 'Collectivism and theoretic and ideological abstractions about equality – always the product of the urban mind – were antipathetic to the whole body of Shakespeare's beliefs.'[59] If the 'organic Shakespeare' was 'the least recognised of all the Shakespeares',[60] recognition might help cure the modern writer: 'if the intuitive sense of beauty is murdered, then the result must be the kind of chaos, unreality and vicious ugliness such as are displayed in the novels of Sartre the Existentialist, reflecting the underlying spirit of modern civilisation . . . the only cure I can see is for every writer to cultivate a piece of land, if only to grow bulbs in it.'[61]

Arguments for a gardening Sartre do not, however, set up rural culture as a simplistic alternative to urban complexity, rather the rural is presented as having its own sophistication. Massingham watched dancers at Whitchurch in Buckinghamshire: 'if anybody labours under the delusion that Morris dancing is a simple rustic affair, leave the poor thing in his ignorance! The elaborate footwork, the swaying of the body, the movement of the arms . . . the interweaving figures make up an intricate whole which is as far from simplicity as it well could be.'[62] We now turn to the detail of organic folk practice.

A Local Organic Song and Dance

Organicists set the rural body against the urban body; the one organic, composed and rooted, the other artificial, chaotic and all over the place. A physical folk culture is set up in counterpoint to 'cinemas, football pools, and hire-purchase of radios'.[63] If Massingham celebrated the complexities of Morris dancing, a culture of folk dance and song was developed most fully by Gardiner.[64] Springhead was to foster a folk culture of ritual, control and order, folding people into their land and its seasons with the result that the cosmopolitan would hold no charm. There is no sense of any carnivalesque disruption in the Springhead year; Gardiner remains local king for 365 days, leading his folk-rural life against the jazz-urban: 'When . . . local communities collapse the sources of art and of all that makes for culture become sealed . . . Witness the cult of Negroid-American music. Art cannot be divorced from human beings; nor can it be divorced from the soil.'[65] Rolt echoed Gardiner's words on contemporary tunes:

> The international character of cinema 'culture' is nowhere better expressed than in its music, which has become the accompaniment of the modern dance, that dreary cosmopolitan shuffle that knows neither grace nor gaiety . . . travesties of tunes plucked carelessly from their roots in a dozen regional civilisations of which they were once the expressive flower.[66]

However, just as the Arts and Crafts movement was criticized, so too was the folk song and dance revivalism of Cecil Sharp. Georgina Boyes's account of Gardiner's work with the Travelling Morrice, founded in 1924, and the Morris Ring of 1934, reveals a self-styled, pure folk-fundamentalist who opposed Sharp as a purveyor of urban folk-picturesque, accusing him of: 'handing his discoveries over to the classrooms, permitting the Morris dance to be done by women, drawing an artificial distinction between "traditional" performers and imitators'.[67] For Gardiner songs and dances went with labour as physical exercise, and were central to his workcamps: 'Discussion divides men; ideas confuse and confound men; but song and work unite men and clarify their minds.'[68] Gardiner drew on his German exchanges and on the sword dances performed by the

40 'Plough Monday, 1939: The Killing of the Fool'. From R. Gardiner, *England Herself* (London, 1943).

miners of the North Riding of Yorkshire. The aesthetic of dance here lies in corporeal participation more than visual spectacle: 'above all we concentrated on the rhythmic intensity and flow of the dance. The basis of the dance is the circuit of energy whose current passes from man to man through the linking swords. We made a conscious endeavour to stimulate this current, concentrating our minds and senses so that the tension should at no point be broken.'[69] Dancing implied tuning your body to the actions of others, to the seasons (sword dancing was for mid-winter, the Morris for the spring), and to the region. On Plough Monday Gardiner made sword dance circuits of the county, dancing in public (illus. 40) in Blandford, Dorchester ('a startled crowd'), Cerne ('more for the glory of the day and the place than for onlookers'), Sherborne ('a fiery performance by the Monk's Conduit'), Stalbridge, Sturminster and Shaftesbury ('a large-crowded welcome'): 'such purposeful travel and the enactment of the dance brings about a sharp interchange between actors and *genius loci* ... At the end of such a day one had an extraordinary feeling of being in touch with a whole region, of having recalled to life its hidden genii, and of being nourished by their subtle favours.' The physical tour and dance gives rise to the region. The day would culminate with speeches from the likes of Lymington, such that: 'Wessex became plough-minded again.'[70]

If dance and song could cultivate the folk, other methods could help generate 'an advance guard in search of true values'.[71] The hike, restyled from weekend rambling to a 'Marching in Downland', could train elite bodies. In the mid-1920s and late 1930s Gardiner would assemble young men for a 25-mile-a-day engagement with the seasons, the landscape and pre-Conquest English history, all to the rhythm of marching songs, fifteenth-century carols sung by watchmen sitting by twilight fires and evening readings of Lymington's *Famine in England*. The new elite would sleep in haylofts, and occasionally patronize the local: 'At Woolstone below White Horse Hill we enjoyed the cheer of an inn kept by a homely Berkshire ex-policeman and his amply-bosomed wife. They regaled us with mugs of Wantage ale.'[72] Gardiner labelled one of these eastward-bound treks 'the Hike on London',[73] a ritual, rucksacked, small-group version of the March on Rome.

As with principles of regional culture and economy, restrictions of form are seen as crucial to the production of an organic culture. Gardiner took the polyphonic music used in his camps as a symbol of formal discipline: 'to realize the point at which life enters and becomes form ... to experiment with a form of social and facultative discipline of which the polyphonic music was a perpetual symbol ... To live in such forms and to bend oneself to their discipline is an experience giving unusual refreshment.'[74] Duncan similarly valued generative confinement: 'But this much learnt: the attempt to work within the limits of nature, both of cattle and men, requires confining and fencing within defined limits or there is chaos and poor harvest; a dance without tempo, verse without structure – which is what impotency is.'[75] As with preservationists we find an attempt to channel desire, in this case in part to reclaim the pleasures of male bodily movement from lax and/or feminine association. Gardiner thought women were happy not to be allowed to participate in certain dances: 'They in their hearts want what we want more than anyone; look how they kindle at the show of any genuine touch of real manhood!'[76]

If the work of Llewelyn and John Cowper Powys serves as the organicist Formby equivalent in relation to physical ruralism in general, then their brother Theodore offers a contrary version of local folk body culture, with less stable, even dissolute, authority. In Powys's Dorset village stories, written and set not far from Springhead, desire and authority mingle in confused fashion. Squires and vicars are figures of slack morality, of dreamy reflection, of anything but firm and controlled cultural leadership. When in Powys's most successful novel, *Mr Weston's Good Wine*, God comes as a wine merchant to Folly Down, announcing his presence with a neon sign set on a tumulus, time stops and the village shifts into a semi-drunken dream where wishes come true or people get their come-uppance. Powys Country is a tiddly Springhead, with folk bodies stumbling into awkward clinches, cross-class gropings and rapes.[77] Authority fails – ceases to function, falls from grace – as desire unchannels itself. Powys Country offers an uneasily adjacent, off-beam version of organic England.

Canal Culture

Organic culture could also be detected outside the straightforwardly rural and agricultural. There were other folk pursuing other crafts. Here we consider one example which, unusually for organicist initiative, had immediate popular cultural impact.

In 1944 Tom Rolt's *Narrow Boat* presented canals as the site of a working, yet passing, organic culture. The book had a Foreword by Massingham, who had helped get it published;[78] when he first saw the manuscript he might almost have thought he was reading his own words, since Rolt was searching out a forgotten space of organic Englishness and interweaving descriptions of humdrum objects with giant statements on civilization. Rolt described a 1939–40 journey from Banbury through Midland England with his wife Angela on the narrow boat 'Cressy', following non-beaten tracks forgotten by all but the remaining boat people, 'outpaced and forgotten in the headlong fight of modern progress'. Rolt found that even in 'the heart of a town' one could walk down an alley into another time where 'traditions and customs survive'. Here was a deep England as culturally distant as the furthest village: 'Most people know no more of the canals than they do of the old green roads which the pack-horse trains once travelled.'[79] *Narrow Boat* celebrated a vernacular landscape, ordinary enough to be overlooked and to be valued for its lack of 'show villages'.[80]

Rolt sought a knowledge of canal culture via participation rather than observation, distancing himself from the anthropological investigations of working-class culture by Mass Observation. He dismissed its practitioners as 'earnest intellectuals' who were wandering in the 'unexplored jungles of factory and public house' and reporting in 'that pseudo-scientific jargon beloved of the modernist': '"mass-observation" creates the mass-mind.'[81] *Narrow Boat* is dedicated to 'the Vanishing Company of "Number Ones"', owner-operators of boats rather than company employees: 'modern conditions are all against the old race of owner-boatmen.'[82] Sometimes Rolt finds the Number One to be 'a perfect specimen of true Romany stock',[83] but generally, while presenting them as a breed apart, he does not define boat people by ethnicity. Rolt deploys what Sibley terms the 'benign stereotype' of the nomad,[84] accommodated yet distinct within an 'English tradition', 'part of the soul of England'.[85] Number Ones are to be distinguished from 'the new poor without pride who are the product of industrial cities' and who are replacing them in company boats: 'Soon they will be an extinct race. Their traditional and graceful dress is fast disappearing, a shoddy, shameless poverty is taking its place.'[86] The true nomad

41 'Painting the Can'. From L.T.C. Rolt, *Narrow Boat* (London, 1944); illustration by 'BB' (D. J. Watkins-Pitchford).

is good by being paradoxically in place, settled on the canal, mobile yet established within a stable social order.[87]

If the canals contained a folk they generated a culture, a folk art of water cans and painted castles and flowers. Rolt contemplated Mr Tooley of Banbury painting his can: 'his must surely be the only surviving natural art in this country which has not been commercially exploited and debased' (illus. 41).[88] There was also an oral culture focused on the pub: 'an institution which the milk-bar, the cinema and the social club can never replace, but the brewers have transformed it into a sordid drink-shop as characterless as their liquor'.[89] True canal pubs with authentic beer are contrasted to the 'monster "gin-palace"' which Rolt has to resort to near Leicester, with its 'execrable' drink and 'an effete young man crooning into a microphone, his accent a curious blend of natural Leicestershire and cultivated American'.[90] At the Canal Tavern in Shardlow, though, there is true culture, with singing Englishmen and women whose 'spontaneity' has survived 'the repressive effects of Puritanism and the Enclosure Acts': 'nearer to the spirit of an older and happier rural past than all the "olde innes" with their sham timbering and bogus brasses. The scene in the bar would have delighted Hogarth or Rabelais.'[91]

Rolt is fully aware of one of the spurs to oral tradition: 'He cannot read the newspapers, which is small loss to him, and he seldom has time or inclination for the cinema. Like our rural ancestors with their country songs, festivals and dances, he has to provide his own amusement.'[92] To paraphrase Richard Hoggart, who had little more time for milk bars than Rolt, here were the uses of illiteracy: 'education has so far done little for the unemployed townsman except to make his tragic existence more intolerable.'[93] Rolt's philosophy, set out in *High Horse Riderless* (written before *Narrow Boat* but published after, and with fewer sales), set husbandry against technocracy, whether on the canals or the land, and defined 'sense of place' against centralization. The canal tradition was 'a living force', although not one which would survive a postwar settlement shaped by 'economists and scientific planners'.[94] We can see emerging here a fault line which over the following decades would come to dominate commentary on English landscape in an increasingly elegaic, melancholy, hopeless manner. Traditional vernacular is lined up to do hopeless battle against a rational, large-scale, anti-natural modern world. Rolt moors by the junction of the River Sow, which runs clear from the Staffordshire hills, and the Trent, which has been polluted by the Potteries: 'For several hundred yards below their confluence the smoky line of demarcation between the two streams is clearly visible, and constitutes a striking natural commentary upon the old age and the new.'[95]

There is, of course, some irony here. Rolt, an engineer who would go on to pioneer industrial archaeology, was fully aware of the canal's role in driving the Industrial Revolution, and indeed he found the most lively working canal culture in the 'Industrial Landscape' of the Potteries: 'through open cabin doorways we caught the gleam of polished brass knobs and rails, while many of their crews were dressed in the true tradition, captains in corduroys, broad-belted, their wives wearing the graceful full-skirted dresses, tight-waisted and most elaborately pleated.'[96] Rolt sustains his organicist and anti-modern reading here in two ways, first by setting up the Potteries as a 'genuine' industrial landscape far from Priestley's Third England, with the canal through Stoke the antithesis of the Great West Road, and second by positing some continuity from before the machine age: 'the canal – the spell which loosed the machine – has not merely fallen into obscurity, but has become the last remaining stronghold of a people whose way of life has survived the whole course of the revolution substantially unchanged, and who therefore retain to this day many of the characteristics of the pre-machine age peasant.'[97]

If, however, the industrial landscape could tug Rolt's argument away from organicism in one direction, the picturesque begins to draw it in another, particularly through the visual imagery of *Narrow Boat*. Both Rolt and Massingham stressed that the book was not idyllic country literature: 'To regard Mr Rolt's book as nostalgic is, therefore, wholly to misinterpret it. He is pleading for something that is part of the soul of England.'[98] In his guide to *Worcestershire* Rolt likewise took an 'ecological' standpoint against both 'the neat maps and diagrams of the "Town and Country Planners"' and the country dreams which would not be 'an honest picture of Worcestershire to-day. It would be much truer to show a tarmac motor-road, a row of council houses and a combine harvester in the field opposite.'[99] Rolt had wanted *Narrow Boat* to be illustrated by Angela Rolt's photographs, but in the event these merely formed the basis for the images by the well-known country book illustrator Denys Watkins-Pitchford ('BB'). Rolt later commented of the pictures: 'it is impossible to rid this type of illustration from the suspicion of romanticism.'[100] Two of Watkins-Pitchford's scenes resurfaced in their original photographs in Rolt's 1950 *Inland Waterways of England*. Watkins-Pitchford's frosty, icicled 'Winter

PLATE XLIII.—"NUMBER ONES"

(a) Mr. John Harwood of the *Searchlight*

(b) Mr. Joseph Skinner of the *Friendship* in his cabin

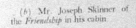

42 'Number Ones'. From L.T.C. Rolt, *Inland Waterways of England* (London, 1950).

on the Oxford Canal' becomes a prosaic picture of a wooden draw-bridge on a dull winter day. An image of dark pottery-kiln-mystery at Burslem similarly becomes a grey site of warehouse dereliction. And while in *Narrow Boat* the rendering of people is oblique or dis-tant, mysterious, in *Inland Waterways* they are full face to the camera (illus. 42), clearly belonging to today, clearly present, yet evidently enjoying a different life to the non-boating reader. The photograph gives both clarity and a different kind of cultural distance, a starker kind of noncommunication.

Worries over picturesque association also stemmed from the success of *Narrow Boat*. Rolt's work is exceptional within organi-cist literature in having an immediate and considerable effect, and the characteristic organicist stance of embattled melancholy was put to popular test by a canal leisure boom, fostered by the Inland Waterways Association which Rolt helped launch in spring 1946. Rolt broke off from the group as his arguments for trading boatmen and boatwomen were overwhelmed by the opportunities for revival through leisure.[101] Canals began to attain an inorganic popularity, such that in August 1950, 50,000 people attended a canal boat rally at Market Harborough. In the pre-popularity days of 1939 Rolt had to battle through a weedy canal to get there, commenting: 'Such troubles only give an added zest to the navigation of little-used canals such as this.'[102] Easy popular navigation was somehow less satisfying.

Soil and Health

Diagnosis

You do not breed good men and women on tinned meat, canned tomatoes, foreign eggs with a rubber stamp on them, imported bananas with a band round them, or 'breakfast foods,' milled, grilled, baked-up, dried-up, puffed-up, roughed-up, packed in cardboard, kept for months, and sold at the pistol

point of publicity campaigns ... Food from our own soil, fresh, unspoilt, full of irons and the salts of the earth – English beef, Southdown mutton, new milk, wheat with the grain in it, green vegetables and fresh fruits – these are the guarantee of health, the aids of the good doctor, the enemies of the quack.
JAMES WENTWORTH DAY, *Facing Adventure*[103]

Artificial manures lead inevitably to artificial nutrition, artificial food, artificial animals, and finally to artificial men and women.
ALBERT HOWARD, *Agricultural Testament*[104]

England and the Farmer gives a chapter to 'Diet and Farming', *The Natural Order* to 'Feeding Ourselves'.[105] The organic English rural body is defined not only through labour and culture but through consumption. Farming, as 'the external mechanism of human biology',[106] becomes a national 'health service',[107] though in ways set against the vision of a modern planned society which would produce the NHS.

Organicists were wary of the fitness schemes discussed earlier in the book: 'If there has been an apparent improvement as a result of the National Fitness Campaign, it is apparent only, for exercise alone can do little more than produce an appearance of health. The desire to take exercise ought to be a consequence of health, not a consequence of a consciousness of ill health.'[108] Not only did we 'have no science of health, only a science of disease',[109] but the nation had a false sense of the norm, leading to the acceptance of sickness: 'An average always tends to become accepted as a normal after a time, and the true normal gets lost and forgotten ... Man may have forgotten what should be his normal state.'[110] For Northbourne and others health encompassed the mental and spiritual as well as the physical and was 'a state of balance internal and external, a unity, a wholeness, a power'.[111] The continued stress on the primacy of physical experience, however, led organicists to regard diet as the basis of health, with farming at its root. Lionel

Picton traced dietary deficiency back to earth: 'people continue to consume the toxic food with the slow establishment of degenerative disease.'[112] Wentworth Day also asked whether toxicity might move up the food chain into the body: 'Can the use of toxic chemicals on the farm and on stored food, such as potatoes or grain, result in poisonous residues getting into our food and eventually poisoning us, the human beings who started the whole vicious circle?'[113]

Organicists again style themselves as providing a dissident diagnosis, looking to the wisdom of 'primitive' peoples and unorthodox scientists, and to their own taste. Northbourne thought that modern life might be altering a good sense: 'taste is the sense on which we rely in fact for the final decision as to what is good for us or not, and when it is perverted that which is good may become unacceptable.'[114] Massingham's tongue remained, however, an 'infallible test' – 'I know the difference in taste between food grown by natural and organic manuring and that grown by artificials' – and his Indore gardening methods offered the 'taste-proof of composted crops'.[115] Kinship colleague Laurence Easterbrook wrote to him confirming the taste test: 'One member of the family, . . . who formerly hated parsnips, has become a complete convert since growing them with compost produced a soft succulent vegetable that almosts melts in the mouth.'[116] Massingham lamented that 'nine-tenths (probably a much higher percentage) of the entire population of Britain never knows the natural, essential taste of any vegetable.'[117]

Behind the taste test lay organic experiment. Sir Albert Howard's journal *Soil and Health*, issued from 1945 until his death in October 1947 as a successor to Picton's wartime *News Letter on Compost*, sought to counter 'the vast mass of interested propaganda . . . The creation of an army of compost-minded crusaders is certain to encounter opposition.'[118] The cover showed English white cliffs, a green and brown patchwork of fields, three villages grouped around their spires, and SOIL AND HEALTH emblazoned sans serif in an orange sky. The journal, which was in effect Howard's personal communiqué, mixed original and reprinted pieces on land pioneers, the use of sewage sludge in farming, the role of disease in removing the unfit, nutrition and dental health, the effects of diet on the mood of workers, the DDT danger, juvenile delinquency, 'murdered bread' and the worldwide 'March of Compost'.

If Howard's work was seen to confirm composting as a way to health, for proof on the capacity of diet to work over or despite genetic disposition organicists looked to Sir Robert McCarrison. Lymington began *Alternative to Death* by stating:

> When McCarrison discovered that rats fed on the equivalent diet of many of our city dwellers grew diseased, nervous, treacherous, quarrelsome, and cannibalistic, but that similar rats fed on the fresher, whole, simple diet of some Indian hill tribes were fertile, gentle, and healthy, he thumbed a long nose at the last two centuries of 'progress'.[119]

Northbourne also considered human–animal comparisons: 'We are not rats. But they would be less suggestive if the people whose diets were given to the rats were not now so very subject to the same kinds of troubles as those which appeared in the rats.'[120] A two-way imperial traffic again operates, connecting English organicism with global analysis. In his 1936 Cantor Lectures to the Royal Society of Arts on 'Nutrition and National Health' McCarrison suggested that diet was central to the 'Building of An A1 Nation'.[121] In a presentation style taken from physical anthropology and imperial survey (illus. 43),[122] McCarrison traced the differences in physique between Indian ethnic groups to diet. Photographs of human types, passive under the camera, unreflectively consuming their traditional regional diets, line up alongside dead rats whose different sizes show the effects of diet abstracted from human bodies. The anonymous rat acts as a cipher of human difference. Elsewhere rats in isolation stand for 'Sikh' and 'Poorer Class European' (illus. 44), the one eating fresh and raw food, the other living under a canned, boiled and white bread regime. The former, growing big, 'lived happily

DIET AND PHYSIQUE OF INDIAN RACES.

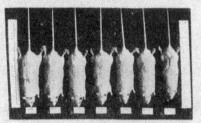

Hunza Hillman: Diet: whole cereal grains (mainly wheat), milk, vegetables and abundant fruits–apricots, etc; meat occasionally.

Average representatives, showing weight in grams of 7 groups of rats fed from the same early age on certain national diets of India. The best of these diets (Sikh) was composed of whole wheat, butter, milk legumes, vegetables with meat occasionally. The worst (Bengalis and Madrassis) is one composed mainly of rice.

Tibetan Hillman: representative of dandy carriers, rickshaw men, etc. Very hard worked. Average protein intake 175 grams daily, of which over 60% is derived from animal sources. The heat value of their diet may be as much as 6,000 calories daily (M¢Cay).

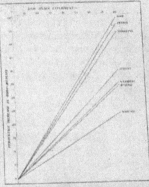

East coast cultivator: Diet: rice with dhal and vegetables and a small amount of fish, milk, and butter. Protein from 50 to 70 grams daily: calories 2,400 to 2,750 (M¢Cay).

Percentage increase in body-weight of 7 groups of young rats, of the same initial aggregate weight fed on certain national diets of India. (vide photograph above).

Nepalese Hillman (Goorkha). Protein 120 to 130 grams, of which less than one third is derived from animal sources. Calories 3,000 to 3,200. Such people eat largely of the better class cereals–wheat, maize and good millets (M¢Cay).

Bengali: Diet: rice, dhal, vegetables, oil with a little fish and perhaps a little milk. Protein, 50 grams daily: Calories 2,300 to 2,500 (M¢Cay)

Mahratta

Sikh
(M¢Cay)

Pathan

Typical of rice-eating Madrassi. Diet contains little or no animal protein. Calories low. (M¢Cay)

FIG. 1. NOTE FINE PHYSIQUE OF RACES (MAHRATTA, SIKH, PATHAN) WHOSE DIETS ARE WELL CONSTITUTED, AND POOR PHYSIQUE OF THOSE (BENGALI, MADRASSI) WHOSE DIETS ARE ILL-CONSTITUTED. NOTE SIMILAR EFFECT IN RATS FED ON THESE DIETS. FROM LEFT TO RIGHT THE RATS REPRESENT SIKH, PATHAN, MAHRATTA, GOORKHA, KANARESE, BENGALI, MADRASSI.

43 'Diet and Physique of Indian Races', From Sir Robert McCarrison, 'Nutrition and National Health', *Journal of the Royal Society of Arts*, LXXXIV (1936).

SIKH DIET versus DIET OF POORER CLASS EUROPEAN.

The former diet consisted of whole wheat flour chapatties, butter, whole milk, dhal (legume), fresh raw vegetables ad libitum and fresh meat with bone once a week.

The latter diet consisted of white bread and margarine, tinned meat, boiled vegetables, tinned jam, tea and sugar with a little milk.

44 'Sikh Diet versus Diet of Poorer Class European'. From McCarrison, 'Nutrition and National Health'.

Two rats of the same age and initial body-weight: the one (left) fed on the Sikh and the other (right) on the poor European diet.

Two rats of the same age and initial body-weight: the one (left) fed on the Sikh and the other (right) on the poor European diet.

Two rats of the same age and initial body-weight: the one (left) fed on the Sikh and the other (right) on the poor European diet.

The rats shown above are representative of 20 in each group. Duration of experiment 187 days. Average initial body-weight, both groups 125 grams: average final body-weight: Sikh 188 gms: poor European, 118 gms. Common diseases in the latter group were pneumonia and gastro-intestinal ailments.

together'. The latter, staying small, 'were nervous and apt to bite the attendants; they lived unhappily together and by the sixtieth day of the experiment they began to kill and eat the weaker ones among them'. McCarrison feeds on and fuels a discourse of urban barbarism in the 'poorer class Britisher': 'It is not unreasonable ... to expect that, other things being equal, similar results will arise in man from the use of these diets.'[123] Animal conclusions extend easily to the human when the latter is regarded as animalistic; a different class of human to the all-too-human scientist.

Goodness

In response to scenarios of dietary decline organicists offered principles of 'wholeness' and freshness, with natural unprocessed foods grown under a rule of return which created a wholefood England. Discussing the lapse into 'subnormal health' Massingham elegiacally listed lost local cooked meats, fish and cheeses before concluding: 'We are, to some extent, what we eat.'[124] Picton cited Sir Thomas Browne's *Religio Medici* on bodily substance: '*All flesh is Grass* is not only metaphorically but literally true, for all these creatures we behold are but the herbs of the field, digested into flesh in them or more remotely carnified in ourselves.'[125] Examples of surviving vegetable-animal-human wholeness were tracked down in the 'Whole Diets' of the rural Chinese, Tristan da Cunha, the Faroe Isles and the Eskimo. Again, the Hunza are the key non-Western example,[126] McCarrison, Howard and Wrench finding a healthy 'shut-away people'[127] with a lacto-vegetarian diet which gives 'health and the constant cheerfulness of wholeness ... There are many other examples of this health still extant on the globe, all of them in places remote from our Western civilization.'[128]

Wholeness demanded not only organic farming but local freshness. Long-distance food transport was, thought Beach Thomas, 'senseless and un-English ... even suicidal'. As if pre-empting more recent studies of the geographies of food production and consumption, Beach Thomas tracked a vegetable:

Trace a single cabbage. It is grown at Sandy ... conveyed to Covent Garden ... bought there by a greengrocer in Newbury ... It has become a battered and flaccid and even ill-smelling lump by the time it reaches the kitchen of some Berkshire home ... The feeding of the country people from central markets and by imported tins has ruined the health of consumers and brought loss to the producers.[129]

Northbourne also warned of the destructive effects of modern food production: 'Sterilization means killing, in order to remove the likelihood of unwanted change. It is the very opposite of freshness. The excellence of freshness consists in the existence of susceptibility to change. It implies liveliness.'[30] Local freshness was also to break an alienating fetishism of the commodity, breaking through packaging to get back to earth. Duncan made a philosophy of his breakfast: 'Tinned beans, Kentucky Ketchup, Canadian Salmon – these are our taboos and they have the advantage of giving a precise breakfast application to a vague philosophy.'[31] Organic self-sufficiency was the local path to national rescue:

> I like seeing my own dinner growing on the pasture I have sweated to drain, and no amount of economists and their planning can substitute that kind of *spiritual* pleasure with cheap beef or canned mutton. All this chatter about the democracies having a degenerate culture! This will not be the case if the inhabitants of this island will grow their own bread, bake it and eat it, instead of reading their culture and letting others live to feed them. Is not culture the way you bake your bread? Does it not begin there?[132]

Wartime could again be seen to have triggered some hopeful practice. If organicists were wary of the effects of general plough-up, the extension of domestic cultivation was welcomed as a means of making production and consumption adjacent. Philip Oyler was happy with the new gardening: 'pastures have been turned under by the plough and lawns by the spade and thousands of people have experienced a mental as well as physical delight in eating fresh food that they themselves have grown.'[33] If in the short run not everyone could be self-sufficient, Lymington thought that some female re-education could have dramatic results: 'Such education in housekeeping as she has had has been to stress calories or vitamins and germs rather than to tell her what foods could make up a balanced, wholesome diet, which would banish constipation, bad teeth, soft bones, and all the troubles which spring from them."[134] Explaining the inclusion of recipes from female acquaintances in his *Thoughts on Feeding*, Picton likewise allied the male thinker and the domestic cook: 'she and she alone redeems his theories from sterility and renders his philosophy effective."[135]

Organic diet mixes two kinds of wholefood pleasure, a delight in basic roughage and an exploration of strange or forgotten tastes. Josef Craven records the eccentric ex-Edinburgh lawyer Alexander Stewart Grey, a former member of Chesterton's Distributist League, who organized squats in London mansions. He was converted to spiritualism after a visit from the ghost of a lodger who had died from eating an overripe kipper, and afterwards played safe by eating linoleum from the floors.[136] If Grey does not feature in the general organic literature, there too we find an embrace of the strangely wholesome. Picton repeatedly stressed the virtues of turnip juice, while Oyler explored an exotic English drinking tradition:

> raw milk from tuberculosis-free cows, which is both food and drink, teas made from camomile, lime flowers, and various beneficial herbs, cordials made from strawberries and other fruits and berries, mead, cider, perry, beer (a food as well as drink, when made as in former days of malt and hops – as different from modern beer as real bread is from the present commercial article), various spirits and liqueurs too (if we chose to make them), and wine from grapes, probably the best drink of all for adults.[137]

With milk in mind Oyler suggested a productive use of the roadside at odds with RBA-style planting for beauty: 'Along the roadsides, too, goats can be tethered by the thousand.'[138] In a further example of the organicist tendency to look elsewhere for domestic inspiration, Oyler would in 1950 produce *The Generous Earth*, an account of life in the Dordogne over the previous three decades. Oyler presented a place close to yet far from post-war Britain, a region of true peasant husbandry and healthy eating, with locally produced food central to the relationship of people and land. Lord Northbourne provided a Foreword, retained for the 1961 Penguin edition, setting the book in its organicist context. *The Generous Earth* is in effect the organicist equivalent to the neo-romantic, post-war discovery of Mediterranean culinary and cultural pleasures by Elizabeth David, John Minton and others.[139]

Organic dietary concern focused on bread as the symbolic national staple. Duncan considered his loaf: 'I bake a loaf of bread. Is this an economic action, a spiritual ritual, a biological necessity or a work of art? Is it not obvious that the *whole* is contained in any *part?*'[140] Like many preservationists, organicists held white bread to be 'a scandal and curse to civilization',[141] and praised wartime increases in the extraction rate of flour for the Ministry of Food's 'National Whole-meal Loaf'.[142] Picton and Massingham argued, though, that milling interests would force a move back to white in peacetime. Organic knowledge is again set against 'science and vested interest', removing wheat-germ, 'the vital element of bread', in a 'perversion of natural laws and processes which we are foolish enough to call "the conquest of nature"... A nation ... that tampers with and adulterates its bread is aiming a mortal blow at it own heart.'[143] Picton lamented the social aspiration to white bread as a sign of purity and luxury, and gave stories of white bread illness and wholemeal cure.[144] The threat was not only to individual health but to national demography. Correlating 'Bread and the Birth-rate', Picton detected a plunge after the removal of non-white elements of grain through steel roller milling after 1872; a graph showed the birth rate subsequently rising and falling with the percentage extraction in the loaf: 'It is already certain that our numbers in the next three decades will not be maintained ... Fresh complete food with the normal content of the E vitamins ... will conduce to our regeneration.'[145]

Experiment

Such diagnoses and prescriptions were accompanied by local experiment. Considering 'Our Murdered Bread', the first issue of *Soil and Health* reported from the frontline in 'The Battle of the Loaf'.[146] Pioneering firms and local groups stood out against white standardization; electric-driven stone mills were grinding humus-grown wheat at Stonefield Maternity Home, Blackheath; wartime medical work in West Ham used wholemeal;[147] the Bolton Adult Education Society had been inspired by a Howard lecture into 'The Bolton Experiment', in which home-baked wholewheat bread was accompanied by subscriptions to *Soil and Health* and bulk purchasing of *The Living Soil* and *An Agricultural Testament*. Allinson's bakery stood out from the commercial white background in sponsoring the stone-ground Allinson Challenge Trophy.[148] Two larger examples of dietary resistance emerged, however, as key organicist experiments, one covering a county, the other focused in a city.

Under Picton's guidance, the County Palatine of Cheshire Local Medical and Panel Committees brought together Howard's ideas on composting and McCarrison's ideas on diet and maternal mortality in a *Medical Testament*. This was launched in Crewe town hall on 22 March 1939 with speeches by Howard and McCarrison before 600 of 'the more intelligent public', including farmers, doctors, teachers: 'Sir Albert Howard was an iconoclast. And that night, in the minds of his audience, the images of chemical agriculture and pest control, to whose shrines three generations of farmers have been assiduously directed, lay shattered to fragments.'[149] Reproduced in Picton's *Thoughts on Feeding*, Balfour's *Living Soil* and the *British Medical Journal*,[150] the *Testament* offered remedies for the 'c3 population' with their 'bad teeth, rickets, anaemia, and constipation': 'the new knowledge of nutrition compels our profession to return to the Hippocratic view – in so far as it has abandoned it – that a physician is a naturalist'. Doctors should 'take cognizance of the other links of the cycle of nature' by attending to food and its origins.[151]

Exchanges in the *BMJ* letters page bolstered the Panel's self-image as a professional yet dissident body. Wrench, Howard, Picton and others wrote in support, before Richard Bomford of New York cautioned: 'let us not abandon scientific method for mysticism ... Is it possible to be at one time compost-minded and *compos mentis?*'[152] Organicists seized on this as a statement of misguided orthodoxy, and an exchange of authority and counter-authority followed over several months.

Diet was the Panel's central concern: 'Probably half our work is wasted, since our patients were so fed from the cradle, indeed, before the cradle, that they are certain contributions to a c3 nation. Even our country people share the white bread, tinned salmon, dried milk regime.'[153] Picton made motherhood the prime target: 'It is needful to give life a good start. May I make a comparison from rice cultivation? ... Human beings are in like case: it is the seed bed that matters most.'[154] The Panel promoted breastfeeding as a free gesture of dependence, whereby woman could choose to be tied to baby and home. Women are presented as grounded in natural process, with the doctor like a farmer overseeing lactation: 'The dairymen know all about this, and the yield is at its peak with eight-hourly milking, neither less nor more.'[155] Picton tried to sell wholemeal to local midwives by showing them two cages of guinea pigs. One group was fed on white bread and was 'quiet and docile' and happy to be stroked, the other on wholemeal and was more lively on release: 'Out they came in a wave, racing about in all directions, which flustered the assembled midwives and instantly convinced them of the claim for wholemeal.'[156] The *Testament* gave parables of ante-natal consumption. In one a young woman moves from the town to marry a farmer and yet the new diet of fresh food is too late to make her body fit to bear her child, which is born sick and dies. Farm life and diet produces a better baby the next time.[157] In another a village doctor introduces a strict ante-natal dietary regime of fruit, green vegetables, oily fish, eggs, porridge and not too much meat, and the Panel's special 'Fertility Bread' made from locally grown wheat with added raw wheat germ. Children follow a similar diet, and the results are 'splendid . . . They are sturdy-limbed, beautiful-skinned, normal children.'[158] The Cheshire village becomes a eugenic environment.

When the Bolton Adult Education Society called themselves 'The Bolton Experiment', they alluded to the second substantive organicist dietary initiative, the 'Peckham Experiment' in South London. Focused on the Pioneer Health Centre founded in 1926 by G. Scott Williamson and Innes Pearse, the Peckham Experiment was housed from 1935 in a modernist building designed by Owen Williams. Closed during the War, the Centre reopened until it was taken over by the London County Council in 1950.[159] In its setting Peckham shows how organicism could connect to elements of the modernist concern for health discussed in Chapter Two, but it is very different to local authority health centres of the time, being marked out especially by its concern for soil, organic food and motherhood. The tendency in discussions of Peckham has been to focus on either architecture or health and to dismiss soil as an unfortunate eccentricity on the part of the organizers.[160] I would suggest, however, that if one is trying to understand Peckham as a site of holistic philosophy, then one cannot isolate particular dimensions of its work at the expense of others.

The Centre was a family club based on weekly subscription, giving primary health care and recreation facilities. Stapledon hailed it as 'Tracing new paths in biology': 'almost for the first time, we see biology being definitely applied in the service of man . . . The supreme teaching of the Peckham researches is that "Nature is that which we obey."'[161] Balfour also welcomed 'the only scientific inquiry into the nature of Health in Man that has so far been made': 'organism and environment, *both* living, must grow and develop together, *each* deriving its sustenance from the other. Thus to cultivate health one must first cultivate a vital environment.'[162] For Howard, Peckham and Cheshire were 'islands of health . . . in an ocean of indisposition': 'Elaborate statistics will be superfluous as the improved health of these communities will speak for itself and will need no support from numbers, tables, curves and the higher mathematics. Mother earth in the appearance of her children will provide all that is necessary."[163] Citing *The Living Soil* and asking 'Is the environment alive?', Pearse and Lucy Crocker described Peckham's version of biology: 'This is the functional picture of life in flow. It is to be seen in a progressive *mutual synthesis participated in by both organism and environment*. It is wholeness – Health."[164] Williamson and Pearse became Council members of the Soil Association, with Williamson also chairing its Panel of Experts, and Centre Manager C. D. Wilson its Secretary. From 1935 the Centre had its own farm at Bromley Common in Kent producing 'vital foods';[165] Howard foresaw a piece of frontier India in south London:

> One of the most important contributions of these Peckham pioneers has been to unearth the beginnings of a c3 population. The next step will be to see how far these early symptoms of trouble can be removed by fresh food grown on fertile soil. For this the Centre must have: (1) a large area of land of its own on which vegetables, milk, and meat can be raised, and (2) a mill and bakehouse in which whole-meal bread, produced on Cheshire lines from English wheat grown on fertile soil can be prepared. In this way a large amount of food resembling that of the Hunza hillmen can be obtained.[166]

Organic principles of food production were extended in the Peckham vision of society as soil: 'Tilling the familial and social soil of man is becoming a science and art ... Whether it is sought in virgin ground or in the weeded fallow from which disorder has been cleared, Health is a cultivator's problem, and that cultivator can ultimately be no other than the biologist."[167] Organic practice is set up against a contemporary planning labelled as mechanistic: 'To planned expansion there is then an alternative – organic growth."[168] The health centre would plant organicism in an anti-organic city:

In these times of disintegrated social and family life in our villages, towns, and still worse in cities, there is no longer any place like this. Nevertheless, man has a long history of such spaces that have met the needs of his social life and the tentative adventure of his children as they grew up: – the church, the forum, the market-place, the village green, the courtyard; comfortable protected spaces where every form of fruitful social activity could lodge itself.

The Centre is just such a place, not modelled on the past, not traditional, but planned to meet certain biological necessities only now beginning to be understood.[169]

Cultivating an organic social space, the Centre took a largely artisanal 'sturdy sample of society',[170] excluding the sick, the disabled and overly reflective intellectuals: 'This is a point of very great importance, where . . . a technique of homoculture is contemplated.'[171] Soil, family and community are to be nurtured together. Through the Centre and its sharing of biological knowledge nuclear families would come to know their bodies, couples would make decisions on birth control and rethink home as a social soil, a 'zone of mutuality' reflecting a human instinct for 'nesting' and stemming the prevailing 'Ebb of the Instinct for Nurture in Womanhood'.[172] A fable of familial transformation told of 'Mr. and Mrs. X' and their two children; overweight, slovenly, constipated and sweaty before joining, but now slim, fit, brisk and happy.[173]

The Centre, like the Cheshire Panel, aimed to produce new bodies, and here we find parallels with preservationist cautions over bodily display, but key differences in bodily aesthetics. The design of the Centre facilitated internal visibility, with a central swimming pool visible through glass and a general open plan beyond the consulting rooms. Both biologists and members could survey others' bodies in 'a building designed to be furnished with people and with their actions'.[174] The Peckham biologists anticipate and head off associations of voyeurism and exhibitionism by emphasizing the membership of married couples, and by presenting the Centre as a space for healthy 'Courtship and Mating':

> we have made possible for such young people an environment rich in diversity of every kind, in knowledge and in action, where a continuity of association can be maintained; making preparation for their falling in love by cultivating, tilling and composting the social soil, keeping it alive and healthy in order that adolescence may achieve its growth, differentiation and maturation for mating.[175]

This would be a courtship without bodily eroticism, which was put down by Pearse and Crocker as a symptom of 'generalised devitalization, avirilism and decadence' reflecting 'disorders of the body – worms, urinary and rectal disorders, constipation, etc.'.[176] The bodies on display to the biologists were to be happy yet unself-conscious in their own physical experience. As 'A vignette of life in the centre' Pearse and Crocker described a newly married couple gingerly approaching the swimming bath. The man goes in while the woman, 'shy at being left on her own', finds a quiet corner and watches: 'He too is shy – almost too self conscious to return her greeting.' She sees an older couple come in: 'Mother is very stout; how can she have the courage!' Should she learn to swim?: 'No, I should never have the courage to go in that bath with everyone looking.' But with her husband coming out 'bucked and refreshed', they begin talking to strangers and even dance a little: 'Those unused to move in any society find themselves gently lapped by the tide of its action.'[177]

Communal activity here provides self-realization through the forgetting of one's own visibility. If the National Fitness Movement presented bodies in conscious formation, Peckham looked for 'order in anarchy',[178] not through an unmonitored and ruleless environment (Williamson wrote that 'I am the only person with authority and I use it only to prevent anybody from using authority over

45 Peckham Gym. From I. Pearse and L. Crocker, *The Peckham Experiment* (London, 1943).

anybody else'),[179] but through one geared to produce a spontaneous coordination. With the exception of one image of a keep-fit class, the photographs in *The Peckham Experiment* show unregimented bodies, a free milling of people into healthy wholeness (illus. 45). In the gym, boys and girls swing in no apparent order, with spontaneity valued as an expression of sensible function rather than confusion: 'He swings *where there is space*.'[180] No leaders are required to demonstrate the moves, while the biologists oversee from elsewhere in the building. In its creative order out of chaos the bodily aesthetic of the Peckham gym is the urban leisure equivalent of a bodger's workshop.

Excrement and its Uses

If eating and its relationship to the soil preoccupies the organicists, so too does excretion, in relation to both the healthy passage of waste from the human/animal body and its potential utilization on the land. The nation might recycle itself through a regular rule of return.

A parent in the eugenic Cheshire village testified to the Panel that: 'No white bread comes in this house: it's all wholemeal and there's no trouble with constipation.'[181] Picton, for whom constipation was 'the root of evil', recommended more than one bowel movement per day: 'It is a passageway and should be kept empty. It is not a depot, and health charges demurrage. Particularly it should be empty through the hours of sleep.' Raw food was the 'key to cure': 'Diet so drastic is no laggard in delivering its benefit.'[182] One of Picton's wholemeal fables was of the Channel Islands under German occupation, where wholemeal had reduced constipation, only for it to return since liberation and the return to white.[183] Theorizing that constipation led to mucus being produced as a lubricant, Picton suggested that 'Colds come to all, but stay especially with the constipated.'[184] Another fable of 'The Starch Eater, The Gradient, And The Gorilla' warned against flatulence.[185]

The frontline against constipation was the domestic kitchen: 'How many of our cooks realize that constipation is not a human heritage, but evidence of an unbalanced diet? And how many of them realize that the health of the country depends far more on them than on the medical profession.'[186] An advertisement for '100% Whole Wheat Meal' homebaking flour in *Soil and Health* is billed as 'A message of hope to the Intelligent Housewife!' as opposed to white-breaded constipation, 'the poisoner of body and mind'.[187] The Hunza have a further walk-on part in organic England as an example of regularity. Lacking the resources for gluttony, McCarrison suggested that they were only conscious of their abdomen when hungry: 'their buoyant abdominal health has, since my return to the west, provided a remarkable contrast with the dyspeptic and colonic lamentations of our highly civilized communities.'[188]

Excrement is also valued within the agricultural rule of return: 'Grow something, put it in at one end of an animal, let something come out at the other end, put it on the soil, grow something again and put it back into the animal and there, plus a non-acid soil, is the very basis of all sound agriculture.'[189] Dung is detached from associations of dirt, reclaimed from being matter out of place to being a pleasant substance of value. Picton wondered that: 'No-one thinks of the grease and grime which smear the hands and overalls of a working engineer as reprehensibly dirty; but humanity feels fastidious and shrinks from any prolonged contamination with filth of organic origin.'[190] Things were different in Gardiner's Dorset: 'Manure is very nearly a fetish at Springhead.'[191] The by-products of a healthy human animal become something to care for, Lymington arguing that: 'The faeces of a nation fed from its own soil and seas on fresh healthy foods should be one of the most valuable fertilizers to that soil in the future.'[192] Lymington admired the Japanese attitude to people as 'the equivalent of livestock as producers of organic fertilizer',[193] and suggested the elevation of manure to the academy: 'There should be a Chair in Oxford for the right uses of dung.'[194] In a later radio discussion he would be put down as a member of the 'back to the earth-closet school'.[195]

For Picton excrement could also underscore an organic connection between city and country, healing a cultural divide in its passage between the two:

> Picture to yourself a world of constant cleanliness, a world in which the rubbish and waste are not only removed from house and town, where the reign of sweetness and light is perpetual; but also recombined, with promptness and intelligence, into the herb of the field, the fruit of the orchard, and the fresh green produce of the costermonger's barrow.[196]

Picton fondly remembered watching horse manure going out of town as a child: 'These to-and-fro processions stood in the mind of a little boy as symbols of the husbandry of life.'[197] Howard concurred with his own remembrance of things passed: 'The night soil and urine of the population is at present almost completely lost to the land.'[198] Human excreta was not to be returned raw to the land but in properly composted form. Massingham cited Reginald

Reynolds's unorthodox history of sanitary practice, *Cleanliness and Godliness*, in his argument on the folly of banishing waste from sight or mind: 'Only one county (Hampshire) has made (in 1943) 1,000 tons of compost from 3 in. sewage sludge sandwiched between 18 in. surplus straw ... In all the others destructors and incinerators are ... "burning up the land on which we live."'[199] Reynolds, discussing Wrench, McCarrison, Howard and the Cheshire Panel, drew out 'The Dialectics of Dung':

> the study of sewage is by nature dialectical, the existence of sewage as dirt being not absolute, but relative to its station; and the method of dialectics has been correctly described as the study of things *in motion*. So whatever truth there may be in the doctrines of metempsychosis, ... there is a true law of reincarnation in what Dr. Wrench calls *The Wheel of Health*.[200]

Picton did not stop at dung. Corpses could also make compost. Picton proposed shallow burial and the removal and reinterment of bones after swift decomposition: 'at once seemly and economical of land'.[201] When young, Picton had seen 'the whole hope of the future' when visiting a Dr Dowson who, inspired by Vivian Poore's *Rural Hygiene*, had two small boxes of earth on either side of his front door, each containing a dead guinea pig, one buried deep, the other buried shallow. The former stank, the latter didn't.[202] Like guinea pigs, English bodies could go shallowly back to the land to make humus.

Breeding

> A clear definition of the aim of national life is essential if we are to set any course. That aim I should define as full, vigorous, healthy and independent life for all who prove worthy of it in the body politic ... all those whose hereditary make-up renders

them capable should possess beauty of body and serenity of mind.
LYMINGTON, 'The Policy of Husbandry'[203]

We cannot afford to shelter always those who would be careless of our soil and future . . . Like the husbandman, we
must distinguish between the weed and the desirable plant.
LYMINGTON, *Alternative to Death*[204]

Organic England was also a genetic landscape. While not all
organicists profess genetic arguments, such questions are registered
in all organicist collections, and fit with a general sense of the country as a healthy, socio-sexual landscape and the city as degenerate.
Lymington saw in city life a 'denial of breeding values', with 'the
instinct to choose a lifelong partner and home-maker with health
and stamina, both physical and spiritual' being 'warped into attrac-
tion which mistakes a spurious sex appeal for true vitality, and the
mutual capacity to enjoy tinsel amusements with the character to
share life'.[205] The city becomes a concoction of artificial materials,
unEnglish ideology, ill-health and unnatural thrusting: 'Concrete
and chromium, Communism, drugs and movement by perpetual
explosion in the cylinder are not the natural lot of man any more
than is the degeneration of the tremendous creative forces of sex
to the mean and loveless licence of the contraceptive.'[206] In the
country, by contrast, 'when people are in true harmony with Nature
there is least often unsound mating among human beings'.[207] The
Peckham biologists similarly set organic health against an urban
landscape of family breakdown and ill-breeding, in which young
people left broken homes 'ill-nurtured, to escape into the unfamiliar
welter of a society disintegrated as the family from which he issued,
there to breed his like again'.[208]

Such moral geographies of city and country should not imply,
however, that this was a vision of a rural sexual landscape constrained
by respectable convention. Duncan, on the Devon/Cornwall border,
found country folk anything but conventionally prim:

It used to be a ritual here until quite recently for a young man to choose a girl and to spend the night with her on a new-made haystack. To do this was respectable. The couple were considered engaged if the girl became pregnant. Even now most girls here are carrying a child when they are married, and so far they have resisted efforts to conform with the usual conception of respectability. For 'no farmer can afford to marry a barren woman, and divorce is a bad thing'.[209]

Such practices were seen to contribute to a country landscape of genetic health: 'For hundreds of generations the country people have reared large families and produced the best stock of the nation. A farmer has bred a son with a similar eye to the work of his farm as in breeding a colt.'[210] Such eugenic arguments do not necessarily map onto ethnic arguments, but invariably organicism projects categories of ethnic alienness and belonging onto human genetic health, with the people of England becoming a human stock and the country holding ancestral variety and soundness as a counter-weight to urban deterioration. Simply living out of town was not enough here; one had to be close to the soil: 'A rural population can in fact only be strong when it lives directly out of and with the land it cultivates, and as little as may be through the medium of money.'[211] Northbourne's anti-monetary demographic strength echoed Stapledon's analysis of the country as a national gene pool: 'The country ... provides those foundation stocks that are necessary to maintain the vigour and inherent peculiarities of every race. The British countryside in short carries in its population the genes, unsullied and uncontaminated, that maintain and perpetuate our national vigour and our national characteristics.' Stapledon speculated that any scheme of rural resettlement would genetically summon the pure: 'The country may, I think, be regarded as a magnet which attracts to itself the national stock ... those who return will be overwhelmingly pure English, pure Scotch and pure Welsh in their ancestry.'[212] And if the country was a genetic-attractor, then it could also become a genetic-exporter: 'a healthy countryside might be looked upon as a national investment, since it would certainly be exploited to provide a first-grade stock for the towns to draw upon'.[213] If Stapledon drew on a knowledge of plant breeding in his human commentary, Lymington extended his commentaries on *British Farmstock* to English people. If the country showed 'how close breeding makes fine types of stock', and the city how 'the cross breeds multiply and batten on the breeds of English culture', then it would be 'the sound who will return to the soil, not the weakling or the parasite'.[214] Cue the wartime organicist land pioneers? Cue Moral Rearmament?

This and the previous chapter have shown how in wartime and beyond organicist argument moved across soil, family, health, genetics, craft, song, dance, regionalism, wholefood and conservative revolution, with reformed English ecologies nurturing organic English bodies, and land and society restored. Whatever its breadth, though, organicism had relatively little effect at a national scale. We now turn to visions in war and reconstruction which had sweeping, national, concrete consequences.

PART III

Landscapes of War and Reconstruction

5

Landscapes of War

War shook up the geography of England, unsettling people and their objects, transforming landscapes, moving things to where they weren't before. A study of the shifting formations of landscape and Englishness through these decades can hardly ignore the War, but this chapter is not simply a potted general history of events on the home front.[1] The argument here is that particular events of war are both articulated in terms of planner-preservationist Englishness and give also that Englishness a chance to gain a position of considerable cultural and political power in war and reconstruction. Here we consider how various consequences of war – the transformation of agriculture, the evacuation of city children and mothers, the bombing of cities – altered the terrain on which this modern Englishness moved, and opened up a space for it to claim and exercise authority.

Impacts

Mobilizing the Land

In 1945 the Ministry of Information's *Land at War*, with its anonymous text by Laurie Lee, reviewed the agricultural War effort.[2] Images of conflict and the pastoral are brought together, the Ministry harnessing the cultural power of country tradition and yet suggesting that its landscape needed shaking up: 'When, in

1939, we turned again to the land, we found it no more prepared for war than we were ourselves.' What was to be 'Britain's battlefield' consisted of crumbling barns, weedy fields and depopulation with, apart from an 'advance guard' of 'modern and progressive' farmers, a 'general apathy': 'Land is a pretty good mirror of man's state of mind . . . A countryside of weeds and broken hedges will point surely to the demoralization of the community living upon it, just as well-ordered cultivations will show its self-confidence and power.' If land was a national symbol, it afforded a different symbolism now: 'By the second year of the war it was obvious to everyone that the countryside was astir in a big way. Never had the fields looked so well ordered, or the hedges so trim and well cared for . . . it was as if some vast empty mill had reopened its shuttered doors and was slowly returning to its original business.'[3]

A modern vision of the country is mobilized, with the plough as the chief 'weapon of war'.[4] Between 1939 and 1945, 6,500,000 acres were ploughed up, drawing on a dormant reserve of fertility, with Stapledon's ley-farming ideas a key influence on policy. Farmer-author A. G. Street broadcast that Stapledon's 'signature' was 'written plain in living green upon our countryside from John O'Groats to Land's End'.[5] New ploughs were supplied and old ploughs brought out of retirement, presented in *Land at War* as the eccentric agrarian counterparts to Dunkirk's little ships. The Ministry stressed that 'farming *is* a modern industry', reclaiming the land into a progressive national identity, with waste lands – bog, fen, moor – which might now rank as prime natural habitat retaken in 'a sort of desert warfare'.[6] Close-up images show machines taking the land in hand: 'Teeth of the Gyrotiller. Cut of the Plough. Rake of the Harrow. Press of the Roller. Drill of the Planter. Arms of the Reaper'. The tractor becomes 'the king-pin of mechanization, the heart of the modern farm';[7] 56,000 were in use in 1939, 203,000 by 1946, still under half the number of farm horses, but with the trajectory of change in place. A 'mechanized regiment' of 'Tractors on Parade' lines up for the camera at wheel height, fresh from the

46 'Tractors on Parade'. From Ministry of Information, *Land at War* (London, 1945).

British factory and ready for any earth (illus. 46): 'So power came to the land, such power as it had never seen before ... Through it, agriculture found its feet again, stretched out, and tested its new strength. It will never again be a country cousin.'[8]

This is power driven by the modern knowledge of technical and cultivation officers, whose task is modernizing the agricultural mind. Improved stock breeding is seen to transform the herd from tripper-like to hiker-like animals: 'In place of the occasional mixed herds of happy-go-lucky, lump-backed, ill-conditioned animals, you could now see more and more clean, beautifully formed cattle coming on to the land.'[9] Agriculture also becomes a site of modern planning, with a human chain of command from the Minister in Whitehall through the County War Agricultural Executive Committees (War Ags), set up at the outbreak of war, through district and parish to the farmer, with local knowledge moulding abstract production targets to the fit of the land: 'And the Parish Representative, who knew every yard of the valley, went to the farmer at the end of the lane. "Bob," he said, "how about that 17-acre field-for wheat?" And

Farmer Bob said "Aye."[10] The National Farm Survey of 1941–3, styled as a 'second Domesday Book', classified all land according to potential productivity and actual management.[11] Farmers were graded A, B or C, with the state having the power to take over Grade C farms (around 5 per cent of the total) if the farmer was not prepared to rectify matters. The Survey form listed possible reasons for failure: 'old age. Lack of Capital Personal Failings. If personal failings, details:-'.[12] State assessment and eviction focused issues of private rights and public control, with a Farmers' Rights Association seizing on cases such as the Hampshire farmer shot by police while resisting eviction.[13] *Land at War* carefully presents War Ags as *locally* constituted bodies, calling them 'a form of self-government' welcomed by 'brother farmers', and 'perhaps the most successful example of decentralization and the most democratic use of "control" this war has produced'.[14] Others, such as Wentworth Day, would view them as unwelcome, unEnglish and persisting for too long after the War:

> All through the War the so-called experts of the County War Agricultural Executive Committees – some of whom had never farmed in their lives or had lost money at it and were therefore glad to get a paid job – ordered farmers about . . . they told the farmer what to grow, and, if he disobeyed, they kicked him out of his house and land – without the right of appeal to an independent tribunal. They are still with us.[15]

Land is also mobilized via a human transfusion: 'new crops, new ways, new farms – but also new men'.[16] The Ministry recorded the labourer having 'put off his smock and put on the mechanic's overall'.[17] New men were needed to replace the 50,000 members of an already ageing workforce who went into the armed forces in the first two years of the War.[18] The Ministry, however, ran into an iconographic problem with a lack of available imagery of young male landworkers. The frontispiece of *Land at War* shows an old worker resolutely holding a bit of harvest, a picture which might have come from any illustrated country guide to olde England. There is an awkward balance between mechanical modernity and human age in terms of agricultural masculinity. Indeed youthful farm imagery focused less on new men than on new women.

The Women's Land Army (WLA) was set up in June 1939 and directed by the Chair of the Women's Institutes, Lady Denman. Entirely staffed and run by women, it was employing over 19,000 by August 1941 and 87,000 by August 1943.[19] The role of the WLA gave a focus for the argument on the role of urbanites in the country and the connection of women to the land. H. V. Morton went typically over the top in wartime: 'Land girls, like women in general, are of two kinds: true and false. The false are those who, having appreciated rural scenery during periods of prolonged drought, believe they would like to go back to the land.'[20] Like Morton, Vita Sackville-West, in her official account of the WLA, concluded that 'true' land girls, like true visitors, went beyond the picturesque: 'in the peculiar metropolitan beauty of Covent Garden, she may once have bought her pound of apples cheap, thinking no more of what had gone to produce them . . . But she knows now.'[21] Girls are seen to be transformed in body through land work, *Land at War* commenting that: 'Compared with the ruddy, strong-limbed village lasses, these paler, streamlined, town-bred girls seemed much too fragile for the rigours of outdoor work.'[22] While many land girls were former factory workers, the occupations highlighted in official accounts are 'streamlined' service jobs not demanding physical strength: 'She has been a shop-assistant, a manicurist, a hair-dresser, a shorthand-typist, a ballet-dancer, a milliner, a mannequin, a sales-woman, an insurance-clerk.'[23] Adaptation from Third England to the farm is taken to demonstrate both country hospitality and hidden urban capacity. It also, though, connects to a mechanization of agriculture which, far from being a mark of masculinity, is seen to enable the feminization of land work: 'It is astonishing that a machine of such size could be operated by girls at all.' The machine, and by implication the girls, can replace 'a whole gang of men'.[24]

Women's land work triggered controversy in terms of its natural-ness and social acceptability, debates which echoed those surrounding women's wartime factory labour.[25] Was this an exceptional situa-tion which would revert to 'normal' in peacetime? Should women receive equal pay, or would this signal job 'dilution'? Were women independent social beings, or should they be classified as ultimately dependent on fathers or husbands and therefore not due full reward? Discussions of the Land Army tend to assume that girls will return whence they came, or stay and adopt a more traditional and feminine role of farmer's wife, shepherdess, dairy maid or teacher of 'rural domestic economy'. Sackville-West thought that, while the 'cream of the Land Army' might be given smallholdings, even those who had found their 'true vocation' in farming would give way to men in physical ability and wages: 'the ratio would work out at three women equalling two men ... It thus seems extremely unlikely that women will oust men to any great extent on the farms, and indeed no reason-able person would wish them to do so.'[26] Some, she thought, might board a 'new "Mayflower"': 'what could be more desirable than that the stock of these fine girls should mix with their consanguineous friends in Canada, Australia, New Zealand?'[27] Whether abroad or at home, absorption was the ideal. In Wiltshire, the Mayor of Wilton, Edith Olivier, told of the good assimiliation of 'a girl whose face might have belonged to one from the Forest of Arden; it was sur-prising to learn that she was a Londoner ... New blood such as this, naturally absorbed into a village, will enrich the local breed and make a better blend in future.' Olivier's words were illustrated by Cecil Beaton's photograph of 'A land-girl from London who adapts herself to the village mould as though born to it' (illus. 47).[28] A sturdy trunk, a rooted body, with breeding potential. This girl against a tree does threaten conventional country womanhood.

However, if the ideal was absorption, imagery often made the land girl stand out from farm and fields. With some exceptions, an

47 'A land-girl from London who adapts herself to the village mould as though born to it ...'. From Edith Olivier, 'The English Village in War-Time', *Geographical Magazine*, XIV (1942); photo by Cecil Beaton.

aesthetic of fresh-aired beauty predominates in Sackville-West's official history and elsewhere. Bodies are reshaped by new labour, with the female body moving out of the streamlined office in a reverse Cinderella transformation and harvesting a new glamour. Whether seen in posed shots or snapshots the land girl is almost always long-haired and recognizably feminine, and never accompanies male workers, although many of those billeted individually on farms would have worked alongside men. The Land Army is marked out from the rest of the agricultural workforce, including the 55,000 regular pre-war female land workers.[29] It blends with the land but not with its people. Commentary on the WLA certainly recognized possibilities of socio-sexual disorder, with class and sex mixing in judgements as to whether land girls were suitable for the country: 'The coming of the land girl ... was a source of some perplexity to the farmer. To his wife also.'[30] The iconic distinction of the Land Army is a means to contain potential social disruption. Likewise the interview-based recruitment process, controlled by local representatives who were generally of middle age and upper or upper-middle class, filtered recruits. While more 'proper' candidates tended to be directed to individual billeting with farmers, the less right sort of girl was likely to be one of those 22,000 resident by January 1944 in 696 often isolated hostels, run by the WLA, the YWCA or the War Ags and supervised by a Warden and Forewomen; a kind of gang-labour Youth Hostel. Lectures advised on work, leisure and 'Social Hygiene (Y.D.)'. While forming 'the centre of the social life of the neighbourhood',[31] the hostel aimed to provide as moral a landscape as its pre-war leisure counterpart.

Land at War also presented a land mobilized through the efforts of rural women: 'still close to the tradition of communal farm work ... The women went back to the land.'[32] Voluntary groups took food to field workers under the Rural Pie Scheme, with 1,250,000 snacks a week being delivered in 5,000 villages by October 1944.[33] The WI mounted a fruit-preserving campaign in 1940 and 1941, supported by the Ministry of Food. Associations of femininity, community and fruitfulness came together: 'Jam. It seemed the perfect solution ... Groups of WI jam makers, or preservation centres as they came to be called, sprang up all over the country ... something which country-women with their traditional knowledge of jam-making could do and do well.'[34] Non-agricultural land could also be mobilized, since rural, urban and suburban dwellers could 'Dig For Victory' in gardens or allotments, whose numbers had almost doubled to 1,400,000 in 1943.[35] Rather than presenting an army of land technicians, the imagery of male and female domestic digging called up an amateur spirit of improvisation. Muddling agrarianism migrates from the farm to the urban allotment as country farming turns professional.

Moving People

The new labour allocated by the War Ags for harvest could include urban workers, proving to the Ministry that, 'the hereditary link with the land is still unbroken, even among the most urbanized communities.' If allotments bridged a town-country gulf in one direction, harvest work did so in another: 'they tore off their shirts, took a good swig of country air, and plunged into the corn and cabbage as if for a salt-sea bathe.'[36] Landscape once more becomes an occasion for citizenship. There were, however, other town-country bridges viewed as less harmonious exchanges. In September 1939 city moved to country on a scale and in a manner rather different from the pre-war excursions. 1,473,000 children, the younger ones with their mothers, moved in three days from bomb-threatened areas to 'safe' reception areas. Evacuation crossed boundaries of social geography. Two Englands met, one often deemed more English than the other, and anger, sympathy, kindness, rejection, abuse or friendship followed.

Government committees had been considering evacuation since 1931, in the light of arguments such as that made by Churchill in the Commons in 1934: 'We must expect that, under the pressure of continuous air attack upon London, at least 3,000,000 or 4,000,000 people would be driven out into the open country around the metropolis.'[37] The Anderson committee report of 26 July 1938 formed the basis of the September 1939 scheme. Perceived urgency led to some trains being filled up regardless of destinations, and reception areas often took an unexpected mix of children. As the official historian of social policy Richard Titmuss commented, 'Few places in Britain were immune from this upheaval.'[38] Many evacuees quickly returned; 43 per cent of unaccompanied schoolchildren, 86 per cent of accompanied children, 88 per cent of mothers. Only 500,000 were left in the reception areas by January 1940.[39] Whatever its social variety, public debate addressed evacuation as a working-class movement into the country. Citizen and anti-citizen walked abroad once more, Harry Batsford commenting: 'It is pitiable that so many English folk – possibly, God help us, a large majority – should be so desperately out of touch with the real England ... Many of these people are by now hopeless cases, but it is still possible for a number to learn to "see" the country.'[40] Morton, while noting that in terms of bombs and shelters 'The War was far away from rural England', found an indirect presence: 'strange women from the cities were in the habit of coming into the tap room in the evening and drinking half a pint, or even gin, like a man. Such a thing had never happened before in the village, and no one liked it.'[41] Wartime uprooted accepted geographies, with debates over pre-war leisure amplified; some condemning a selfish, rural middle class, others a sinful, urban, working class.[42] Evacuation became the main source of conflict on the Home Front and was so prominent that by May 1940 Richmal Crompton had managed to publish a 'William' story on it. In *William and the Evacuees* the village children are jealous of the evacuees' presents and parties, and want to be 'vacuated' themselves. William tries to place himself and his friends in a large, luxurious country house: 'Dear Sir, I am sending you sum evackueys tomorro. Please have everythin ready, Luv from, Mister Chamblane.'[43] The plot is uncovered and William exits to buy bullseyes.

The fact that bombs did not immediately fall opened up evacuation as a site for social survey.[44] It became variously a 'window through which town life was seen',[45] a revelation of urban poverty 'quite unknown to the ordinary citizen',[46] a 'laboratory experiment in State control' giving a 'golden opportunity ... for the redistribution of our abominably congested population from the abominable nineteenth-century conurbations which contain it'.[47] Surveys focused on three issues: billeting arrangements, the behaviour of urban children and the behaviour of urban mothers. For the Fabian Society, regretting that 'our greatest social experiment is left largely to the caprice of amateurs', billeting 'involved inevitably an enormous number of individual difficulties which it could not possibly solve, because so many of them were inherent in the very structure of English society'.[48] Chaotic billeting revealed the need for expert planning. Billeting worked through social distinctions on the part of chooser and chosen, with the selection process often containing all the humiliations of picking teams at school: 'in many areas, they were walked or paraded around while householders took their pick. "Scenes reminiscent of a cross between an early Roman slave market and Selfridge's bargain basement ensued"... farmers picked strong-looking lads, and the presentable, nicely dressed children were quickly chosen.'[49] While reception areas were themselves socially stratified, evacuation rapidly became a symbolic issue of urban working-class behaviour in a middle-class setting, the Fabian Society noting: 'what the evacuation scheme did was to make the countryside and the comfortable classes suddenly and painfully aware, in their own persons, of the deep and shameful poverty which exists to-day in the rich cities of England.'[50]

Mythic urban monsters entered the home, and hygiene and propriety seemed to fly out of the window. While surveys noted that billeting officers might be 'intimidated by the local gentry into assigning children to poor homes and leaving the wealthier behind', and that 'many well-to-do people deliberately closed their houses and evacuated themselves rather than accept evacuees'[51] (or in the case of larger country houses hurried to invite 'safe' non-military and non-evacuee guests such as private schools),[52] evacuation was dramatized in terms of the plight of the middle-class recipients of the urban poor. In Evelyn Waugh's *Put Out More Flags* local lady Barbara Sothill is, as billeting officer, transformed 'from one of the most popular figures in the countryside into a figure of terror'.[53] Waugh portrays a class and ethnic nightmare with the 'Connollys' of Birmingham, three children of unknown parentage: a dumb young girl, a rogue of a boy and a randy, boozy, 'ripely pubescent' teenage girl.[54] Waugh's Connollys barely exceed much official commentary on the behaviour of urban children. The wi's *Town Children Through Country Eyes* commented on hygiene, food habits, clothes, upbringing and intelligence: 'many of the guests arrived in a condition and with modes of life or habits which were startlingly less civilized than those they had accepted for a life-time.'[55]

In such reports trauma is seen to afflict the family, not the child: 'The habits of most of the children were unspeakable', 'In some cases, clothes were stitched on and had to be cut off', '*Nottingham. They all used bad language and had no idea of telling the truth and were quite undisciplined.*'[56] The assumption is that while the city would be horribly bewildering to a country child, the country should be a place of pleasant unfamiliarity to the city child; not a place of boredom, loneliness and dullness. However, what was good to one side – in environment, in manners – might be mystifying and alienating to the other, the Fabian Society noting that: 'Many children were brought home because the parents felt they were being taught good manners that would alienate them from their homes.'[57] The estimated average 10 per cent of evacuees who were unclean or verminous generated the most publicity, although a rapid clear-up of lice and scabies through medical examinations[58] prompted condemnation of slum conditions rather than of the children. Enuresis was more controversial. While initial bed-wetting could be forgiven as resulting from the shock of upheaval, deliberate acts of urination or defecation in the corners of rooms, on curtains, on beds, indeed seemingly anywhere but in an outdoor lavatory, were harder to understand: 'The children relieve themselves any time and anywhere', 'The play meadow by the end of the first week was worse than any stock yard.'[59] Worse than animals, urban children transgress the rules of normal country life, with 'un-housetrained' children coming from 'apparently good homes' as well as slums: 'dirty habits of this nature are practically unknown among country children.'[60] Ritchie Calder pointed out 'the difficulty which town-bred children had in learning the cloacal geography of the country cottage. Nor is it easy to convince country people that it is the cleanest families in, for example, the Glasgow slums, who refuse to use the communal closet serving a whole tenement.'[61]

In matters of cloacal geography and country knowledge, however, children are seen as open to redemption. Edith Olivier repeated her analysis of Land Army absorption: 'These visiting children soon become real country children; feeding the cows and pigs and driving with the donkey cart which takes the milk to market: in fact, working and playing side by side with the children who belong to the place.'[62] A counter-narrative of evacuation emerges, especially in relation to boys outdoors, whereby children's natural innocence, suppressed by the city, is released in the country. Children initially terrified at the size of cows and surprised to see apples on trees gain a 'great interest in country life, particularly on the part of the boys', with a consequent 'immense improvement in ... health and manners'.[63] The Fabian Society found children connecting to intellectual, spiritual and physical cultures of landscape: 'They have grown in stature, increased in weight, and there is a marked difference in their nervous condition ... they quickly became part of the countryside – almost indistinguishable from the village children.'[64] Evacuation is restyled as homecoming: 'the country is a child's spiritual home', 'to this close contact with nature, the town child has responded with the enthusiasm of one who has been deprived of its heritage.'[65] The Fabians dreamed of a material reclamation of heritage:

> In the first two or three weeks many people believed that a social revolution had begun. Some thought that the child from the slums, introduced to country food, country air, and better surroundings ... would get such a taste of 'the good life' that he would never go back either physically or spiritually, but would remain in the village dominated by the Tory landowner until he had driven that landowner from his seat.[66]

For urban mothers it was a different story. Titmuss ascribes the high rate of return home of mothers and accompanied children to anxieties about homes and boredom on the part of women 'dyed to the colour of a different environment'.[67] Mothers with children were often treated as lodgers rather than guests, and asked to vacate the house during the day: 'I have seldom, if ever, since the war, been in the busy, crowded Exeter High Street without seeing these mothers and children wandering about looking miserable.'[68] If children could adapt to country manners, no possibilities of redemption were held out for mothers. Evacuation was seen as revealing a moral and economic crisis in young inner-urban motherhood. While some showed sympathy towards mothers who were forced to go out to work rather than look after their children, more commonly mothers were blamed for their own sins. The WI suggested that: 'The mothers fell into two types (a) the frankly dirty and shiftless mother, (b) the mother who though passably clean or even smart herself yet seemed too indolent, bored or incompetent to train her children or look after her home.'[69] WI members had 'found it hard to be sympathetic to women who could neither cook, sew nor conform to the ordinary standards of human decency and whose one idea of enjoyment was to visit the public-house or cinema'. While prepared to allow that 'this state of affairs is a serious slur on our educational system',[70] charity stopped at current mothers: 'The appalling apathy of the mothers was terrible to see. "Pictures" and cheap novelettes were their one desire. Had no wish to knit, sew or cook.' Urban women serve to elevate country motherhood: 'After this experience I think England ought to be proud of her country women for their cleanliness, good housewifery and decent standards', 'General feeling was of shame that such people are being bred in our big cities.'[71]

Two species of urban women preoccupy the country in early wartime. The feckless, urban mother, always cast as working class, lodges unhappily in the village, shifting off to the nearest town whenever possible. The land girl works proudly as a townswoman fit for war effort and country life. While evacuated children might be helped into citizenship, evacuated mothers are a lost cause. A reconstruction of cities away from slumdom into a bright future of modern housing, gardens and community centres might make a proper place for growing children, but for their mothers? Would they even appreciate such improvement? If they belonged in the slums, would they be happy when the slums had gone? From such questions emerge many of the tensions of post-war paternalistic town and country planning, whose landscape offered inclusive citizenship only by marking out an irredeemable human residue.

Bombs

In view of the recent Blitz, it would be useful for all members of the AA to be familiar with the roads leading out of London and their ramifications.

Especially it is necessary in view of the great importance this Association holds of the doctrine of the Resurrection of the Body, in the light of recent air raid deaths. This doctrine extends to all domestic animals including cattle (we are not sure of sheep and goats).

London woman's dream, describing a notice on an Automobile Association map given to her in the bath, reported to Mass Observation in January 1941.[72]

There were 60,000 civilian air-raid casualties in Britain during the War, with 40,000 before December 1941, and half of them in London. Bombing built up during the summer of 1940, and began on a large and sustained scale in September. 2.25 million cases of homelessness for a day or more had been recorded by the end of June 1941, some more than once, with 1.4 million in the London region. Such suffering gave momentum to the calls for post-war reconstruction. What Calder terms the 'myth of the Blitz',[73] of collective suffering and collective heroism, served to underpin calls for a *collective* and *planned* reconstruction.

Visions of egalitarian peace fed on a sense that initially the establishment was prepared to countenance an unequal degree of

suffering according to class. On early tours of East End bomb damaged sites, royalty were booed; after Buckingham Palace was winged
the Queen was reported as saying: 'I'm glad we've been bombed.
It makes me feel I can look the East End in the face.'[74] While the
Dorchester converted its Turkish bath into a shelter with reserved
spaces, including one for Foreign Secretary Lord Halifax, buildings
such as the Tilbury shelter in East London held 10,000 a night in
its basement, with two lavatories for women and none for men.[75]
Nigel Balchin's 1942 novel *Darkness Falls from the Air* dramatized
the uneven predicament of the East and West Ends: 'The grill room
at the Piccadilly is two floors underground, and you had to strain
your ears to hear anything of the guns. When the band was playing
you wouldn't have known anything was happening.'[76] The use of
tube stations as deep shelters was initially forbidden as it was seen to
be detrimental to morale and so, as Titmuss recalled, 'the ordinary
people of London took it in their own hands to open the tubes as
a refuge for the night'.[77] Shelterers' organizations emerged, often
communist-influenced, to campaign for improvement via lobbying
or mass trespass. If evacuation showed the anti-citizen abroad again
in the country, bombing brought grouse moor tactics to the city.

The Ministry of Information's 1942 official history of Civil
Defence, *Front Line*, presented common, rather than cross-class,
suffering: 'The Blitz was aimed at the people.'[78] *Front Line* demonstrates Calder's analysis of the 'myth of the Blitz' moving in a
leftward trajectory, with heroism located in the people and any
mistakes put down to a bungling establishment.[79] Balchin's novel,
too, captures such an outlook, with his progressive civil-servant
hero, frustrated by establishment attitudes and musing on a possible clean slate: 'As I got near the office I suddenly wondered what
would happen if they'd written the place off in the night. I thought
it might be quite a good thing if they had. But they'd need to do it
in daylight, so as to get most of the staff, if it was going to be any
good.'[80] *Front Line* shows once-subversive sentiments becoming
official. J. B. Priestley had earlier been taken off the air in part for

his implicit criticism of the establishment in his radio 'Postscripts' which hailed 'citizen warriors' fighting a 'citizen's war'.[81] *Front Line*, though, could officially contrast the Battle of Britain's 'triumph of the few' with the Blitz as 'The Achievement of the Many': 'The first was the more brilliant; but the roots of the second struck very deep. Before the war it was the British people, the many, who discerned Hitler for what he is.'[82] The implication is that in earlier days an elite few had held another view of Hitler; the state realigns itself with the people away from an older establishment. Reconstruction debates would presume such an alliance.

For an official patriotic text, *Front Line* remarkably contains no pictures of royalty. Indeed, aside from one Churchill quote, there are no names in the publication. Here is a nation constituted through

48 Ministry of Information, *Front Line 1940–1941* (London, 1942), front cover.

shared and anonymous suffering and heroism: 'Those whose deeds and stories are recounted in these pages speak now, as then they acted, not for themselves but for Britain.'[83] If there is a hero it is the auxiliary fireman, *voluntarily* battling with fire, and only pausing for a cup of tea at 'All Clear'.[84] *Front Line's* cover (illus. 48) shows such a figure looking up. John Taylor suggests that such imagery represents a wartime 'new line of sight' of vigilance, resilience and optimism, eyes looking not only for potential bombs and death but into a brighter future.[85] While explicit class commentary is absent in such accounts, the non-appearance of the well-off clears a space for reconstruction in the anonymous name of the common people. In *Front Line* photography emerges as the apposite language to capture common experience. As Taylor notes, such dramatically peopled imagery contrasts markedly with the theatrical art of empty ruins found in architectural portfolios such as James Pope-Hennessy's *History Under Fire*, illustrated by Cecil Beaton.[86] *Front Line* mixes action snapshots and posed tableaux of the everyday, presenting photography as a medium able to catch, in a direct and democratic fashion, the process of wartime life. The bulk of photographs are uncredited. There is a contrast with the sense of intrusion found in accounts of artists commissioned by the War Artists' Advisory Commission to record war damage. In one such account John Piper arrived at Coventry Cathedral to find that 'the ugly mood of the crowd watching bodies being dug from the rubble persuaded him to seek a discreet vantage point in a nearby office building'.[87] In contrast to the photograph, associated in the public mind with quick and functional journalistic record, the time taken to sketch or paint suggests an aesthetic intrusion into common life. Henry Moore described sketching tube shelterers: 'I had to behave as though I wasn't trying to look; they were undressing, after all ... I would have been chased out if I'd been caught sketching.'[88] In only one image in *Front Line* does an individual catch the camera's eye; the camera is by implication within rather than detached from the scene that it records, a technology on active service.

The Blitz not only underpinned reconstruction in its stress on collective experience, but also in focusing debate on the city. Firstly, and we shall return to this in terms of the detail of rebuilding plans in a later chapter, it literally cleared a space for rebuilding. Secondly, it allowed the mobilization of city life as communal rather than degenerate. If evacuation suggested that something had to be done, the presentation of community under bombs implied that cities had earned a right to reconstruction. The city as an organic whole rises out of the bombsites, with attack described in *Front Line* in anatomical terms: 'The enemy sought to destroy the bodily life of the capital: to cut the nerves, pierce the veins, sever the muscles.'[89] The 'arteries' of the city are sustained; men reconnect cut wires under the pavement, and everyday life continues to be coordinated, with a milkman shown delivering across a bomb site, a postman collecting from a box left standing in the mess.[90] The city becomes a body to be cherished, with London remoralized from an evil octopus into a civic whole, focused on St Paul's, which miraculously survived the flames in the raid of 29 December 1940, 'The Stroke at the Heart': 'I saw the Dome and Cross of St Paul's, silhouetted in sharpest black against the red flames and orange fumes, and it looked like an enduring symbol of reason and Christian ethics against the crimson glare of unreason and savagery.'[91] As the cathedral of reason St Paul's could easily translate into a symbol of future order, not least because a key reference point for reconstruction debates in London and elsewhere would be Wren's 1666 plan for London after the fire.

Beyond the civic 'heart' lay an apparently organic city, a *gemeinschaft* metropolis of suburban community. Civil Defence was presented as 'an affair of streets and neighbourhoods', with wardens caring for places through local knowledge, 'knowing his neighbourhood and its people as a good gardener knows his rose-beds'.[92] Titmuss noted problems of local 'stubbornness': 'Homeless people were reluctant to move from familiar places; they clung to their "villages" in London.'[93] This vision of a locally loyal people is bound up with the last great mobilization of the Cockney as a national hero.

The Ministry stated, despite several reports to the contrary, that: 'Nothing has affected the unconquerable optimism of the Cockney nor has anything restricted his ready if graveyard humour.'[94] There is a tension here though in that, as Stedman Jones has argued, it was an 'archaic and nostalgic notion of the "cockney" spirit which was enlisted',[95] one fixed in a particular urban habitat, to be praised so long as it didn't wander elsewhere, either up West or out into the country. And if this urban habitat was to be transformed through reconstruction as well as bombing, Cockneys might even find themselves out of place at home in a modern peace. In 1946 Bill Brandt would photograph East London pubs for the progressive weekly magazine *Picture Post*. If war had mobilized the Cockney, the fitting title for this series was 'The Doomed East End'.[96]

Beyond London the bombing was often of equal or greater intensity but shorter duration, with some morbid inter-urban rivalry arising concerning degrees of suffering and recognition. In January 1943 the *Bristol Labour Weekly* complained that *Front Line* had neglected the city: 'I think I am right in saying we began with raids in June 1940 – weeks before London.'[97] *Front Line*'s general message was of uneven but shared national suffering; a Welsh boy singing 'God Save the King' for six hours under rubble to guide his rescuers, Red Clydeside showing itself to be part of a United Kingdom despite earlier doubts ('Was the Clyde whole-hearted about the war?'[98]) There was even 'The Countryman's Blitz': surplus bombs tipped, senseless isolated attacks, mistaken massive raids on Somerset fields.[99] There is another kind of city-country Blitz movement, however, which gets little space in the official story. In *Front Line* 'trekking' out of the city for the night appears only as an exceptional response in isolated cases.[100] Other accounts, though, present trekking as far more common. Tom Harrisson considered it 'a sound response to environmental collapse, an ecological adaptation to disturbances on an unprecedented scale', and Titmuss found it to be 'the chief feature which distinguished social behaviour in the provincial from that in the London raids'.[101] Rural authorities surrounding provincial cities struggled to provide shelter, and many trekkers slept rough in buildings, ditches and hedges; emergency *Wandervogel*. In Plymouth 30,000 people or more left each night for two weeks after the first raid in April 1941; a Society of Friends report recorded a new country life: 'The YMCA canteen stopped on the Yelverton Moors on the night of the 26th April and called out for customers. These appeared in no time from among the ditches and heather of the open moor.'[102]

Plans in Wartime

> Never before . . . in the history of mankind has been presented
> such a magnificent opportunity – it may never come again – to
> provide pleasant homes for all in beautiful towns and villages and
> in noble cities, set against a thriving and unspoiled countryside.
> GILBERT MCALLISTER, *Homes, Towns and Countryside*[103]

Themes of 'never before' and 'never again' emerge well before 1945 – never again a return to the poverty and perceived chaos of the 1930s, never again such an opportunity to make a new country. Well before the military outcome is clear, plans are drafted for a reconstructed world to come. No sooner are buildings flattened than visions of replacements emerge. We here explore some of the broad cultural meanings of planning in wartime in relation to the optimistic visions of the future and the tensions generated by attempts to combine planning and Englishness.

Future Gazing

Late in 1941 readers of the *Geographical Magazine* encountered advertisements for soap (illus. 49 and 50). Pears targeted the geographical public less for their personal hygiene than for their love of planning. Soap is sold on a clean new world of future roads

THE TOWN OF THE FUTURE

■ There can be no doubt that our future towns will be as different from those we knew before the war as a radiogram is different from our first crystal set. And just as our admiration for the elegance and the greater efficiency of the modern does not in any way impair our affection for the old-fashioned, so we need have no regrets when we come to live in the town of the future.

Towns and cities damaged by the war are already considering their rebuilding plans. Residential districts, we are told, will be designed on the garden city principle of villas or semi-detached houses each with its own garden; or ten-storey blocks of flats surrounded by communal lawns, flower walks and rose arbours. It is gratifying to note that experts are planning for a 'green and pleasant land' with plenty

of space, light and fresh air. In the past, towns and cities have straggled and sprawled, capturing parts of the countryside with the same inevitable disappointment as the caging of a wild bird. The town of the future will be erect and compact, with the trees, the grass and the flowers of the countryside brought to its front doors. Schools and playgrounds for the children will be included as an integral part of the communal plan. These will be so positioned that children will not have to cross main roads on their way to school. The Shopping Centre, in view of its supreme importance to housewives, will receive

very special attention. Architects, remembering the British climate, will develop the arcade principle for greater all-the-year-round convenience, specially appreciated on wet shopping days.

Ancient buildings will be restored and records and relics of a glorious past preserved. The town of the future will retain its cherished character, its unique individuality and its historical associations, yet it will sparkle and shine in its new pride.

New buildings, new services, new homes, rising up from the ruins of the old, will make for happier family life in Britain after the war. The better environment will invite us to make the most of our longer leisure and will encourage us to seek new interests within the pleasant, comfortable and healthy precincts of our new homes.

Pears

RENOWNED AS THE LEADING TOILET SOAP SINCE 1789

49 Pears Soap advertisement: 'The Town of the Future', *Geographical Magazine* (October 1941), back cover.

and towns. Just as Pears, 'the leading toilet soap since 1789', was modern with a heritage, so radically different towns might be set harmoniously in a green and pleasant land, with family-centred communities, fine shopping centres for the housewife and trunk

ROADS OF THE FUTURE

"They shall beat their swords into ploughshares and their spears into pruning hooks." And out of the factories where bombers and fighters are now made will stream motor cars by the hundred thousand

As our present system of roads is admitted to be inadequate, even for current requirements, it is certain that one of the very first items on the agenda for reconstruction will be the building of new and better roads to accommodate the increased traffic that must be expected in the future

A network of great highways will be constructed to link up our important cities and towns with the capital. The purpose of these trunk roads will be to speed a nation on wheels directly to its objective in the minimum of time with the maximum of safety but with due regard to the separate needs of different types of road user. It is not inconceivable that the petrol-driven car will be superseded by one controlled by radio. Aerials along the roadsides would provide the motive power with varying wavelengths for different destinations. Thus, if the first part of a journey is along radio road A.1, the car is tuned to the wavelength of that road, and it the ultimate destination is along the A.3 road, then the car is returned to the new wavelength when branching off from A.1.

Our post-war main roads will connect us with distant friends and relations; they will open up new ways of enjoying our leisure; they will lead us to better health through recreation and to a keener appreciation of our fellow countrymen through more frequent and more widespread travel.

The roads of the future will give much happiness and a wider outlook to every man, woman and child, while upon these broad highways the whole life of the nation will expand. The roads of the future lead straight into the dawn of a New Age.

Pears

RENOWNED AS THE LEADING TOILET SOAP SINCE 1789

50 Pears Soap advertisement: 'Roads of the Future', *Geographical Magazine* (November 1941), back cover.

roads connecting new settlements. Radio-controlled cars on the 'Roads of the Future' would tune into their destinations, powered by waves from roadside aerials: 'The roads of the future will give much happiness and a wider outlook to every man, woman and child, while upon these broad highways the whole life of the nation will expand. The roads of the future lead straight into the dawn of a New Age.'

Reconstruction played across what Addison terms a 'massive new middle ground', a 'progressive Centre'[104] of politics and culture which encompassed government itself, where home ministries tended to be dominated by Labour members of the Coalition, radio discussion programmes such as the Brains Trust starring Joad and Julian Huxley, magazines such as *Picture Post*[105] and planning and architectural journals. While this is by no means a homogeneous field, it is unified by assumptions of cultural and political authority, with change expected to be dramatic and yet managed and often culturally conservative. Crucially the state is pictured as potentially rising, via planning, above sectional politics, just as the reconstructed city would rise from the mess of war.

From 1939 the Town and Country Planning Association sought a popular 'Planning Front',[106] issuing twelve 'Rebuilding Britain' booklets by Williams-Ellis, Mumford and others, providing annual reviews on 'Planning and Reconstruction', lobbying politicians, running conferences and staging exhibitions. Had the Luftwaffe targeted the TCPA's March 1941 conference at Lady Margaret Hall in Oxford (attended by 181 delegates), they might have taken out the following stars of planning and architecture, all of whom feature in this book: Abercrombie, Barlow, Dower, Eden, Fitter, Holford, Jellicoe, McAllister, Mauger, Morris, Osborn, Pepler, Scott, Silkin, Stamp, Stapledon, Taylor: 'That a gathering of such weight was possible at this grave time was notable . . . Every session was fully attended; and the informal discussions . . . went on throughout all the meals and far into every night.'[107] Architects, sociologists and geographers also came together to map out the future in the *Architects' Journal*'s series on *Physical Planning*,[108] while the RIBA's Reconstruction Committee projected a planned country in its *Rebuilding Britain* exhibition, opened by William Beveridge at the National Gallery in February 1943: 'Now is the opportunity for making the New Britain that we all desire.'[109] Prewar planner-preservationism gathers pace and power in calls for 'A National Plan', a restructuring of 'inefficient urban agglomerations', and an end to the 'anarchy in our present surroundings': 'Peacehaven. It must be the saddest monument to the Great Peace that was ever built.'[110] Citizenship would also proceed from planning: 'We have not merely put a blight on our landscape, we have put a blight on ourselves.'[111]

On the RIBA catalogue cover uniformed soldiers hovered over London, looking east over a place to be remade (illus. 51). These men could be representative citizens from anywhere: city

51 *Rebuilding Britain*, issued by the Royal Institute of British Architects (London, 1943), front cover.

dwellers looking on home, Northerners looking at London, Scots over England, countrymen over the Smoke. If rebuilding Britain proceeds from authority in London, its principles are to apply everywhere. There are tensions of authority, though, in this montage technique. Wrenched out of one photo into another's mid-air, are these soldiers truly embedded and involved in planning? On the one hand the RIBA declared that 'The people of Britain will get the reconstruction they deserve',[112] on the other that: 'it may be asked, why architects are qualified to assume such wide responsibilities in the service of the community. The answer is that architects are the only men trained to plan and design all kinds of buildings.'[113] Throughout reconstruction literature people are called to place their trust in an expert authority. Elsewhere in *Rebuilding Britain* a disembodied, cut-out, cloth-capped man with pipe is presented as a reminder to new authority: 'The people on this page are not experts in building and planning, but they know something about their own needs. It is up to them, and to all of us, to express our needs; and it is up to the experts to make sure that they don't forget for whom they are planning.'[114] An alliance of experts and people is forged only through a reminder of separation. In a strange mixture of Lord Kitchener's First World War recruiting finger and the 'It Could be You' gesture of today's National Lottery, *Rebuilding Britain* features a hovering hand pointing to a crowd where only the tops of heads and hats are visible: 'It's up to you.'[115]

'These Dashed Vista-Mongers': Blimping Reconstruction

The 'Never Again' refrain was not unanimous. Not everyone thought that the future should be in the hands of experts and indeed some defiantly unreconstructed voices saw reconstruction as threatening rather than building on English tradition.

John Betjeman anticipates the language of later critiques of modern planning in his 1943 *English Cities and Small Towns*, concluding that while bombing might have 'built up an affection for the old towns of England among those many who formerly thought little about them', there remained a danger of peacetime planning:

> Much rubbish about 'opening up vistas,' 'rural slums,' 'post war reconstruction,' has been appearing lately in the press ... These old towns of England are numerous enough to survive a decade of barbarian bombing. But their texture is so delicate that a single year of over enthusiastic 'post war reconstruction' may destroy the lot.[116]

The later refrain of Prince Charles and Betjeman himself that planners rather than the Luftwaffe had been the chief force of destruction in English towns is aired in advance. 'Reconstruction' is put into quotation marks to suggest both common currency and unEnglish jargon, cutting against historic texture. Planners are assumed to be abstract. A similar sense of Englishness as resident in something beyond planning came in the wartime governmental 'Recording Britain' scheme whereby artists recorded largely English representative scenes and special sites, producing a deeply trad- itional watercolour memorial to an Englishness off the beaten track; eccentric, obscure, out of time.[117] This was hardly a record of the roots of a future planned England; country Englishness was to be valued as a thing of the past.

The most public symbol of anti-reconstruction was David Low's *Evening Standard* cartoon character Colonel Blimp, who served to register that non-enthusiasts for reconstruction were reactionary and out-of-date. For Labour's Stafford Cripps the efficient coordination of the war effort meant that 'from now on we have said good-bye to "Blimpery"'.[118] In January 1943 Low produced a spoof article by Blimp with a domestic hit-list which included socialist bishops, Beveridge and planners: 'you've got these dashed vista-mongers wanting to tell people what to do with their own land.'[119] Low allied Blimp with mythic anti-planning forces: the 'Anti-Beveridge League', the 'Anti-Plan Society', the 'Perish-Priestley Party'.[120] A more complex relation of reconstruction, Englishness and patriotism came in Powell and Pressburger's film *The Life and Death of Colonel Blimp*, made in 1942 and released in June 1943.[121] Churchill and the MOI sought to ban it; Low's cartoon comment on 'The Blimp Crisis' showed a government private viewing with rows of civil service Blimps aghast at seeing their double on the screen.[122] The film, however, is far from being simply 'anti-Blimp'. Through the often sympathetic character of General 'Sugar' Candy, Powell and Pressburger question where patriotism resides in the battle between new and old authority. The film can be seen as a complex allegory of reconstruction, just as their 1944 film *A Canterbury Tale* could be regarded as an allegory of organicism, with a similarly ambivalent conclusion as to the form to be assumed by patriotism.[123]

We first see Candy laid out on a slab, corpse-like, in the Turkish Bath of the Royal Bathers Club. He wakes as a regular army unit storms the Club, jumping the gun in a mock battle against Candy's Home Guard units, ignoring the order that 'war starts at midnight'. Candy asks on whose authority they are there. The army lieutenant replies: 'On the authority of these guns and these men.' Blimp explodes: 'Authority! Authority! How dare you, sir.' Candy's is the static, composed and establishment authority of the Club, whose interior doesn't have to change for the subsequent 40-year flashback. By contrast the new army has sped into London along the West Road, dispatch riders zooming in formation to a swinging jazz score. The flashback shows Candy as having been out of kilter for 30 years, and misreading the current war. His BBC Postscript on 'Dunkirk – Before and After' is pulled when he plans to tell the nation that he would rather lose than play unfairly; he is replaced by J. B. Priestley. Organizing the Home Guard he is undermined by the new army's pre-emptive modern strike. In a sequence which shows the cultural detail in Powell and Pressburger's work Candy features on the cover of *Picture Post* as Home Guard organizer, and the face of Blimp covers a W. H. Smith news-stand. The magazine shows 'A Lecture on Soldiering: Candy, V. C. at a Provincial Factory'.

The article has the same page layout as Tom Wintringham's 1940 *Picture Post* article 'The Home Guard Can Fight', showing training at the magazine's proprietor Edward Hulton's Osterley Park, with Candy's head substituted for Wintringham's in the pictures of Guard trainers.[124] There, however, the similarity ends. The socialist Wintringham, who is credited with popularizing the phrase 'The People's War', conceived of the Guard as a democratic anti-Blimp force: 'As I watched and listened I realised that I was taking part in something so new and strange as to be almost revolutionary – the growth of an "army of the people" in Britain – and, at the same time, something that is older than Britain, almost as old as England – a gathering of the "men of the counties able to bear arms".'[125]

Sympathy grows for Candy/Blimp in his decline. Powell and Pressburger said of Blimp's character: 'We think these are splendid virtues: so splendid that, in order to preserve them, it is worth shelving them until we have won the war',[126] and they leave the viewer with a decent old man trying his best and displaying the human qualities lacking in the new war machine. The implication is that in a war fought for a new world in a new way, a certain valued mode of Englishness may be lost. Blimp, with his Edwardian manners and walrus moustache, is beached. At the end of the film Candy walks to the bombsite that was his old home. A water tank occupies the site, and the words of his late wife when they moved in in 1919, that they would remain there until the floods come, fill his head: 'Now here is the lake, and I still haven't changed.' Obstinacy or resolution? Blimp unable to adjust to a new world, or Blimp resilient against bombs and setbacks? An Englishness which is doomed, or one which should last? Powell and Pressburger's Blimp is a powerfully complex figure, both for those recognizing themselves in him, and for those who thought he was their simple opposite.

Is Planning English?

The Blimping of reconstruction turns on the question of whether planning is English. If the entire project of planner-preservationism rested on the assumption that it could be, even within the planning movement there were doubts and a sense of caution over the wrong associations in wartime. These were expressed in repeated distinctions made between English and German versions of order. Thus the *Architects' Journal* contrasted 'One Approach to Planning', an image of Hitler and a Nazi rally, with 'Another Approach to Planning', a works Joint Production Committee meeting.[127] We can explore the Englishness or otherwise of planned order through a popular wartime fantasy plotline, that of Nazis in an English village.

In 1942 H. V. Morton produced *I, James Blunt*, a fictional diary of a retired ironmonger, active in 'Labour Affairs' before the War, and now living in a Surrey village under Nazi occupation. Morton wrote the story as a warning against complacency, imagining that with the USA refusing to come into the War in Europe, in 1944 England would fall for German peace propaganda. England is occupied and Englishness overrun. Blunt's wife is killed: 'but England is no longer England, and you are happier where you are, my dear, under the lilac tree I planted in Foxton churchyard.'[128] The Royal Oak pub is renamed the Oak, all pictures of English history are removed, Waterloo Bridge becomes Goebbels Bridge and British legends are banned: 'the scientific extermination of British nationality would be the first act of a victorious Germany.'[129] St Paul's makes way for the Nazi Party offices. Children are taught as Germans, adults are deported to the colonies and Britain, in a bizarre echo of organicist ideals, is to become an agricultural state feeding the continent. Nazi order overruns a gentle Englishness.

In such accounts Englishness begins to appear in conflict with modern order *per se*, as in *Picture Post*'s July 1940 contrast between a peaceful German Sunday afternoon, with troops parading down a street, and 'Sunday Afternoon in England', a village street with sheep and a church behind.[130] A similar contrast structured Alberto Cavalcanti's 1942 film *Went the Day Well?*, a story of disguised Nazi paratroopers occupying an English village.[131] The idea of Nazis and the English village becomes a powerful narrative through which to evoke the values at stake in the conflict. Inadvertently though it begs the question, if planned order is an enemy, should peace bring planned and orderly reconstruction? Distinctions are, of course, made between different forms of order achieved through different structures of authority, but such differences are not always so neatly specified, and a tension persists which, as we shall see, would haunt reconstruction debates after the War. If planner-preservationists continued to hold pastoral Englishness and planned order together, others reflected on contradictions. The most complex exploration of village Englishness and authoritarian order, which deserves more detailed discussion here, comes in Rex Warner's 1941 novel *The Aerodrome*. In Warner's story the hero-narrator Roy moves between the village in the valley and the aerodrome on the hill, between earth and 'air values', rural and urban minds, community and planning, squirearchy and totalitarianism, English rural order and fascism, English rural muddle and fascism.[132] A complex inter-familial plot links Roy to the Air Vice-Marshal. *The Aerodrome* has been read as an appeal for the decent contingencies of the village against the aerodrome's oppressive order,[133] but the story is more complex, with drome and village dialectically related. As Warner puts it: 'If there had been guilt in the village, there had been guilt also at the aerodrome, for the two worlds were not exclusive, and by denying one or the other the security that was gained was an illusion.'[134]

Warner even refuses easy visual oppositions of drome and village. The aerodrome blends in, its irregular hangars appearing 'merely as rather curious modifications of the natural contours of our hills', its main depot 'constructed so as to appear indistinguishable from a country church'. Similarly the values of airbase and village are complicit in their harsh structures of authority. The rape of village girls by airmen is not a source of controversy in the village:

'these occurrences were common enough among ourselves'.[135] The distinction then is less between the communitarian and authoritarian than between old and new power, with the village order of squire and rector presented as in decay: 'the very presence of the Aerodrome on the hill, the very sound and sight of the machines crossing and recrossing our valley, seemed somehow to have dissipated the cohesion of our village and to have set up a standing threat to our regime'.[136] The new authority aims in effect to plough up the rural mind: 'We in the Air Force look upon things very differently from those who have been used to dictate your ideas to you. Muddle, inefficiency, any kind of slackness are things which we simply do not tolerate.'[137] If this is fascism it is a fascism of logic rather than unreason, of scientific modernity in all its masculine vanity, a totalitarianism of cleanliness and 'new order'.[138] The Air Vice-Marshal speaks in the drome chapel: 'Reflect, please, that "parenthood", "ownership", "locality" are the words of those who stick in the mud of the past to form the fresh deposit of the future. And so is "marriage". Those words are without wings. I do not care to hear an airman use them.'[139] Roy is attracted and joins the drome, and when at the end of the story he moves back to the village, it is a different place. The Marshal and drome may have gone but so too have English village values: 'no corner of the country that had felt the force of his ideas could afterwards relapse wholly into its original content.'[140] English rural muddle is not enough. Bear Roy and the Marshal in mind when we return in the following chapter to planner-preservationists seeking both to preserve local heritage and survey the land from the air to plan it.

Warner writes from the Left, and his work brings out tensions within the Left's attempts in wartime to unite planning, restructuring and a communitarian cultural conservatism valuing the landscapes of everyday life.[141] If planning was the means to a better world, would it over-order ordinary English life and community? From early in wartime socialist commentators such as Priestley and Orwell sought to promote the planned reconstruction of a 'new world order'[142] in the service of a common Englishness defined by *unplannable* virtues of community, improvisation, the everyday, the amateur.[143] Could the two cohabit? Contradictions of order and everyday life run through Orwell's 1941 *The Lion and the Unicorn: Socialism and the English Genius*, and his 1947 *Britain in Pictures* volume on *The English People*,[144] which sought to define a socialist Englishness of new authority and old community. Orwell located cultural value in everyday working-class life rather than national abstractions and monuments: 'It is a culture as individual as that of Spain. It is somehow bound up with solid breakfasts and gloomy Sundays, smoky towns and winding roads, green fields and red-pillar boxes.'[145] Englishness is 'somehow' located in that which cannot be pinned down and ordered: 'All the culture that is most truly native centres round things which even when they are communal are not official.' Orwell picks out common vernacular spaces, 'the pub, the football match, the back garden, the fireside'.[146] Are these the spaces of planned reconstruction? Will the future 'task of bringing the real England to the surface'[147] kill this valued vernacular muddle?

Such contradictions are resolved through a sense of educated yet conformist everyday life. Orwell suggests a conservative transformation, with an England under common ownership remaining a family, if no longer, in his phrase for the current state of the nation, 'a family with the wrong members in control'.[148] Educated citizenship is the key term here, just as in debates over country leisure. Orwell indeed picks on just this example when seeking to show how the current situation indicated a lack of discrimination in *The English People*: 'In the main they see no objection to "ribbon development" or to the filth and chaos of the industrial towns. They see nothing wrong in scattering the woods with paper bags and filling every pool and stream with tin cans and bicycle frames.'[149] The English needed to care for themselves differently: 'Nearly all of them love their country, but they must learn to love it intelligently.'[150] We will return to the potentially contradictory combination of intelligence and love in a later chapter.

Electing the Plan

The election of June 1945 confirmed the strength of a planned vision of the future. Many commentators had detected a shift to the Left in public opinion during the War, fuelled by the 'Never Again' theme, by the perceived success of the Soviet planned economy, and by the work of educational bodies such as the Army Bureau of Current Affairs.[151] All political parties felt obliged to speak the language of planning; the electoral issue was who could be trusted to plan. While Conservatives argued that Churchill should be given the chance to 'finish the job', the party was associated with a 'never again' past of poverty and appeasement. Churchill misjudged the national mood in his opening election broadcast with a Blimpish comparison between his recent coalition partners and the common enemy. Labour's election would, he argued, concentrate state power to such an extent that they would fall back on 'some form of Gestapo, no doubt very humanely directed in the first instance'. Attlee replied by suggesting that Churchill had 'wanted the electors to understand how great was the difference between Winston Churchill the great leader in war of a united nation, and Mr Churchill the party leader of the Conservatives'.[152] A series of Conservative attempts to link Labour's socialism to Hitler's National Socialism followed, with planning presented as a road to totalitarianism suppressing the British 'spirit of adventure'.[153]

By contrast Labour's manifesto *Let Us Face the Future* had no reservations about planning: 'We stand for order, for positive constructive progress as against the chaos of economic do-as-they-please anarchy.'[154] Labour recalled a lost peace after 1918, and sought to mobilize the nation over the 'sectional interest' of big business: 'We need the spirit of Dunkirk and the Blitz sustained over a period of years.' As for 'drastic policies of replanning': 'All parties say so – the Labour Party means it'. The argument that 'Labour will plan from the ground up'[155] suggested not only community over bureaucracy but a literal rebuilding. A Labour poster (illus. 52) envisaged a

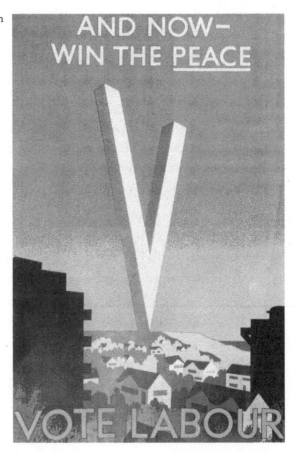

52 'And Now – Win The *Peace* – Vote Labour'. Labour Party election poster, 1945.

AND NOW–
WIN THE PEACE

VOTE LABOUR

new country: 'And Now – Win The *Peace*'. A monumental V stands on the hilltop, above a new landscape of houses, gardens and flats. Vote Labour for a new landscape.

The Labour victory, with an overall majority of 146, was unexpected. This was not, however, a radical move into the unknown. Labour's programme, feeding off the planning experience of wartime in which Labour politicians had been key players, presented a new world already familiar, even familial, with the right members in control. It does not diminish the achievements of the post-war administration to say that it came to power in part through very conservative values of security, competence and trust. Even the contrast of flamboyant Churchill and modest Attlee could turn to Labour's advantage here. An opponent said of Attlee that had he announced the Revolution in the Commons, 'it would have sounded like a change in a regional railway timetable'.[156] Electing Labour could suggest a retention rather than a dangerous introduction of planning. As Raphael Samuel puts it: 'A great deal of what passed for Labour thought at the time was in fact a kind of civil service idealism.'[157] Addison similarly comments: 'The demand for jobs, homes, and social security was the very reverse of revolutionary, but it was none the less radical, for these modest needs had never been satisfactorily met by the system of parliamentary capitalism. The Labour Party reaped the benefit.'[158] As the 'Win the Peace' poster shows, in such a conservatively radical scheme a modest semi could be an adequate signifier of a brave new world.

6

Geographies of the Reconstruction

In its broadest sense the setting of a nation's life and work is the geographical environment – the surface configuration, climate, soil, resources, peopling and present utilization of the land. Hence a planning authority must have regard to geography, and a geographer whose life-time study is 'the inter-relatedness of things' has a right to speak upon planning.
EVA TAYLOR, 'Britain After the War'[1]

The test of a real society is its ability to differentiate in detail while remaining fundamentally homogenous.
THOMAS SHARP, *Exeter Phœnix*[2]

This chapter addresses reconstruction as a geographical project. As we have seen, reconstruction was a live word from early in wartime, and here it refers to a sensibility rather than a chronological category. This sensibility is geographical in both its spatiality and its concern for symbolic landscapes. Reconstruction is taken to be an inherently spatial project, encompassing all aspects of the built and non-built environment: wild uplands, low farmland, villages, cities, streets, houses, chairs, kitchens, gardens. Reconstruction is presented as a national project immanent in national space. Additionally, in the bulk of reconstruction literature, the human and nonhuman environment is taken to be symbolic of the nation, with a characteristic slippage here between Englishness and Britishness, whether tapping the symbolism of traditional sites or establishing new symbols for a new country. The detail of reconstruction legislation has been covered by many writers[3] and will be touched on here where appropriate. Legislation is not, however, the structuring device of this chapter. The New Towns Act 1946, the Town and Country Planning Act 1947 and the National Parks and Access to the Countryside Act 1949 are here placed alongside planning tracts, architectural polemic, nature writings, topographic guides, radio broadcasts, educational manuals and children's books, in order to show how reconstruction operated through a broad discursive space whose various elements were mutually constitutive. Chapter Seven will explore the cultivation of appropriate modes of belonging in this new England – planned community, stable family and landscaped citizenship. Here, though, we focus on the visions of region, city, country and nature which made up the geographies of reconstruction.

This chapter gives more space than earlier ones to urban questions. Planner-preservationism was not simply a rural discourse, indeed it runs right across the geographies of reconstruction, and thinking in these terms allows us to avoid treating different dimensions of post-war landscape in isolation. There is certainly a tendency in some discussions of landscape and Englishness to isolate certain elements of wartime and post-war imagery so as to suggest a nostalgic rural vision of the nation; the landscapes of Englishness become swallowed up in a generalized vision of 'Deep England', and differences within ruralism (as well as connections between the rural and non-rural) may be missed.[4] The argument here is that reconstruction works through a town and country geography, mixing tradition and modernity. To take one example, in Stanley Badmin's 1943 Puffin Picture Book *Village and Town* (illus. 53 and 54), children are guided from 'The First Houses' through local vernacular, eighteenth-century design,

53–4 S. R. Badmin,
Village and Town
(Harmondsworth,
1943), front and
back covers.

nineteenth-century mess and the modern present to 'The Future'
of town and country planning and high-rise environmental harmony: 'We could do all that and much more if we made plans in
advance, instead of muddling along as we do now, allowing people
to build more or less where and what they fancy whether it is ugly
or not ... Look at your own home town. Surely something better
must be built next time?'[5]

Regions, Countries, Cities and Buildings

The Region: Planting the City

Town and country came together in the region, which emerges as a key scale for the articulation of a new authority in reconstruction. A key body in this process was the Barlow Commission on the Distribution of the Industrial Population, set up in 1937 with Abercrombie as a member, which reported in January 1940.[6] The Commission began from the premise that the economy was regionally imbalanced. Geographer Eva Taylor's 'coffin' metaphor for the interwar boom region stretching from London through the West Midlands[7] suggested that such uneven development could precipitate national death through constraining growth elsewhere. Regional thinking becomes the means to integrate rather than fragment the nation, socially and economically. A Central Planning Authority was proposed to balance the nation via regional policy, and balance city and country within each region. The concentration of development in the south-east and the Midlands during the War was also seen to present a ripe target, 'an urgent strategical problem'.[8]

Through such reports the planner-preservationist vision of an ordered England begins to gain governmental power, although Abercrombie considered that the Commission's Report did not go far enough towards state planning. Abercrombie put his name to a 'Dissentient Memorandum' and a minority report. The latter gives an early example of balanced reconstruction as a war aim:

> A strong and well-balanced industry, a healthy and well-housed population, good educational and recreational facilities, the absence of slums, of poverty and of unemployment are the necessary environment for individual freedom in a well-ordered community. The nation has not only to maintain freedom for her citizens, but to make that freedom something worth enjoying.[9]

The Barlow Report was followed in 1942 by the Uthwatt Report on land values and the Scott Report on rural land use; the two were summarized in a 'Penguin Special' under the title *Country and Town*.[10] Government reports and Puffin books echo one another; we return to the Scott Report below. While reconstruction plans commissioned by individual British city authorities often had a specific urban brief, those by central government and non-governmental groups (such as the West Midland Group on Post-War Reconstruction and Planning) took the region as the necessary scale for reconstruction. They were inspired by the regionalism of u.s. planners such as Lewis Mumford, the work of the Tennessee Valley Authority, and by the writings of Patrick Geddes, mentor to both Abercrombie and Mumford.[11] A consideration of Abercrombie's 1945 *Greater London Plan*, prepared for the Ministry of Town and Country Planning as a follow-up to the *1943 County of London Plan*, shows how regionalism, urbanism and preservationist ruralism could combine, yet could also generate tensions over what should happen to the country.[12]

Abercrombie planned for new transport links, a rebuilt city and ten New Towns each taking 60,000 excess Londoners. He wanted to plant development in the region: 'It is not satisfactory to build millions of houses, even good ones, if they are in the wrong place.'[13] Abercrombie looked to maps produced by planner Raymond Unwin in the 1930s, one showing the current situation of haphazard green spaces left between crazy building, the other presenting a future ideal, with a 'continuous green background of open country in which are embedded at suitable places compact spots of red, representing building'.[14] In the *Greater London Plan* the planner appears as a regional gardener, planting New Towns, trimming pre-war housing sites: 'these slabs of housing should be welded into real communities, their ragged edges rounded off, social and shopping centres properly planned, and local green belts provided.'[15] For Abercrombie this regionalism went hand-in-hand with his cpre ruralism, for good agricultural land was to be maintained, and pleasant and lively country living and recreation provided. Regional planning and rural Englishness are interwoven. Abercrombie assumes that Barlow will be implemented so that the *Greater London Plan* will be part of a general effort to prevent uncontrolled regional growth 'sucking in' an 'undue proportion'[16] of the national population. A regional discourse, tying London into its region and reducing its pull on the nation, restores the city to its proper place as a regional, national and imperial centre: 'at one end the community of the Capital of the Empire, at the other the communities of simple people whose work and existence happen to lie within this imperial metropolitan region'.[17]

Abercrombie plans to hold country and city in regional balance. The *Greater London Plan* also, however, shows the potential for dissonance within this harmony of scales. As New Towns are planned, and bits of the country in the south-east are again to be settled by evacuated Londoners, we find regional planning and rural Englishness lining up against one another, with the region viewed less as a scale for town–country balance than as part of an international planning language writing itself over old English fields and villages. Abercrombie's regional–rural balance begins to totter, most notably at Stevenage.

Beautiful Stevenage

> Abercrombie Proposes . . . The Ministry Discloses . . . Stevenage Opposes.
> HAROLD ORLANS, *Stevenage*[18]

Nikolaus Pevsner's 1955 Reith lectures on *The Englishness of English Art* ended up in the New Towns. Harlow's Town Centre and Stevenage's New Town Square with its clock tower, preserved silver birches and Fine Fare supermarket stood as the latest examples of 'Picturesque Principles Applied to Urban Conditions'.[19] Modernity and tradition are reconciled, Englishness and planning cohabit. For others, however, Stevenage Square signified modernity trampling on tradition, remote town planning stamping on the English country. In March 1946 the Minister of Town and Country Planning, Lewis Silkin, announced Stevenage as the first New Town. Seven others had been designated in the Greater London area by December 1949. The first London family moved into Stevenage on 2 February 1951. Much of the following is derived from Harold Orlans's 1952 *Stevenage: A Sociological Study of a New Town*,[20] a book whose treatment of ruralism and Englishness anticipates more recent critical analyses of national heritage: 'The industrial revolution made her an empire, but is still not fashionable in Britain. The foreign visitor has heard much about the lovely thatch-roofed village, the stage on which so large a portion of English ideology is enacted, but when he comes to England he will search hard before he finds one.'[21]

On 1 May Stevenage Council posted a five-foot New Town plan in a High Street shop window. On the same day a Stevenage Residents' Protection Association was formed, later growing to 1,200 members. Local opinion was split, with just over half opposing the New Town in a referendum. Opposition set ruralism against urbanism, locality against remote state planning. Rural concern was in part about loss of high-quality agricultural land, with even Stamp tempering his usual reconstruction enthusiasm in a letter to *The Times*: 'Not a single one of the proposed new towns ventures away from a lowland agricultural site ... I am not convinced that our descendants will appreciate having been provided with "new towns to starve in".'[22] More prominent in local debate was a cultural objection, driven by what Orlans termed 'The Rural Cult', a 'disease' reflecting 'the generic desire of the middle classes to keep their property from being depreciated, and their culture contaminated, by contact with the working classes'.[23] A leaflet was circulated on 'The Battle of Stevenage': 'this gracious old Market Town with roots in the fifteenth century ... crucified on the cross of progress'.[24] Anti-New Town campaigning focused around Aston, where the unelected Development Corporation, with Clough Williams-Ellis as its first Chairman, had established their HQ. Local squire V. A. Malcolmson argued in the *Hertfordshire Express* that even if Aston would be in Stevenage's Green Belt this would not 'inoculate' it against an 'urban mentality':

> There are those who seek happiness in life in the peace and beauty of rural surroundings and their recreation in country sports, natural history and rambles, and who derive inspiration from poetry, art and literature of an elevating and instructing character; on the other hand there are those, mainly newcomers . . . who seek their pleasures in cinemas, dance halls, night clubs and public houses, but little weight need be attached to their views.
>
> It is impossible to reconcile these two outlooks on life . . . I can see no good reason why the old residents of Stevenage should have a population of this class thrust upon them, completely re-moulding their mode of life and aspirations, and bringing in its wake the strain and unrest of a dominating industrial city.[25]

Evacuation was seen by the local press to offer a warning experience: 'The return of London evacuees is leaving Stevenage quiet at the moment, but it will not be quiet for long if Prof. Abercrombie gets his way.'[26] A language of evacuation is indeed built into the *Greater London Plan*, with the Outer Country concentric zone seen as 'the chief reception area for overcrowded London': '415,000 persons require decentralizing.'[27]

Abercrombie's CPRE track record counts for little here. In the anti-New Town campaign a rhetoric of the rural and the homely is turned against this preserver of the countryside and planner of new houses: 'The Stevenage we love will never be the same. We are not against New Towns but we don't want to be interfered with. It isn't English at all.'[28] The planner becomes a jargon figure, signifying 'the tyranny of control from Whitehall over our homes'.[29] The Hertfordshire Society sought to ensure that 'the materialistic aims of "planners" do not conflict with the claims of agriculture, or our rural heritage'.[30] Orlans indeed found planners to be disconnected from everyday life: 'One informant told of two Corporation planners who "when gazing into a shop full of china rabbits, were appalled by the standard of public taste, and wanted to evolve some scheme for improving it".'[31] Contemporary cartoons showed besuited planners in an office throwing darts at a map to designate New Town sites, or standing on a hill admiring a landscape: 'Magnificent View, Isn't It – On A Clear Day One Can See Eight Satellite Town Sites And Twenty Six Regional Board Headquarters.'[32] Survey and sweeping rhetoric here denote not good expertise but remote power. The New Towns Committee's declaration that 'Our responsibility is . . . to conduct an essay in civilization'[33] sounded arrogant to those who regarded such plans as writing over an already meaningful landscape. Silkin declared to a town meeting: 'Stevenage will in a short time become world-famous. (*Laughter*) People from all over the world will come to Stevenage to see how we here in this country are building for the new way of life.'[34] Silkin's visit on 6 May 1946 drew local predictions not only of urban but of racial alien-ness: 'I was informed yesterday, on what seemed good authority, that one of the largest synagogues in England is to be built in the New Town. Is this likely? Could any of your readers inform me?'[35] Hanging boards renamed the local station as 'SILKINGRAD',[36] while the town meeting turned Silkin's rhetoric of sacrifice for a better future back on him: 'I want to carry out in Stevenage a daring exercise in town planning. (*Jeers*) It is no good your jeering: it is going to be done. (*Applause and boos. Cries of "Dictator"*).'[37] The Minister's tyres were let down as he spoke. The Residents' Protection Association collected £40 to support their endangered species.

Rural Englishness and remote planning came together in a radio broadcast by E. M. Forster, who had earlier written of the area in *Howard's End*. Forster described the commandeering of a landscape unchanged for five generations: 'Commandeered for what? Hadn't the war ended?' A satellite town has been announced, and 'doomed' people now moved 'in a nightmare': 'Meteorite town would be the better name, for it has fallen on them out of a blue sky.' Forster agreed with 'the voice of planning and progress' in relation to the rehousing of the urban poor, but found himself in 'a collision of loyalties. I cannot free myself from the conviction that something irreplaceable has been destroyed, and that a little piece of England has died as surely as if a bomb had hit it.'[38] The words 'England' and 'little' spark a series of oppositions: progress and tradition, planning and locality, big government and small people, force and peace, alien out-of-nowhere satellite towns and rooted historic Englishness. Virtue occupies a little, peaceful England, and the efforts of an Abercrombie simultaneously to preserve rural England and plan a region lose cultural sense. At Stevenage a language of opposition to modern planning on behalf of landscape begins to emerge. It was to govern the terms of the debate in subsequent decades.

A Tidy Phoenix: Urban Restyling

On the city scale bombing opened up a space for reconstruction: for literal building, for symbolic renewal and for the exercise of a planning authority. The partial implementation of Wren's plan for London after the 1666 fire recurs as a nationwide reference point of missed opportunity. In Exeter Thomas Sharp warned against hasty rebuilding: 'It would be an exact repetition of what happened in the rebuilding of London after the Fire.'[39] Sharp termed his plan *Exeter Phœnix: a plan for rebuilding*. On the cover (illus. 55) the cathedral survives behind shells of housing. An orange phoenix rises bearing a message for the citizens: 'a plan for rebuilding by Thomas Sharp'. One is to assume that the bird hasn't stolen the plan for nesting material: 'Given the will, the citizens of Exeter have the power and the opportunity to create the city they desire. Exeter, like the fabled phoenix, can rise renewed from its own ashes.'[40] Any sense

55 Thomas Sharp, *Exeter Phœnix: a plan for rebuilding* (London, 1946), front of the dust-jacket; design by F.H.K. Henrion.

that the phoenix might be a dangerously fiery symbol of peace is defused by its transformation into an active, serving messenger of reconstruction. Mythic energy is channelled, a controlled warmth comes from the disorder of the fire, the process of rebuilding is to be tidily new, guided by a planner styled as a roving expert who can nevertheless connect to a particular place.[41] The image of the phoenix enables a resolution of the tensions between history and modern rebuilding, and the national and local range of the planner. A universal mythic creature *rising from its own particular ashes* connected local history and splendid newness, general urbanism and particular site. Sharp declared that: 'Cities have personalities and characters as men have: and the planner must try to catch the personality and character of the place he is planning before he can begin to formulate his plans.'[42] The consultant planner, like the phoenix, is to rise above the place and its people, able through detachment to escape sentiment. Sharp demonstrated his relation to place in a consideration of bombed Georgian buildings: 'their ruins now contain the quintessence of Exeter's problems of reconstruction. Should these places be rebuilt exactly as they were before the blitz? Should they be rebuilt in a "medieval" form? Or should they, in their turn, be entirely modern, and of our own day?'[43] For Sharp the phoenix did not imply restoration: 'The result would not be Exeter, or any live city. It would be a dead museum; and a fake museum at that.'[44] Abercrombie suggested a similar spatial resolution of past and present in his *Plan for Plymouth*: 'The break, the contrast between the two, should be consciously stressed. Our aim would be to make new Plymouth as modern as possible, but to keep old Plymouth as antique as is compatible with practical use and sanitariness.'[45] Functionality is to be put to one side only in the occasional preservation of ruins: as a memorial to lost lives,[46] and as a reminder of a pre-war world left behind. *Architectural Review* editor J. M. Richards surveyed *The Bombed Buildings of Britain*: 'To posterity they will as effectually represent the dissolution of our pre-war civilization as Fountains Abbey does the dissolution of the monasteries.'[47] Reconstruction is assumed to herald a civilizational shift.

In reconstruction the physical hand of the planner becomes emblematic, as an ethical instrument of steady and unshaking design, bold decision, erasure and redrawing. The cover of Ralph Tubbs's *1942 Living in Cities* (illus. 56)[48] shows the future in the planner's hands. History travels from a harmonious 'Long Ago' through nineteenth-century chaos and wartime bombing to a 'Tomorrow?' whose clean, set-squared lines pick up once more the cruciform order of the cathedral. If the planner's hand here designs the future, elsewhere it could rub out. In the 1943 film *When We Build Again* an architect played by Thomas Sharp works over a map of Birmingham with an eraser,[49] and a parallel gesture concludes an extraordinary series of drawings by 'Batt' (Oswald Barrett) in C. B.

56 Ralph Tubbs, *Living in Cities* (Harmondsworth, 1942), front cover.

Purdom's *How Should We Rebuild London?* (illus. 57).[50] The titles of the drawings recalled the religious rhetoric of the Beveridge Report. A soldier is shown returning to a world of rubble, land speculation, inertia, reminders of the failure of the Wren plan and promises of new 'Technics'. In a drawing labelled 'Purpose' the soldier, armed with copies of the Uthwatt Report and the *County of London Plan*, rolls his sleeves up over his scarred arms and faces a city map. In 'Vision' he wipes the suburbs clean from the plan, leaving a newly road-ringed city and clearing 'Exploitation', 'Chaos', 'Inertia' and 'Evil'. Such ethical hand movement pertains across the spectrum of planning, from the most radical visionaries to the more conservative figures such as Sir Charles Bressey, whose plans for London featured in the GPO Film Unit's 1940 *The City*.[51] One could not design a more conservative individual than Sir Charles: stilted and establishment in voice, moving slowly but surely across his office to engage in awkward dialogue with the off-screen Cockney narrator.

57 'Vision'. From C. B. Purdom, *How Should We Rebuild London?* (London, 1945); drawing by 'Batt' (Oswald Barrett).

This man hardly seems desperate for a new world. When, however, Sir Charles sits down with his plans, his hands become dynamic. Lines of new roads are swept across the map of congested streets. The chair swivels and Sir Charles's arms swing, pointing to diagrams and dreams of a new city. And then he gets up and staggers to the door, saying goodnight to the narrator while staring at a fixed point just off camera, an aged figure once more.

There are, of course, tensions in such sweeping planning authority, as shown in the Stevenage example and in the last chapter, and the proximity of planning and bombing could indeed imply some uneasy affiliations. While the planner sought to achieve a different and more discriminating overview to that of the bomber pilot, there are overlaps of aerial perspective. In Sharp's *Oxford Replanned* a page headed 'Mutability' outlined threats to the city from fire, war, traffic and the motor industry, none of which Sharp could regard as part of the 'real' Oxford. 'Mutability' was illustrated by a German aerial photograph from April 1941 outlining an offshoot of the Morris works in North Oxford as a target.[52] The constructive and destructive powers of planning and bombing might seem unnervingly adjacent to those who did not belong in Sharp's ideal Oxford.

Building Modern Englishness

Definitions of architectural modernity and tradition have been a source of contention in recent years, not least with regard to work of the immediate post-war period. To some this appears to be a period of renewed English tradition, to others a time of appropriately English modernism, to others again, it is the point of modernism's dilution.[53] For our purposes the key issue is the way in which the architecture of a modern Englishness in reconstruction sought to define itself as combining tradition and modernity, whether in city or country. Planner-preservationism realizes itself in influential architectural form. While some architectural practitioners did indeed define themselves as modernist as opposed to traditionalist or vice-versa, those considered here placed themselves in a middle ground built out of negotiations between tradition and modernity via fitness for purpose. The speculative mock-Tudor villa and the thatched petrol pump remained excluded from the well-mannered variety called for by Sharp: 'Harmony in variety: variety in harmony: form without formality: order without repression or regimentation – all this we can express in our towns of tomorrow. And in expressing it we shall be but renewing the English tradition.'[54]

Modernism, tradition and Englishness combined in the influential work of Pevsner and his colleagues at the *Architectural Review*. In admiring Stevenage New Town as an example of a modern picturesque, Pevsner sought to extract the picturesque, 'England's one great contribution to the art of landscape',[55] from associations of the anti-functional: 'There is an English national planning theory in existence which need only be recognized and developed. It is hidden in the writings of the improvers from Pope to Uvedale Price and Payne Knight.'[56] Such commentary gathers Englishness into modernism, modernism into Englishness. If, as Pevsner argued, architectural modernism had been 'prepared step by step in England' yet only 'made abroad',[57] in contemporary planning it was coming home, rooting itself, just as Pevsner himself was making a home in England.[58] Pevsner looked to the picturesque neither to ruralize the city nor to encourage garden cities – these 'failed in not being truly urban' – but to plan according to the particularities of place: 'In planning and architecture today "each case on its own merit" is called functionalism ... the informal then is at the same time the practical and the English.'[59] Wren's plan of 1666, John Wood's Bath, William Holford's plan for the City and St Paul's, modern high- and low-rise LCC housing at Roehampton, all showed how one might 'design functionally and Englishly'.[60] Sharp echoed Pevsner in presenting such planning as 'the rebirth of an art which is of significance to the whole community': 'By analogy with an equivalent art practised by the eighteenth-century Improver of land (we, after all, are Improvers of cities) it might be christened TOWNSCAPE.'[61]

Negotiations of the modern and traditional structure the architectural geographies of reconstruction from city centres to the smallest villages. The Ministry of Housing and Local Government's 1953 guide to *Design in Town and Village* brought together essays by Holford on 'Design in City Centres', Frederick Gibberd on 'The Design of Residential Areas', and Sharp on 'The English Village'.[62] Principles of function and order extend across country and city. In 1946, alongside his plans for reborn cities, Sharp, then President of the Town Planning Institute, produced *The Anatomy of the Village*. In it he put forward as being 'in character' a 'Modern Street' from Stratford-on-Avon, designed by modernists F.R.S.

and F.W.B. Yorke: small brick terraced houses, flat-roofed, simple, bare, unadorned by front gardens.[63] For Sharp 'urbanity' though not 'urbanness'[64] was the requirement in country building; mock rusticity would be out of place:

> Respect for tradition is an excellent thing, provided that the tradition respected is a genuine living tradition. A true tradition is subject to growth and development. It is not a pool which has welled-up at some particular moment of time, and has remained stagnant ever since. It is a flowing eddying widening stream that is continually refreshed by new tributaries, a stream whose direction is subject to change by new currents created by new conditions.
>
> The tradition that is invoked to restrict activity in the countryside to the kind of activity which was common in the past is a false tradition. Any suggestion that new village building should *imitate* that old kind of building . . . any attempt to achieve, by planning, the exact effects which have resulted solely from a lack of planning; these would not only illustrate a sense of tradition gone morbid, they would also be doomed to failure from the beginning.[65]

If Sharp could term the village 'The Place of Precedent', this entailed a particular relationship to history: 'Though we may learn from our old villages many *principles* of design . . . our modern villages should not attempt to imitate the old but should perform their modern functions in a frankly modern way.'[66]

Reviews of post-war building presented the countryside as moving into a new architectural era matching social and technological change. Paul Mauger's 1959 *Buildings in the Country* devoted its front cover (illus. 58) to a group of council houses by Tayler and Green at Hales in Norfolk, which in their 'contemporary vernacular expression' showed a modern architectural sense of place: 'The use of the local pantiles and of several different facing materials on the

58 Paul Mauger, *Buildings in the Country* (London, 1959), front of the dust-jacket.

walls of houses in a single terrace – a regional trait – has become characteristic of their work.'[67] For Pevsner such houses 'could almost be called post-modern'.[68] Mauger's back cover showed another new landscape, an aerial view of Calder Hall nuclear power station. Mauger worried over the persistence of temporary buildings here, but was confident about the potential of the new power architecture: 'We are beginning to see the exciting shapes of rationally designed buildings rising from the flat riverside or coastal country in which most of them occur.'[69] Mauger's book surveyed country buildings on the principle of 'fitness to their surroundings',[70] whether power stations, Sharp's designs for villages in Kielder Forest, petrol stations, factories, hotels, farm buildings, public housing, schools, health centres or crematoria. All of them were seen as new structures in tradition: 'the traditional in architecture always has been and still is, the particular contribution of the day which gave it birth.'[71]

A New Country[72]

In this section we consider specifically rural visions and plans, beginning with schemes for revitalizing rural settlement before moving on to questions of agriculture and landscape design.

Fables of Settlement

C. S. Orwin begins his 1945 book *Problems of the Countryside* with a Rip Van Winkle figure, sleeping from 1880 to 1940.[73] On waking in his village little has changed, save for the closure of the black-smith and wheelwright. Rip feels quite at home. Only the odd car and tractor puzzle him. The nearby market town, though, is different, with new traffic, housing, industry and amenities. The people there are younger. The town moves forward, the village is stuck. At the close of the book another Rip sleeps from 1940 through a generation, and wakes to a new landscape: 'there was now a spaciousness and order . . . which was new.' Larger fields, trimmer hedges, technical change, all 'seemed to promote a greater activity on the land'. On the farm mud is resurfaced by concrete, and old barns and sheds are gone: 'the homestead impressed him . . . with its air of order and efficiency.' Holdings have been amal-gamated, villages expanded: 'the isolated cottages in the fields . . . seemed to have disappeared.' Here is rationalization through an economic and social logic of a plan rather than a market. The church is still there, but the 'ugly Victorian vicarage-house' has been changed into a Community Centre, now 'the focus of all the social activity of the village', with tennis courts, a Village Hall for drama, a clinic and a library, a Youth Hostel, a canteen. The vicar is content with 'a smaller, labour-saving vicarage-house'. A new school admits 'light and air', replacing the gloomy Gothic schoolroom of Rip's childhood:

> Rip Van Winkle had an impression of a virile, well-knit society, as though there had been a blood transfusion into the old body corporate, which had caused it to expand and to develop, both physically and mentally. There was a vigour and activity about the place which it had never suggested as he remembered it, and he found it good.[74]

Newness similarly transfuses the old body in Keith Jeremiah's 1949 book *A Full Life in the Country*, a survey and plan 'infusing new life and new blood' into Sudbury and District in Suffolk.[75] A Foreword by Lewis Mumford told of 'the restoration of a garden'. The district had been preserved only by neglect, bypassed by nineteenth-century industry and economically depressed for years, only for 'the stones rejected by the nineteenth-century builders' to become 'the very corner-stones of the new order'.[76] The book's dust-jacket pictured the rural life of the future (illus. 59). Tree, leaf, blossom and fruit weave the country into a natural coherence, forming the spine of the book. Farming and crafts are shown revitalized. Nuclear families bloom: 'It is essential for the constant renewal and vitality of country life that there should be plenty of happily settled families.'[77] Public institutions – a new school, a modern health centre, a church in the background – focus life outside the home. Transport connects the region. The hunt still hunts, but English sport also flourishes on the modern playing field. Cricket and modernism cohabit within a frame of trunks and branches.

Such visions of the full settled life work alongside an emphasis on connectivity. In rural reconstruction commentary the pre-war philosophy of road-building persists, in part as a means to order settlement. Sir Charles Bressey moved beyond London's traffic both to embrace the 'unpretentious homeliness' of village lanes and decry the lack of ambition shown by mere individual village bypasses:

59 Keith Jeremiah, *A Full Life in the Country: The Sudbury & District Survey & Plan* (London, 1949), dust-jacket; design by R. Tilbrook.

> Our road map displays too many of these disconcerting bulges – a separate blister to each village. This gives rise to confusion and untidiness ... a comprehensive relief route of the 'bowstring' variety is more satisfactory, taking, in its ideal form, a straight course over open country, bye-passing a whole series of villages which are studded along the curve of the bow.[78]

Settlement is to make up a country network. In a diagrammatic vision suggesting not an imposed, rigid geometry but a modern pattern emerging from local roots, Jeremiah proposed 'village clusters' as a modern and rational means to maintain 'the sense of local patriotism – of being and belonging – which ... is of importance to human self-respect'.[79] Less rational settlement, such as the 'straggle' at Belchamp Otten near Sudbury, 'should be permitted to die out in the course of years'.[80] Mumford played off earlier ideal settlement geographies in praising Jeremiah's scheme:

When William Morris, in *News from Nowhere*, imagined an ideal future for England he wiped out London and peopled the country with Sudburys. In the nineties that doubtless seemed to most people an archaic, backward looking, ideal; but when one translates Morris's picture into the milieu of the electric grid, the motor bus and car, the wireless and television, it comes closer to the desirable and possible future than, say, Mr. Wells's early dreams of a population living in a sort of gigantic Crystal Palace.[81]

Academic settlement geography joined the quest for a rational and hierarchical order of places. Robert Dickinson extended his pre-war analyses of East Anglian settlement to identify 'community units' through a mapping of market areas and administrative hierarchies: 'the geographical anatomy of this society must be thoroughly analysed so as to discover and rectify its maladjustments.'[82] In such work we find the first British use of the work of the German geographer Walther Christaller, whose theoretical hexagonal patterns of service centres on an isotropic plain will be lodged in the memory of many former school geographers.[83] The irony is that Christaller and his ideas were then being employed in the Reichs Office for Spatial Planning, where plans were being formed to 'rationalize' settlement and population in occupied Eastern lands.[84] Again the English village connects, however unwittingly, to Nazism, with parallel network models set in different geometries of power.

New Land

Schemes for the land in reconstruction projected a wartime trajectory of agricultural change into a future of technology, prosperity and aesthetic order. This is a very different vision to that of the organicists. Indeed for Orwin the organicist vision was itself one of the *Problems of the Countryside*:

a school of thought, a good deal in evidence at the present time, which makes the welfare of the land its first object rather than the welfare of the human beings upon it ... it may be doubted whether the prophets of the new pantheism could maintain it if they spent day after day and week after week in mucking out cowsheds, spreading dung, milking night and morning, in return for £3. 10s. a week and an ill-equipped cottage.[85]

Technologically and/or politically progressive commentators proposed a different future. A socialist agricultural lobby argued for nationalization and technological transformation with the state as the best modern landlord, able to 'take long views'.[86] Daniel Hall, who joined Orwin in chiding the organicist 'Dream of Agricultural Retrogression', presented land nationalization as progressive evolutionary growth: 'The scheme here proposed is but an orderly progression along the line British farming has been following throughout all its history.'[87] Public ownership appears a far from revolutionary strategy, and could appeal beyond the political Left as a means to efficiency and stability.[88]

Other socialist visions foresaw a less corporate modernity, and indeed could echo the more co-operative decentralized variants of organicism. F. W. Bateson's collection *Towards a Socialist Agriculture* suggested that: 'Socialism, in the sense of publically planned, democratic co-operation rather than of national ownership, will alone provide the conditions under which such technical efficiency can be attained.'[89] For Bateson, the Statistical Officer for the Buckinghamshire War Ag, the War had given the country 'a large-scale experiment ... in State Socialism in the agricultural sphere'.[90] For inspiration regarding a 'Socialist national agricultural plan'[91] the country should look to co-operative programmes in Denmark, Ireland and Palestine: 'The Labour Party missed a great opportunity in neglecting agricultural co-operation. Socialism, suitably translated, might well have become the motive force – the religion, as it were – of a communal agriculture in this country comparable to that in the new Jewish colonies in Palestine.'[92] International inspiration here mixes with an English radical counter-history, where the heroes are not great improving landlords but the *Village Labourer* as documented by the Hammonds, with John Clare alongside as the poet of common dispossession. Inspired by the pooling of farming equipment in war, Bateson's poetic 'Lines on the Buckinghamshire Parish Machinery Pools' envisaged a different agrarian future:

> This lovely evening, my shouting children
> (All Brill was playing rounders in the garden),
> The zooming efficient bombers in the sky
> Conspired with meditations on the Pools
> To a daydream of a New England, like William Blake's,
>
> The manor houses gutted, hollyhocks
> Self-sown upon the guilty staircases,
> Where liberté, égalité were facts,
> And from apocalyptic chariot descending
> Fraternité bestrode the Aylesbury market.[93]

Socialist argument had little effect on the Labour Government's 1947 Agriculture Act, which cemented a partnership of government and farmers through guaranteed prices and security of tenure for tenant farmers. Malcolm Chase suggests that the Act reflected both an ideological shift and a pragmatism regarding the disruption of food production in a time of acute shortage (bread rationing was introduced from 1946 to 1948).[94] Labour legislation aligned with 'progressive' farming in the technocratic rather than political sense, technocracy defining itself as a discourse able to hold technology and politics apart. Ministry publications, the National Agricultural Advisory Service with its network of experimental farms, and such friendly media as *The Archers*, broadcast from January 1951 on the BBC Light Programme,[95] gave modern agricultural advice. D. H. Robinson's *The New Farming* presented technology as carrying farming forward: 'At no time in the history of agriculture has the agricultural mind been so receptive to scientific teaching, provided that it can be grafted on to the business of farming.'[96] Robinson pictured stock improved through scientific breeding and helicopters moving low over corn to spray 'selective weed-killer'.[97] Science gives a smooth connection to the land, with the farmer refigured as a skilled scientific operator.

In the middle of this field of debate, with helicopters on one side, and humus farming on the other, sat Dudley Stamp. The Committee on Land Utilization in Rural Areas was set up in October 1941 under Lord Justice Scott,[98] with Sharp as Secretary and Lady Denman of the Land Army and WI on the committee. Stamp was the dominating figure, *The Economist* commenting that the Scott Report might 'more properly be called' the 'Stamp Report'.[99] Stamp championed the report as 'A New Charter for the Countryside'[100] and advocated 'a *prosperous* and *progressive* agriculture' as the cornerstone of a 'national estate' under a Central Planning Authority.[101] War had shown the way: 'From an atmosphere of neglect the countryside has assumed an air of busy thriving prosperity; it has put aside the bedraggled condition which in many parts cloaked its beauty and the landscape has largely resumed its former well-kept appearance.'[102] The anti-picturesque line is stressed – 'we do not want a countryside which behind a smiling face hides much human poverty and misery'[103] – but also the role of agriculture in preserving beauty. The country would not be completely transformed:

the future changes will be of the nature of simplification of farm boundaries, field shapes and sizes, of gradual reorganization according to the needs of increasing mechanization or of improved methods of husbandry, or in response to changing demands, rather than a complete change to entirely new types of farming such as some have envisaged. In our opinion a radical alteration of the types of farming is not probable and no striking change in the pattern of the open countryside is to be expected.[104]

For critics on Left and Right this was not 'progressive agriculture' but compromise, and the Report was not a seriously modern document. Stamp was the target of criticism, and indeed was worried that the Report was being 'tarred too heavily with the preservationist brush': 'I am sufficiently young to look forward to a future which we shall enjoy. I believe that we shall have a countryside not visualized as yet ... We must get away from the purely preservationist idea. Nature, which includes human beings, is essentially dynamic and never static.'[105] For Orwin, though, there was little sense of agrarian or industrial dynamism in the Report.[106] The dissenting minority report by liberal economist S. R. Dennison took Stamp to task for an ignorance of market conditions, a false equation of the rural with the agricultural, and a treatment of farming and villages as 'museum pieces'.[107] The detail of Dennison's argument is beyond this study, but his vocal criticism allowed Stamp to reassert an alliance of planning and preservation by putting Dennison down as 'a Professor of Economics trained in the laissez-faire school'[108] who showed a misguided sense of value: 'there are human values impossible to assess in monetary and economic terms.'[109] Stamp promoted his geographer's viewpoint over economics; *The Economist* turned his argument round in their comment on the Stamp Report: 'those people who have long felt that the organization of the teaching and degrees of the University of London gave too much opportunity for good geographers to claim authority and a hearing as bad economists have gained a further reinforcement for their criticisms.'[110]

Two systems of valuing land and people clash and indeed the Scott/Stamp Report shows the potential contradictions, as well as the political power of planner-preservationism. This may derive from the Report being a committee document and therefore a compromise between contradictory viewpoints. However, my own suspicion is that *The Economist*'s 'Stamp Report' label is appropriate, and reflects a general slackness of aesthetic and political argument in Stamp's work. Crucially the Report manages to potentially disconnect use and beauty. While stressing that beauty and use were 'in no sense incompatible', it maintained that they were easily separable concepts, with new uses to be judged according to whether they 'offend by reason of bad taste or incongruity with the old'.[III] The aesthetic is upheld as crucial, yet is potentially disconnected from matters of social and economic function, opening up the Report to accusations of arbitrary elite aesthetic 'taste' and anti-functional aestheticism. In the Scott Report and elsewhere, Stamp, buoyed by a faith in planning authority, tends to sail over such complexity, only to end up in cultural and political knots: 'a full life for the individual as well as for the nation can only be achieved by affording opportunities for the legitimate development of differing tastes and differing ideals, always remembering that the development of the individual must not be at the expense of the community and that minorities have rights.'[II2] We will return to questions of authority and taste in the following chapter.

Absent Squires and New Landscapers

One site and person are conspicuously absent from the new land of reconstruction: the country house and the dominant squire. However much planners might celebrate an eighteenth-century spirit of design, the country house is not a site of future significance. Joad concluded in 1946 that: 'The country house set in its park belongs already to the past.'[II3] Celebrants and critics considered the country house doomed as a private realm. If Evelyn Waugh's *Brideshead Revisited*[II4] is the most celebrated evocation of private beauty ruined through public occupation, Kenneth Clark had similarly assumed of country houses in late 1939 that 'these will be largely abandoned after the war and will either fall into disrepair or be converted into lunatic sanatoria'.[II5] As Patrick Wright has argued, the National Trust Country Houses Scheme, run by James

Lees-Milne from 1936 and gathering momentum through and after the War, is conducted in an atmosphere of salvage.[116] Lees-Milne mourned a Trust acquisition in 1946:

> This evening the whole tragedy of England impressed itself upon me. This small, not very important seat in the heart of our secluded country, is now deprived of its last squire. A whole social system has broken down. What will replace it beyond government by the masses, uncultivated, rancorous, savage, philistine, the enemies of all things beautiful? How I detest democracy. More and more I believe in benevolent autocracy.[117]

Wright places such country house lament at the origin of later heritage assumptions:

> This polarity between traditional nation and modern society set the private values of the aristocratic house against the public egalitarian tendencies of the reforming present. It set the ancestral continuities of the aristocratic family off against the social-democratic ideas of citizenship. It set high national culture off against the procedural and bureaucratic realities of the modern State.[118]

When the architects of reconstruction did attend to the country house, as when Hugh Dalton as Labour Chancellor supported the Trust's work through the National Land Fund, it was as something to be preserved as a site of historic and aesthetic value only because its time had gone and would not come again. A powerless country house would not inhibit progress.

The spirit of eighteenth-century design could still be called upon in proposals to replace houses. Thomas Sharp envisaged 'Flats in a Country Park' (illus. 60), Corbusierian structures in a Brownian landscape:

60 'Flats in a Country Park'. From T. Sharp, *Town Planning* (Harmondsworth, 1940); sketch by Colin Allan.

What an inspiring ideal … this is! – that on the site of a mansion, from whose windows one solitary family and its dozen retainers once enjoyed the unique beauty of an English country park, there should rise the communal home of five hundred or a thousand people sharing that beauty as their own and at the same time maintaining an essential feature of the English countryside for others to look at and enjoy.[119]

Landscape design could be reworked by new professional landscapers associated with the Institute of Landscape Architects, founded in 1929; among its members were Sylvia Crowe, Brenda Colvin, Nan Fairbrother, Geoffrey Jellicoe. For Stamp, concluding his review of the historic relationship between *Man and the Land*, Jellicoe's 1946 scheme for the Hope Valley Cement Works in the Peak District showed 'The Twentieth-Century Landscape Architect At Work',[120] working not for an owner's private pleasure but for the public good. Crowe similarly imagined a future England as 'one great estate'[121] to be supervised by 'landscape counsellors':[122] 'The days when nature and the farmer between them could look after the English landscape are over.'[123] Landscape architects extend a planner-preservationist imagination into new techno-landscapes, Crowe's studies of roads and power condemning contemporary disorder but embracing the 'New Shapes' of curving bypasses, geodesic domes, radio masts, nuclear power stations: 'new shapes are evolving which relate not to the human scale, but to cosmic forces, the sea, the clouds and the mountains.'[124] Landscape design is defined as the practice of an ordering modernism, resolving any contradictions of the natural and new: 'How can we explore and enjoy the new experiences which science has opened up for us without losing touch with the organic world of which we remain a part? How can we explore, yet not destroy the wild flowers, travel faster than sound, yet still hear the birds' song?'[125] In his scheme for the Harwell nuclear research laboratory Jellicoe shaped excavated waste into hills echoing the barrows of the surrounding downland, and named them after Greek gods.[126] A rather different, and to contemporary eyes perhaps more recognizable, sense of past and present, nature and science, is found in John Betjeman and John Piper's 1949 *Architectural Guide* to Berkshire: 'On a moonlit night, the thatch and tile, stone and brick, elms and barns of old Harwell village compared with the blue electric glare and bright sinister workshops of the Atomic Research Establishment form an instructive contrast between past and present.'[127] The modern and traditional, the scientific and natural, divide; we will return to such realignments at the conclusion of this book.

New Nature

Versions of a Patriotic Nature: Tawny Pipit

A key element in the geography of reconstruction was a new form of nature conservation. Concern for nature *per se* was by no means new in this period, but in its institutional power and cultural form one can consider this conservation as bringing into being a 'new nature', set alongside the new country, the New Town, the new city. We will consider the forms of citizenship cultivated by this new naturalism in the following chapter, alongside a discussion of the landscaped citizenship to be generated through National Park policy. We can begin to approach this new nature through a humorous film.

In the 1944 comedy *Tawny Pipit*, directed by Bernard Miles, *Anthus campestris* nests in England for only the second time.[128] 'Mr and Mrs Pipit' choose a field on a scarp above Lipsbury Lea, and versions of patriotic nature are humorously played out. A brewery sign on the pub wall locates Lipsbury Lea as being within range of Garne's Brewery, Burford, Oxon. Eccentric ornithologists, a more eccentric old colonel, sensible ornithologists, locals with some rustic knowledge, a jolly vicar, malicious egg collectors, village urchins and bemused civil servants come together in an Ealing-style comedy.

The birds trigger a laudable but eccentric national and local patriotism. When an over-enthusiastic, bird-watching corporal declares that the eggs 'belong to England, sir', his solid and handsome captain comments, 'Talk about war aims.' Local pride is expressed by a village lady singing a tribute song to the vicar: 'It's a very great honour we're all agreed / That they came to Lipsbury Lea to breed.' After some soul-searching the villagers decide it is permissible for the word 'breed' to feature in a church song: 'I always think it's alright as long as it's just eggs.' The Colonel, a figure of fun far less complex than Powell and Pressburger's Blimp, addresses the village on the need to welcome feathered visitors who 'can't help being foreigners': 'now then, this love of animals and of nature has always been part and parcel of the British way of life and its going to go on being [applause].' Laudable eccentricity extends to the ancient members of the 'Association of British Ornithologists', roused from a meeting by the announcement that *Anthus campestris* is here again. Ornithology denotes academic, unworldly reflection; indeed care for birds also seems to help care for ornithologists, an equally pleasantly useless element of English life. The villains are the head of the County War Ag who wants to plough up the nesting field, and egg collectors in the shape of a couple disguised as a Methodist minister and his wife, and a 'fifth columnist' in the Association.

There are two unambiguously admirable figures in *Tawny Pipit*. The birds are discovered by Bancroft, a Battle of Britain pilot, DFC, DSO, recovering after being shot down, and his nurse Hazel. He is the experienced birdwatcher, although she makes the initial spot. Just before the end he proposes marriage, and the pipit/human breeding/coupling theme is confirmed as he flies over the field in his Spitfire, saluting the hatched birds. It is through Bancroft and Hazel that the audience spy the birds, the screen reshaped through their binoculars to home in on the nest. These younger watchers are clearly marked out from the Association's older ornithologists as energetic people of field study, seeking birds in the landscape rather than the library. Bancroft's ability to read maps and landscape is established in the opening sequences as he and Hazel look across the vale; we will return to the fostering of an observational citizen-scientist in the final chapter. *Tawny Pipit* effectively underwrites one mode of naturalism against another, modern observation overtaking eccentric otherworldliness.

This alignment of *Tawny Pipit* and a new naturalism is underlined by the presence as Technical Advisors to the film of Julian Huxley, James Fisher and Eric Hosking, leading figures in the new nature conservation and members of the Editorial Board of the influential Collins *New Naturalist* series, alongside John Gilmour and Dudley Stamp.[129] We conclude this chapter by considering this new naturalism's tactical combination of nature reserve and nature display, and its extension of ecological understanding to the city as well as the country.

Reserving Nature

Nature-in-reconstruction is valued through a complex form of eco-logical patriotism. While new naturalism took pride in national flora and fauna, it theoretically disqualified eco-jingoism:

> Natural historians have written ... of 'English' birds or 'English' plants as though England were divorced from the stream of the world's living things ... the habit of writing of Rutland flowers or Cornish birds, as if nuthatches had to show a passport for crossing the Tamar ... Those habits of the mind – habits of the parish – cannot very well survive evolutionary theory and ecological understanding.[130]

Science undercuts a nativist naturalism with another mode of plant and animal patriotism. While nature as species-object might not be essentially English, the stress on ecology implied a unique com-plexity and variety of habitat to be valued, a network of organisms set within a national legislative space of which the naturalist, as fellow organism, was a citizen. This is a very different deployment of ecology to that of organicist argument. Figures such as Huxley, Stamp, Arthur Tansley and Max Nicholson connected new natur-alism with progressive planning,[131] with nature established as a matter for scientific understanding, and science to be supported by but independent of the state.[132] While elsewhere in this book questions of landscape and Englishness play against a complex institutional landscape of power over land, new naturalism manages to carve out an institutional space mapping directly onto specific areas of land to be reserved. Formal lobbying for legislation began early in the War; the Society for the Promotion of Nature Reserves' June 1941 Conference on 'Nature Preservation in Post War Reconstruction' produced a Nature Reserves Investigation Committee, while a parallel committee of the British Ecological Society under Tansley proposed a 'National Wildlife Service'.

When in August 1945 the parliamentary Hobhouse Committee set up a Wild Life Conservation Special Committee, ecological new naturalists dominated.[133] The Committee proposed a 'Biological Service' and 73 National Nature Reserves; the Nature Conservancy was formed in 1949 with Tansley as Chairman. Nicholson was Director-General from 1952, and other new naturalists such as J. A. Steers, E. B. Ford and later Stamp served on the Board. While the Nature Conservancy commended the work of private owners and local Trusts, the concept of the nature reserve was recast as an ecological research arena of state responsibility, a living laboratory representative of national habitat.[134]

Reserves were to be one element in a modern, well-ordered landscape, alongside scientific farming. While the Wild Life Committee noted that 'the dissemination of powerful new insecticides, such as DDT, raises urgent issues of supervision if lasting harm is to be prevented'[135] in the immediate post-war years modern agriculture in general was not envisaged as a quantitative or qualitative threat to non-farmed nature. Tansley argued that: 'The great extension of agriculture during the War has not on the whole diminished the beauty of the countryside – rather the contrary is true ... It is scarcely probable that the extension of agriculture will go much further, for the limits of profitable agricultural land must have been reached in most places.'[136] While lack of human effect was sometimes a basis for designation, reserves were often sites of human impact and control. The Committee posed 'one simple question: What has to be done to enable man to control nature so as to maintain or establish a series of varied and most delicately balanced conditions?'[137] If, as Tansley insisted, an environment of human intervention was not necessarily an inferior ecosystem to natural climax vegetation,[138] the reservation of nature could imply the controlled creation of new habitats. Thus Minsmere Level in Suffolk was reserved despite being a coastal grazing marsh flooded by the military in 1940 for defence purposes and heavily bombarded: 'the general effect of this rough treatment was to make Minsmere exceedingly attractive to birds."[139] Similarly, at Nottingham Sewage Farm the Committee found that periodic flooding created fine habitat: 'in 1945 the first recorded breeding of the Black-winged Stilt in the British Isles occurred here.'[140]

If reserves did not signify 'pure nature', then scientific management was in no sense unnatural: 'Some nature lovers who have little actual acquaintance with the ways of nature and her reactions to human activities constantly advocate a policy of "letting nature alone" in nature reserves."[141] For the Committee this particular sense of managed ecology implied that the scientist should be in control: 'To place these functions in the hands of laymen would be to court failure on a large scale."[142] While reserves would attract visitors in the same way as 'both ancient monuments and living museums', their primary purpose would be scientific research, as well as economic gain: 'our proposals ... would prove a most profitable business transaction.'[143] The reserving of 'geological monuments',[144] for example, mixed national pride in rock with commercial opportunity: 'The staffing of the British and Colonial Geological Surveys, and the supply of a steady flow of trained geologists for industrial work at home and overseas, require that there shall be available in this country a sufficient number of representative areas for geological study.'[145]

Nature on Display

The assertion of science as the primary source of value in reserves did not imply an intent to reserve nature purely for the scientist. The reserving of nature must be understood in relation to efforts to display nature to a wide public, thereby cultivating a broader scientific citizenship; the spaces of reservation and display are dialectically constituted. The *New Naturalist* series and related publications translated scientific expertise into lay understanding of topics ranging from *Butterflies* to *Britain's Structure and Scenery*, from the microscopic to the mountainous.[146] Visual imagery was a key mode of communication. Photographic editor Eric Hosking recruited around 20 photographers for the series, and 2,500 pictures had been accumulated by April 1946.[147] While the books mixed colour and black-and-white images, Collins foregrounded what was for the time an unusual investment in colour: 'The plants and animals are described in relation to their homes and habitats and are portrayed in the full beauty of their natural colours, by the latest methods of colour photography and reproduction.'[148] The *New Naturalist* series extended Collins's collaboration with colour reproduction firm Adprint, with whom they had produced gardening texts and the *Britain in Pictures* series, which included Fisher's *The Birds of Britain* and Gilmour's *British Botanists*.[149] Colour extended to the distinctive *New Naturalist* covers by Clifford and Rosemary Ellis, which gave the series a distinctly modern aesthetic.[150] If, however, the declared aim of colour photography was to provoke wonder through accuracy, reproductive quality was for some reviewers a blindspot: 'The colour of some is too crude to be pleasing or, indeed, representative of the scenery they portray.'[151] Peter Marren notes alarm at landscape scenes with purple hills and over-blue lakes, described by Cyril Connolly as: 'strangely unreal, and cold as landscape wrapped in cellophane'.[152]

New naturalism presented itself as a modern practice in an English tradition, with photography updating earlier forms of encounter with nature. Ernest Neal described *Exploring Nature with a Camera* in these words:

> The love of hunting is probably one of man's most deeply-seated instincts, and nature photography satisfies that instinct to the full. It provides all the thrill of the hunt without the ugliness of destruction to mar it; it forces you to pit your wits against the cunning of the fox or the elusiveness of the otter if you are to succeed. It increases your powers of observation and, above all, it makes you better acquainted with the fascinating wild things all around, and that is an abiding joy.[153]

61 'A pylon hide, erected to photograph a tawny owl by flashlight'. From Eric Hosking and Cyril Newberry, *The Art of Bird Photography* (London, 1948).

FLASH-LAMP

NEST

Hosking and Cyril Newberry, who published accounts of their photographic work in the conservative rural journals *Country Life* and *The Field*, looked for trophies of *Birds in Action*: 'bird photography is primarily a sport, and, much as we hope that our pictures will prove of interest and value, it is the exhilaration of getting them which provides one of the major incentives to the work.'[154] Earlier discourses of what James Ryan terms 'camera-hunting'[155] are reworked to mark out a cultural space both modern and traditional. A tension arises, though, from attempts to make photography a popular field pursuit. While texts such as Hosking and Newberry's *The Art of Bird Photography* and *Birds in Action* include introductory essays on technique, this remains a specialist practice. Neal's book ends with a glossary running together 'Biological and Photographic

Terms':[156] ecology, elytra, exposure, extension, focal length, food chain, geometrid (the last a type of moth, not a camera stand). Ecology and photography are popularized as specialisms, with clear distinctions retained between the dedicated practitioner and the everyday snapper. Hosking's photography is evidently an extraordinary art, catching views beyond everyday sight, dependent on spending a long time in a hide by a nest (illus. 61), and demanding a mastery of high-speed flash, night or day, in the service of 'A Revolution in Bird Photography'.[157] Some of Hosking's most celebrated imagery gave seven views of a barn owl flying in and out of a grain hopper, each time gathering a vole, shrew or mouse, and setting off a photo-cell trip to demonstrate the 'Heraldic attitude of a Barn-Owl in flight'.[158] We shall see in the next chapter how the 'citizen-scientist' promoted by new naturalism was a figure primarily of field observation, but in one sense such a display of nature begins to shift the relationship between observation, photography and books. The naked outdoor eye could hardly compete with the flash camera. As photography and other televisual and cinematic media develop, nature is increasingly revealed as wonderful on the page or screen.[159] Field study is left with a diminished outdoors.

Human Ecologies, Urban Nature

If new naturalism sought an ecological understanding of species in environments, then that species could be human, and the environment urban. In his guide to *Watching Birds* Fisher suggested that: 'We must see ourselves first as animals living in this country in an ecological relationship with the wild creatures around us.'[160] It is mainly geographers who contribute studies of human ecology to the *New Naturalist* series, linking environment and human character, discussing human physical types, and describing human progress in terms of environmental change: 'We believe that the study of the natural history of man in Britain can contribute to the view that he must be regarded as one with nature. We believe that the search for a true relationship of man and his environment can alone save our beautiful islands from wrongful changes.'[161] H. J. Fleure's *A Natural History of Man in Britain* displayed 'folk-life' and physical types, such as 'J. James, from the Plynlymon district, showing features akin to those of man of the later Paleolithic age', and 'Charles Darwin, showing features similar to those of the beaker-making immigrants of about 1900–1800 BC',[162] as part of a paleolithic-to-the-present evolutionary story. Fleure argued for a co-operative cultural evolutionism, and while concerned about the individualism of modern society saw signs of hope in the post-war revitalization of 'small-group-membership' over individualism: 'the old deep-rooted tendencies have shown their vigour once more in the efforts to create the Social-Service State.'[163]

An emphasis on human ecology extended to a naturalism of the city as a site of human–animal–vegetable co-operation. Nicholson's account of *Birds and Men* set out to nail a myth: 'the old conception of a rich primeval bird life being steadily impoverished by civilization is ceasing to be true ... civilization is enriching and diversifying our bird life in some ways while reducing it in others.'[164] While not denying that human action could harm birds, Nicholson's general story, and this in a book written before the Clean Air Acts, is of adaptation: 'the Metropolitan Police District is rapidly becoming one of the best mainland areas in Great Britain for seeing rare birds.'[165] Nicholson described smart starlings warming themselves by 'smoke-bathing' on chimneys, and aggressive blue tits raiding milk bottles and tearing paper:

> the paper-tearing practice which suddenly developed on a large scale in 1949 has no obvious explanation ... the destruction of magazines, lampshades, cartons, wallpaper and other material inside inhabited houses is potentially a much more serious persecution of men by birds, which it is to be hoped will not be widely imitated.

62 'A Coal-Tit flies from its nesting hole.' From Eric Hosking and C. Newberry, *Birds in Action* (London, 1949).

Nicholson hints at Hitchcock-like terror: 'The question is, what will blue tits start to attack next?'[166]

The key new naturalist exponent of an urban ecology was Richard Fitter. In his *London's Natural History*, *London's Birds* and *Birds of Town and Village*, animals exploit the vernacular landscape; images show a coal tit exiting a petrol tin, a flycatcher entering an old kettle, a wren nesting in broccoli (illus. 62).[167] Humans and non-humans cohabit: 'man is himself a part of nature; the biological function of Buckingham Palace is the same as that of a bird's nest.'[168] Fitter relates history not as an erosion of nature but as a human-natural ebb and flow. While Fitter can use Cobbett's language of London as a cancerous growth – 'The Wen Begins to Swell', 'The Wen Bursts' – urban growth is never presented as straightforward destruction. Rather, built-up areas 'constitute a true biological unit within which the influence of man on natural communities is at its most intense'.[169] Fitter's revisioning of city nature also entails a reclamation of English urban naturalist writing. Richard Jefferies is cited not for his agrarian works, his nature-mysticism or his apocalyptic vision of a poisonous city in *After London*, but for his urban ecology of *Nature Near London* and *The Open Air*: 'So it happens that, extremes meeting, the wild flower, with its old-world associations, often grows most freely within a few feet of the wheels of the locomotive.'[170] Jefferies, Fitter noted, 'liked London and its birds much more than most of his latter-day fans'.[171] *London's Birds* (illus. 63) opens with a Jefferies quotation stating that, 'London is the only *real* place in the world.'[172] Like London's birds, Fitter suggests, English nature writers and English citizens could happily nest in the city:

> Much nonsense has been written about every Englishman being a countryman at heart . . . The illusion that all cockneys are pining for the delights of rural life has largely been exploded by the experience of the evacuation in 1939, when no group came back to their homes more quickly than the London mothers, bored to death by a combination of nothing to do and the quiet of the country.[173]

Urban nature also implied a revision of ecology away from a privileging of native species. Fitter works with distinctions of native

63–4 Nature in London: R.S.R. Fitter, *London's Birds* (London, 1949), dust-jacket; Rose Macaulay, *The World My Wilderness* (London, 1950), dust-jacket; design by Barbara Jones.

and alien, but does not try to imply a judgement over the right to belong. A principle of ecological openness is also extended to human society: 'London welcomes strangers of all countries and colours ... It was a popular victory when the West Indian cricketers beat England at the Oval in 1950.'[74] Like Jefferies, Fitter highlights the Oxford ragwort as a welcome intrusive species, along with more exotic plant visitors:

> it is the bombed cities, and London, above all, which have given the ragwort its greatest triumphs of colonization. In several places among the ruins saplings of native sallow and of Chinese buddleia have grown ten or more feet high, and cherry-trees originating in office-workers' lunches and numerous Trees of Heaven (*Ailanthus*), also from China, push their way up through the miniature forests in the Temple ... the London Rocket ... which grew in profusion in the ruins after the Great Fire of 1666, has been rediscovered in the ruins made by the great fires of 1940–41.[175]

London's Natural History lists 126 flowering plants and ferns from bombed sites,[176] and concludes with a chapter on 'The Influence of the War'. In it newly open ground lets in flora and fauna, craters hold pond life, birds are not bothered by aerial warfare: 'the fact that a swift circled around during a fierce air battle over the Roding valley in 1940 may be imputed to relative unconcern in the swift.'[177] Fitter even spots that common species, the observant geographer: 'Dr. Dudley Stamp informs me that in Sloane Square the pigeons have developed an interesting technique of bathing in static water tanks. He has often watched them take off from the edge and flutter half in the water across to the other side.'[178]

Spontaneous regeneration could, however, generate tensions in relation to planned reconstruction. In the plant world bombing triggers unexpected and chaotic growth rather than planned order. Nature reconstructs itself with a transgressive waywardness, potentially jarring with plans for a new English nature. Nature-in-ruins could indeed be deployed as a symbol of something other than orderly reconstruction. In the work of neo-romantic artists such as John Minton the presence of nature and children in ruins denotes anarchic and innocent spontaneity, outside a rational new order.[179] In Rose Macaulay's 1950 novel *The World My Wilderness*, set in 1946 (illus. 64), the bombsite 'wilderness' around St Paul's serves as a site to dramatize oppositions of civilization and barbarism, respectable Englishness and black marketeers, responsible adulthood and wild childhood, order and disorder. Nature-in-ruins belongs with the second term in each case:

> The children stood still, gazing down on a wilderness of little streets, caves, and cellars, the foundations of a wrecked merchant city, grown over by green and golden fennel and ragwort, coltsfoot, purple loosestrife, rosebay willow herb, bracken, bramble, and tall nettles, among which rabbits burrowed and wild cats crept and hens lay eggs.[180]

Macaulay's book may end with archaeologists and planners beginning to reclaim the waste, 'civilized intelligence … at work among the ruins',[181] but nature itself does not require such reconstruction. This is a different city phoenix, of plants and feral beasts, which hardly needs a planner, and in which only unruly humans, anticitizens, belong.

7
Citizens in Reconstruction

Town and country planning is now recognized as the essential basis for orderly progress towards an orderly environment for living.
THOMAS SHARP, *English Panorama*[1]

This chapter considers the senses of citizenship cultivated within the geographies of reconstruction. We move from models and critiques of community to the open air as a site for the physically, morally and spiritually healthy walker and the citizen-scientist. Anti-citizenship continues to stalk the land, and visual education is prescribed as a cure. New Towns, new houses and National Parks form zones for citizenship in reconstruction, key sites within an orderly environment for living.

The Anatomy of Home and Community

Cultivating Community

The choosing of sites for new communities is always an exhilarating side of the planner's work.
PATRICK ABERCROMBIE, *Greater London Plan*[2]

Reconstruction aimed to promote 'balanced community': the neighbourhood unit in cities, the ideal village anatomy in the country.

Community is set up as a social and geographical model cutting across class. Abercrombie set Welwyn's 'social integration and visual seemliness' against mono-class estates: 'Welwyn . . . shows a much healthier combination of human types.'[3] The Minister of Town and Country Planning Lewis Silkin was likewise 'very concerned indeed not merely to get different classes . . . living together in a community, but to get them actually mixing together . . . Unless they do mix, and mix freely, in their leisure and recreation, the whole purpose of . . . a mixed community disappears.'[4] The Minister of Health Aneurin Bevan also condemned 'castrated communities': 'we have to try and recapture the glory of some of the past English villages, where the small cottages of the labourers were cheek by jowl with the butcher's shop, and where the doctor could reside benignly with his patients in the same street.'[5] A village model is here upheld as a basis for a Left urbanism, although a rhetoric of community could appeal across the spectrum from High Tory to radical socialist. In his Stevenage study Orlans captured the mix of consensus and volatility inherent in such a benignly flexible concept:

> many . . . planners merely translated into sociological terms and architectural forms middle- and upper-class ideologies of a conservative or liberal-reformist nature . . . the 'balanced community' concept thus served the forces of law and order, middle-class morality, and the social and political *status quo* . . . For other planners (and, formally, for the Socialist Government), the 'balanced community' concept was part of a utopian Socialist creed . . . Indeed, this was often all that the Conservative Stevenage home-owner saw.[6]

City and regional plans deploy a benign visual rhetoric of community, mapping neighbourhood units as informal friendly blobs shaped into topography, happily evolved places rather than arbitrary functional zones (illus. 65). New Town planner Frederick Gibberd declared that: 'The process is diametrically opposed to the all too

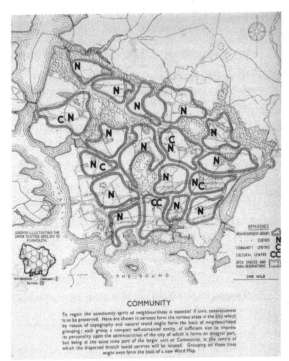

65 'Community'. From J. Paton Watson and P. Abercrombie, *A Plan for Plymouth* (Plymouth, 1943).

COMMUNITY

To regain the community spirit of neighbourliness is essential if civic consciousness is to be preserved. Here are shown in cartoon form the various areas in the city which by reason of topography and natural trend might form the basis of neighbourhood grouping; each group a compact self-contained entity, of sufficient size to impress its personality upon the administration of the city of which it forms an integral part, but being at the same time part of the larger unit or Community, at the centre of which the dispersed branch social services will be located. Grouping on these lines might even form the basis of a new Ward Map.

common practice of superimposing some theoretical pattern on the landscape, and may be distinguished from it by the term "organic layout".[7] The *County of London Plan* styled the city as a set of communities 'grouped organically round the heart of London',[8] while the *Plan for Plymouth* gave a nod to anarchist Kropotkin's evolutionary principle of mutual aid: 'It is not generally appreciated that it is the community spirit developed from that inherent characteristic of all races in the form of mutual aid which has been mainly responsible for the development of art and knowledge in the best periods of progress.'[9] The city is reshaped from a spreading wen into a nest of social spaces: Residential Units, Neighbourhood Groups, Community Groups.

In the country community might similarly revive through new organization and leadership, extending the pre-war efforts of RCCs and wis. If, as the Scott Report put it, the 'cardinal problem' was 'how to refocus cultural life within the village itself',[10] a village hall or Social Centre might be the solution. Orwin's research team found 'a sorry tale in the Survey area of lapsed troops of Guides and Scouts, of vanished Girls' Clubs, and of abortive attempts at informal gatherings for various purposes'.[11] Walter Gropius argued for village halls as the key organ of the communal anatomy: 'Since these small community centres are instruments of such vital importance to the human development of the group, they should be given priority over any other rehabilitation scheme, even over housing. Like the powerhouse of an industrial plant, they generate the current for the vital arteries of the group.'[12] Beyond such specific gathering points, the planning process itself could be a means to cultivate community. A basic tenet of the physical planning derived from Abercrombie's mentor Geddes was that survey should precede plan, with survey itself generating citizenship. Cecil Stewart's *The Village Surveyed* described a participatory study of Sutton-at-Hone in Kent.[13] Stewart, recruited by Sir Stephen Tallents, local resident and former secretary of the Empire Marketing Board, considered his role: 'The planner, through his study of social structure and social institutions, has the opportunity of resolving many social conflicts which are wasteful of community energy, and by presenting new objectives may release important reserves of social energy for the ultimate development of the community.'[14] Village meetings and an exhibition guided the survey, and children produced 'My Plan for My Village' essays: 'We might have a park near our house and a picture palace near by ... and a little fish and chipe [sic] shop further down the road.'[15] Boys were found to have the most sweeping visions of community development: 'Generally, they seemed much more destructive than the girls, half of them suggesting more or less wholesale demolition.'[16]

Visible Community

For its cultivation community required literal building, which needed to be visible. Social and physical planning are assumed to reinforce one another. Thus Gibberd proposed that the Municipal Offices in Harlow New Town should rise appropriately high: 'The accommodation for the officials is planned as a tall office block, say 140 ft high, to dominate the composition and express a grand civic scale. The town might follow the example of Patrick Geddes and make it an "Outlook Tower," in which one could view the town and the surrounding region.'[17] The *Plan for Plymouth* suggested that 'to-day the loss of community spirit is largely due to lack of conveniently sited meeting places', and envisaged Neighbourhood Centres as a 'development of the medieval community around the village green'.[18] Abercrombie here gestures towards the garden common scheme of his early teacher Sir Charles Reilly, which had been adopted as a planning model by the Labour Party. In the 'Reilly Green' plan a community building acted as a focus for houses around a green space.[19] Abercrombie thought that such focused schemes were the first step towards a new non-vicarious living: 'With the return of "community" will come the spirit of companionship unknown to the youth of yesterday who vainly sought it in the car or the cinema.'[20]

In his village studies Sharp developed this emphasis on focal buildings into a discussion of the 'Psychology of Plan Shapes'.[21] Diagnosing problems in 'The Village of To-day' with social flux and formal slackness, Sharp suggested that any attempt at social reordering would be helped by a programme of visual settlement psychology which would make plan form 'immediately apprehensible'.[22] Sharp's ground-level photographs and aerial views, like Hugh Casson's cover drawing for *The Anatomy of the Village* (illus. 66), are set slightly off-centre to any village axis, indicating a cradling formality with views in and out closed off to provide 'a kind of psychological refuge and a visual satisfaction'. Closure would

66 Thomas Sharp, *The Anatomy of the Village* (Harmondsworth, 1946) front cover; design by Hugh Casson.

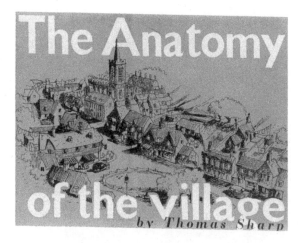

heighten the sense of local 'climax': 'if that inward view is terminated on one of the public buildings, then the sense of climax will be heightened, and the traveller cannot but be aware that he is entering a well established community.'[23] Christaller's argument for a regular settlement geography is again echoed: 'The stronger and more purely the location, form, and size express the centralistic character of such community buildings, the greater is our aesthetic pleasure, because we acknowledge that the congruence of purpose and sense with the outer form is logically correct and therefore can be recognized as clear.'[24]

For a model example of community building the Scott Report looked to the Village Colleges of Cambridgeshire as 'very near the ideal'.[25] The colleges were established in the 1920s and 1930s under the direction of Henry Morris, head of the county's Education Committee, and they became a touchstone of rural reconstruction debates in terms of both architecture and citizenship.[26] Harry Rée's biography of Morris presents a complex character whose personality embodied many of the contradictions of planner-preservationist thinking, in terms of both authority and aesthetics. Rée describes a man impatient with bureaucracy yet believing in the capacity of local government, a socialist who pursued an aristocratic lifestyle,

THE COUNTRYMAN'S
COLLEGE

BRITAIN ADVANCES

THE VILLAGE COLLEGE
CARS SHOULD BE LEFT IN THE
CAR PARK AND BICYCLES
IN THE RACKS

DOGS MUST NOT BE BROUGHT
INTO THE COLLEGE

67–70 Village College Life. From H. C. Dent, *The Countryman's College: Britain Advances* (London, 1943).

a homosexual who was 'repelled by the effeminate' and was convinced of the virtues of family life.[27] Morris held that contemporary civilization had failed to achieve an 'art of living' in either city or country,[28] and responded with a progamme of fresh air, fresh food, exercise and the incorporation of art into everyday life. The leading educationalist H. C. Dent reviewed Morris's work in the British Council's *Britain Advances* series under the title *The Countryman's College* ('16 Other Titles to be announced later including booklets on Electric Railways, Mothercraft . . .') (illus. 67–70). Morris was attempting 'to arrest the decay of our rural civilization in England' through 'the adoption of the rural region as a cultural and social unit'.[29] The Village College, serving a cluster of settlements, acted as a school for children, adult education centre, pre-natal and infant welfare centre, library, social centre, health centre, gym, pool, employment bureau and recreation ground, all under the supervision of a collegiate 'Warden'. Morris argued that through such an institution: 'A new type of leader and teacher with a higher status and of superior calibre would at last be possible in the English countryside.'[30] Service on the college Board of Managers could provide 'a most valuable training in practical citizenship. It is, in fact, democracy in action.'[31] In their review of reconstruction work Gilbert and Elizabeth McAllister found in the Village College a communal space of right living – 'Ballet, bee-keeping, gymnastics, art, domestic science, choral singing, first-aid and discussion classes are only a few of the activities at Impington.'[32] The arts of right living varied, however, between men and women and boys and girls. Boys are shown advancing over the school field with hoes, keeping bees and displaying themselves gymnastically indoors and out. Girls learn to sing indoors under a master's baton and folk dance in dainty rings outside. Men work wood. Girls stir sauce on a modern hob. An old woman occupies herself in the library. People discuss things. There are no dogs: 'THE VILLAGE COLLEGE. CARS SHOULD BE LEFT IN THE CAR PARK AND BICYCLES IN THE RACKS. DOGS MUST NOT BE BROUGHT INTO THE COLLEGE'.

Right living also demanded an appropriate architecture. Morris, Dent suggested, had 'ever before him the vision of an England made beautiful in all its ways';[33] he lent his own art to the colleges, and commissioned murals and sculptures. The style of the Village College developed from various sources, ranging from County Architect H. H. Dunn's conventional mix of Georgian and classical at Sawston (1927–30) through to the modernism of Linton (1938) and Impington (1938–40). Dent commented approvingly, 'as the scheme has progressed . . . the design has become increasingly functional.'[34] Impington, designed by Walter Gropius and shown on the cover of Dent's book, was the most prominent meeting of rural Englishness and international modernism. Morris met Gropius in 1934 in a Belsize Park flat designed by the modernist architect Wells Coates; Rée recounts a description of the occasion: 'Enlightened architect met enlightened educationalist; result: orgasm.'[35] Gropius agreed to design Impington with Maxwell Fry for a reduced fee on a site donated by the Chivers family, whose jam-making factory was in the village. School rooms faced south-east across open fields 'to catch all the morning sunshine'.[36] Cost frustrated Morris's attempts to get a Henry Moore family group for Impington to register the linkage of family and community; it went to a Stevenage school instead. Moore wrote of Morris: 'the Family Group in its differing forms sprang from my absorbing his idea of the village college – that it should be an institution which could provide for the family at all its stages.'[37] An anatomy of community could shelter an ideal of domesticity. We now turn to the family in reconstruction.

Home Life and the Ironing of the Social

An anatomy of domesticity was central to such models of community. The home-in-reconstruction is invariably woman-centred, with the woman a home-centred wife.[38] If the open air could be a space of good citizenship for men and women, at home clear distinctions of gender were reasserted. In the context of wartime upheavals in employment, whether in factories, the forces or agriculture, such arguments presumed a return to 'normal' after an exceptional war-time role reversal. A new Englishness is housed in a profoundly traditional new domesticity. One should not assume that all women sought such a return to the home and when they did this did not necessarily signify a desire to reassert traditional domestic roles or separate male and female spaces. Those advocating a return to a model feminine domesticity were thus not simply reflecting some general mood but making a contentious moral argument.

If the woman was to be rerooted it would be in a modern home, a space of new design and technology. There are varying degrees of technological enthusiasm in reconstruction literature, but in general a movement for an interior design of fitness for purpose and 'Utility' furniture[39] goes alongside an upgrading of the housewife to a mother-technician. In the planner-preservationist collection *Homes, Towns and Countryside*, Gilbert MacAllister set the range of reconstruction:

> From the planning of the kitchen to the planning of the nation. Through it all the emphasis is on space for living. Space is the fundamental condition of good planning and of the satisfying life. No kitchen, however well equipped, will make up for lack of living-space. But the antithesis, in a world of abundant production, is forced. We can have all this and gadgets, too. The lightening of the drudgery of the housewife is a major post-war objective. Only so can woman take her rightful place with man in society and share with him the adventure of living, the seeking after beauty, truth and goodness, which are the essential aims of the civilized man.[40]

In the same volume Leopold Friedman discussed 'The Culture of Living', envisaging the machine as 'the Slave not the Driver'. Peace would create 'the right psychological conditions for an entirely changed outlook towards domestic problems', with a demand for efficiency and modernity from women who in the War had operated machinery and experienced 'a new mode of life': 'We should think in terms, in the modern engineering sense, of "time study" and "deskilling" of jobs when determining the space and the mechanism required for the labour necessary to run our homes, thus freeing our housewives as much as possible for continued self-education, education of children, social activities and relaxation.'[41] This is not a move away from motherhood, but an assertion of the house as a machine-for-traditional-living-in: 'She it is who gives the home that personal touch, makes it a place to which the tired husband is happy to return; those little displays of flowers, the arrangement of the ornaments, splashes of colour, spring from a fresh mind and lively spirit, not tired and overburdened by the sombre worries of mere existence.'[42] *Homes, Towns and Countryside* showed an image of 'Lunchtime in a Welwyn Home' (illus. 71). Man and woman sit at table by an open window letting in fresh air from the garden and the woods beyond: 'The worker in a smaller industrial town such as Welwyn has a choice at lunchtime; he can eat either at home or in the canteen.'[43] A child leans over the window sill. We are to assume that this is a married couple eating a meal prepared by the wife while their son plays safely outside. This image could not be captioned, 'lost child begs for food as lovers grasp a quick snack'.

The child is a key figure here. The reconstructed home was to be a site for breeding. Denise Riley has traced the prevalence of pro-natalism, especially in 1945 and 1946, regarding family policy issues from healthcare and communal babysitting to 'streamlined rational kitchens'.[44] Fears over a declining birthrate crossed the political spectrum, serving to reinforce a model of homely motherhood as the fitting role for married women. As Riley puts it: 'The effect of the universal stress on the Mother was to create two irreconcilable parties: the housewife-mother and the woman worker.'[45] The geographies of domestic reconstruction operated through such assumptions. Riley considers Orwell's *The English*

71 Lunchtime in a Welwyn Home. From Dennis Hardy, *From New Towns to Green Politics* (London, 1991).

People to be 'an exact compendium of attitudes which one can find throughout a wide selection of British periodicals, articles, books and broadcasts in the 1940s'.[46] Orwell called for measures to 'encourage childbearing and to save women with young children from being obliged to work outside the home', and thought that pet ownership, the 'cult of animals', had contributed to a lower birthrate: 'Britain today has a million and a half less children than in 1914, and a million and a half more dogs.'[47] Beveridge couched the welfare state in similar terms, warning in 1943 that, 'If the British race is to continue there must be many families of four or five children.'[48] Labour's *Let Us Face the Future* followed this demographic line: 'A healthy family life must be fully ensured and parenthood must not be penalized if the population of Britain is to be prevented from dwindling.'[49] It is in this context that we should understand Friedman's statement that: 'the concentrated effort and strain of war-work will make a greater need for relaxation for our war-workers in the years of peace. If we are to preserve the health and future generations we shall do well not to overlook this.'[50] Pro-natalism becomes a central issue in arguments over house and flat development, especially for garden city lobbyists, for whom flats were simply 'birth-control barracks'.[51] *Homes, Towns and Countryside* hailed 'the instinctive desire for more space, more sunlight, more air' as a 'healthy movement' in accordance with 'the deepest needs of men and women; it is in accordance with the essential requirements for children'.[52]

The most prominent pro-natalist was Mumford:

> The prime desideratum of town planning must be to provide an urban environment and an urban mode of life which will not be hostile to biological survival: rather to create one in which the processes of life and growth will be so normal to that existence, so visible, that by sympathetic magic it will encourage in women of the child-bearing age the impulse to bear and rear children, as an essential attribute of their humanness, quite as interesting in all its possibilities as the most glamorous success in an office or a factory.[53]

This passage forms part of Mumford's critique of the *County of London Plan*, which he saw as proposing too many flats, though he later praised the *Greater London Plan* for removing this flat bias.[54] Houses and gardens were essential to foster the 'Primary Orientation: The Family': 'It may be a little while yet before the future Londoner can make love to his wife in a summer-house in his garden as William Blake, certainly no man of affluence, did; but that might at last be held up as an ideal, if we are as earnestly committed to the rehabilitation of family life as we ought to be.'[55] For Mumford the family ideal implied that the career woman and the mother were mutually exclusive:

All over the world, millions of women have been driven to take jobs outside the family and to renounce the responsibilities and pleasures of domesticity in favour of a biologically sterile existence. The family as such was disparaged; the office and the factory became emblems of woman's emancipation – that is, of her sexual deprivation and her biological futility.

Mumford called women back to 'the stable, reassuring environment of home and garden and nearby countryside'.[56] Upholding principles of femininity implied keeping women in the home: 'Our too masculine, too mechanical, too life-denying society has come to its terminus. Perhaps the best slogan for the coming age is that for the lifeboats: women and children first.'[57]

The house was not the only environment for the cultivation of domesticity. New Town communities as a whole were designed to cater for the new-trad woman. In the *Greater London Plan* Abercrombie reflected on the development of new settlements:

> Womenfolk are inclined to be more critical than the men, and where employees have returned to London this has usually been due to their womenfolk's dislike of the new surroundings. This emphasizes the necessity for providing good cheap shopping, social and entertainment facilities in the reception towns from the start; it is these services that are so much missed by the women.[58]

A promotional film for Stevenage showed a young woman with a wicker basket leaving her modern house, catching a convenient bus and entering a pedestrianized centre with trees, shops, a boy sailing a model yacht in a clean fountain, a dog safely left tied to a post, a pram being pushed by. A smooth social arrangement connects the home to the commercial centre.[59] The *Greater London Plan* offered similarly smooth-centred images (illus. 72), Peter Shepheard picturing a future Ongar as pedestrian, if hardly bustling, and with

72 'Ongar Town Centre'. From P. Abercrombie, *Greater London Plan 1944* (London, 1945); design by Peter Shepheard.

orderly blooming tulips, four women, a child, a cat and a dog going about their daily lives: 'The bus route is just off the picture to the left.'[60] Such civic images contain within them a domestic model, community and domesticity fitting in with one another to produce an orderly everyday life, an ironing of the social. Ironing, a core practice of good household management, serves as a metaphor for uncreased living.

Faulty Anatomy

In July 1953 the *Architectural Review* announced the 'Failure of the New Towns', the production of 'lopsided and amputated suburban communities',[61] overly ironed out and non-civic. From within the broad movement for planned reconstruction criticism emerges of the results of reconstruction. The journal's editor, J. M. Richards, diagnosed an 'anti-architectural planning',[62] a Garden City-lobby triumph of over-dispersal with no sense of layout, enclosure or design. Art editor Gordon Cullen concluded that New Town 'prairie planning' produced a spaced-out uniformity rather than a careful composition, commenting: 'If buildings are the letters of the alphabet they are not used to make coherent words but to utter the desolate cries of AAAAA! or OOOOOO!'[63] Here were non-town New Towns; a Cullen montage showed an old man bending down, sketching a small town on a new suburban pavement: 'This citizen drawing out once more the traditional English design for urbane living, upon the empty pavement of an imaginary new town.'[64] The mix of modernity, tradition and locality stressed in geographies of reconstruction is seen to be lost in what Ian Nairn termed 'Subtopia': 'Subtopia: Making an ideal of suburbia. Visually speaking, the universalization and idealization of our town fringes. Philosophically, the idealization of the Little Man who lives there (from suburb + Utopia).'[65] Nairn reinstated the distinction between town and country in the face of these new developments, claiming, 'Subtopia smudges over this vital difference.'[66] Once more a model of citizenship is integral to this landscape and the 'Little Man' is put down along with his place. Nairn would return to such matters in his 1964 collection *Your England Revisited*: 'Here is part of a new estate near Bristol – indifferent design, wasted space, no thought and no love. No wonder there are Teddy Boys.'[67]

Such commentary in part reflects competing philosophies of urban density, with lobbyists for mixed house and flat development renewing their battles with Garden City campaigners. I would suggest we also find here a clash between two forms of environmental fantasy, which turn on the place of women within stark or mysterious environments. The distinction emerges in a comparison of two commentaries on housing areas, one by J. M. Richards, the other by Garden City lobbyist Frederic Osborn. Richards's *The Castles on the Ground*, a 1946 account of 'The Anatomy of Suburbia', is generally regarded as a strangely generous view of the suburb for its time. Richards made the usual criticisms of lower-class 'sporadic building of a suburban kind that threatens to engulf the countryside',[68] but welcomed a well-appointed 'true suburbia'. The latter is defined as a place of shady and winding green avenues, of fantasy and mystery rather than Subtopian uniformity: 'In the suburbs fantasy is functional.'[69] The true suburb suggested to Richards a need for 'a modern aesthetic that allows romance and fantasy to flourish, as distinct from one dictated solely by rational scientific planning'.[70] True suburbia is defined as the 'proper *milieu*' of the modern woman, where the 'bored housewife' could achieve 'a fuller life through fantasy as well as fellowship'.[71] Her right environment was certainly not the New Town which are accused of, 'marooning the unhappy housewife on the distant rim of their sentimental green landscapes so that she has to tramp for miles with her shopping basket and is altogether cut off from the neighbourliness of closely built-up streets'.[72] Richards could dream that in the true suburb the housewife could dream.

While Richards delighted in shaded romance, Garden City lobbyist Frederic Osborn preferred a clear visibility. Two kinds of visual pleasure clash as two planners dream different dreams of the suburban woman. Osborn's New Town was a place demanding the exercise of an authoritative eye: 'Sheds, fowl houses, rabbit pens, amateur-designed porches, unauthorized trellises, etc., require the constant vigilance of the administration. They can spread like a rash, and once established are difficult to clean up.'[73] This space of visible moral order could still, however, be a place of dreams. Clear visibility could itself spark fantasy. In Osborn's poem 'To Julia on Washing Day' a planner's eye wanders in a New Town landscape, taking in a neighbour's underwear:

> When as your silks in dainty rows
> Hang empty on the line
> I would that what they oft enclose
> Were mine.

> Unbidden wishes they awake;
> Wild dreams of frustrate love
> Wherein you slip things on – and take
> Them off.

Yet when we meet I must not say
What thoughts I bubble with;
At most I murmur: 'Lovely day,
Miss Smith!'[74]

Citizens Outdoors

Spaces of Citizenship

> The townsman has discovered the countryside. The new methods
> of transport have laid it open before him. Nothing will keep him
> out of it now. Nor should anything. The countryside, too, must be
> recognized and utilized as a home – the home of countryman and
> townsman alike … But it must be recognized that the townsman is
> more powerful than he was. He is no longer a prisoner. He is free.
> If he is not given the freedom of the countryside he will take it,
> and with strong damaging hands. The power is his now. He could
> be brutally dominant if he chose.
>
> THOMAS SHARP, *Town Planning*[75]

The interwar art of right living governs the discourse of country
leisure in war and reconstruction. Sharp seeks a balance between
pure desire and preserved purity, a taking of pleasure in control. If
urban people have the power and right to move, that power needs to
be channelled, for the benefit of their selves and the country. While,
as we have seen, reconstruction could be articulated at the regional,
civic and domestic levels, debates over leisure and landscape continued to play on a national map, with the nation the scale of both
planning and meaning. Yet again the nation makes sense in terms
of something beyond itself, Stamp and the Scott Report declaring
the countryside to be 'the heritage of the whole nation – indeed,
also of the Dominions and the English-speaking world'.[76] Here
was a source of belonging for the white imperial citizen, even the
American cousin.

Organizations such as the YHA thrived during and after the War, despite many hostels closing in coastal or reception areas. Membership climbed from a low of 50,000 in 1940 to 100,000 in 1943, 150,000 in 1945 and 230,000 in 1948.[77] The 1940 *Handbook* optimistically retained information on hostelling in Europe, although it did note under Denmark, Finland, Norway, Rumania and 'Germany (Including Austria)' that: 'In the present circumstances, members will not be able to use hostels in these countries.'[78] In the *Handbook* a Holiday Fellowship advertisement showed a group of hikers pointing to a 'Summer Holidays 1940' map of Britain: 'Holidays are the chief exception to the rule of not spending.'[79] The YHA issued its first calendar in 1947, its first diary in 1948 and Oliver Coburn's *Youth Hostel Story* on its 'Coming of Age' in 1950 (illus. 73). The open-air movement comes to maturity in reconstruction, maintaining the mapping-scouting-fieldwork art of living. As Jack Cox, editor of the *Boy's Own Paper*, put it, the aim was 'camping with a purpose'.[80] In 1951 the open-air ethos was laid down in *The Country Code*, drawn up by the National Parks Commission, with ten maxims for gate-shutting, dog-controlling, plant-protection, solid and liquid waste disposal, stile-using, etc. The *Code* established its rules through glimpses of agricultural knowledge and practice so that the visitor would see good behaviour as rural economic sense as well as politeness: don't pollute streams, don't let your dog savage valuable lambs. Seventy thousand copies had been sold by 1959.[81] Warning illustrations by James Lucas showed the young as both future citizens and country hazards: wandering through corn, clambering on walls, tossing litter, carefree yet careless. Above the heading 'Live and let live' two young couples are shown singing their way down a nighttime village street. A dog barks and a resident shouts from an upstairs window: 'The countryman ... has to keep early hours.'[82] The city that never sleeps meets the country that goes to bed early.

Such a coding of landscape conduct lay at the heart of campaigns for National Parks, which were established under the 1949

73 Oliver Coburn,
Youth Hostel Story
(London, 1950),
cover; design by
Conroy Maddox.

National Parks and Access to the Countryside Act. In 1942 John
Dower had surveyed possible parks for the Ministry of Town and
Country Planning, submitting his report in May 1945.[83] Dower
defined his task in geographical terms: 'when I have been asked
to explain the functions of the Ministry of Town and Country
Planning in which I serve, I have found the best short explanation
is to say that our job is, or ought to be, creative geography'.[84] In
July 1945 Lewis Silkin set up a National Parks Committee under
Sir Arthur Hobhouse, including Dower, Williams-Ellis and Julian
Huxley, whose July 1947 report formed the basis for the 1949 Act.[85]

Ten out of the twelve parks suggested by the Hobhouse Committee were established within ten years, the exceptions being the South Downs and the Norfolk Broads.[86] Parks were generally in upland areas with elements of 'wild' landscape, yet urban access was a key requirement: 'at least one of them is quickly accessible from each of the main centres of population in England and Wales.'[87] National Parks take their place in reconstruction legislation as regulated spaces for a landscaped social-democratic citizenship.

Labour was enthusiastic about the open air. In his 1946 Budget speech Hugh Dalton looked forward to National Parks:

> There is still wonderful beauty to be found in our country. Much of it has been spoiled and ruined beyond repair; but we still have a great wealth and variety of natural scenery in this land. The best that remains should surely become the heritage, not of a few private owners, but of all our people, and, above all, of the Young and the Fit, who shall find increased opportunities of health and happiness, companionship and recreation, in beautiful places.[88]

Dalton, dubbed 'the Red Rambler of the Pennines',[89] was well known as an open-air activist, acting as President of the Ramblers' Association in 1948 and walking the proposed Pennine Way with Tom Stephenson, Barbara Castle and others.[90] The Home Secretary Chuter Ede was President of the Southern Area of the Ramblers' Association, Silkin had addressed ramblers' rallies, Stephenson, a former colleague of Silkin in the Independent Labour Party, acted as Press Officer at the Ministry of Town and Country Planning from 1943, and was initially secretary of the Hobhouse Committee's sub-committee on footpaths and access, which also included Dower.[91] Stephenson recalls a Labour leadership committed to the open air as a democratic right for the people, but notes disappointment with the 1949 Act for not following Dower and Hobhouse in proposing free rights of access to uncultivated land. Priorities of food production, together with a sympathy among key figures such as Dalton with the rights of landowners, led Labour to ally themselves with farming interests.[92] In his foreword to *The Country Code* Trevelyan similarly warned of farmer–visitor tension: 'If the simple rules of conduct laid down here are neglected by visitors to the country, food production and country life will be hampered, and the farmer will regard the holiday maker from town as his enemy. This must reduce the opportunities for free enjoyment of the countryside for visitors.'[93]

Introducing the second reading of the National Parks Bill on 31 March 1949, Silkin concluded: 'This is not just a Bill. It is a people's charter – a people's charter for the open air.'[94] In what sense were these popular spaces? As in the interwar period, citizenship works in relation to anti-citizenship. Joad's 1946 *The Untutored Townsman's Invasion of the Country* reiterated interwar arguments on right and wrong living in the context of a likely 'Post-War Invasion' driven by prosperity, cars and holidays: 'Is it not clear that the scale of the invasion of the country by the towns will be beyond anything that most of us have experienced and beyond what most of us have imagined?'[95] Dower, President of the Ramblers' Association in 1946, argued for a tutored invasion. Addressing the Town Planning Institute, he suggested that while any theory limiting beauty to the few had 'no place in democratic practice', there were certain standards of freedom: 'Needless to say, liberty should not mean licence; public enjoyment should be subject to a reasonable standard of good behaviour.' Planning should not cater for 'ignorant and insensitive elements in the visiting public':[96] 'it will be by no means easy ... to resist the inevitable demand of the "urban-holiday-minded" that they should have their share in the National Parks programme.'[97] Quoting as 'the first shot in the campaign for British National Parks' Wordsworth's talismanic comment in his *Guide to the Lakes* on the Lake District being 'a sort of national property, in which every man has a right and interest who has an eye to perceive and a heart to enjoy',[98]

Dower excluded the hearts and eyes of the urban-holiday-minded. This is not simply a zoning of pleasures for mutual tolerance, but an assumption of an unbridgeable cultural geographical divide whereby the 'urban-holiday-minded' person could not conceivably take meaningful pleasure in the non-urban. The question was not simply access, but meaningful access:

> For all who want to spend their holidays gregariously . . . National Parks are not the place. They had far better keep away, and (some of them, perhaps, after an unsuccessful experiment or two) pretty certainly will keep away – provided that any proposals to establish, within National Parks, the kinds of facilities they desire are firmly resisted.

A close watch should be mounted for such thin-ends-of-wedges as 'a garden pleasure-ground (small bar attached)'.[99] Dower issued the usual warnings on the 'minority' of bad visitors, 'typically . . . charabanc parties, ill-controlled children's outings and other "excursion" groups'.[100] A landscape for citizenship demanded a policing of the anti-citizen. A people's charter should nurture the right kind of popularity.

Arguments for citizenship are again bound up with assertions of cultural authority, which work through a particular social aesthetic. Dower acknowledged that 'the landscape is so fundamentally a thing of "values", of aesthetic and spiritual rather than scientific and material assessment',[101] and like Cornish he assumed a principle of latency: 'The driving force of the aesthetic instinct is within ourselves; it needs only to be released by the attitude of receptive, disinterested love.'[102] Dower quickly, though, distanced such love from decadent aestheticism. The eye needed training like a rambler's body: 'it can, I am convinced, be greatly broadened and deepened if we train it appropriately and exercise it strenuously.'[103] How though, if landscape was a matter of values, was value to be defined and love encouraged?

the key to success is that enough of us – and especially of those who have some relevant authority or influence as governors, administrators, technicians, and writers – should care enough about the task, and should go humbly and seriously to school with Nature herself as mistress and inspirer, and with the great minds that have been applied to the loving study of nature as guides and interpreters. It is my robust faith that, if we do this with heart and mind, it will not be long before we are sufficiently sure and united to assume a leadership which the rest of our fellow-countrymen are sufficiently ready to follow.[104]

Dower's call for 'a team of experienced landscape lovers', an emotionally committed committee, exercising a classically masculine mode of engaged control over the beauty of a feminized nature, epitomizes the dialectic of commitment and detachment, embodiment and elevation, love and science, which lay at the heart of the preservationists' social aesthetic. Dower also suggested a geography of love. Local landscape lovers would be useful, but might have limited sense: 'many of them are simple folk with little power of expressing their opinions, and most of them are more or less lacking in comparative experience, and therefore tend to be unreliable outside the region or regions in which they have lived and observed.' The key was to mix the simple and local with those – Cornish is given as an example, Dower would presumably be another – who could bring a national comparative aesthetic geography to bear, those 'very few who . . . have visited, studied, and appreciated the whole of England and Wales'.[105] If a national space was to be planned, national standards of creative geography should be exercised: 'We shall have to be up and doing to encourage the right sort of recruits and to give them the right sort of condensed training.'[106]

While aesthetic judges might take one kind of training, the urban-holiday-minded might be offered another. Dower proposed 'more and better Blackpools and Brightons, and . . . popular holiday camps'.[107] The latter were upheld as an interim coastal pleasure zone, a staging-post on the way to citizenship. Stamp stated: 'I would rather see five thousand in a camp than those five thousand spread about in two thousand bungalows.'[108] The herded herd could camp with a purpose. Political and Economic Planning's 1942 report on *Planning for Holidays* saw quantitative increase threatening qualitative decline, and argued that planned reconstruction was therefore necessary to check 'permanently' the pre-war 'spoilation of the coast'.[109] Coastal and inland holiday centres, including converted large country houses 'no longer inhabited by their traditional owners',[110] would be a useful channelling device: 'it will ... be necessary to divert a considerable number of holiday-makers away from the coast.'[111] Joad gave guarded praise to Butlins as a method of 'interim canalization':

> A holiday camp supplies a certain sort of delight which is best enjoyed in company. I say 'delight' but, in fact, it is a whole way of life that is offered, complete with riding and swimming, with tennis and dancing and shopping, with 'mateyness' and heartiness during the week and religious services and more 'mateyness' on Sunday.

Spatial concentration in camps minimized scenic destruction while giving campers 'a chance to open their eyes to the fact and presence of beauty ... You cannot, after all, jump overnight from the Blackpool holiday in a mob to the mountain holiday with two or three.'[112] PEP also welcomed camps as a wholesome demographic space: 'they should be developed on sound lines under enlightened management. They will then become an important national asset, not least as places where young men and women who may have few social opportunities in their daily lives can meet, mix, and plan to marry.'[113]

Campers and camp-owners may not have discerned such schemes of scenic and sexual induction, but one should not automatically assume an opposition between elite scheming and unreflective mass pleasure. Rather we find different relations of order and happiness, bodily discipline and bodily pleasure, with the two not necessarily opposed or even in tension. The holiday camp as a site of pleasure, in contrast to certain kinds of seaside resort, is far from being a liminal marginal zone where anything can go.[114] Camps boomed after the War, attracting half a million visitors by 1947, predominantly from the affluent working class, mixing the outdoor ethos of fitness and health with the indoor fun of the resort, and in a controlled fashion releasing women from the burdens of cooking and cleaning and childcare.[115] Orderly pleasure was not only the prescriptive dream of an elite. In the progressive weekly *Picture Post*, Hilde Marchant, reporting Billy Butlin's message that 'within such a highly organized setting, the individual gets a greater opportunity for self-expression', was sympathetic to the Butlin ethos of self-formation through communal dancing, communal roller-skating, organized rambling, Radio Butlin wake-up calls and mass keep-fit: 'They are expected to take part each morning in army style keep-fit exercises. They do so. And they like it.'[116]

The Citizen-Scientist

Matters of citizenship, aesthetics and vulgarity also occupied those seeking to promote physical and biological field study. If nature conservation, whether of plant, animal or mineral, was a matter of national heritage, the study of the natural world could be a means to good citizenship. Whether considering specially reserved nature, where restricted access would, thought the Wild Life Conservation Special Committee, deter 'trippers and casual picnic parties',[117] or observing the everyday country or city, citizen-scientists might form themselves outdoors. And just as nature might be reserved, so should the conduct of those studying it. Discussions of nature conservation generally miss the models of human conduct constituted alongside the animal, vegetable and mineral. In new naturalism a deep attachment to nature is to be achieved through a reserved detachment, with observation the primary method of connection. We can approach these issues via a study in coastal geography.

Between April 1943 and April 1945 J. A. Steers surveyed the coast of England and Wales for the Ministry of Town and Country Planning: 'we have only one coast and it is neither a local, nor even regional, but a national possession. It is the consciousness of the coast as a whole which needs quickening.'[118] Steers followed the Scott Report in arguing for the maintenance or restoration of the coastguard's path as a giant, long-distance footpath. Steers sat on the Wild Life Conservation Special Commitee, and was President of the Norfolk and Norwich Naturalists' Society in 1940–41; his physiographic studies sought to register a cultural value in coastal features.[119] In June 1944 Steers addressed a Royal Geographical Society audience which included Stamp, Dower, Tansley, Holford and the Minister of Town and Country Planning W. S. Morrison. He argued that:

> The whole matter is basically one of geography ... people have a great desire to visit the seaside, either in vast numbers ... or in ... more manageable masses ... or as individuals on the remoter coasts. It is the last type of coastal region which is likely to become more and more *popular in the right sense*. Let us think of national authority as a coordinator and a judge.[120]

The 'more popular' resorts had 'acted as safety valves', saving other places for 'the walker and naturalist'.[121] A threat came, though, from 'Areas of bad scattered development' – plotland shacks and bungalows – which might spoil even these sites: 'hideous settlements ... long lines of jerry-built wooden erections ... the drive for seaside holidays has overreached itself'.[122] Here was coastal popularity in the wrong sense: 'education must begin at school, and might well be associated with the teaching of geography. This is the subject above all directly concerned with the study of landscape, and intelligent knowledge and appreciation of the local region by school pupils should do much to guarantee the proper use of the countryside in the future.'[123] Morrison commended Steers: 'He not only gives us the facts, but proceeds by his paper to "point the moral".'[124] Tansley responded that: 'If we want our future citizens to value our national heritage of natural scenery and wild life, it is up to us to see that the young get the necessary training.'[125]

Two books summarized Steers's survey: *The Coastline of England and Wales*, introduced by Stamp and Abercrombie, and the popular format *A Picture Book of the Whole Coast of England and Wales*, introduced by Scottish naturalist Frank Fraser Darling and designed to comprise 'a "lantern" lecture on coastal physiography'.[126] To regard such works as cultural documents is not simply to connect 'scientific analysis' and non-scientific 'sentiment'. Rather their text, photography and cartography mobilizes a particular cultural authority of science. Stamp, Abercrombie and Fraser Darling present Steers as providing an 'unbiased academic assessment'[127] which nevertheless has planning application: 'a scientific survey made by a geographer who is alive not only to the changing face of Nature but to human works, good and bad'.[128] A delicate interplay of science and cultural policy is set up, with Steers offering 'a geographical background to the assessment of our coastal scenery, and so to the proper use and enjoyment of our coasts'.[129] Science rises into a background authority, to be brought down to earth to plan and judge.

Steers's RGS cultural commentary had been accompanied by slides of disfiguring shacks, mines and quarries. Neither book contains such imagery. While a fold-out map indicates 'areas of bad scattered development' through small cross symbols clinging like limpet mines to a vulnerable outline of the nation, the photographs present specimens of good coastal geography with hardly a human presence. The need for preservation is underlined by pure physical geography. Images of spits and beaches and bars and cliffs present beauty underwritten by geographical science. Fraser Darling made the photographic agenda explicit:

Mr Steers saw other things in the course of his travels ... and he has another collection of photographs, which would be no adornment to a book. Mr Steers can disturb complacency in forthright fashion whenever he cares by exhibiting this other collection ... Vast stretches are ruined by a display of vulgarity and the results of thoughtless behaviour ... Scottish coasts are generally more fortunate through the saving mercy of more violent weather. The mock Tudor and the Moorish would blow away.[130]

The omission of such imagery registers the *Picture Book* as a document of scientific vision; the inclusion of such commentary serves to reinforce an association of scientific geography, beauty and cultural health. Preservation might ensure that 'a hundred years or more hence, competent photographers not yet born may take their stereoscopic colour-print cameras and come back with as good a collection as Steers, the patient geographer, has given in this book'.[131]

Alongside Steers on the Committee was the geological popularizer Arthur Trueman, whose *Geology and Scenery in England and Wales* set out geology in straightforward text, sketch and diagram: 'For geology is preeminently the layman's science. In it more than in any other science there is opportunity for a beginner to make original observations, to weigh up evidence, to co-ordinate his facts and in general to acquire a truly scientific outlook.'[132] This is not a romanticized geology of writhing rocks and mysterious fossils; rocks are the subject for a cool reading by a firmly located citizen-scientist: 'many never know an area until something of its meaning becomes clear to them, just as some may never feel comfortable in a strange town until they have seen a map of its streets.'[133] Trueman hoped to provide 'a basis for a wider appreciation of the scenic features',[134] although he was wary of 'the worst results of popularity'.[135]

Moves for geographical field study focused on the Council for the Promotion of Field Studies (later the Field Studies Council), formed in 1943, with Tansley as its first President. Field centres were established in areas of prime ecology and geology; Flatford Mill in Suffolk in 1946, followed in 1947 by Juniper Hall in the Weald, Dale Fort in Pembrokeshire, and Malham Tarn in Yorkshire. Geographer S. W. Wooldridge argued for field teaching to 'build up the power to read a piece of country'[136] and to 'develop the art of seeing' by using the local area as a 'laboratory': 'geography begins at home.'[137] Wooldridge parodied Wordsworth in promoting the Council's work:

> One traverse in a Surrey Vale
> (or if you prefer it Yorkshire Dale)
> Will teach you more of Man,
> Of Man in his terrestrial home,
> Than all the text books can![138]

Wooldridge worked closely with Geoffrey Hutchings, Warden of Juniper Hall and active in the interwar movement for regional survey.[139] Hutchings designed the dust-jacket for their *London's Countryside*, depicting a classic fieldwork scene with a bearded rucksacked man discoursing before students and a spread-out landscape (illus. 74).[140]

Field study similarly ran through new naturalism:

> Some writers today complain that 'modern natural history' is 'too scientific'... Do these people really believe that the search for truth is less important than the search for poetry or art or aesthetic satisfaction or 'happiness'? Do they not understand that the purest source of these imponderables is in the realms of fact ... ? Once facts are despised, fancies replace them; and fancies are poisonous companions to the enjoyment and appreciation of Nature.[141]

New naturalism sought to cultivate field observation through books, lectures, clubs and broadcast media, taking nature into living rooms

74 S. W. Wooldridge and G. E. Hutchings, *London's Countryside* (London, 1957), dust-jacket; design by G. E. Hutchings.

to encourage movement into the field. The BBC radio children's panel programme 'Nature Parliament', chaired by popular personality 'Uncle Mac' (Derek McCulloch), ran from January 1946 with a panel of naturalists which included James Fisher and Peter Scott: 'here, then, is a team of real experts that will leave no stone unturned, no reference book unthumbed in excited interest, combined with honest endeavour, to candidly answer the pertinent, complicated, exacting and penetratingly imaginative questions posed by young listeners.'[142] An ideal new naturalist citizen-scientist emerges, an energetic figure of field study, young in outlook, able to read the wider landscape as well as specific species, loving nature through a scientific appreciation, like Bancroft in *Tawny Pipit*. The directness of observation is held to make it a democratic form of nature knowledge, potentially open to all rather than restricted to a scholarly cognoscenti. James Fisher produced a cheap pocket-sized Penguin on *Watching Birds* in 1940:

Some people might consider an apology necessary for the appearance of a book about birds at a time when Britain is fighting for its own and many other lives. I make no such apology. Birds are part of the heritage we are fighting for. After this war ordinary people are going to have a better time than they have had . . . It is for these men and women, not for the privileged few to whom ornithology has been an indulgence, that I have written this little book.[143]

Birdwatching should not be an arena of social discrimination:

All sorts of people seem to watch birds. Among those I know of are a Prime Minister, a President, three Secretaries of State, a charwoman, two policemen, two Kings, two Royal Dukes, one Prince, one Princess, a Communist, seven Labour, one Liberal, and six Conservative Members of Parliament, several farm-labourers earning ninety shillings a week, a rich man who earns two or three times that amount in every hour of the day, at least forty-six schoolmasters, an engine-driver, a postman, and an upholsterer.[144]

The democracy of new naturalism is expressed in Fisher's plainness of language. A 1940 book on birdwatching could easily have been filled with arch analogies on aeroplanes and war, or dreams of natural flight as an escape from present circumstances, but beyond the Preface Fisher restricts his language to bird observation and its necessary equipment – small library, note system, camera, field-glasses: 'E. M. Nicholson has a very neat light leather gadget which slides up and down the straps and which fits just over the eyepieces to protect them when it is raining.'[145] Fisher's is a language without plumage: 'My attitude towards bird watching is primarily scientific, or so I like to think. Those of you who want passages, purple or otherwise, on the aesthetic of bird watching, will not find them here.'[146] This is not to say, though, that *Watching Birds*, like Fisher's subsequent series on *Bird Recognition*, does not have its own aesthetic, but in this case it is one of sensible prose, maps, diagrams, tables and charts.

Fisher sets up a particular spatial relationship between amateur observation and expert knowledge, with the amateur providing a local pair of reliable eyes through which national records can be built up: 'improvements in our knowledge of classification can come from his own work.'[147] Fisher presented twelve stages through which the fledgling watcher might be socialized into scientific service: becoming vaguely interested, being puzzled, identifying species, speculating – 'he probably begins to widen his circle of ornithological friends' – and eventually contributing to 'field-character description' in the *Handbook of British Birds*. The beginner could join local societies, carry out preliminary local surveys, note sightings, set up nest boxes, establish sanctuaries. Brian Vesey-Fitzgerald described the local naturalist in the *New Naturalist* journal: 'the local naturalist must know his own country ... To be a really good local naturalist you must know the geography of your district as well as you know the geography of your house.'[148] Fisher suggested that, 'Bird scientists will be able, with their armies of lay helpers, to conduct a great Mass Observation of birds.'[149] New naturalism and the social survey movement of Mass Observation connect in their combining of the amateur and the professional, their stress on close detachment, their assessment of organisms in their environment. Julian Huxley had written the Foreword to Mass Observation's initial 1937 pamphlet, and Fisher was a friend of the Mass Observation founder Tom Harrisson, who had begun his career as an ornithologist, carrying out a key early bird survey of the Great Crested Grebe.[150] New naturalism and Mass Observation also overlap in the emphasis placed on the 'sociality' of organisms and on nature as a community. Fisher argued against theories of bird behaviour asssuming aggressive territoriality, positing instead that 'bird sociality' was 'fundamental' to evolution: 'birds are social animals.'[151]

History also offered model surveyors, most notably Gilbert White, the eighteenth-century parson naturalist of Selborne. English pastoral is again harnessed for modern effect. In 1941 and 1947 Fisher produced new editions of White's *Natural History*, presenting him as a proto-modern observer, an earlier citizen-scientist.[152] While in H. J. Massingham's introduction to *The Writings of Gilbert White of Selborne* in 1938 White appears as an organic visionary, and Selborne an ecological and social organism,[153] Fisher's 'A New Judgement on Gilbert White' revealed a naturalist field-worker, anticipating Darwinian insights and contemporary theories:

> White has been elevated to the fountain-head of a tradition – of elegant nature writing – which has developed into a mockery of the honest language of the *Natural History* ... The epithet applied to writers in this tradition is usually charming. Charming nature writing. Oh, the critics and reviewers, the weekly columnists, the nature correspondents, who find Nature 'charming'; who find White's Selborne 'charming'; who find the emotional, romantic outpourings of Jefferies 'charming'; who find the humourless introspection, the self-conscious pessimism, the nostalgic obscurantism of Hudson 'charming'; and who lump them altogether in their charming paragraphs to charm those to whom the country is a plaything![154]

Fisher recognizes that White also loved gardening and the picturesque, but this is 'quite a different person from Gilbert White the naturalist ... no more than the salt in his dish'.[155] The new naturalist White is in 'the real tradition of British field-workers, of observers'.[156]

Visual Education, Design for Life

We conclude with a body crossing the outdoor and indoor spaces of citizenship, embedding visual education in a wider design for life. The Council for Education in the Appreciation of Physical Environment was formed in September 1942, following a deputation by the CPRE and TCPA to the President of the Board of Education R. A. Butler.[157] Renamed in October 1945 as the Council for Visual Education, with Abercrombie as its first President, the Council focused on schools, guiding the 'instinctive interest of all children in the matter' through 'drawing, history, geography, mathematics, hand-work and projects' to give 'some understanding of the opportunities which will arise in the post-war reconstruction period, so that they will not tolerate the kind of development which took place in many areas after the last War'.[158] Beyond school the CVE worked towards 'a more beautiful and better planned environment for the everyday life of the people'.[159] In relation to economic and cultural issues of planning and design, it suggested, 'the future of England ... must mainly depend upon the standard of popular appreciation'.[160]

The CVE resembled the CPRE in its structure, with architectural, planning, design and educational bodies brought together in a council of expertise, an informal visual establishment. Constituent bodies included the CPRE, TCPA, Architectural Association, RIBA, DIA, Institute of Landscape Architects, Society for the Protection of Ancient Buildings, British Film Institute, Town Planning Institute and Workers' Educational Association. The Council co-opted members from the Ministries of Health, Education and Town and Country Planning, and the Arts Council. Herbert Read and F. J. Osborn were vice-chairs, Clough Williams-Ellis vice-president. The Executive included William Holford and Noel Carrington, while others active included Kenneth Clark, Henry Morris, architects Oliver Hill and Hugh Casson, planners Elizabeth and Gilbert McAllister, and John Betjeman. The Council worked through school exhibitions, toys, models and games including 'Matchbox Village' and 'Matchbox Town', 'a fascinating and instructive game'.[161] There were also lectures and films, teacher-training courses and pamphlets.[162] From 1954 a school essay competition attracted around

75 W. F. Morris,
'The Future Citizen
& his Surroundings'
(London, 1946),
pamphlet cover;
design by E.
Warne-Browne.

THE FUTURE CITIZEN
& HIS SURROUNDINGS

by

W. F. MORRIS

C.V.E.
6d.

1,000 entries each year on such themes as 'My Favourite Street' and 'Beautiful Buildings I Have Seen'.

W. F. Morris's pamphlet on *The Future Citizen and his Surroundings* set out the cve's programme for raising 'the uneducated taste of the great majority'.[163] The pamphlet's cover, by E. Warne-Browne (illus. 75), showed a young boy, a young girl and a younger girl walking in the country by a stile, village and church: a latent family on a rambling survey. Just as cve vice-chair Osborn praised Vaughan Cornish as one whose direct way of seeing could help the citizen 'regain something of the direct appreciation of the child' ('When he looks at a tree, he *sees* the tree'),[164] so Morris judged that: 'The capacity for good judgement in aesthetic matters is latent in most children, but is warped or suppressed by bad surroundings or strong misleading suggestions in youth or adolescence.'[165] As part of 'the endeavour to make of the pupil a good citizen – ideally a citizen of the world, but in any case a citizen of his own country', the child 'should be taught impatience with things unnecessarily drab or sordid, and should be infected with a desire to remove or improve them'.[166] Studies of local settlement could relate ideas of 'Citizen and Town Planning', while a 'Hobbies Club' could make 'a relief model of a given area, as it is and as it might be, to illustrate, for example, the differences between heterogeneous ribbon building and planned settlement'.[167] In his foreword R. A. Butler commended local survey: 'The teaching method known as "the project" has on occasion been used in order to familiarize children and young people with the history and topography of their own district ... Such a method can be used to even greater advantage if the aesthetic importance of the pupil's surroundings be ever stressed.'[168] For Butler all this had a direct economic implication in a competitive post-war world: 'We can prevail only through qualities of distinction, and what is more distinctive than originality of Design? The Art School far from being considered in the past the agreeable and rather light-hearted shelter for the dilettanti, will become the Training Establishment for our Export Commandos.'[169]

Subsequent CVE pamphlets addressed art, architecture and design. Hervey Adams's *Art and Everyman* carried a Foreword by Williams-Ellis arguing that, 'it is through the schools alone that we can break into this vicious circle of shoddy education and debased public taste.'[170] Adams sought to cultivate 'intelligent opinion'[171] so that the modern would be welcomed: 'we cannot put the new wine of present day social and economic needs into the old bottles of old-fashioned appearances to which we may perhaps sentimentally cling in our love for the "olde-cosye-worlde". New needs, new materials, and new scientific discoveries inevitably create new kinds of appearances."[172] Charles Reilly's *Architecture as a Communal Art* simultaneously upheld the English village, the country town, the interwar municipal estate and the most modern architecture as examples of communal art against speculative building's 'vulgar individualism'.[173] The cover showed Charles Holden's modernist 1932 Arnos Grove tube station: 'Our younger architects are already ceasing to be commercial travellers in the past styles and are becoming instead prophets of the new."[174] In the CVE's final pamphlet Nikolaus Pevsner addressed *Visual Pleasures from Everyday Things*. Visual pleasure, Pevsner argued, derived from order and design, and every element in the environment, however mundane, should therefore embody such principles. Seeking to embed a feeling for beauty in everyday life, Pevsner quickly marked out the aesthetic from associations with the 'soft' or 'cissy',[175] thereby distancing beauty from conventional modes of femininity or effeminacy, yet also criticizing the mode of strong and Puritan masculinity which would assume such associations. The visually bright citizen would revel in a designed country: 'Visual education . . . is concerned with things in nature as much as with man-made things. Possibly only one in a thousand today knows what to do with his eyes beyond using them for utilitarian purposes . . . Very few realize that any tree, any leaf, any stone – and also any pot, any rug, any spoon – can be regarded aesthetically."[176]

Visual education was not, of course, confined to the CVE, and one final example will underline the nature of the citizen under cultivation by showing how visual education could extend not only to trees and spoons but also to the presentation of the self through the body. Penguin's *The Things We See* series began with Alan Jarvis's 1946 *The Things We See: Indoors and Out*. The things to see included bodies. Jarvis considered 'The Impulse to Decorate', whether on people or buildings. Jarvis presented positive images of an extravagantly coated Hungarian cowherd and a Zulu woman, which for him only confirmed that 'enjoyment of the things we see needs practice'.[177] The practised eye would not always be so tolerant,

Vulgarity

WE CANNOT RESIST wanting to go beyond the example of ornament inappropriately applied and to give an example of a crude shape poorly decorated. Following our principle that words alone may confuse, the example is reinforced with a visual contrast which defines the meaning of vulgarity. By vulgarity in people we mean just this kind of coarseness of body, cheapness of ornament, and insensitive application of make-up (4). The parallel in the case of the pottery is exact, in its florid shape and crude cosmetic decoration (5).

76 'Vulgarity'. From A. Jarvis, *The Things We See: Indoors and out* (Harmondsworth, 1946).

though. In a study of 'Ornament' Jarvis highlighted 'inappropriate' decoration, juxtaposing an ornate teapot or a tattooed male back: 'It is amusing to note that an undecorated pot is called by the potter a *body*, and to see that in this case the ornament of the body adds as little in the case of the teapot, as does tattooing in the other.'[178]

And when it came to 'Vulgarity' (illus. 76), people and pots again flaunted the same lack of principle. Jarvis showed dainty floral jugs by Elsie Collins and a heavily made-up woman photographed by John Deakin:

Vulgarity
We cannot resist wanting to go beyond the example of orna-ment inappropriately applied and to give an example of a crude shape poorly decorated. Following our principle that words alone may confuse, the example is reinforced with a visual contrast which defines the meaning of vulgarity. By vulgarity in people we mean just this kind of coarseness of body, cheapness of ornament, and insensitive application of make-up. The parallel in the case of the pottery is exact, in its florid shape and crude cosmetic decoration.[179]

Citizens, like pots, should attend to their own bodies with a care for the responsive environment generated. Crude jugs and crude women, such things to see, indoors or out, were hardly objects of visual culture. Neither person nor pot were responsible, both showed misguided beauty on a wronged anatomy. Just like a straggling vil-lage, a brash house, or a shack on a coast, here was a lack of visual education, an absence of order, a wrong design for a wrong life.

PART IV

Festivals and Realignments

8

Landscape and Englishness
in an Altered State

In writing this book I have had a sense of veering between cultural proximity and cultural distance. Sometimes the material has seemed, to this reader at least, to echo today, while at other times there seems barely any connection. The aim of this final chapter is to consider the gap between past and present, and to give an account of how relations of landscape and Englishness have shifted from the time of reconstruction to now. We begin with a discussion of the 1951 Festival of Britain, which acts as a summation of the planner-preservationist vision but also allows us to detect fractures in the landscape of modern consensus. We then draw out the various challenges to this landscape which emerge during the 1950s and 1960s, particularly in melancholy evocations of a threatened vernacular Englishness. Traditional landscape, local heritage and pastoral anti-modernity line up against visions of a planned and ordered country. We conclude by considering the contemporary resonances of organicist and planner-preservationist argument, whether in Green engagements with nature, or social democratic formations of nation and citizen.

Festival

In the summer of 1951 the Festival of Britain offered a national vision aligning the modern and traditional, city and country, reconstruction and citizenship, history and the future. The Festival is perhaps the fullest expression of a progressive sense of landscape and citizenship and yet it also shows the sense beginning to unravel under attack from without and through tensions within. The national focus of the Festival was the exhibition on the South Bank of the Thames in London. Ian Cox's *Guide to the Story it Tells*,[1] price 2/6, described the event, and advertisers sought to connect their products with the festive spirit. Visitors opening the front cover would find a garish advertisement for Benedict Processed Peas: 'No other peas are quite the same, So ask for Benedict by name.' There seems something symbolic about the prominence of tinned peas in this brochure of national identity. Here was a modern vegetable for the modern Festival family; a brilliant bowl of processed green, with a knob of butter on top, took up half the page. At the bottom a cartoon strip showed a man returning to his modern home for domestic delight: 'Oh! How Tender, How Delicious/ Sweet and Plump And So Nutritious.' The wife serves Benedict, all sit down to eat and husband and daughter smile: 'Yes! If You Would Your Family Please/ Make Sure By Buying Benedict Peas.'

The general message of both exhibition and brochure – in the details of displays, in the accompanying advertisements – was of a modern country of humans, animals, vegetables and minerals, built on tradition and to be moulded through modern planning in industry, home, science, city and country. The *Architectural Review* hailed the South Bank as 'the first modern townscape', an 'Exhibition as Landscape' realizing the best principles of reconstruction.[2] In Poplar in East London an exhibition of architecture and planning showed a model new community, Lansbury, named after the former Labour leader and local MP, with mixed houses and flats. Standing out from the new Lansbury harmony was 'Gremlin Grange', a how-not-to-do-it house, with crooked mock-Tudor frontage and unscientific demeanour.[3] The Festival has been subject to a variety of readings,[4] but the broad message was of movement into a new world under the guidance of those whom Gavin and Lowe term

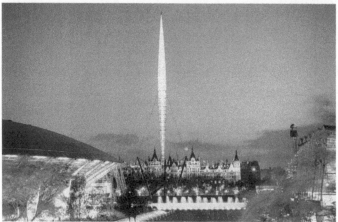

77–9 Festival of Britain, 1951.

'heroes of the social democratic age', a new generation of planners, designers and architects, figures of rationality who could lift public authority above sectional interest.[5] A specific example can illustrate the percolation of such ideas through everyday national life. In 1951 my uncle, who was training by correspondence class to be an architect in Norwich, and later to work in the City of Norwich architecture department, went to London for a week (illus. 77–9). His imagination already caught by the plans on paper for Norwich and elsewhere,[6] the South Bank, with Lansbury thrown in, was the word made flesh. Photographs show Roy Foyster in Festival mood, and record the sights: Ralph Tubbs's proto-space age Dome of Discovery, the largest dome in the world and one holding stories of national science and exploration, Powell and Moya's Skylon shot at night, the rational kitchens of the 'Homes and Gardens' pavilion. Delight in the modern was a popular force even outside the pages of journals and reviews.

The Festival went far beyond London. One exhibition toured Northern and Midland cities, another went round the coast on board the Festival ship 'Campania', and Glasgow and Belfast had specific shows.[7] The *Geographical Magazine*'s 'Festival Number' offered a souvenir map prepared under the direction of Eva Taylor and featuring 'What do they talk about?', a 'map-guide to local conversation gambits when touring Festival Britain'; when in Nottingham try the modern Boots factory, when in Yarmouth try the herring season, when in Plymouth try the New Town Plan, when in Burton try beer.[8] Collins issued a series of regional *About Britain* guides suggesting itineraries for drives and describing town and country. The general editor Geoffrey Grigson introduced their 'newness':

> These guides have been prompted by the Festival of Britain ... If the country includes Birmingham, Glasgow or Belfast, it includes Stonehenge. If it contains Durham Cathedral, it contains coal mines, iron foundries, and the newest of factories

devising all the goods of a developing civilization. If it includes remnants of medieval forest, it includes also the new forests of conifers transforming acres of useless land . . . On the Downs in Wiltshire we can stand on a minute plot of ground on which the Iron Age farmer reaped his corn with a sickle, and watch a few yards away a combine harvester steadily devouring ripe acres of wheat.[9]

In places around the country Festival public halls and seats on greens can still be found today, 1951 inscribed into the local landscape. Over 2,000 places held Festival events; over 100 village bus shelters were erected.[10] The Festival organizers nominated Trowell in Nottinghamshire as the 'Festival Village', not for its picturesque beauty but for its ordinariness: 'This is but one village chosen from a thousand, chosen not for its beauty, but as an example of what a small community has done to celebrate the Festival and to make itself a better place in which to live.'[11] Trowell had an exhibition, a cricket match in Victorian dress, a garden competition and a new playground. The national organizers blotted their image of local concern, however, by reflecting in their *1952 Story of the Festival of Britain* on the efforts of 'Trowell in Northamptonshire'.[12]

We can take one example in detail to show the texture of the Festival beyond the showpiece exhibitions. The Didcot Celebrations focused on a day of Carnival, with a parade led by the Reading Military Band and a Carnival Queen contest. The entrants were to be aged between fifteen and twenty-five, single, resident for at least twelve months and selected by a panel from submitted photographs and personal interviews. The Queen received a five-guinea prize, with her four chosen attendants getting a guinea each. Festival Minister Herbert Morrison sent a standard national greeting to the town:

I welcome the strong Festival spirit which Didcot is showing and hope that the programme of celebrations will be a success.

It is not enough for us to try to preserve old customs and picturesque survivals from the past. In addition to this we of the present generation ought to create new amenities for posterity, and to see that we leave behind us, each in our community, legacies by which we will be proud to be remembered. I hope that this Festival year will start something which will grow in strength in the future.[13]

J. B. Priestley's 1951 novel *Festival at Farbridge* echoed this small town affair, with a pageant, parade and Festival Ball, and a Festival Centre painted a shocking pink: 'a pink that defied the tradition, the elements, the whole economic and aesthetic outlook of the South Midlands'.[14] Didcot also searched for 'Mr. Festival', not a Mr Local Universe but a lurking presence on Carnival Day:[15]

Can You Spot Mr. Festival?
£1 PRIZE
For the FIRST Person to Spot Him
??????

Description. Tall, well built. Age twenty-five to thirty-five, Fair. Wearing a sports coat and flannels. A person answering to the above description will be in the following places on August Monday – **Along the Route of the Carnival, 2 p.m. to 3 p.m. In the Park from 3 p.m. to 6 p.m** And if he has still not been correctly challenged **At the Carnival Ball in the Coronet Ballroom from 9 p.m. to 1 a.m**.

If you see anyone who you think might be MR FESTIVAL at the above places during the times stated you must challenge him with these exact words:

'YOU ARE MR FESTIVAL, AND I CLAIM THE PRIZE.'

The FIRST Person to correctly challenge Mr. Festival will receive a prize of **One Pound**.

There will be some Consolation Prizes.

Two Rules to Remember
1. You Must Be in Possession of a Handbook.
2. You Must Challenge in the Exact Words.

What might have happened? Perhaps the money was gone by 2.30 pm. Perhaps others wearing the not-uncommon sports coat and flannels were continually propositioned. Or Mr Festival may have hung around the park, being addressed in words slightly off the mark, until, repairing via various bars to the Coronet Ballroom (amid more men in sports coat and flannels) he resorted, after several Martinis, to approaching girls: 'Guess who I am. Go on, guess who I am!' A late licentious Mr Festival who, when asked by the constabulary for his name, insisted they guess it.

Realignments

Other Versions of Festival

In earlier chapters we began to see how internal contradictions could lead a seemingly coherent vision of a modern landscape and Englishness to unravel through doubts over the Englishness of planning, possible equations of modernization and standardization, or an overwriting of one kind of English ruralism by a planned regionalism. Similarly, if the Festival aimed to present a picture of a country planned and preserved, it could also prompt critiques of that narrative, and contained within it some tensions. Reviewing the South Bank exhibition, Dylan Thomas picked up on a prevailing delight in eccentricity, shown in the 'Lion and Unicorn' pavilion celebrating 'British Character'. Here were future visions of strange and colourful invention rather than cool grey reason: 'what everyone I know, and have observed, seems to like most in it is the gay, absurd, irrelevant, delighting imagination ... the linked terracotta man and woman fly-defying gravity and elegantly hurrying up a w.c. wall."[16] Along the Thames the Festival Pleasure Gardens at Battersea evoked an Englishness of past quirkiness, with Rowland Emett's miniature 'Far Tottering and Oystercreek Railway' going nowhere in particular for fun.[17] Emett had first shown the railway in drawings for *Punch*, and here, as in *Punch*'s Festival issue of April 1951,[18] we find a rather different sensibility of the nation. *Punch* offered a spoof 'Bouverie Street Exhibition', complete with an 'Arcade of Sublime Domesticity' and an Emett-drawn fun fair of trains and flying saucers. Cartoons contrasted 'The Native Village – 1851' and 'The Native Village – 1951', one ribald and rustic, the other with a green covered by regular prefabs, a welfare clinic with a queue, a bus stop with a queue and a sign reading 'Site For Library'.[19] *Punch* imagined a 'Merrie Effort' whereby Rural Emergency Powers would be assumed in order to schedule 'Merrie Areas' in rural England. In a demonstration 'Central (Intensive Reconstruction) Area' the 'return to medievalism' would be 'rigorous and complete'; initially Rutland was earmarked for 'this hard core of Merriment', but the 'Merrie Board' had settled on a corner of Herefordshire between the Wye and Wales, where all post-Tudor buildings would be demolished or re-styled with 'the official prefabricated "glove" frontages'.[20]

In such sideshows to the Festival the tensions of planning and Englishness identified earlier in the book begin to form into opposing camps which would realign the culture of English landscape in subsequent decades. If Didcot's *Official Handbook* opened with a message of modernization from Morrison, rather different images of authority followed: the Lord Lieutenant of the county pictured in his garden in plus fours, the local MP, Sir Ralph Glyn, with a message blaming the petrol engine for two world wars.[21] Two years later the Coronation would help reinvigorate an imperial, deferential, High Historic sense of nation, whatever the efforts made by figures such as Stamp to align planning and 'The Second Elizabethan Age'.[22] And if *Punch* could satirize the Festival's modern domesticity, another set of domestic values were the focus of the 1951 feature film *The Happy Family*, in which the Lord family, played by Stanley Holloway, Dandy Nicholls and a young George Cole, among others, barricade and defend their home on the South Bank exhibition site against Ministry eviction orders. Posh and lazy civil servants pass the buck as Mr Lord speaks for other English values: 'As I see it, in order to show the world how we've really progressed in England, and to show them what sort of people we really are, you're prepared to use force to turn me and my family out of our house, is that it, Mr Filch?' The rhetoric of rural Stevenage moves to inner London, although at one point a radical protesting heritage threatens to overtake the story. Mrs Lord's mother is revealed to have been a Suffragette, Dandy Nicholls contacts Robespierre through a ouija board and George Cole talks of an English revolutionary spirit last manifested in the 1945 election. However, Stanley Holloway as the father figure is quick to gather the fight back into more conservative language, toasting not revolution but 'The Family', and lining up English domesticity against the planning State: 'Alright, let's drink to us. To living quietly and being left alone, and not being led about like sheep. To our Englishman's castle, and to all the millions of little castles belonging to little people all over the country. That's nicer than revolution, ay? Let's drink to the family, our happy family, and thank God for it.'

English Melancholy and its Humours

The Collins's Festival *About Britain* guides also featured writers more commonly seen at odds with the values of Grigson's progressive introduction. Two of the guides were written by historian W. G. Hoskins, a key figure in the emergence of an anti-modern, anti-state, anti-progress culture of landscape from the late 1940s.[23] Hoskins produced numerous national and local landscape histories and topographic Guides, most famously *The Making of the English Landscape* in 1955, and would become a minor TV celebrity in the

1970s with his BBC2 series on English landscape. For Hoskins land-scape was a document, 'the richest historical record we possess',[24] and its meaning was being eroded by modernity. In 1963 he reworked *Punch*'s Merrie Areas scheme in the Shell Guide to *Rutland*:

> The one thing everybody knows about Rutland is that it is the smallest county in England. Perhaps most people also know by now that, being small, it is fighting for its independence against the urban theorists who seem to dominate the world of planning today. Rather than being exterminated in favour of a larger unit with no historic meaning, it should be set aside at once as England's first Human Conservancy. We have Nature Reserves of various kinds for the protection of rare animals, birds, and plants. Only the human being is not pro-tected against incessant noise, speed, and all the other acids of modernity. Rutland is still largely untouched ... still a picture of a human, peaceful, slow-moving, pre-industrial England ... One would like to think that one day soon at each entrance to this little county, beside a glancing willow-fringed stream, there will stand a notice saying *Human Conservancy: Abandon the Rat-Race at This Point.*[25]

In Hoskins's lament for landscape the very language of planning becomes urban, alien and theoretical, contrasting with a topo-graphic language which is down-to-earth and made up of local detail. Modernity is acid, meaningless, place-dissolving. National designations regarding nature and the human are effectively mocked. Hoskins has no real hope that his ironic Conservancy proposal will come to pass. This is a culture of landscape which, unlike the organicism of earlier chapters, holds out no hope of conservative transformation. Indeed it is defined by and delights in its melancholy, gently transcribing what is left of the country before modern acid dissolves England's local variations (illus. 80). Hoskins was a key figure in the promotion of local history, which he offered

80 Milton Keynes, Buckinghamshire. From W. G. Hoskins, *Midland England* (London, 1949).

as a therapeutic practice of rooting and belonging, with place the means to cultural depth: 'Some shallow-brained theorists would doubtless call this "escapism", but the fact is that we are not born internationalists ... We belong to a particular place and the bigger and more incomprehensible the world grows the more people will turn to study something of which they can grasp the scale and in which they can find a personal and individual meaning.'[26]

In the concluding chapter of *The Making of the English Landscape* Hoskins, having taken the reader from the earliest times to the nineteenth century, pauses briefly to consider 'The Landscape Today': 'Since ... the year 1914, every single change in the English landscape has either uglified it or destroyed its meaning, or both ... It is a distasteful subject, but it must be faced for a few moments.'[27] For two pages, before closing the book with a detailed description of the deep local history legible from his Oxfordshire window, Hoskins presents an alliance of planning, science, industry and the military tearing up the country. Country houses and parks are broken up: 'if it stands near a town, the political planners swarm into the house, turn it into a rabbit-warren of black-hatted officers of This and That, and the park becomes a site for some "overspill" – a word as beastly as the thing it describes.' Here is Hoskins's new Englishness:

> England of the arterial by-pass, treeless and stinking of diesel oil, murderous with lorries; England of the bombing-range wherever there was once silence . . . England of high explosive falling upon the prehistoric monuments of Dartmoor. Barbaric England of the scientists, the military men and the politicians: let us turn away and contemplate the past before all is lost to the vandals.[28]

Hoskins signals the emergence in recognizable contemporary form of a series of powerful cultural oppositions; urban against rural, national and international against local, individual against state, shallow theory against deep particularity, planning against landscape, modernity against tradition. Hoskins also crucially sets past against present. History becomes a site not for tracing continuities from past through present to future, for finding a tradition with which to align the modern, but an escape hatch. History stops at the modern world.[29] No matter that all of the landscapes discussed by Hoskins – deserted medieval villages, parliamentary enclosures, country parks – are the product of historical change, in this landscape sensibility modern change becomes somehow different in its erasure of meaning, rubbing out the historic document of landscape. And with change being so powerful as to be unstoppable, turning away is the only possible sensible gesture, away from an England of roads, bombs and planners and towards a humbler ground of deserted village and obscure country church, of ridge and furrow and bench ends. England of the branch-line:

the railway has been absorbed into the landscape, and one can enjoy the consequent pleasure of trundling through Rutland in a stopping-train on a fine summer morning: the barley fields shaking in the wind, the slow sedgy streams with their willows shading meditative cattle . . . the warm brown roofs of the villages half buried in the trees, and the summer light flashing everywhere. True that the railway did not invent much of this beauty, but it gave us new vistas of it.[30]

England of Rutland, England of Trumptonshire (my first experience of English pastoral), England of the Emett Railway, England of *The Titfield Thunderbolt*, the 1953 Ealing comedy in which the local residents fight the closure of the oldest branch-line in the world by running the railway themselves and bringing out of the local museum an ancient engine; amateurs against experts, locality against bureaucracy.[31] Railway preservation emerges in the 1950s as part of a developing popular heritage culture, with Tom Rolt of *Narrow Boat* fame a leading player.[32] Branch-line salvage, branch-line history, can find virtue in not connecting to a wider network, operating locally, back and forth and not beyond, rescuing and revering something passed by, bypassed, by the modern world.

The gesture of turning away from the present has, of course, had enormous contemporary effect, its particular formulation of despair acting as a powerful force for conservation. In relation to the material considered earlier in this book, though, the significance of figures such as Hoskins lies in their cultivation of a melancholy way of seeing England, departing from the earlier preservationist style. Hoskins may be as angry as Sharp or Williams-Ellis, moving his Englishness across the full range of humours – melancholy, bile, phlegm – but he cannot supplement his anger with a national plan for improvement. Hoskins, like his Shell Guide editors and fellow practitioners of 'church-crawling' John Betjeman and John Piper,[33] moves around England for different ends, seeking out places where planning is not in evidence and should not be necessary. Thus in

Rutland Hoskins finds a site for slow pleasure, a place where slow motoring is still possible and where roadside picnics 'in the French style' can be taken. Hoskins suggests that white wine should be chilled in advance and decanted into a flask to keep it cool:

> So one is all set for a good morning among the churches: not more than three in a morning is sufficient for enjoyment, and perhaps another one or two after tea: and the afternoon perhaps spent in lying in a field in the Midland sun, quietly unwinding. I have found Tixover churchyard a pleasant place for an afternoon doze ... A week of this treatment in Rutland sends one back ready to fight politicians and jacks-in-office with one hand tied behind one's back.[34]

As in Betjeman's work it is crucial that this melancholic humour and underdog English spleen is mixed with authoritative observation. If Hoskins were simply grumbling about the modern world and recommending churchyard boozing then his cultural impact would have been rather different. He is able, though, to present himself as knowing more than the average tourer, and far more than the average planner. Modern expertise is countered by experienced and knowledgeable observation, enabling the writer to spot the bumps in fields that others never notice, the fonts overlooked by run-of-the-mill guides. Hoskins's Guides are detailed documents of cultural value and erosion, illustrated by photographs showing specific landscape features rather than general rural scenes.[35] An expert authority is countered not by bumbling amateurism but by another authority, itself held to be more English. If the landscape is regarded as distinctly English, then so too is the way of seeing which offers topographic literacy.

This then is an Englishness whose melancholy derives from knowing too much, from being all too aware, from holding a country in regard yet feeling, as that other melancholy church-tourer Philip Larkin put it in his 1972 poem 'Going, Going', 'That it isn't going to last'. Larkin's poem gathers up pollution, mass leisure, speculative development, regional planning and a sense of town-iness spreading over everything to suggest a country sold off for profit and pleasure: 'And that will be England gone.' Englishness is located in meadows, lanes, choirs and guildhalls, in many ways a more restricted landscape than that described in Larkin's poetry in general, which moves over a range of humdrum vernacular spaces. Larkin's suggestion in the poem that perhaps the only bits of England left will be 'the tourist parts' indicates that, like Joad in an earlier period, this version of the English landscape is recog-nized as mythic in terms of being a tourist fantasy as well as a conservative cultural icon.[36] 'Going, Going' was first published as the Prologue to the 1972 Department of the Environment report *How Do You Want to Live? A Report on the Human Habitat*;[37] the Ministry excised its verse critical of business and government, and its auctioneer title. The poem indeed cuts against the grain of the whole report, which mixed modernism and conservation in one of the last official expressions of planner-preservationism. The cover photograph by Lord Snowdon was in full 1970s style, showing a young woman with lank hair and a damp dress emerging from a misty pond. Larkin's view of this hybrid of the Pre-Raphaelite and the Prog. Rock poster is not recorded.

Other Environments

I have highlighted the work of Hoskins and others in part to sug-gest that it is through evocations of a vernacular rather than elite landscape that the progressive planning ethos is most effectively challenged in the 1950s and 1960s. Others have stressed how in this period the elite landscape of the country house is mobilized by the National Trust as a threatened symbol of tradition against a social-democratic modernity.[38] This was certainly so, but in the light of Peter Mandler's work on the successful economic adaptation of the privately owned country house in the 1950s and 1960s[39] it would be a mistake to project the Conservative polemics of the 1970s, defending the wealthy against progressive taxation measures relating to land and property, back over previous decades as a *dominant* image of counter-modern Englishness.[40] The work of the Trust's James Lees-Milne certainly began to lay down a language of benighted elite heritage,[41] but a more interesting and powerful challenge to a landscape of modern consensus came through variants of vernacular Englishness.

Such a process went far beyond topographic and architectural writing. Indeed if thinking about Englishness through landscape allows a connection across different cultural fields, then we should look beyond these obvious sources of environmental commentary. To take one example, the 1950s see a reworking of pastoral Englishness around issues of science and technology, with wayward and/or alien science the effective successor to wartime Nazis in the English village. John Wyndham's 1957 *The Midwich Cuckoos* finds alien children in an English village seeking to usurp the human role as evolutionary leader. Filmed as *The Village of the Damned*, Wyndham's story plays on oppositions of vernacular Englishness and alien governmental and out-of-this-world science. As a place of 'simple ordinariness' Midwich approaches Hoskins's Rutland Conservancy: 'had there been posts at the entrance to the village bearing a red triangle and below them a notice / MIDWICH / DO NOT DISTURB / they would have seemed not inappropriate.'[42] Potentially demonic science also appears in Hoskins's 'Landscape Today', with 'the obscene shape of the atom-bomber, laying a trail like a filthy slug upon Constable's and Gainsborough's sky'.[43] While Geoffrey Jellicoe could landscape primeval hills around the Harwell Laboratory, or Sylvia Crowe could wonder at the cosmic 'New Shapes' of Dounreay, others highlighted a nuclear anti-landscape. As Meredith Veldman has shown, a version of English pastoral fuelled the Campaign for Nuclear Disarmament from the late 1950s, not least in its style of protest, with walks between London and Aldermaston conducted in an atmosphere of pilgrimage.[44]

One of CND's leading socialists, historian E. P. Thompson, would go on to deploy a language of vernacular Englishness in theoretical argument in his 1965 essay 'The Peculiarities of the English', setting up an English historical materialism against abstract, continental theory. Thompson reflected upon the appointment of Perry Anderson to the editorship of *New Left Review*:

> we discovered that we had appointed a veritable Dr. Beeching of the socialist intelligentsia. All the uneconomic branch-lines and socio-cultural sidings of the New Left which were, in any case, carrying less and less traffic, were abruptly closed down. The main lines of the review underwent an equally ruthless modernization. Old Left steam engines were swept off the tracks; wayside halts ('Commitment,' 'What Next for CND?', 'Women in Love') were boarded up; and the lines were electrified for the speedy traffic from the marxistentialist Left Bank.

Thompson risks labelling himself a Titfield Thunderbolt of the Left, living on 'a branch-line which, after rigorous intellectual costing, had been found uneconomic'.[45] Thompson may be far from Hoskins in politics, but as in Hoskins's Rutland abstraction appears as un-English distraction from a rich material palimpsest. Such examples begin to indicate a broader field of landscape and Englishness, extending beyond specific commentary on buildings and fields. This is not the place to write the cultural history of Englishness in the post-war era, but some general realignments can be noted. As Raphael Samuel's essays on 'Retrofitting' and 'Retrochic' have shown, during the 1950s, 1960s and 1970s the everyday environment shifts, indoors and out, from a modernist ethos of clean design to a style of life picking and choosing from the past, a new temporality of everyday living. Rational interiors retreat, neo-vernacular moves in. Goodbye to the drip-dry, non-iron Terylene shirt and the geometric, tufted, nylon carpet, hello to the trad. shag pile and bean bag.[46] New pop cultures generate versions of Englishness to complement, attack or parody those of more traditional cultural commentators, whether through urban social realism, camp country-house indulgence or counter-cultural pastorals.[47] Connections are there to be made between, say, Alan Sillitoe's *Saturday Night and Sunday Morning* and contemporary planning visions of the city,[48] or between John Betjeman's jolly-but-sad heritage laments and the 1968 Kinks LP *The Kinks Are The Village Green Preservation Society*: 'We are the Office Block Persecution Affinity / God save little shops, china cups and virginity.' During the late 1960s and 1970s a radical environmentalism evolves in part through a self-made landscape of free festivals, Albion Fairs and rediscovered ley lines, restyled from Alfred Watkins's practical trackway system into lines of earth energy.[49] If the DoE's 1972 *Human Habitat* report could suggest that modernity remained manageable, its cover image per-haps belonged more to this self-styled alternative vision of the land, with nature redirected away from national scientific conservancy into a space of holistic and often mystical understanding.

An emerging Green Englishness connected to a revitalization of movements for organic farming. From the 1963 publication of Rachel Carson's *Silent Spring*,[50] documenting the effects of pesti-cides and herbicides on wildlife, agriculture is restyled as an enemy of landscape and nature. The farmer passes from landscape guardian to being, in the title of Marion Shoard's influential 1980 book, the chief agent in *The Theft of the Countryside*. The cultural significance of this break in association of productive land use and cultural value cannot be overstated. Shoard opened her account by stating:

> England's countryside is not only one of the great treasures of the earth; it is also a vital part of our national identity . . . Although few people realize it, the English landscape is under sentence of death . . . The executioner is not the industrialist or the property speculator . . . Instead it is the figure traditionally viewed as the custodian of the rural scene – the farmer.[51]

In the same year Richard Mabey's pioneering discussion of cultures of nature, *The Common Ground*, also detected new lines of conflict, a landscape other than 'the green fields of St George's England versus the dragons of Mammon and industry'. The enemy was now within: 'We were not prepared for this.'[52] Earlier images of planner-preservationism, of saints patriotically defending landscapes, are recycled in revised form. And as modern farming becomes a dragon, so organicism returns with a public impact which is much more significant than that in the 1930s and 1940s; recent years have seen the republication of elements of organicist literature from the earlier era.[53] Some interwar organicists lived to see the revival of organic thinking. In 1968 Rolf Gardiner, still at Springhead and still farming organically, spoke in Cerne Abbas church on 'Harvest Thanksgiving', and looked forward to 'the Postmodern age, which will be different, and based on laws of true sanity and thrift', the 'Aquarian or post-modern Age of man the gardener and husbandman'.[54] This may be one of the earlier and lesser-known definitions of post-modernism, but whether or not we accept Gardiner as a post-modern theorist this organicist vision of landscape and Englishness may well be more recognizable to many today than the planner-preservationist belief in the capacity of public authority to generate a modern Englishness. As the status of Nature and the distinction of organism and mechanism, human and machine, becomes ever less certain,[55] organicist thinking gains popular appeal by offering a solid, natural, moral ground. What is needed, though, is perhaps less an appeal to a foundational Nature than a recognition, as indeed Mabey suggested in *The Common Ground*, that what it is to be natural has always been a matter of culture, just as cultures have always been constituted through non-human objects, organic or inorganic. As argued in the Introduction to this book, landscape allows an analytical movement across such a reconstituted field, and it is hoped that the discussion of organicist material in earlier chapters will have shown the cultural complexity of a movement claiming affinity with natural order. It turns out that far from being a simple ground of value, the category of Nature can be complex, unstable, even transgressive of its supposed boundaries, as befits what Raymond Williams termed 'the most complex word in the language'.[56] As Richard White puts it in his discussion of attempts by environmental historians to appeal to a stable Nature, 'Historians thought ecology was the rock upon which they could build environmental history; it turned out to be a swamp.'[57] Nature as a category tends towards its own deconstruction.

It remains the case, though, that a concern for wholefood, folk culture and the mutual constitution of living organisms through organic cycles is perhaps more familiar today than a faith in the capacity of the state to generate a modern and beautiful landscape. As this book was being completed, however, visions of a new Englishness and geographies of the reconstruction became somewhat less distant. The occasional gestures of the Major Conservative government towards a selectively quoted Orwellian village and suburban Englishness were buried under the landslide of a new/New Labour administration, elected in part through the votes of suburb and village. If the new government still seemed to associate the modern with the values of the market, there was at least the odd reference in some quarters to the virtues of the 1945 programme, if not in terms of public ownership then in a sense that there might be some value in asserting public authority over private action. A language of community and citizenship mixing a Labour and Liberal heritage became central to a sometimes moralistic argument on the relations between individual and society, government and people. One could again imagine the philosophy of, say, the Council for Visual Education registering with government: teach children civics, nurture public spaces, promote modern design. While, however, a re-invigorated social democratic politics may seek to reconstitute public culture, the extent to which this is to work through a sense of nationhood is unclear. Herbert Morrison's grandson may be behind the year 2000 successor to the 1951 South Bank Exhibition, but many of the debates concerning what exactly should be experienced under the Millennium Dome relate to a quite proper confusion over whether this is to be a specifically national event and, if it is, what exactly that nation is, whether styled as British or English. The language of globalization tugs the argument in one way, suggesting that the nation-state might be a redundant political and cultural unit, while in another direction the clear alignment of nationhood and public culture in Scotland and to a lesser degree Wales questions the value of making an exhibition of a British nation in London. To say nothing of a rumbling English regionalism manifested primarily in terms of economic strategy but with varying degrees of cultural articulation across the country.[58] Such arguments will not be resolved through one exhibition, although that event will certainly serve as a refracting device for national definitions. Formulations of Britishness and Englishness are, however, perhaps more likely to be reshaped through the actions of a Scottish Parliament or a Welsh Assembly than a passing millennial show.

If the significance and nature of the national scale is a matter for debate, it remains the case that the material considered in this book provides a reference point for arguments over the built and non-built environment. The attempt to renew a social-democratic discourse of governance effectively reopens many of the landscapes considered in earlier chapters. The terms of debate regarding who has the authority to judge the future of landscape shift as a culture of individual entrepreneurial rights is challenged, however tentatively. Controversies over house building in the Green Belt recall the New Town arguments of reconstruction, with the party political battle more acute given the new electoral geography of small town and rural England after 1997. One should perhaps, though, be more cautious in tracing parallels between then and now in relation to landscape and citizenship. The countryside may still be upheld as a symbol of national identity, but does it follow that environmental practices signify national citizenship? Open-air movements may prosper and birdwatching thrive, and both may be bound up with moral geographies of personal, local and even global improvement, but such activities no longer operate within a moral geography of nation and state whereby citizen and country are to progress for mutual improvement. Different scales of local and global value pertain, and it remains to be seen whether it is possible or desirable for landscape and Englishness to once more come into alignment through the body of the citizen.

REFERENCES

Passport to Plenty: Preface to the 2016 Edition

1 Tom Nairn, *The Break-Up of Britain* (London, 1977), chapter 6: 'English Nationalism: The Case of Enoch Powell'. Bill Schwarz takes Powell's 1968 Wolverhampton 'rivers of blood' speech as the starting point for *The White Man's World* (Oxford, 2011), the first volume of his *Memories of Empire* trilogy exploring 'the fate of England as Greater Britain rose and fell', p. 32. Powell serves to focus Schwarz's argument on Englishness, whiteness and the end of empire: 'At the very moment of decolonization, a language of racial whiteness assumed a new prominence *at home*', p. 12. See also Wendy Webster, *Englishness and Empire, 1939–1965* (Oxford, 2005). On Englishness and postcolonial migrant identities see Divya Tolia-Kelly, *Landscape, Race and Memory: Material Ecologies of Citizenship* (Farnham, 2010).

2 Frank Cottrell Boyce, 'Foreword', in Humphrey Jennings, *Pandaemonium, 1660–1886: The Coming of the Machine as Seen by Contemporary Observers* (London, 2012), p. viii. *Pandaemonium* was first published in 1985. *The Silent Village* (1943) was the story of a Nazi massacre of Czech villagers, filmed in South Wales. On Jennings (1907–1950) and the documentary film movement (and including a chapter by Wendy Webster on *The Silent Village*) see Scott Anthony and James Mansell, eds, *The Projection of Britain: A History of the GPO Film Unit* (London, 2011).

3 'Icons of England' was removed from government websites after the 2010 general election, which returned a Conservative/Liberal Democrat coalition; a seemingly dormant website is maintained at www.icons.org.uk.

4 Jeremy Paxman, *The English* (London, 1999); Robert Colls, *The Identity of England* (Oxford, 2002); Krishan Kumar, *The Making of English National Identity* (Cambridge, 2003); Andy Medhurst, *A National Joke: Popular Comedy and English Cultural Identities* (Abingdon, 2007).

5 Patrick Wright, *On Living in an Old Country* (Oxford, 2009); Patrick Wright, *A Journey through Ruins* (Oxford, 2009); Robert Colls and Philip Dodd, eds, *Englishness: Politics and Culture, 1880–1920* (London, 2014).

6 Patrick Keiller, *The View from the Train: Cities and Other Landscapes* (London, 2013),

pp. 7–8. See also Keiller's book, linked with a 2012 installation at Tate Britain on 'The Robinson Institute', *The Possibility of Life's Survival on the Planet* (London, 2012).

7   David Matless, 'The Predicament of Englishness', *Scottish Geographical Journal*, CXVI (2000), pp. 79–86.

8   John Fowles, 'On Being English But Not Being British', in *Wormholes: Essays and Occasional Writings* (London, 1998), pp. 79–88.

9   Paxman, *The English*, pp. 265–6.

10 Edward Carpenter, *Towards Democracy* (London, 1905), pp. 54–8.

11 Another recent analysis of landscape, Englishness and the modern is given by Alexandra Harris in *Romantic Moderns: English Writers, Artists and the Imagination from Virginia Woolf to John Piper* (London, 2010). See also the pioneering study of landscape and modernity on England's first motorway by Peter Merriman, *Driving Spaces: A Cultural-historical Geography of England's MI Motorway* (Oxford, 2007).

12 Andrew Saint, *A Change of Heart: English Architecture since the War, a Policy for Protection* (London, 1992); see also David Matless, Brian Short and David Gilbert, 'Emblematic Landscapes of the British Modern', in David Gilbert, David Matless and Brian Short, eds, *Geographies of British Modernity* (Oxford, 2003), pp. 250–57.

13 Andrew Saint, *Towards a Social Architecture: The Role of School Building in Post-War England* (London, 1987).

14 Nigel Whiteley, 'Modern Architecture, Heritage and Englishness', *Architectural History*, 38 (1995), pp. 220–37, quotation p. 220.

15 Bridget Cherry, 'The "Pevsner 50": Nikolaus Pevsner and the Listing of Modern Buildings', *Transactions of the Ancient Monuments Society*, 46 (2002), pp. 97–110; Bridget Cherry and Simon Bradley, eds, *The Buildings of England: A Celebration* (London, 2001). On Pevsner's life and work see Susie Harries, *Nikolaus Pevsner: The Life* (London, 2011).

16 Nikolaus Pevsner, *The Leaves of Southwell* (Harmondsworth, 1945). David Matless, 'Topographic Culture: Nikolaus Pevsner and the Buildings of England', *History Workshop Journal*, LIV (2002), pp. 73–99.

17 From notes on a talk given by George Shaw at Nottingham Trent University, 19 November 2010. George Shaw, *The Sly and Unseen Day* (Gateshead, 2011), the catalogue of a show at the Baltic gallery, includes an essay by Michael Bracewell, terming Shaw's art 'a sustained enquiry into the nature of time, place and memory', p. 9. Bracewell is notable for commentary on pop culture and Englishness, see *England is Mine: Pop Life in Albion from Wilde to Goldie* (London, 1997). Georges Perec, *Species of Spaces and Other Pieces* (London, 1997).

18 Belbury Poly, *The Owl's Map* (2006, GBX007 CD; www.ghostbox.co.uk)

19 July Skies, *The Weather Clock* (2008, MMM027 CD); *The Weather Clock (EP)* (2008, MMM027L CD); www.julyskies.com/wordpress2.

20 British Sea Power, *Childhood Memories* (2002, RTRADESCD069 CD); *The Decline of British Sea Power* (2003, RTRADECD090 CD). 'The Land Beyond' appears on the album *Open Season* (2005, RTRADCD200 CD). Penny Woolcock, *From the Sea to the*

Land Beyond (2012, DVD BFIVD967). John Betjeman's 1970s LPS *Betjeman's Banana Blush* (1974, VCCCD19), *Late Flowering Love* (1974, VCCCD21) and *Sir John Betjeman's Britain* (1977, VCCCD20) appeared on the Charisma label, alongside another variety of charismatic spoken-word Englishness, Vivian Stanshall's *Sir Henry at Rawlinson End* (1978, VCCCD18). A recent, caustically absurd musical counter-history of England and Ireland is given by Cathal Coughlan, Luke Haines and Andrew Mueller in *The North Sea Scrolls* (2012, FPCD032). Hear also the shuffle of Englishness, land and war in P. J. Harvey, *Let England Shake* (2010, LC00407).

21 John Lowerson, 'The Mystical Geography of the English', in Brian Short, ed., *The English Rural Community* (Cambridge, 1992), pp. 152–74; David Matless, 'A Geography of Ghosts: The Spectral Landscapes of Mary Butts', *Cultural Geographies*, 15 (2008), pp. 335–58. The cultures of archaeology are the subject of Kitty Hauser's studies, *Shadow Sites: Photography, Archaeology, and the British Landscape, 1927–1955* (Oxford, 2007) and *Bloody Old Britain: O. G. S. Crawford and the Archaeology of Modern Life* (London, 2008). See also Adam Stout, *Creating Prehistory: Druids, Ley Hunters and Archaeologists in Pre-War Britain* (Oxford, 2008).

22 Rob Young, *Electric Eden: Unearthing Britain's Visionary Music* (London, 2010).

23 'The Full English: Unlocking Hidden Treasures of England's Cultural Heritage', online at www.efdss.org/efdss-the-full-english.

24 Laura Cannell, *Quick Sparrows Over the Black Earth* (2014, BRAWL008 CD). Alasdair Roberts has issued several albums of traditional and self-penned songs since 2001, including *Alasdair Roberts* (2015, DC613 CD) and *Too Long in This Condition* (2010, DC421 CD).

25 Anthony Newley, 'Strawberry Fair', *The Decca Years, 1959–1964* (2000, 466 918-2 CD). *The Strange World of Gurney Slade* appeared on Network DVD in 2011 (VFD54035). In 1960 Newley was at the height of his fame as singer and stage and screen actor; Garth Bardsley, *Stop the World: The Biography of Anthony Newley* (London, 2010).

26 Robert Macfarlane, 'Glimpses and Tremors', *The Guardian*, 11 April 2015; Jez Butterworth, *Jerusalem* (London, 2009).

27 Richard Mabey, *The Common Ground* (London, 1980), p. 27.

28 Sue Clifford and Angela King, *England in Particular* (London, 2006); David Crouch and David Matless, 'Refiguring Geography: Parish Maps of Common Ground', *Transactions of the Institute of British Geographers*, XXI (1996), pp. 236–55; Richard Mabey, *Flora Britannica* (London, 1996). Other key Mabey works include *Food for Free* (London, 1972), *The Unofficial Countryside* (London, 1973), *Gilbert White* (London, 1986), *Nature Cure* (London, 2005).

29 Peter Hamilton, *An English Eye: The Photographs of James Ravilious* (Oxford, 2007, first published 1998); the book has a foreword by Alan Bennett. Ravilious was the son of the painter Eric Ravilious.

30 Philip Conford, *The Origins of the Organic Movement* (Edinburgh, 2001); Philip Conford, *The Development of the Organic Network: Linking People and Themes, 1945–95* (Edinburgh, 2011).

31 Paul Kingsnorth, *Real England* (London, 2008), p. 285.

32 Paul Kingsnorth, *The Wake* (London, 2014).

33 Paul Kingsnorth, 'Rescuing the English', *The Guardian*, 14 March 2015.

34 Helen Macdonald, *H is for Hawk* (London, 2014); Robert Macfarlane, *The Wild Places* (London, 2007); Mark Cocker, *Claxton: Field Notes from a Small Planet* (London, 2014); Mark Cocker and Richard Mabey, *Birds Britannica* (London, 2005); David Matless, 'Nature Voices', *Journal of Historical Geography*, xxxv (2009), pp. 178–88.

35 Mark Cocker, *Crow Country* (London, 2007), focuses on rook-life in the Yare Valley; Tim Dee, *Four Fields* (London, 2013) has Fenland fields as a running thread.

36 Jason Orton and Ken Worpole, *The New English Landscape* (London, 2013), p. 10; Nick Papadimitriou, *Scarp* (London, 2012). Regional cultural landscape is the focus of David Matless, *In the Nature of Landscape: Cultural Geography on the Norfolk Broads* (Oxford, 2014); David Matless, *The Regional Book* (Axminster, 2015).

37 Seamus Heaney, 'Englands of the Mind', in *Finders Keepers: Selected Prose, 1971–2011*, pp. 77–95, quotation p. 95. The collection also includes 'Through-other Places, Through-other Times: The Irish Poet and Britain', pp. 364–82, where Heaney reflects on his inclusion in the 1982 *Penguin Book of Contemporary British Poetry*, and his 1983 response of 'An Open Letter', containing a phase alluded to earlier in this preface: 'be advised, / My passport's green. / No glass of ours was ever raised to toast *The Queen*', p. 370.

38 Nairn, *Break-Up of Britain*, p. 259.

39 Alasdair Gray, *Unlikely Stories, Mostly* (London, 1984). Gray's slogan paraphrased Canadian poet Dennis Lee. Gray later reflected: 'the only people who think their nation can only be made worse, not better, are likely to be very rich'; Alasdair Gray, 'Work As If You Live in the Early Days of a Better Nation', *The Herald*, 5 May 2007.

Introduction: Versions of Landscape and Englishness

1 M. Foucault, 'Nietzsche, Genealogy, History', in P. Rainbow, ed., *The Foucault Reader* (Harmondsworth, 1986), pp. 76–100, p. 82.

2 H. V. Morton, *In Search of England* (London, 1927), p. 231.

3 *Broadland by Car* (Norwich, Jarrold White Horse Guide, n. d.), p. 25.

4 Broads Authority, *The Broads . . . Last Enchanted Land* (Norwich, Broads Authority leaflet, *c.* 1989); my emphases.

5 Broads Authority, *No Easy Answers: Draft Broads Plan 1993* (Norwich, 1993), p. 107.

6 David Matless, 'Moral Geography in Broadland', *Ecumene*, 1 (1994), pp. 127–56; J. Taylor, A *Dream of England: Landscape, Photography and the Tourist's Imagination* (Manchester, 1994), pp. 90–119; M. Ewans, *The Battle for the Broads* (Lavenham, 1992).

7 The Broads Conference, *Norfolk and Suffolk Broads: Report on the Preservation and Control of the Broads Area* (Norwich, 1947), p. 5; also see John Arrow, 'The Broads as

a National Park', *Architectural Review*, CVI (1949), pp. 86–100; Ewans, *op. cit.*, pp. 99 and 185 takes a similar line.

8   W.J.T. Mitchell, ed., *Landscape and Power* (Chicago, 1994), p. 1; this argument is critically discussed in the geographer Don Mitchell's fine book *The Lie of the Land: Migrant Workers and the California Landscape*, which addresses arguments over the definition of landscape at length, touching on a similar body of work to that addressed here. In working out its 'labour theory of landscape', though, the book tends to reinforce a distinction of material struggle and aesthetic spectacle. My argument would not be against the importance of the former, or against the sense that beauty has often been deployed to place oppression out of sight; but I would be concerned that making such a distinction a general principle of analysis risks labelling the material world as a site devoid of imagination. Mitchell takes as his model the work of Carey McWilliams, who crops up in this book in a somewhat surprising context in Chapter Three below.

9   Stephen Daniels, 'Marxism, Culture, and the Duplicity of Landscape', in R. Peet and N. Thrift, eds, *New Models in Geography*, vol. II (London, 1989), pp. 196–220, qu. p. 197. 'We should beware of attempts to define landscape, to resolve its contradictions; rather we should abide in its duplicity', *ibid.* p. 218. For a contrasting view see Don Mitchell, *op. cit.*, p. 2: 'The more the word landscape is used, the greater its ambiguity. And the greater its ambiguity, the better it functions to naturalize power.' This, of course, begs the question as to the model of power used; my own work is informed by a Foucauldian sense of power as productive and not to be equated with domination; see David Matless, 'An Occasion for Geography: Landscape, Representation and Foucault's Corpus', *Environment and Planning D: Society and Space*, X (1992), pp. 41–56. On landscape see also B. Bender, ed., *Landscape: Politics and Perspectives* (Oxford, 1993); S. Daniels, *Fields of Vision: Landscape Imagery and National Identity in England and the United States* (Cambridge, 1993); D. Cosgrove and S. Daniels, eds, *The Iconography of Landscape* (Cambridge, 1988); D. Cosgrove, *The Palladian Landscape: Geographical Change and its Cultural Representations in Sixteenth Century Italy* (Leicester, 1993); E. Hirsch and M. O'Hanlon, eds, *The Anthropology of Landscape: Perspectives on Place and Space* (Oxford, 1995); S. Schama, *Landscape and Memory* (London, 1995).

10 B. Latour, *We Have Never Been Modern* (London, 1993), trans. Catherine Porter, pp. 5–6; see also the discussions in M. Serres and B. Latour, *Conversations on Science, Culture, and Time* (Ann Arbor, MI, 1995). A historical materialist formulation of relational thinking in terms of nature, culture and space is found in D. Harvey, *Justice, Nature and the Geography of Difference* (Oxford, 1996). Don Mitchell, *op. cit.*, p. 33, also takes landscape as a Latourian quasi-object, but in the sense of it being a material form which represents social and environmental relations to us in an 'obfuscatory' way. On the development of such themes in cultural geography see David Matless, 'New Material? Work in Cultural and Social Geography, 1995', *Progress in Human Geography*, XX (1996), pp. 379–91, and David Matless, 'The Geographical Self, the Nature of the Social and Geoaesthetics: Work in Social and

Cultural Geography, 1996', *Progress in Human Geography*, XXI (1997), pp. 393–405.

11 J. Hawkes and J. Hawkes, *The Spotters Book of Broads Hire Cruisers* (New Radnor, 1995).

12 R. Samuel, *Theatres of Memory* (London, 1994); and see my review of Samuel's book in *Transactions of the Institute of British Geographers*, XXI (1996), pp. 711–13.

13 A. Randall and R. Seaton, *George Formby* (London, 1974), p. 151.

14 *Eastern Evening News*, 10 June 1991.

15 On Englishness in the late Victorian and Edwardian period see R. Colls and P. Dodd, eds, *Englishness: Politics and Culture, 1880–1920* (London, 1986).

16 Matless, 'Geographical Self', *op. cit.*; for an excellent account of genealogies of subjectification which accords with the Foucauldian approach taken here, see Nikolas Rose, 'Identity, Genealogy, History', in S. Hall and P. Du Gay, eds, *Questions of Cultural Identity* (London, 1996), pp. 128–50. Rose emphasizes a 'spatialization of being', and the study of the 'repertoires of conduct' activated by particular spaces, pp. 143–4.

17 Felix Driver, 'Moral Geographies: Social Science and the Urban Environment in Mid-Nineteenth Century England', *Transactions of the Institute of British Geographers*, XIII (1988), pp. 275–87; Matless, 'Moral Geography in Broadland', *op. cit.*; David Matless, 'Visual Culture and Geographical Citizenship: England in the 1940s', *Journal of Historical Geography*, XXII (1996), pp. 424–39.

18 An interesting discussion of material relating to the themes of Part II and chapter 2 of this book can be found in Frank Trentmann, 'Civilization and its Discontents: English Neo-Romanticism and the Transformation of Anti-Modernism in Twentieth-Century Western Culture', *Journal of Contemporary History*, XXIX (1994), pp. 583–625. Trentmann's essay provides a concise introduction to many of these issues, and I would generally follow his analysis, although he plays down the modernity of the open-air material and misses the distinction of citizen and anti-citizen made within the movement. The key difference in terms of this book's overall argument is that the connection to modern visions of a planned landscape, and thus to a coherent modern vision of Englishness, is not made.

19 Daniels, *Fields of Vision, op. cit.*; A. Light, *Forever England: Femininity, Literature and Conservatism Between the Wars* (London, 1991); Taylor, *Dream of England, op. cit.*; P. Mandler, *The Fall and Rise of the Stately Home* (London, 1997); also D. Gervais, *Literary Englands* (Cambridge, 1993) contains useful discussions of Orwell, Waugh, Eliot, Leavis, Larkin, Betjeman and others.

20 The best discussion of heritage remains P. Wright, *On Living in an Old Country: The National Past in Contemporary Britain* (London, 1985); also P. Wright, *A Journey Through Ruins* (London, 1991); P. Wright, *The Village that Died for England: The Strange Story of Tyneham* (London, 1995); Samuel, *Theatres, op. cit.* For an equation of heritage and decline see R. Hewison, *The Heritage Industry* (London, 1987), and for an effective response to Hewison's polemic Patrick Wright and Tim Putnam, 'Sneering at the Theme Parks: An Encounter with the Heritage Industry', *Block*, XV (1989), pp. 45–55. Englishness is presented as a cultural preoccupation restrictive

of a Thatcherite 'industrial spirit' in the work of Corelli Barnett and Martin Wiener; see M. Wiener, *English Culture and the Decline of the Industrial Spirit, 1850–1980* (Cambridge, 1981); C. Barnett, *The Collapse of British Power* (London, 1972); C. Barnett, *The Lost Victory: British Dreams, British Realities* (London, 1995). Wiener and Barnett argue for a persistence of aristocratic values at the core of the British state; while such arguments have much force they tend effectively to blur distinctions between very different forms of political Englishness, and to hold out an ideal type of liberal ideology as an implied alternative, one which has difficulty coming to terms with the prominence of patriotism and nationalism in the Thatcherite project of the 1980s and beyond. For a very different High Tory vision of Conservative Englishness see N. Everitt, *The Tory View of Landscape* (London, 1994). For an argument which essentially inverts Wiener and Barnett, see D. Edgerton, *England and the Aeroplane: An Essay on a Militant and Technological Nation* (London, 1991).

21 Work by Patrick Wright, Raphael Samuel and Alison Light cuts across some of these assumptions, but the kind of preservationist modernity examined in this book has not been given detailed consideration.

22 Alex Potts, 'Constable Country Between the Wars', in R. Samuel, ed., *Patriotism*, vol. 1 (London, 1989), pp. 160–86.

23 David Matless, 'Doing the English Village, 1945–90: An Essay in Imaginative Geography', in P. Cloke, M. Doel, D. Matless, M. Phillips and N. Thrift, *Writing the Rural: Five Cultural Geographies* (London, 1994), pp. 7–88.

24 P. Bishop, *An Archetypal Constable: National Identity and the Geography of Nostalgia* (London, 1995); Light, *op. cit.*

25 For essays on national identity, English, British or otherwise, in this vein, see H. Bhabha, ed., *Nation and Narration* (London, 1990); E. Carter, J. Donald and J. Squires, eds, *Space and Place: Theories of Identity and Location* (London, 1993), R. Samuel, ed., *Patriotism*, 3 vols (London, 1989); 1. Chambers, *Border Dialogues: Journeys in Postmodernity* (London, 1990), pp. 14–50.

26 D. Horne, *God is an Englishman* (Harmondsworth, 1969), p. 22; Wiener, *op. cit.*, pp. 40–2.

27 Alun Howkins, 'The Discovery of Rural England', in Colls and Dodd, *Englishness*, *op. cit.*, pp. 62–88.

28 On such distinctions, see S. Smiles, *The Image of Antiquity: Ancient Britain and the Romantic Imagination* (New Haven, 1994).

29 Denis Cosgrove, Barbara Roscoe and Simon Rycroft, 'Landscape and Identity at Ladybower Reservoir and Rutland Water', *Transactions of the Institute of British Geographers*, XXI (1996), pp. 534–51.

30 H. V. Morton, *In the Steps of St Paul* (London, 1936), p. 173. Morton's *In Search of Ireland* (London, 1930) suggested as recommended reading accounts of the victory of Sinn Fein and the fight for Irish independence. On relations of Englishness and Ireland in the period leading up to independence and just after, see D. G. Boyce, 'The Marginal Britons: The Irish', in Coils and Dodd, *Englishness*, *op. cit.*, pp. 230–53.

31 S. Gikandi, *Maps of Englishness: Writing Identity in the Culture of Colonialism* (New York, 1996), p. xii.

32 See especially Gilroy's essays 'The Peculiarities of the Black English' and 'Art of Darkness: Black Art and the Problem of Belonging to England', in *Small Acts: Thoughts on the Politics of Black Cultures* (London, 1993); also P. Gilroy, *'There Ain't No Black in the Union Jack': The Cultural Politics of Race and Nation* (London, 1987). On the photography of Ingrid Pollard, see Taylor, *Dream of England, op. cit.*; Phil Kinsman, 'Landscape, Race and National Identity: The Photography of Ingrid Pollard', *Area*, XXVII (1995), pp. 300–10. On the work of the Black Environment Network and issues of landscape and ethnicity, see Julian Agyeman and Rachel Spooner, 'Ethnicity and the Rural Environment', in P. Cloke and J. Little, eds, *Contested Countryside Cultures* (London, 1997), pp. 197–217.

33 Foucault, 'Nietzsche, Genealogy, History', p. 88: 'History becomes "effective" to the degree that it introduces discontinuity into our very being . . . "Effective" history deprives the self of the reassuring stability of life and nature.'

34 Michel Foucault, 'Truth and Power', in *The Foucault Reader, op. cit.*, pp. 51–75, p. 59.

35 There is an enormous literature on Foucault. For good general introductions, including discussions of genealogy, see H. Dreyfus and P. Rabinow, *Michel Foucault: Beyond Structuralism and Hermeneutics* (Brighton, 1982); L. McNay, *Foucault: A Critical Introduction* (Cambridge, 1994).

36 Foucault, 'Nietzsche, Genealogy, History', p. 76.

37 *Ibid.*, p. 94.

38 See also David Matless, 'Effects of History', *Transactions of the Institute of British Geographers*, XX (1995), pp. 405–10.

1 *Ordering England*

1 C. Williams-Ellis, *England and the Octopus* (London, 1928); the book was republished by the CPRE in December 1996.

2 P. Fussell, *The Great War and Modern Memory* (Oxford, 1975); Howkins, 'Discovery of Rural England', *op. cit.*

3 Clough Williams-Ellis, 'Introduction', in H. H. Peach and N. Carrington, eds, *The Face of the Land* (London, 1930), pp. 11–24, qu. p. 11.

4 For earlier versions of these arguments, see David Matless, 'Ages of English Design: Preservation, Modernism and Tales of Their History, 1926–1939', *Journal of Design History*, III (1990), pp. 203–12; David Matless, 'Definitions of England, 1928–89: Preservation, Modernism and the Nature of the Nation', *Built Environment*, XVI (1990), pp. 179–91; David Matless, 'Appropriate Geography: Patrick Abercrombie and the Energy of the World', *Journal of Design History*, VI (1993), pp. 167–78; for a reading of similar material which misses the modern element, see D. N. Jeans, 'Planning and the Myth of the English Countryside, in the Interwar Period', *Rural History*, I (1990), pp. 249–64.

5 CPRE *Annual Report* (London, 1928), p. 13.

6 P. Kirkham, *Harry Peach, Dryad and the DIA* (London, 1986); Peach and Carrington, *Face of the Land, op. cit.*; the DIA's work is praised in F. R. Leavis and D. Thompson, *Culture and Environment: The Training of Critical Awareness* (London 1933), pp. 135–6.

7 A. Bertram, *Design* (London, 1938), p. 93.

8 J. M. Keynes, 'Art and the State', in C. Williams-Ellis, ed., *Britain and the Beast* (London, 1937), pp. 1–7, qu. p. 1.

9 Williams-Ellis, in *The Face of the Land, op. cit.*, pp. 15–16.

10 Williams-Ellis, 'Our Physical Environment', in C.E.M. Joad, ed., *Manifesto*, (London, 1934), p. 216.

11 Williams-Ellis, in *The Face of the Land, op. cit.*, pp. 15–17.

12 T. Sharp, *Town and Countryside* (London, 1932), p. 221; see also Vaughan Cornish, 'The Scenic Amenity of Great Britain', *Geography*, XIX (1934), pp. 195–202.

13 P. Abercrombie, *Town and Country Planning* (London, 1933), pp. 199–200. See also Cornish's own landholding efforts, described in V. Cornish, *The Scenery of Sidmouth* (Cambridge, 1940).

14 P. Abercrombie, 'The English Countryside', in W. A. Robson, ed., *The Political Quarterly in the Thirties* (London, 1971), pp. 36–52, qu. pp. 41–2.

15 John Moore, 'The Cotswolds', in *Britain and the Beast, op. cit.*, pp. 86–90, qu. p. 89.

16 Williams-Ellis, in *The Face of the Land, op. cit.*, p. 16.

17 V. Cornish, *The Scenery of England* (London, 1932), p. 22.

18 Williams-Ellis, *Octopus, op. cit.*, p. 108.

19 V. Cornish, *National Parks, and the Heritage of Scenery* (London, 1930), p. 4; Thomas Sharp, 'The North-East: Hills and Hells', in *Britain and the Beast, op. cit.*, pp. 141–59, qu. p. 159.

20 Abercrombie, 'The English Countryside', *op. cit.*, p. 44; G. M. Trevelyan, *Must England's Beauty Perish?* (London, 1929).

21 Williams-Ellis, *Octopus, op. cit.*, p. 108; Williams-Ellis had modified this view by the time he produced *On Trust for the Nation*, a tribute to the Trust's work in 1947 (London).

22 Martin Auster, 'Construction of the Planning Idea: Britain, the USA and Australia 1929–1939', *Planning Perspectives*, IV, pp. 207–23; C. Williams-Ellis, *Architect Errant* (London, 1971).

23 S. Baldwin, *On England* (London, 1926), pp. 5–6.

24 Bill Schwarz, 'The Language of Constitutionalism: Baldwinite Conservatism', in *Formations of Nation and People* (London, 1984), pp. 1–18.

25 Cornish, *National Parks, op. cit.*, p. 9.

26 Sharp, *Town and Countryside, op. cit.*, pp. 217–24.

27 Williams-Ellis, in *The Face of the Land, op. cit.*, p. 20.

28 R. Benewick, *The Fascist Movement in Britain* (London, 1972); L.P. Carpenter, 'Corporatism in Britain', *Journal of Contemporary History*, XI (1976), pp. 3–25; R. Skidelsky, *Politicians and the Slump* (London, 1967).

29 J. Herf, *Reactionary Modernism: Technology, Culture and Politics in Weimar and the Third Reich* (Cambridge, 1984), p. 2.

30 CPRE Archive, Museum of English Rural Life, University of Reading, File 335, letter, G. M. Jack to A. Cleghorn, 30 September 1935.

31 Joad, *Manifesto*, *op. cit.*; R. Wilford, 'The Federation of Progressive Societies and Individuals', *Journal of Contemporary History*, XI (1976), pp. 49–82. Membership never exceeded 600. The Federation's journal *Plan* was edited by Woodcraft Folk leader Leslie Paul.

32 Abercrombie, *Town and Country Planning*, *op. cit.*, p. 18; Abercrombie, 'The English Countryside', *op. cit.*, p. 12.

33 *The Face of the Land*, *op. cit.*, p. 108.

34 O.J.R. Howarth, *The Scenic Heritage of England and Wales* (London, 1937), p. 44; J. Sheail, *Rural Conservation in Interwar Britain* (Oxford, 1981), pp. 16–17.

35 Geoffrey Boumphrey, 'Principles of Town and Country Planning', in *Manifesto*, *op. cit.*, pp. 250–70, qu. pp. 268–9.

36 Sharp, *Town and Countryside*, *op. cit.*, p. 11.

37 Abercrombie, *Town and Country Planning*, *op. cit.*, p. 178; D. Hardy, *From Garden Cities to New Towns* (London, 1991).

38 V. Cornish, *The Preservation of Our Scenery* (Cambridge, 1937), p. 46.

39 Boumphrey, 'Principles', *op. cit.*, p. 266.

40 Sheail, *Rural Conservation*, *op. cit.*, p. 9; P. Hall, *Cities of Tomorrow* (Oxford, 1988), chapter 3.

41 J. Carey, *The Intellectuals and the Masses: Pride and Prejudice among the Literary Intelligentsia, 1880–1939* (London, 1992); V. Cunningham, *British Writers of the Thirties* (Oxford, 1988); A. Light, *Forever England: Femininity, Literature and Conservatism Between the Wars* (London, 1991); P. Oliver, I. Davis and I. Bentley, *Dunroamin: The Suburban Semi and its Enemies* (London, 1981); D. Ryan, *The Ideal Home Through the 20th Century* (London, 1997).

42 John Gloag, 'The Suburban Scene', in *Britain and the Beast*, *op. cit.*, p. 199.

43 Carey, *The Intellectuals*, *op. cit.*, p. 53.

44 Sharp, 'The North-East', *op. cit.*, p. 145.

45 Peach and Carrington, *The Face of the Land*, *op. cit.*, pp. 133–4; on Slough, see Earl of Mayo, S. Adshead and P. Abercrombie's survey for the CPRE on *The Thames Valley* (London, 1929), p. 5.

46 J. Betjeman, 'Slough', in *The Collected Poems* (London, 1958), first published in *Continual Dew* (1937).

47 J. B. Priestley, *English Journey* (London, 1934), p. 401; see also J. B. Priestley, *Our Nation's Heritage* (London, 1939).

48 Light, *Forever England*, *op. cit.*

49 Rod Brookes, '"Everything in the Garden is Lovely": The Representation of National Identity in Sidney Strube's Daily Express Cartoons in the 1930s', *Oxford Art Journal*, XIII (1990), pp. 31–43. Brookes notes of Prime Ministerial radio broadcasts that 'Baldwin's self-presentation as the Little Man was central to this "domesticated" Englishness', p. 32. See also Schwarz, 'Language of Constitutionalism', *op. cit.*, p. 9. On community and domesticity, see L. Davidoff,

J. L'Esperance and H. Newby, 'Landscape with Figures: Home and Community in English Society', in J. Mitchell and A. Oakley, eds, *The Rights and Wrongs of Women* (Harmondsworth, 1976), pp. 139–75.

50 D. H. Lawrence, 'Nottingham and the Mining Countryside', in A.A.H. Inglis, ed., *A Selection from Phoenix* (Harmondsworth, 1971), pp. 103–11, qu. p. 111; T. Sharp, *Town Planning* (Harmondsworth, 1940), pp. 15–16.

51 G. Orwell, *Coming Up For Air* (Harmondsworth, 1962), p. 15 (first published 1939).

52 *Ibid.*, p. 176.

53 *Ibid.*, p. 180.

54 *Ibid.*, p. 192.

55 Morton, *In Search of England*, op. cit., pp. 5–6.

56 Priestley, *Our Nation's Heritage*, op. cit., p. 165; see also C.E.M. Joad, *The Book of Joad* (London, 1935), pp. 201–3; on the Restriction of Ribbon Development Act 1935, see Sheail, *Rural Conservation*, op. cit., pp. 133–6.

57 Abercrombie, *Town and Country Planning*, op. cit., pp. 14–15.

58 Patrick Abercrombie, 'The Many-tentacled Town: The Vision of Emile Verhaeren', *Town Planning Review*, III (1912), pp. 133–49, qu. p. 144; on Abercrombie and Verhaeren, see Matless, 'Appropriate Geography', op. cit. See also Patrick Geddes's citation of Verhaeren in *Cities in Evolution* (London, 1915), p. 26, p. 342.

59 Abercrombie, 'The Many-tentacled Town', op. cit., p. 148.

60 R. G. Stapledon, *The Land: Now and Tomorrow* (London, 1935), p. 11; Williams-Ellis, in *The Face of the Land*, op. cit., p. 12.

61 Geoffrey Boumphrey, 'Shall the Towns Kill or Save the Country?', in *Britain and the Beast*, op. cit., pp. 101–12, qu. p. 103.

62 *Ibid.*, op. cit., p. 104.

63 Matless, 'Definitions of England', op. cit.; J. B. Harley, 'Maps, Knowledge and Power', in D. Cosgrove and S. Daniels, eds, *The Iconography of Landscape* (Cambridge, 1988), pp. 277–312; Cunningham, *British Writers of the Thirties*, op. cit., pp. 192–206; on the air-view in archaeology, see chapter 2 below.

64 Peak District Advisory Panel, *Housing in the Peak* (Sheffield, CPRE, 1934), p. 20.

65 Moore, 'The Cotswolds', op. cit., p. 88.

66 Peach and Carrington, *The Face of the Land*, op. cit., pp. 28–30; Abercrombie, *Town and Country Planning*, op. cit., p. 205.

67 On plotlands, see the excellent study by Denis Hardy and Colin Ward, *Arcadia for All: the Legacy of a Makeshift Landscape* (London, 1984).

68 W. Holtby, *South Riding* (London, 1936), pp. 43–4. Holtby died in 1935; she was an equal rights feminist and ILP supporter, and close friend of Vera Brittain. See V. Brittain, *Testament of Friendship: The Story of Winifred Holtby* (London, 1940; republished by Virago 1980). *South Riding* was a best-seller and filmed twice, first in 1938. Holtby described the novel as about the battles between those who want to plan and those who do not, 'a more profound cleavage than between mere Conservatism and Socialism, to my way of thinking' (Brittain, *Testament*, p. 416). *South Riding* was written in a rented cottage in Withernsea on the Holderness

coast. You can still find shacks in the area, for example at Skipsea, lingering on fast eroding cliffs.

69 Holtby, *op. cit.*, p. 230, p. 357.

70 *Ibid.*, p. 217.

71 *Ibid.*, pp. 114–15.

72 Williams-Ellis, *Octopus*, *op. cit.*, p. 66; also Abercrombie, *Town and Country Planning*, *op. cit.*, p. 23.

73 Abercrombie, *Town and Country Planning*, *op. cit.*, p. 239.

74 Abercrombie, 'The English Countryside', *op. cit.*, p. 37.

75 Hardy and Ward, *op. cit.*, pp. 91–5.

76 Abercrombie, 'The English Countryside', *op. cit.*, p. 37.

77 Thames Valley resident quoted in Hardy and Ward, *op. cit.*, p. 170.

78 Earl of Mayo *et al.*, *op. cit.*, p. 60.

79 Joad, *The Book of Joad*, *op. cit.*, p. 192.

80 Marshall, *op. cit.*, p. 166; Sharp, *Town and Countryside*, *op. cit.*, p. 158.

81 G. Greene, *Brighton Rock* (Harmondsworth, 1943; first published 1938), p. 89; see especially pp. 231–45.

82 Williams-Ellis, *Octopus*, *op. cit.*, pp. 141–2.

83 See also George Barker's poem 'Vision of England "38"', where St George faces a dragon 'astride the South in coils / Of insatiable economic appetite': 'O my green girl given to the rape of the banker, / The careerist politician and the vague thinker'; in G. Barker, *Collected Poems, 1930–1955* (London, 1957), p. 66.

84 Abercrombie, *Town and Country Planning*, *op. cit.*, pp. 178–9.

85 Peach and Carrington, *The Face of the Land*, *op. cit.*, p. 26; Williams-Ellis, in *The Face of the Land*, *op. cit.*, p. 18.

86 P. Abercrombie, *The Preservation of Rural England* (London, 1926), p. 14.

87 Cornish, *National Parks*, *op. cit.*, p. 4.

88 Vaughan Cornish, 'Harmonies of Scenery: An Outline of Aesthetic Geography', *Geography*, XIV (1928), pp. 275–83, pp. 383–94, qu. p. 276.

89 Cornish, *The Scenery of England*, *op. cit.*, p. 76; on the role of settlement geography in the 1930s and 1940s, see chapter 6 below.

90 Peach and Carrington, *Face of the Land*, *op. cit.*, p. 81; see also Abercrombie, *Preservation of Rural England*, *op. cit.*, pp. 5–8, and *England's Green and Pleasant Land* (London, 1925), published anonymously by J. W. Robertson-Scott, who founded and edited *The Countryman* magazine in 1927; extended edition credited to Robertson-Scott published by Penguin in 1947. On the work of RCCS and other groups, see D. Matless, 'Ordering the Land: The "Preservation" of the English Countryside, 1918–1939', unpublished PhD thesis, University of Nottingham, 1990, chapter 6; M. Brasnett, *Voluntary Social Action: A History of the National Council of Social Service, 1919–1969* (London, 1969).

91 M. Kelly, *Village Theatre* (London, 1939), p. 127.

92 A. Howkins, *Reshaping Rural England: A Social History, 1850–1925* (London, 1991); H. Newby, *Country Life: A Social History of Rural England* (London, 1987).

93 F. G. Thomas, *The Changing Village* (London, 1939). Thomas presented RCC work as of variable quality, sometimes radical and challenging, sometimes warranting the charge of 'merely joining forces with the reactionaries in national life', p. 75.

94 Patrick Abercrombie, 'Geography, the Basis of Planning', *Geography*, XXIII (1938), pp. 1–8, qu. p.2.

95 Williams-Ellis, 'Our Physical Environment', *op. cit.*, p. 223.

96 For a summary, see L. D. Stamp, *The Land of Britain: Its Use and Misuse* (London, 1946). On Stamp, see S. Rycroft and D. Cosgrove, 'Mapping the Modern Nation: Dudley Stamp and the Land Utilisation Survey', *History Workshop Journal*, LX (1995), pp. 91–105.

97 Abercrombie, *Town and Country Planning, op. cit.*, p. 179.

98 *Ibid.*, pp. 202–4; also P. Abercrombie, *Country Planning and Landscape Design* (London, 1934), p. 12.

99 Cornish, 'Harmonies of Scenery', *op. cit.*, p. 275; also V. Cornish, *The Poetic Impression of Natural Scenery* (London, 1931); V. Cornish, *Scenery and the Sense of Sight* (Cambridge, 1935); V. Cornish, *The Beauties of Scenery: A Geographical Survey* (London, 1943). On Cornish, see D. Matless, 'Visual Culture and Geographical Citizenship', *Journal of Historical Geography*, XXII (1996), pp. 424–39; D. Matless, 'Nature, the Modern and the Mystic: Tales from Early Twentieth-century Geography', *Transactions of the Institute of British Geographers*, XVI (1991), pp. 272–86; Matless, 'Ordering the Land', *op. cit.*, chapter 1; A. Goudie, 'Vaughan Cornish: Geographer', *Transactions of the Institute of British Geographers*, LV (1972), pp. 1–16. The Institute of Landscape Architects was formed in 1929; see chapter 6 below. Landscape design priniciples are also discussed in W. A. Eden, 'Order in the Countryside', *Town Planning Review*, XIV (1930), pp. 95–103, qu. p. 96.

100 Cornish, *Scenery of England, op. cit.*, p. 7.

101 'The Science of Scenery' (editorial), *Nature*, CXXI (1928), pp. 309–11.

102 Abercrombie, *Preservation of Rural England, op. cit.*, pp. 50–51; on Abercrombie and Feng Shui, see Matless, 'Appropriate Geography', *op. cit.*

103 Abercrombie, *Town and Country Planning, op. cit.*, p. 230.

104 *Ibid.*, pp. 231–2.

105 *Ibid.*, p. 229.

106 Abercrombie, *Preservation of Rural England, op. cit.*, p. 50.

107 Williams-Ellis, *Octopus, op. cit.*, pp. 125–79; Abercrombie, *Town and Country Planning, op. cit.*, pp. 241–48. The CPRE's recent text on *The Cluttered Countryside* (London, 1996), with a related campaign against 'clutter', suggests an almost verbatim revival of this earlier rhetoric, with a concomitant risk for the CPRE of appearing as a petty watchdog body applying a narrow visual language to contemporary landscape.

108 CPRE Archive, Museum of English Rural Life, University of Reading.

109 Peach and Carrington, *Face of the Land, op. cit.*, p. 88.

110 CPRE Sheffield and Peak District Committee, *The Threat to the Peak* (Sheffield, 1931), p. 39.

111 Advertisement for 'Shell and the Countryside' in *Face of the Land, op. cit.*; on Shell, see P. Wright, *On Living in an Old Country* (London, 1985), pp. 56–68.

112 Peach and Carrington, *Face of the Land, op. cit.*, p. 113; on the EMB, see S. Constantine, *Buy and Build: The Advertising Posters of the Empire Marketing Board* (London, 1986).

113 Williams-Ellis, *Octopus, op. cit.*, p. 128.

114 Peach and Carrington, *Face of the Land, op. cit.*, p. 111.

115 Earl of Mayo *et al., op. cit.*, p. 95.

116 H. H. Peach, 'The Advertiser and the Disfigurement of Town and Countryside', *Journal of the Royal Society of Arts*, 20 December 1929, pp. 144–62.

117 Joad, *Book of Joad, op. cit.*, pp. 204–5. On bungalows, see A. D. King, *The Bungalow* (London, 1984), pp. 155–92.

118 L. Dudley Buxton, 'Foreword', in C. Simpson, *Rediscovering England* (London, 1930), p. ix.

119 A. R. Powys, *From the Ground Up* (London, 1937), pp. 95–6.

120 Williams-Ellis, *Octopus, op. cit.*, pp. 174–6.

121 Bertram, *Design, op. cit.*, p. 23.

122 Peach and Carrington, *Face of the Land, op. cit.*, p. 34.

123 Bertram, *Design, op. cit.*, p. 16; A. Bertram, *The House* (London, 1935); O. Lancaster, *Pillar to Post* (London, 1938); O. Lancaster, *Homes Sweet Homes* (London, 1939).

124 Bertram, *Design, op. cit.*, p. 19; also Abercrombie, *Preservation of Rural England, op. cit.*, p. 14; Williams-Ellis, *Octopus, op. cit.*, pp. 131–2.

125 C.E.M. Joad, *A Charter for Ramblers* (London, 1934), pp. 24–5; compare illustration with frontispiece of Hewison, *The Heritage Industry, op. cit.*

126 Peak District Advisory Panel, *op. cit.*, p. 8.

127 Bertram, *Design, op. cit.*, p. 89.

128 Bertram, *Design, op. cit.*, p. 61. A. R. Powys's alignment of 'Tradition and Modernity' could have different implications, presenting bungalows as 'The truly modern domestic architecture of England': 'in the best interests of the countryside, we should cultivate a new kind of pleasure, a pleasure to be had from the seemly assembling into less permanent houses those very machine-made materials which the founders of the Save the Country movement cry down as horrible', *op. cit.*, pp. 80–1.

129 *Ibid.*, p. 112; for the scope of design philosophy, see J. Gloag, ed., *Design in Modern Life* (London, 1934), and see chapter 7 below.

130 Matless, 'Ages of English Design', *op. cit.*; for good general studies, see Gillian Naylor, 'Design and Industry', in B. Ford, ed., *Early 20th Century Britain* (Cambridge, 1992), pp. 254–93; N. Pevsner, *Studies in Art, Architecture and Design*, Vol. 2: *Victorian and After* (London, 1968), pp. 226–41.

131 Kirkham, *Harry Peach, op. cit.*; N. Pevsner, *Pioneers of the Modern Movement* (London, 1936, republished 1960 as *Pioneers of Modern Design*); N. Pevsner, *An Enquiry into Industrial Art in England* (Cambridge, 1937), pp. 159–62 on Peach and the DIA.

132 W. R. Lethaby, *Form in Civilisation* (London, 1957); first published 1922, Mumford provided a foreword to the 1957 edition. Mumford, like Peach, regarded Le Corbusier as an overly academic architect; see Kirkham, *op. cit.*, p. 61.

133 Frank Pick, 'Introduction', in W. Gropius, *The New Architecture and the Bauhaus* (London, 1935), pp. 7–10. Gropius warned against an easy superficial understanding of the new architecture which could follow from 'catch phrases like "functionalism" ... and "fitness for purpose = beauty"' (p. 23). On Pick, see C. Barman, *The Man Who Built London Transport: A Biography of Frank Pick* (Newton Abbot, 1979); Pevsner, *Studies, op. cit.*, pp. 190–209.

134 Peach and Carrington, *op. cit.*, pp. 129–31.

135 B. Luckin, *Questions of Power: Electricity and Environment in Interwar Britain* (Manchester, 1990); also Pyrs Gruffudd, '"Uncivil Engineering": Nature, Nationalism and Hydro-electrics in North Wales', in *Water, Engineering and Landscape*, ed. D. Cosgrove and G. Petts (London, 1990), pp. 159–73.

136 Abercrombie, *Town and Country Planning, op. cit.*, p. 235.

137 Peach and Carrington, *op. cit.*, p. 37.

138 This is a rather different sense of pylon and land to that in Stephen Spender's 1933 poem 'The Pylons', where pylons with their 'quick perspective of the future' run above and detached from an old country. R. Skelton, ed., *Poetry of the Thirties* (Harmondsworth, 1964), pp. 99–100.

139 Daniels, *Fields of Vision, op. cit.*, pp. 220–1.

140 Proceedings of the Countryside and Footpaths Preservation Conference, 12–13 October 1928, CPRE Archive, Museum of English Rural Life, University of Reading, file D 1 22, p. 4; also Trevelyan, *Must England's Beauty Perish?, op. cit.*; G. M. Trevelyan, *The Call and Claims of Natural Beauty* (London, 1931).

141 Sharp, *Town Planning, op. cit.*, pp. 30–1.

142 Gloag, 'The Suburban Scene', *op. cit.*, p. 193.

143 E. H. Fryer, 'Beautiful England as seen by the Motorist on the Road', CPRE Archive, Museum of English Rural Life, University of Reading, file 78; see also Peach and Carrington, *op. cit.*, pp. 54–5.

144 Williams-Ellis, in *The Face of the Land, op. cit.*, pp. 13–15; also Joad, *Charter, op. cit.*, p. 13.

145 Cornish, *National Parks, op. cit.*, p. 91.

146 Williams-Ellis, *Octopus, op. cit.*, p. 162; also G. Boumphrey, *British Roads* (London, 1939), p. 168.

147 Illustrated in *Britain and the Beast, op. cit.*, and Priestley, *Our Nation's Heritage, op. cit.*, p. 166.

148 Boumphrey, *British Roads, op. cit.*, p. 171.

149 *Ibid.*, p. 168.

150 Roads Beautifying Association, *Roadside Planting* (London, 1930), p. 5; also Peach and Carrington, *op. cit.*, pp. 56–8.

151 CPRE Archive, file 241/16.

152 CPRE Archive, file 313. The CPRE had as an affiliated body the Roads of

Remembrance Association, promoting commemorative roadside sculpture.

153 Boumphrey, *British Roads*, *op. cit.*, pp. 174–5.

154 'Roads Supplement', *Architectural Review*, LXXXI (1937), pp. 154–78, qu. p. 169.

155 *Ibid.*, pp. 170–2.

156 Priestley, *English Journey*, *op. cit.*, p. 134.

157 Williams-Ellis, *Octopus*, *op. cit.*, p. 166.

158 Design and Industries Association, *The Village Pump* (London, *c.* 1930), p. 2.

159 CPRE Archive, file 108/15. A competition ran in Oxfordshire in 1932 and 1933. Somerset Rural Community Council published an advisory manual for *Garages and Petrol Stations on Country Roads* (Taunton, 1930).

160 Letter from CPRE Secretary Herbert Griffin to the editor of *The Service Station*, December 1931, CPRE Archive, file 108/15; on thatch and petrol, see also A. R. Powys, *op. cit.*, p. 117.

161 CPRE 1929 Memorandum to the Prime Minister, CPRE Archive, file 237.

162 Trunk Roads Joint Committee, *Report* (London, *CPRE/RBA*, 1937), p. 2; for a parallel argument, see H. Belloc, *The Road* (Manchester, 1923).

163 Boumphrey, *British Roads*, *op. cit.*, p. 156; also Belloc, *op. cit.*, p. 201; Trunk Roads Joint Committee, *op. cit.*, p. 7.

164 *Ibid.*, pp. 151–2; *Architectural Review*, *op. cit.*, p. 155.

165 Boumphrey, *British Roads*, *op. cit.*, p. 180.

166 P. Abercrombie, letter to *The Times*, 15 December 1936.

167 Abercrombie, *Town and Country Planning*, *op. cit.*, p. 180.

168 Boumphrey, *British Roads*, *op. cit.*, p. 55; Trunk Roads Joint Committee, *op. cit.*, p. 2; R.M.C. Anderson, *The Roads of England* (London, 1932), p. 49; Belloc, *op. cit.*, p. 113.

169 A. Watkins, *The Old Straight Track* (London, 1925); Watkins is cited in Boumphrey, *British Roads*, *op. cit.*, and Anderson, *op. cit.*

170 Williams-Ellis, *Octopus*, *op. cit.*, p. 163; also Abercrombie, *Town and Country Planning*, *op. cit.*, p. 145; on U.S. road design, see A. Wilson, *The Culture of Nature* (Oxford, 1992), chapter 1.

171 CPRE Archive, file 241/16. For a critical reading of Moses's later work in New York, see M. Berman, *All that is Solid Melts into Air: The Experience of Modernity* (New York, 1982).

172 Abercrombie, 'The English Countryside', *op. cit.*, p. 38.

173 J. D. Shand, 'The Reichsautobahn: Symbol for the Third Reich', *Journal of Contemporary History*, XIX (1984), pp. 189–200; E. Diemendberg, 'The Will to Motorization: Cinema, Highways and Modernity', *October*, LXXIII (1995), pp. 91–137; W. H. Rollins, 'Whose Landscape? Technology, Fascism and Environmentalism on the National Socialist Autobahn', *Annals of the Association of American Geographers*, LXXXV (1995), pp. 494–520; Rollins rather awkwardly seeks to hold political modernity on the one hand and aesthetics and ecology on the other potentially apart in order to retrospectively identify good 'environmentally friendly' practice.

174 Quoted in Boumphrey, *British Roads*, *op. cit.*, pp. 171–2; and see pp. 176–7 on

Autobahn junctions; also Alan Brodrick, 'The New German Motor-Roads', *Geographical Magazine*, VI (1937–8), pp. 193–210.

175 *Architectural Review, op. cit.*, p. 163.

176 N. Carrington, *The Shape of Things* (London, 1939), p. 133.

177 Boumphrey, *British Roads, op. cit.*, p. 171; Trunk Roads Joint Commitee, *op. cit.*, pp. 12–13.

178 CPRE Archive, file 241/16. Schoenichen was Director of the German Governmental Agency for Preservation of Natural Monuments from 1933 to 1938, and continued to develop plans for National Parks in occupied Central Europe through to 1943; see G. Groning and J. Wolschke-Bulmahn, 'Politics, Planning and the Protection of Nature: Political Abuse of Early Ecological Ideas in Germany, 1933–45', *Planning Perspectives*, II (1987), pp. 127–48.

179 Boumphrey, *British Roads, op. cit.*, p. 171.

180 *Architectural Review, op. cit.*, p. 164.

181 Shand, *op. cit.*, p. 19.

2 *Arts of Living: Landscape and Citizenship, 1918–39*

1 Joad, *Charter, op. cit.*, pp. 157–8.

2 For parallel arguments, see David Matless, '"The Art of Right Living": Landscape and Citizenship, 1918–39', in *Mapping the Subject: Geographies of Cultural Transformation*, eds S. Pile and N. Thrift (London, 1995), pp. 93–122; Matless, 'Visual Culture', *op. cit.*; David Matless, 'Moral Geographies of English Landscape', *Landscape Research*, XXII (1997), pp. 141–56.

3 For an excellent discussion of questions of proper and improper pleasures in the preceding period which anticipates many of the issues raised in this chapter, see Raphael Samuel, 'The Discovery of Puritanism, 1820–1914: A Preliminary Sketch', in J. Garnett and C. Matthew, eds, *Revival and Religion Since 1700: Essays for John Walsh* (London, 1993), pp. 201–48.

4 T. Eagleton, *The Ideology of the Aesthetic* (Oxford, 1990).

5 Joad, *Charter, op. cit.*, p. 12.

6 Ian Jeffrey, 'Along Imaginary Lines: The Train in Modern Art and Literature', in Nottingham Castle Museum, *Train Spotting: Images of the Railway in Art* (Nottingham, 1985), pp. 20–36; Christopher Harvie, 'The English Railway Enthusiast', in H.-J. Diller, ed., *Englishness* (Heidelberg, 1992), pp. 107–22.

7 Joad, *Charter, op. cit.*, p. 97.

8 K. Grahame, *The Wind in the Willows* (London, 1908).

9 W. Plowden, *The Motor Car and Politics, 1896–1970* (London, 1971), p. 267.

10 Joad, *Charter, op. cit.*, p. 39. In his discussion of Shell posters in *On Living in an Old Country*, Wright notes that in this period, 'the countryside takes its shape around the passage of the motor car', p. 62.

11 S. Cooke, *This Motoring* (London, 1931), p. 160.

12 *Ibid.*, p. 150. Cooke was Secretary of the AA from its establishment in 1905 to 1942.

For Plowden, *This Motoring* contains 'some of the most embarrassing prose of the interwar period' (p. 66). Cooke has a tendency to conclude the many reported conversations with an exclamatory 'Ooh!'

13 Terry Morden, 'The Pastoral and the Pictorial', *Ten*: 8, XII (1983), pp. 18–25; Potts, *op. cit.*, pp. 160–186; Taylor, *op. cit.*; Wiener, *op. cit.*

14 Barbara Roscoe, '"Bradford-on-Avon but Shell on the Road": The Heyday of Motor Touring through Britain's Countryside', in *Rights of Way*, ed. C. Watkins (London, 1996), pp. 89–99.

15 B. Cook Batsford, *The Britain of Brian Cook* (London, 1987). Batsford series included *The Face of Britain, The English Life, The British Heritage*.

16 Morton, *op. cit.*; see David Matless, 'Seeing England with Morton and Cornish: Travel Writing and a Quest for Order', in *'A Land Fit For Heroes': Essays in the Human Geography of Inter-war Britain*, ed. M. Heffernan and P. Gruffudd (Loughborough, Department of Geography Occasional Paper 14, 1988), pp. 110–29.

17 Morton, *op. cit.*, p. 280.

18 *Ibid.*, p. x.

19 H. V. Morton, *In Search of Wales* (London, 1932); Pyrs Gruffudd, 'Selling the Countryside: Representations of Rural Britain', in *Place Promotion*, eds J. Gold and S. Ward (Chichester, 1994), pp. 247–63.

20 Morton, *St. Paul, op. cit.*, p. 46, p. 104.

21 S.P.B. Mais, 'The English Highway', *Geographical Magazine*, V (1937), pp. 65–80.

22 Morton, *In Search of England, op. cit.*, p. 84.

23 *Ibid.*, p. viii.

24 *Ibid.*, p. 258.

25 *Ibid.*, p. 257; Morton echoes Aldous Huxley in *Along the Road: Notes and Essays of a Tourist* (London, 1925), who puts down 'those hypocrites of country heartiness (and they are quite numerous) who tramp and drink ale in little inns, because it is the right thing to do', p. 23.

26 D. MacCannell, *Empty Meeting Grounds: The Tourist Papers* (London, 1992).

27 Morton, *In Search of England, op. cit.*, p. 123.

28 *Ibid.*, p. 273.

29 J. Urry, *The Tourist Gaze* (London, 1990); J. Urry, *Consuming Places* (London, 1995).

30 Taylor, *Dream of England, op. cit.*

31 S.P.B. Mais, 'The Plain Man Looks at England', in *Britain and the Beast, op. cit.*, pp. 212–24, qu. p. 218.

32 R. Titmuss, *Poverty and Population* (London, 1938), p. 288, quoted in G. Jones, *Social Hygiene in Twentieth Century Britain* (London, 1986), p. 132.

33 H. Batsford, *How to See the Country* (London, 1940), pp. 4–5.

34 G. Stedman Jones, 'The "Cockney" and the Nation, 1780–1988', in *Metropolis: London*, eds D. Feldman and G. Stedman Jones (London, 1989), pp. 272–324. The late 1930s Lambeth Walk craze inverts this commentary, with a Cockney inheriting an earldom and doing the Walk at a grand dinner party. 'Natural' working-class behaviour was contrasted to the mannered upper classes; see Mass-Observation,

Britain (London, 1939; republished 1986), pp. 139–84; R. Samuel, *Theatres of Memory* (London, 1995), pp. 390–400.

35 H. Peach, *Let Us Tidy Up* (Leicester, 1930), p. 3; Kirkham, *op. cit.*, pp. 102–3.

36 C.E.M. Joad, 'The People's Claim', in *Britain and the Beast*, *op. cit.*, pp. 64–85, qu. p. 72.

37 Peach, *op. cit.*, p. 17, pp. 23–5, p. 14; CPRE Archive file 254. German parallels are further discussed later in this chapter.

38 Abercrombie, *Town and Country Planning*, *op. cit.*, pp. 243–4.

39 Joad, *Charter*, *op. cit.*, p. 171, also pp. 114–15; and see Cornish, *Preservation of Our Scenery*, *op. cit.*, p. 78; Matless, 'Moral Geography in Broadland', *op. cit.*

40 Lord Horder, 'Quiet: A Physician Prescribes', in *Britain and the Beast*, *op. cit.*, pp. 176–82, qu. pp. 180–81.

41 E. P. Richards, 'Report with Proposals on the Recreational Use of Gathering Grounds', unpublished for CPRE (1935), p. 8; on debates over reservoir pollution see T. Stephenson, *Forbidden Land* (Manchester, 1989), pp. 101–17.

42 Joad, *Charter*, *op. cit.*, pp. 175–6.

43 Cornish, *National Parks*, *op. cit.*, p. 45.

44 Richards, *op. cit.*, pp. 2–3.

45 Cornish, *Scenery of England*, *op. cit.*, pp. 11–12.

46 *Ibid.*, p. 4.

47 The most substantive history of the movement in the interwar period and before is Harvey Taylor's *A Claim on the Countryside: A History of the British Outdoor Movement* (Keele, 1997). Taylor's book is especially valuable in showing how the movement was not an elite cultural phenomenon before the First World War. See also Helen Walker, 'The Outdoor Movement in England and Wales, 1900–1939', unpublished PhD thesis, University of Sussex, 1988; O. Coburn, *Youth Hostel Story* (London, 1951); H. Hill, *Freedom to Roam: The Struggle for Access to Britain's Moors and Mountains* (Ashbourne, 1980); John Lowerson, 'Battles for the Countryside', in *Class, Culture and Social Change: A New View of the 1930s*, ed. F. Gloversmith (Brighton, 1980), pp. 258–80; B. Rothman, *The 1932 Kinder Trespass* (Timperley, 1982); Stephenson, *Forbidden Land*, *op. cit.*; Trentmann, 'Civilization . . .', *op. cit.*

48 Joad, *Charter*, *op. cit.*, p. 59.

49 *Ibid.*, p. 99.

50 Rothman, *op. cit.*; for a less heroic view critical of Rothman, see Stephenson, *Forbidden Land*, *op. cit.*, pp. 153–64.

51 Hill, *op. cit.*, p. 32.

52 *Ibid.*, p. 53.

53 P. Barnes, *'Trespassers Will Be Prosecuted': Views of the Forbidden Moorlands of the Peak District* (Sheffield, 1934). Barnes was Assistant Secretary of the Sheffield and Peak District Committee of the CPRE, and provided photographs for their publications.

54 Hill, *op. cit.*, pp. 76–82; Stephenson, *op. cit.*, pp. 165–8. The clause was opposed

by Attlee and seventeen of those who would be ministers in the 1945 Labour government; see Chapter Seven below.

55 From 'The Manchester Rambler', by Ewan MacColl, reproduced in Rothman, *op. cit.*, p. 9. On MacColl see R. Samuel, 'Ewan MacColl (Obituary)', *The Independent*, 30 October 1989.

56 D. Cannadine, *C. M. Trevelyan: A Life in History* (London, 1992).

57 Coburn, *op. cit.*, p. 3.

58 Lowerson, 'Battles', *op. cit.*, p. 270.

59 W. H. Perkins, quoted in Coburn, *op. cit.*, p. 81.

60 Joad, *Charter*, *op. cit.*, p. 16.

61 *Ibid.*, p. 150.

62 Joad, 'The People's Claim', *op. cit.*, pp. 65–7.

63 *Ibid.*, pp. 79–80; also Williams-Ellis, *Octopus*, *op. cit.*, pp. 73–4; Cornish, *Preservation of Our Scenery*, *op. cit.*, p. 10.

64 Joad, 'The People's Claim', *op. cit.*, p. 74.

65 F. J. Osborn, 'Introduction', in Cornish, *Beauties*, *op. cit.*, pp. 9–14, qu. p. 11.

66 Peach, *op. cit.*, p. 26.

67 A. Ransome, *Coot Club* (London, 1934), p. 65; H. Brogan, *The Life of Arthur Ransome* (London, 1984); Matless, 'Moral Geography in Broadland', *op. cit.*

68 L. Paul, *Angry Young Man* (London, 1951), p. 69. Paul initially moved from the Scouts to John Hargrave's Kibbo Kift Kindred, a guild socialistic ritual movement with green Saxon cowl uniform, which became in the 1930s a vehicle for the Social Credit philosophy of Major Douglas; see J. L. Finlay, 'John Hargrave, the Green Shirts, and Social Credit', *Journal of Contemporary History*, v (1970), pp. 53–71. In his 1927 *The Confession of the Kibbo Kift* Hargrave hailed 'the New Nomads', youth hiking out of the city to regain a contact with land and nature (Glasgow, 1979, revised edition), pp. 88–93. On youth movements, see M. Rosenthal, *The Character Factory: Baden-Powell and the Origins of the Boy Scout Movement* (London, 1986); J. Springhall, *Youth, Empire and Society* (London, 1977); P. Wilkinson, 'English Youth Movements 1908–30', *Journal of Contemporary History*, IV (1969), pp. 3–23.

69 'Gilcraft', *Exploring* (London, 1942, first published 1930), pp. 75–6. 'Gilcraft' was Francis Gidney.

70 *Ibid.*, p. 72 .

71 R. Baden-Powell, *Scouting for Boys* (London, 1953, abridged Boys' Edition, first published 1908), pp. 9–10.

72 Batsford, *op. cit.*; T. Stephenson, ed., *The Countryside Companion* (London, 1939); E. Vale, *See For Yourself: A Field-Book of Sight-Seeing* (London, 1933).

73 Stephenson, *Companion*, *op. cit.*, p. 29.

74 *Ibid.*, p. 18; also Cornish, *Scenery of England*, *op. cit.*, p. 83.

75 Stephenson, *Companion*, *op. cit.*, pp. 33–46; also 'Gilcraft', *op. cit.*, pp. 31–53.

76 Batsford, *op. cit.*, p. 63, pp. 65–6.

77 C. E. Montague, *The Right Place: A Book of Pleasures* (London, 1924), pp. 40–1; quoted in Stephenson, *Companion*, *op. cit.*, p. 33, p. 41; 'Gilcraft', *op. cit.*, p. 41;

Simpson, *op. cit.*, p. 22. On Montague, see O. Elton, *C. E. Montague: A Memoir* (London, 1929).

78 J. P. Browne, *Map Cover Art* (London, 1992); T R. Nicholson, *Wheels on the Road: Maps of Britain for the Cyclist and Motorist, 1870–1940* (Norwich, 1983).

79 David Matless, 'Regional Surveys and Local Knowledges: The Geographical Imagination in Britain, 1918–39', *Transactions of the Institute of British Geographers*, XVII, pp. 464–80; D. Livingstone, *The Geographical Tradition* (Oxford, 1992), chapter 8.

80 Montague, *op. cit.*, p. 43.

81 V. Cornish, *Geographical Essays* (London, 1946), p. 78.

82 Simpson, *op. cit.*, p. 18; also C. Simpson, *The Study of Local Geography* (London, 1930); on citizenship and local knowledges, see Matless, 'Regional Surveys', *op. cit.*, pp. 472–5.

83 *Discovery* (Ledbury, Le Play House Press, 1948, amplified edition, first published 1923); see also *Exploration* (London, Le Play Society, 1939).

84 C. C. Fagg and G. E. Hutchings, *An Introduction to Regional Surveying* (Cambridge, 1930), pp. 31–3.

85 Victor Branford, 'A View of Hastings', *Observation*, I (1924), pp. 31–4, qu. p. 34.

86 P. Geddes, *Cities in Evolution* (London, 1915), pp. 13–14; on Geddes's 'Outlook Tower' in Edinburgh as an expression of this philosophy, see Matless, 'Regional Surveys', *op. cit.*, pp. 465–6; H. Meller, *Patrick Geddes* (London, 1990).

87 O.G.S. Crawford and A. Keiller, *Wessex From The Air* (Oxford, 1928); O.G.S. Crawford, *Air Survey and Archaeology* (Southampton, 1924); L. Deuel, *Flights Into Yesterday: The Story of Aerial Archaeology* (London, 1969).

88 I. F. Smith, *Windmill Hill and Avebury: Excavations by Alexander Keiller 1925–1939* (Oxford, 1965), p. 188; P. J. Ucko, M. Hunter, A. Clark and A. David, *Avebury Reconsidered* (London, 1991); in 1939 Keiller launched a public appeal to pay off the purchase price so that the land could be transferred to the National Trust. Crawford and Keiller were involved in the July 1927 appeal to buy and clear land around Stonehenge; see Peach and Carrington, *op. cit.*, p. 40.

89 G. Clark, *Prehistoric England* (London, 1948, first ed. 1940), p. 107; P. Nash, *Fertile Image* (London, 1951); R. Cardinal, *The Landscape Vision of Paul Nash* (London, 1989); A. Causey, *Paul Nash* (Oxford, 1980).

90 O.G.S. *Crawford, Archaeology in the Field* (London, 1953), p. 51.

91 *Ibid.*, p. 87, p. 208; Crawford reflected on his lack of enthusiasm for the 1914–18 war: 'It would not be correct to say that I was unpatriotic; I had a very deep love of England and of the English countryside. It was rather that patriotism of the flag-wagging kind never appealed to me.' O.G.S. Crawford, *Said and Done: The Autobiography of an Archaeologist* (London, 1955), p. 109. Prehistory at this time tends not to be the occasion for either insular or expansive jingoism: 'We are so accustomed to think of ourselves as islanders that we sometimes tend to forget that Britain is a part of the European continent from which she has at certain intervals in her history become temporarily detached', Clark, *op. cit.*, p. i.

92 Crawford, *Said and Done, op. cit.*, p. 225.

93 Crawford, *Said and Done, op. cit.*, p. 164; also Sir Charles Close, *The Map of England* (London, 1932).

94 L. V. Grinsell, *The Ancient Burial Mounds of England* (London, 1936), p. 75.

95 Crawford, *Said and Done, op. cit.*, p. 74.

96 L. Mulvey, *Visual and Other Pleasures* (London, 1989); G. Rose, *Feminism and Geography: The Limits of Geographical Knowledge* (Cambridge, 1993).

97 Catherine Nash, 'Reclaiming Vision: Looking at Landscape and the Body', *Gender, Place and Culture*, III (1996), pp. 149–69.

98 S. T. Warner, *Lolly Willowes* (London, 1993, first ed. 1926). On Warner's novels, communism, lesbianism and life in Dorset see C. Harman, *Sylvia Townsend Warner: A Biography* (London, 1989); W. Mulford, *This Narrow Place: Sylvia Townsend Warner and Valentine Ackland, Life, Letters and Politics 1930–1951* (London, 1988); Jane Marcus, 'A Wilderness of One's Own: Feminist Fantasy Novels of the Twenties: Rebecca West and Sylvia Townsend Warner', in S. M. Squier, ed., *Women Writers and the City* (Knoxville, University of Tennessee Press, 1984), pp. 134–60; Wright, *The Village That Died For England, op. cit.*, pp. 136–49. Warner later produced a guide to Somerset in Williams-Ellis's *Vision of England* series (London, 1949).

99 Warner, *Lolly Willowes, op. cit.*, p. 88.

100 *Ibid.*, pp. 127–8.

101 *Ibid.*, pp. 159–60.

102 *Ibid.*, pp. 234–5.

103 *Ibid.*, p. 136.

104 *Ibid.*, p. 169.

105 *Ibid.*, p. 247.

106 Watkins was a Liberal councillor, magistrate, photographer, beekeeper, advocate of octaval coinage against post-war decimalisation proposals, and antiquarian. His key ley line texts were *Early British Trackways* (Hereford, 1922), *The Old Straight Track, op. cit., The Ley Hunter's Manual* (London, 1927) and *The Old Standing Crosses of Herefordshire* (London, 1930). On photography, see A. Watkins, *Photography: Its Principles and Applications* (London, 1911). For Watkins's life and work, see R. Shoesmith, *Alfred Watkins: A Herefordshire Man* (Little Logaston, Logaston Press, 1990). For a critique of ley lines, see T. Williamson and L. Bellamy, *Ley Lines in Question* (Kingswood, 1983).

107 *Crawford, Archaeology, op. cit.*, p. 269. Crawford placed Watkins alongside 'Crankeries' such as a character called 'Appian Way' who in the 1920s sought to prove that Britain was the biblical Holy Land, and refused him an advertisement in *Antiquity*.

108 Watkins, *Old Straight Track, op. cit.*, p. 215. The key figure in revising the theory has been John Michell, who provides introductions to Watkins's republished works. On landscape and mysticism, see John Lowerson, 'The Mystical Geography of the English', in *The English Rural Community*, ed. B. Short (Cambridge, 1992),

pp. 152–74. Some of Watkins's followers in the Old Straight Track Club suggested leys might be an energy network to be detected by dowsing, or a construction of Atlantean migrants; see Williamson and Bellamy, *op. cit.*, p. 217.

109 Watkins, *Old Straight Track*, *op. cit.*, p. 218.

110 *Ibid.*, p. 149, p. 197, p. 207, p. 215.

111 *Ibid.*, pp. 12–13.

112 *Ibid.*, p. 219.

113 *Ibid.*, pp. 221–2.

114 *Ibid.*, p. xxi.

115 *Ibid.*, pp. 32–3.

116 Review of Watkins's 1932 *Archaic Tracks Round Cambridge*, quoted in *Shoesmith*, *op. cit.*, pp. 134–5; also see Frank Roe, 'The "Wild Animal Path" Origin of Ancient Roads', *Antiquity*, III (1929), pp. 299–311.

117 Boumphrey, *British Roads*, *op. cit.*, p. 10; Anderson, *op. cit.*, pp. 23–32.

118 *Birmingham Gazette* review of *The Ley Hunter's Manual*, quoted in Shoesmith, *op. cit.*, p. 134.

119 Watkins, *Ley Hunter's Manual*, *op. cit.*, pp. 100–1. The Old Straight Track Club included W. A. Dutt, Norfolk topographer and author of *Ancient Mark-Stones of East Anglia* (Lowestoft, 1926).

120 D. Maxwell, *A Detective in Surrey: Landscape Clues to Invisible Roads* (London, 1932), p. 138.

121 *Ibid.*, p. 88; Watkins, *Old Straight Track*, *op. cit.*, pp. 78–9.

122 Maxwell, *op. cit.*, p. vi.

123 Trevelyan, *Must England's Beauty Perish?*, *op. cit.*, p. 19; also Trevelyan, *Call and Claims*, *op. cit.*; Cornish, *Preservation*, *op. cit.*, p. xi; Joad, *Charter*, *op. cit.*, pp. 89–91, 'Acknowledgement of Animism'.

124 Cornish, *National Parks*, *op. cit.*, A National Park Committee was set up 1929 chaired by Lord Addison, Minister of Agriculture, and reported in April 1931, recommending a National Parks Authority; see Cornish, *Preservation*, *op. cit.*, pp. 1–17 for the CPRE evidence; also Sheail, *Rural Conservation*, *op. cit.*; Lord Addison, *A Policy for British Agriculture* (London, 1939), pp. 274–8. Financial crisis led to the proposals being set aside; a Standing Committee on National Parks was formed in 1935 to continue lobbying.

125 Cornish, *Scenery of England*, *op. cit.*, p. 13; Matless, 'Nature . . .', *op. cit.*

126 Cornish, *National Parks*, *op. cit.*, p. 9.

127 *Ibid.*, p. 5, pp. 13–14.

128 Abercrombie, *Town and Country Planning*, *op. cit.*, p. 223.

129 Cornish, 'Scenic Amenity', *op. cit.*, p. 202. Cornish praised Wordsworth's scientific 'faculty of observation', although he criticized him for being prey at times to 'intellectual associations, which do so much to cramp the proper functioning of the eye . . . although Wordsworth may have been in advance of his time as an advocate of the free play of the senses, he did not go so far as we now believe to be desirable'; Cornish, *National Parks*, *op. cit.*, pp. 84–9.

130   Cornish, *Scenery and the Sense of Sight, op. cit.*, p. xii; Cornish adds, in keeping with his broadly Orientalist embrace of elements of Eastern religion, that a state of receptive contemplation is 'always difficult for the energetic occidental to acquire' (p. xi); see Matless, 'Nature . . .' *op. cit.*

131   Cornish, 'Scenic Amenity', *op. cit.*, p. 202.

132   Cornish, *National Parks, op. cit.*, pp. 24–5.

133   Cornish, *Scenery and the Sense of Sight, op. cit.*, p. 23.

134   Cornish, 'Harmonies', *op. cit.*, p. 275.

135   Morton, *In Search of England, op. cit.*, pp. 258–60; also see his account of the Pedlar's Way, pp. 246–7.

136   Cornish, *Scenery and the Sense of Sight, op. cit.*, p. xi; see also Stapledon, *The Land, op. cit.*, p. 277: 'If I mistake not the meaning of the great pilgrimage . . . then the new age has in fact dawned'; and pp. 114–16 on Stapledon's 'My National Park'.

137   Cornish, *Beauties, op. cit.*, p. 72.

138   Matless, 'Nature . . .', *op. cit.*

139   R. Jefferies, *The Story of My Heart* (London, 1979, first published 1883), p. 65; W. Keith, *The Rural Tradition* (Brighton, 1975).

140   Vaughan Cornish, 'Aesthetic Principles of Town and Country Planning', *Scottish Geographical Magazine*, XLIX (1933), pp. 320–23, qu. p. 323.

141   Cornish, *Scenery and the Sense of Sight, op. cit.*, p. ix. On Cornish's interest in eugenics, centring primarily on the position of the 'white race' in imperial competition, see V. Cornish, 'The Geographical Aspects of Eugenics', *Eugenics Review*, XVI (1923), pp. 267–9; D. Matless, 'A Modern Stream: An Essay in Water, Landscape, Modernism and Geography', *Environment and Planning D: Society and Space*, X (1992), pp. 569–88; K. Dodds, 'Eugenics, Fantasies of Empire and Inverted Whiggism: An Essay on the Political Geography of Vaughan Cornish', *Political Geography*, XIII (1994), pp. 85–99. On climbing, see D. Robbins, 'Sport, Hegemony and the Middle Classes: The Victorian Mountaineers', *Theory, Culture and Society*, IV (1987), pp. 579–601; Peter Hansen, 'The Dancing Lamas of Everest: Cinema, Orientalism and Anglo-Tibetan Relations in the 1920s', *American Historical Review*, CI (1996), pp. 712–47; P. Bicknell, *British Hills and Mountains* (London, 1947) describes a boom in climbing after 1918, with the British Mountaineering Council formed in 1944.

142   R. Baden-Powell, *Rovering to Success* (London, 1922), p. 44.

143   Quoted in E. E. Reynolds, *The Scout Movement* (Oxford, 1950), pp. 151–2; on Rover Scouts, see A. Warren, 'Popular Manliness: Baden-Powell, Scouting and the Development of Manly Character', in *Manliness and Morality*, eds J. A. Mangan and J. Walvin (Manchester, 1987), pp. 199–219.

144   Joad, *Charter, op. cit.*, p. 150.

145   Stephenson, *Countryside Companion, op. cit.*, p. 26.

146   Cornish, *Poetic Impression, op. cit.*, p. 11.

147   G. M. Trevelyan, 'Walking', in G. M. Trevelyan, *Clio, A Muse* (London, 1930, first ed. 1913), pp. 1–18, qu. p. 18; on walking and literature, see A. Wallace, *Walking,*

Literature and English Culture (Oxford, 1993); M. Marples, *Shank's Pony: A Study of Walking* (London, 1959).

148 Trevelyan, 'Walking', *op. cit.*, p. 4, p. 16.

149 Richards, *op. cit.*, p. 2.

150 Stapledon, *The Land*, *op. cit.*, p. 4; on diet, see Peter Bishop, 'Constable Country: Diet, Landscape and National Identity', *Landscape Research*, XVI (1991), pp. 31–6; P. Bishop, *An Archetypal Constable: National Identity and the Geography of Nostalgia* (London, 1995), pp. 15–45.

151 H. Roberts, *The Practical Way to Keep Fit* (London, 1942); also H. Roberts, *Everyman in Health and in Sickness* (London, 1935). Roberts was an East End doctor, Fabian socialist and journalist; W. Stamp, *'Doctor Himself': An Unorthodox Biography of Harry Roberts* (London, 1949).

152 P. Stallybrass and A. White, *The Politics and Poetics of Transgression* (London, 1986).

153 A. J. Cruickshank and P. Stack, *Movement is Life* (London, 1937); on the League, see Jill Julius Matthews, '"They Had Such A Lot of Fun": The Women's League of Health and Beauty between the Wars', *History Workshop Journal*, XXX (1990), pp. 22–54. The motto inverted that of popular Edwardian body builder and exhibitionist Eugen Sandow, *Life is Movement* (London, *c.* 1919).

154 Cruickshank and Stack, *op. cit.*, p. 220.

155 British Medical Association Physical Education Committee, April 1936, quoted in Political and Economic Planning, *The British Health Services* (London, 1937), p. 344.

156 Reproduced in Matless, 'Art of Right Living', p. 110.

157 M. Green, *Mountain of Truth: The Counterculture Begins* (London, 1986), p. 98.

158 Roberts, 'Practical', *op. cit.*, pp. 68–70; see also Len Lye's 1936 film of choreographed hiking *Rainbow Dance*, excerpt shown in the Channel 4 series *The Long Summer* (1995).

159 R. Laban, *Modern Educational Dance* (London, 1948), p. 3.

160 *Ibid.*, p. 6.

161 PEP, *British Health Services*, *op. cit.*, p. 350.

162 Lord Aberdare, 'Fitness and Fresh Air', *The Nottinghamshire Countryside*, II (1938), p. 6.

163 National Fitness Council, *The National Fitness Campaign* (London, 1939), p. 4; S. Jones, 'State Intervention in Sport and Leisure Between the Wars', *Journal of Contemporary History*, XXII (1987), pp. 163–82; John Summerson, 'The Health, Sport and Fitness Exhibition', *Journal of the Royal Institute of British Architects*, XLV (1938), pp. 492–3.

164 John Gloag, 'The Object of the Exhibition', *Journal of the Royal Institute of British Architects*, XLV (1938), pp. 494–5.

165 National Fitness Council, *op. cit.*, p. 8.

166 G. R. Searle, *The Quest for National Efficiency: A Study in British Politics and Political Thought, 1899–1914* (Oxford, 1971); G. R. Searle, 'Eugenics and Politics in Britain in the 1930s', *Annals of Science*, XXXVI (1979), pp. 159–69, including discussion of the role of Keynes and Julian Huxley.

167 V. G. Biller, 'Camping and Caravanning', in Stephenson, *Countryside Companion*, *op. cit.*, pp. 365–77, qu. pp. 364–5.

168 Sir G. Newman, *The Building of a Nation's Health* (London, 1939), p. 230. Such ideas again crossed the political spectrum. On the work of the socialist pioneer of open-air nurseries from the 1900s, Margaret McMillan, see Samuel, 'Puritanism', *op. cit.*, and C. Steedman, *Childhood, Culture and Class in Britain: Margaret McMillan, 1860–1931* (London, 1990).

169 Newman, *op. cit.*, pp. 277–8.

170 A. Bertram, *Pavements and Peaks* (London, 1933), p. 70.

171 *Ibid.*, p. 63.

172 *Ibid.*, p. 51.

173 Coburn, *op. cit.*; M. Burleigh and W. Wippermann, *The Racial State: Germany 1933–1945* (Cambridge, 1991), pp. 201–41.

174 Green, *op. cit.*, pp. 109–12.

175 Newman, *op. cit.*, p. 264, p. 262.

176 *Ibid.*, pp. 277–8.

177 *Ibid.*, p. 264.

178 Gloag, 'Exhibition', *op. cit.*, p. 495.

179 Roberts, *Practical*, *op. cit.*, p. 316; see Roberts, *Everyman*, *op. cit.*, p. 188, against continental militarism.

180 Lord Howard of Penrith, 'Lessons From Other Countries', in *Britain and the Beast*, *op. cit.*, pp. 279–87, qu. pp. 284–5, my emphasis.

181 Anon., 'Strength Through Joy: Suggestion for a Rural Fitness Policy', *The Nottinghamshire Countryside*, II (1938), p. 15.

182 Orwell, *Coming Up*, *op. cit.*, pp. 212–14. In *The Road to Wigan Pier* Orwell had suggested that, 'We may find in the long run that tinned food is a deadlier weapon than the machine gun' (London, 1965, first published 1937), pp. 98–9.

183 Cornish, *Scenery and the Sense of Sight*, *op. cit.*, pp. 24–5.

184 Roberts, *Practical*, *op. cit.*, p. 11.

185 Matthews, *op. cit.*, p. 26.

186 S. Spender, *World Within World* (London, 1953), pp. 92–3.

187 Matthews, *op. cit.*, p. 48; on the recurrence of such issues in relation to swimming, including a discussion of interwar Germany, see C. Sprawson, *Haunts of the Black Masseur* (London, 1992).

188 Joad, *Book of Joad*, *op. cit.*, p. 257.

189 C.E.M. Joad, *The Untutored Townsman's Invasion of the Country* (London, 1946), pp. 149–50.

190 Matthews, *op. cit.*, p. 29.

191 Roberts, *Everyman*, *op. cit.*, p. 203.

192 M. Parmelee, *The New Gymnosophy* (New York, 1927).

193 'In My Little Snapshot Album', by Harper, Haines and Parr Davies, from the film *I See Ice*.

194 Baden-Powell, *Rovering*, *op. cit.*, p. 111.

195 M. Green, *Children of the Sun: A Narrative of Decadence, in England after 1918* (London, 1977); Cunningham, *op. cit.*

196 J. P. Muller, *My Sun Bathing and Fresh Air System* (London, *c.* 1930). Other texts advised on breathing, indoor exercise, and the 'Daily Five Minutes'. On male bodily display, see P. Lewis, 'Men on Pedestals', *Ten: 8*, XVII, pp. 22–9; M. A. Budd, *The Sculpture Machine* (London, 1997).

197 J. Richards, '"Passing the Love of Women": Manly Love and Victorian Society', in Mangan and Walvin, *op. cit.*, pp. 92–122.

198 Cornish, *Geographical Essays, op. cit.*, p. 38.

199 Roberts, *Practical, op. cit.*, p. 113.

200 Keynes, *op. cit.*, p. 6.

201 Williams-Ellis, *Octopus, op. cit.*, p. 22.

202 Joad, *Book of Joad, op. cit.*, p. 134.

203 R. G. Stapledon, 'The Non-Material Needs of the Nation', in Stapledon, *The Way of the Land* (London, 1943), pp. 61–73.

204 A. G. Tansley, *The New Psychology* (London, 1920), p. 295; Tansley's work on both vegetation and the psyche is being explored by Laura Cameron at the Department of Geography, University of Cambridge; see her paper on Tansley, Freud and Wicken Fen, 'Histories of Disturbance', presented at the RGS conference, January 1998.

205 C. C. Fagg, 'The Significance of the Freudian Psychology for the Evolution Theory', *Proceedings and Transactions of the Croydon Natural History and Scientific Society*, IX (1923), pp. 137–64, qu. p. 164; Matless, 'Regional Surveys', *op. cit.*

206 Fagg, *op. cit.*, p. 137; see also C. C. Fagg, 'Psychosynthesis, or Evolution in the Light of Freudian Psychology', *British Journal of Medical Psychology*, XIII (1933), pp. 119–42.

207 G. H. Green, *Psychanalysis in the Class Room* (London, 1921), p. 175; G. H. Green, *The Healthway Books* (London, 1939); W. A. Muir and G. H. Green, *Health and Cleanliness* (London, 1928); Col. R. J. Blackham and G. H. Green, *Keep Fit: A Book For Boys* (London, 1928); D. Sibley, *Geographies of Exclusion* (London, 1995), pp. 20–2.

208 Green, *Psychanalysis, op. cit.*, p. 8.

3 *English Ecologies*

1 C. Henry Warren, 'Corn', in H. J. Massingham, ed., *England and the Farmer* (London, 1941), pp. 51–70, qu. p. 52.

2 Massingham, *England and the Farmer, op. cit.*; the other 'Kinship' collections are E. Blunden, ed., *Return to Husbandry* (London, 1943); H. J. Massingham, ed., *The Natural Order* (London, 1945). On the Kinship, which met regularly until 1947, and related figures, see Rolf Gardiner, 'Can Farming save European Civilisation?', in A. Best, ed., *Water Springing from the Ground: an Anthology of the Writings of Rolf Gardiner* (Fontmell Magna, 1972), pp. 196–203; also Malcolm Chase, 'This Is No Claptrap, This Is Our Heritage', in *The Imagined Past*, eds M. Chase and C. Shaw

(Manchester, 1989), pp. 128–46; Craven, '"Health, Wholeness, Holiness": Radical Right and Fascist Attitudes to the British Countryside, 1918–1939', University of Birmingham M. Phil thesis, 1993; Trentmann, 'Civilization', *op. cit.*; P. Conford, *The Organic Tradition: An Anthology of Writings on Organic Farming* (Hartland, 1988); Philip Conford, 'The Alchemy of Waste: The Impact of Asian Farming on the British Organic Movement', *Rural History*, VI (1995), pp. 103–14; E. Abelson, ed., *A Mirror of England: An Anthology of the Writings of H. J. Massingham* (Hartland, 1988); Wright, *Village that Died, op. cit.*, Chapters 10, 12 and 13. The initial twelve members of the Kinship were Rolf Gardiner, writers H. J. Massingham, C. Henry Warren and Edmund Blunden, agriculturalists Viscount Lymington, Lord Northbourne and J. E. Hosking, conservative historian Arthur Bryant, farmer-novelist Adrian Bell, folk song and dance campaigner and biologist Douglas Kennedy, Philip Mairet and Robert Payne. Later members included Laurence Easterbrook, Michael Graham, Ronald Duncan and Jorian Jenks. Scientists such as George Stapledon, Albert Howard, Lionel Picton and Robert McCarrison were associated with the group but seemingly never members; Payne records an earlier meeting at Lymington's home in 1938 including Ehrenfried Pfeiffer, Howard, McCarrison, Northbourne, Stapledon and Gardiner; V. Payne, 'A History of the Soil Association', Victoria University of Manchester MSc thesis, 1971.

3 Gardiner, 'Can Farming', *op. cit.*, pp. 196–8.

4 John Sheail, 'Pollution and the Protection of Inland Fisheries in Inter-War Britain', in M. Shortland, ed., *Science and Nature: Essays in the History of the Environmental Sciences* (Oxford, 1993), pp. 41–56.

5 H. J. Massingham, 'Introduction', in Massingham, *England and the Farmer, op. cit.*, pp. 6–7.

6 G. T. Wrench, *Reconstruction By Way of the Soil* (London, 1946), p. 13.

7 H. J. Massingham, 'Introduction', in *The English Countryside*, ed. H. J. Massingham (London, 1939), p. 6.

8 H. J. Massingham, *The Faith of a Fieldsman* (London, 1951), p. 267.

9 Massingham, in *The Natural Order, op. cit.*, p. 1.

10 *Ibid.*, p. 8.

11 R. Gardiner, *England Herself: Ventures in Rural Restoration* (London, 1943); G. V. Jacks and R. O. Whyte, *The Rape of the Earth: A World Survey of Soil Erosion* (London, 1939).

12 H. J. Massingham, *Remembrance: An Autobiography* (London, 1941), pp. 82–3. While a number of women were prominent in organicist campaigns, as discussed below, none were members of the Kinship in Husbandry. Whether this constituted a division within the organic movement is unclear and would require further research.

13 E. B. Balfour, *The Living Soil* (London, 1943), p. 173.

14 *Ibid.*, p. 194.

15 *Ibid.*; for another summary of the debate from the organicist side see also M. Graham, *Soil and Sense* (London, 1941); from the artificials side D. P. Hopkins,

Chemicals, Humus, and the Soil (London, 1945). See also the House of Lords debate on 'Agriculture and Food Values', 26 October 1943, initiated by Lord Teviot, later President of the Soil Association, where Lymington made his maiden speech as Earl of Portsmouth; *Hansard: The Parliamentary Debates*, 129 (1943), pp. 291–327, and the commentary by H. J. Massingham, *This Plot of Earth* (London, 1944), pp. 116–17.

16 Payne, *op. cit.*; M. Veldman, *Fantasy, the Bomb, and the Greening of Britain* (Cambridge, 1994), pp. 258–67.

17 Balfour, *op. cit.*, pp. 162–72; A. Howard, *Farming and Gardening for Health and Disease* (London, 1945), pp. 78–80 on 'Unsoundness of Rothamsted'.

18 Balfour, *op. cit.*, p. 17; Howard, *op. cit.*, pp. 33–6 on the 'mycorrhizal association'; also the vitalistic arguments in M. Bruce, *Common-Sense Compost Making* (London, 1946), pp. 68–9.

19 Balfour, *op. cit.*, p. 19.

20 Massingham, *Remembrance, op. cit.*, p. 136.

21 Lord Northbourne, *Look to the Land* (London, 1940), pp. 2–3.

22 H. J. Massingham, 'Work and Quality', in Massingham, *Natural Order, op. cit.*, pp. 31–42, qu. p. 41.

23 H. J. Massingham and H. Massingham, eds, *The Great Victorians* (London, 1930), p. 256, p. 258; also Massingham, *Faith*, pp. 203–5. It should be noted that a rejection of social Darwinism did not preclude a harsh racial evolutionary theory, as in Lymington's vision of 'ecological comity' as a means to evolution via an exclusionary 'comity of breeds and types, custom and language, religion and tradition'; Earl of Portsmouth, *Alternative to Death: The Relationship between Soil, Family and Community* (London, 1943), p. 175 (for simplicity I refer to him in discussion as Lymington even after his elevation to the Earldom).

24 Balfour, *op. cit.*, p. 18.

25 Massingham, *Plot, op. cit.*, p. 101. For other methods see Bruce, *op. cit.*; F. H. Billington, *Compost for Garden Plot or Thousand-Acre Farm* (London, 1942); F. C. King, *Gardening With Compost* (London, 1944); T. J. Barrett, *Harnessing the Earthworm* (London, 1949). For a contemporary skit on things soil-based, and on hiking, by the authors of *1066 And All That*, see W. C. Sellar and R. J. Yeatman, *Garden Rubbish and Other Country Bumps* (London, 1936).

26 Massingham, *Remembrance, op. cit.*, p. 138; A. Howard, *An Agricultural Testament* (Oxford, 1940), pp. 39–52.

27 Bruce, *op. cit.*, p. 46.

28 Northbourne, *op. cit.*, pp. 18–19.

29 *Ibid.*, p. 71.

30 *Ibid.*, p. 70.

31 Howard, *Farming and Gardening, op. cit.*, pp. 81–2.

32 *Ibid.*, p. 87.

33 *Ibid.*, p. 85.

34 J. Jenks, *From the Ground Up: An Outline of Real Economy* (London, 1950), p. 199.

35 Massingham, *Faith, op. cit.*, p. 232.

36 Massingham, *Plot, op. cit.*, pp. 175–83.

37 Quoted in Gardiner, *England Herself, op. cit.*, p. 135.

38 Jenks, *op. cit.*, pp. 203–4.

39 Stapledon, *The Land, op. cit.*, p. 181; also R. G. Stapledon, 'The Case for Land Improvement and Reclamation', *Journal of the Royal Society of Arts*, LXXXIV (1936), pp. 972–94; Stapledon was not an advocate of entirely organic farming: 'Sir Albert Howard and I go so far together but not the whole way' (p. 994), and was generally more open to accommodation with the state and the engineer, but contributed an essay to *England and the Farmer* on 'The Reclamation of Grasslands', pp. 131–52. On Italy, see also Viscount Lymington, 'The Policy of Husbandry', in Massingham, *England and the Farmer, op. cit.*, pp. 12–31.

40 Stapledon, *The Land, op. cit.*, p. 184.

41 Wrench, *Reconstruction, op. cit.*, p. 152.

42 H. J. Massingham and E. Hyams, *Prophecy of Famine* (London, 1953), pp. 131–2; Massingham, *Faith, op. cit.*, p. 76.

43 Massingham, 'Work and Quality', *op. cit.*, p. 41.

44 H. Williamson, *The Linhay on the Downs* (London, 1938), p. 124; a similarly brutal sense of nature is found in Williamson's popular story *Tarka the Otter*. On Williamson's fascism, see below. Massingham's anti-plumage campaigns after 1918 targeted the non-functional luxury use of the animal, with millinery traders damned as 'the knaves and Judases of German Jews they undoubtedly were', Massingham, *Remembrance, op. cit.*, p. 41. When reproducing this extract Abelson, *A Mirror of England, op. cit.*, p. 20, edits out the 'Judases of German Jews' phrase.

45 Wrench, *Reconstruction, op. cit.*, p. 210.

46 Gardiner, *England Herself, op. cit.*, p. 86; Earl of Portsmouth, *A Knot of Roots: An Autobiography* (London, 1965), p. 85; E. Pfeiffer, *Bio-Dynamic Farming and Gardening* (London, 1940). Pfeiffer attended the European Husbandry Meeting organized by Gardiner, Lymington and Hosking in 1950, see Best, *Water, op. cit.*, pp. 199–203.

47 Best, *Water, op. cit.*, p. 268; also R. Gardiner, *Forestry or Famine?* (London, 1949); Bruce, *op. cit.*, pp. 21–2.

48 Massingham, *Plot*, pp. 102–3.

49 Conford, 'Alchemy of Waste', *op. cit.*

50 Wrench, *Reconstruction, op. cit.*, p. 15; G. T. Wrench, *The Wheel of Health* (London, 1938).

51 Massingham, *Remembrance, op. cit.*, p. 99.

52 Sir Albert Howard, 'Soil Fertility', in Massingham, *England and the Farmer, op. cit.*, pp. 32–50, qu. p. 42.

53 Wrench, *Reconstruction, op. cit.*, p. 19.

54 Howard, 'Soil Fertility', *op. cit.*, p. 33; F. H. King, *Farmers of Forty Centuries* (London, 1927).

55 Jacks and Whyte, *op. cit.*, p. 24; though see Massingham, *Plot, op. cit.*, p. 49, for speculations on the effects of deforestation on rain and wind.

56 Northbourne, *Look, op. cit.*, p. 17; Balfour, *op. cit.*, pp. 14–17; Jacks and Whyte, *op. cit.*, p. 213; *The Rape of the Earth* does not address the issue of artificial fertilisers.

57 Jacks and Whyte, *op. cit.*, p. 17.

58 *Ibid.*, p. 18, p. 38.

59 *Ibid.*, p. 213; also Northbourne, *op. cit.*, pp. 13–14; Elspeth Huxley, 'Erosion I: America's Distressed Areas', *Geographical Magazine*, V (1937), pp. 297–311, and 'Erosion II: Man the Desert-Maker', *Geographical Magazine*, VI (1938), pp. 297–312.

60 Earl of Portsmouth, 'Preface', in C. McWilliams, *Ill Fares the Land* (London, 1945), pp. 9–18, qu. p. 16; Massingham, *Plot, op. cit.*, p. 56; Jacks and Whyte, *op. cit.*, pp. 234–5, p. 296.

61 McWilliams, *op. cit.*, p. 15; on McWilliams, see M. Davis, *City of Quartz* (London, 1990), pp. 34–5; Mitchell, *Lie of the Land, op. cit.*

62 Viscount Lymington, *Famine in England* (London, 1938), pp. 92–5; also Viscount Lymington, *Horn, Hoof and Corn: The Future of British Agriculture* (London, 1932).

63 Lymington, *Famine, op. cit.*, p. 20.

64 Jacks and Whyte, *op. cit.*, p. 262, p. 259; only Japan is upheld as a non-Western conservation model; see also K. E. Barlow, *The Discipline of Peace* (London, 1942), p. 106 on Kenya.

65 Jacks and Whyte, *op. cit.*, p. 19.

66 Portsmouth, *Alternative, op. cit.*, p. 12; also Northbourne, *op. cit.*, p. 15; Jacks and Whyte, *op. cit.*, p. 24; Wrench, *Reconstruction, op. cit.*, p. 44; Howard, 'Soil Fertility', *op. cit.*, pp. 33–4; Howard, *Farming and Gardening, op. cit.*, pp. 48–9.

67 Adrian Bell, 'Husbandry and Society', in Blunden, *Return to Husbandry, op. cit.*, pp. 5–9), qu. p. 8.

68 Massingham, *England and the Farmer, op. cit.*, p. 5.

69 Northbourne, *op. cit.*, pp. 22–3, pp. 24–5.

70 Massingham, *Remembrance, op. cit.*, p. 129.

71 Portsmouth, in McWilliams, *op. cit.*, p. 11.

72 Lymington, *Famine, op. cit.*, p. 90.

73 Jacks and Whyte, *op. cit.*, p. 210, p. 215.

74 *Ibid.*, p. 285.

75 Wrench, *Reconstruction, op. cit.*, p. 71, p. 70.

76 Jenks, *op. cit.*; Jorian Jenks, 'The Homestead Economy', in H. J. Massingham, ed., *The Small Farmer* (London, 1947), pp. 149–98.

77 The successor to Alfred Orage's *New Age*; see Massingham, *Remembrance, op. cit.*, pp. 31–3.

78 L. Merricks, *The World Made New: Frederick Soddy, Science, Politics, and Environment* (Oxford, 1996); J. Martinez-Alier, *Ecological Economics* (Oxford, 1987); A. Bramwell, *Ecology in the 20th Century* (London, 1989); J. Jenks and J. T. Peddie, *Farming and Money* (London, 1935).

79 Massingham, *Remembrance, op. cit.*, p. 111.

80 L.T.C. Rolt, *High Horse Riderless* (London, 1947), p. 137.

81 David Bradshaw, 'T. S. Eliot and the Major: Sources of Literary Anti-Semitism in the 1930s', *Times Literary Supplement*, 5 July 1996, pp. 14–16.

82 Portsmouth, *Alternative*, *op. cit.*, pp. 70–2.

83 Viscount Lymington, *Ich Dien: The Tory Path* (London, 193 I), p. 84; Lymington is referring to agricultural co-operative schemes in Ireland. Anti-Semitism is absent from Jenks's 1950 *From the Ground Up*, but a philosophy of roots asserting that 'Husbandry is Fundamental' and critiquing world economy from a position still associated with British fascism risks being accused of not entirely declaring its hand. By contrast Rolt condemns anti-Semitism as a 'disease', *High Horse*, *op. cit.*, p. 107.

84 Lymington, *Famine*, *op. cit.*, p. 148, p. 56.

85 Northbourne, *op. cit.*, p. 41.

86 *Ibid.*, p. 120.

87 *Ibid.*, pp. 124–5.

88 *Ibid.*, p. 126; also Lymington, 'Policy of Husbandry', *op. cit.*, p. 30; Viscount Lymington, 'Notes on Rural Life and Land Tenure', in Blunden, *op. cit.*, pp. 15–19. There is an echo here of the powers of confiscation vested in County War Agricultural Committees, of which Northbourne and Lymington were members; see chapter 4 below.

89 Northbourne, *op. cit.*, pp. 114–15; Massingham and Hyams, *op. cit.*, p. 23.

90 Rolt, *High Horse*, *op. cit.*, p. 142, pp. 152–4.

91 *Ibid.*, p. 142; Massingham and Hyams, *op. cit.*, p. 130.

92 R. Duncan, *Journal of a Husbandman* (London, 1944), p. 92.

93 H. J. Massingham, *In Praise of England* (London, 1924), pp. 147–8.

94 H. J. Massingham, *Downland Man* (London, 1926); Massingham, *In Praise*, *op. cit.*, pp. 147–203; H. J. Massingham, *Pre-Roman Britain* (London, 1927); H. J. Massingham, *Fee, Fi, Fo, Fum: The Giants in England* (London, 1926); H. J. Massingham, 'The Finding of Merlin', *Criterion*, IV (1926), pp. 329–41; also Wright, *Village That Died*, *op. cit.*, pp. 106–17.

95 Massingham, *Downland Man*, *op. cit.*, p. 394; also Rolt, *High Horse*, *op. cit.*, p. 162.

96 Massingham, *Downland Man*, *op. cit.*, p. 61, p. 64.

97 *Ibid.*, p. 256; Massingham, *In Praise*, *op. cit.*, p. 197.

98 Massingham, *Downland Man*, *op. cit.*, p. 255.

99 *Ibid.*, p. 241.

100 *Ibid.*, p. 236.

101 G. Elliot Smith, *ibid.*, p. 19.

102 Massingham, 'The Finding of Merlin', *op. cit.*, p. 337; Massingham, *Fee, Fi*, *op. cit.*, p. 162.

103 Massingham, *Downland Man*, *op. cit.*, p. 50, p. 42. Massingham alludes to his friend W. H. Hudson's *Nature in Downland*.

104 *Ibid.*, p. 112.

105 *Ibid.*, p. 62. Massingham may have been one of O.G.S. Crawford's 'Pyramidiots', Crawford, *Archaeology*, *op. cit.*, p. 269.

106 H. J. Massingham, *English Downland* (London, 1936), pp. 24–5.

107 Massingham, *Downland Man, op. cit.*, p. 329.

108 Balfour, *op. cit.*, p. 13.

109 Massingham, *England and the Farmer, op. cit.*, p. 5.

110 Adrian Bell, 'The Family Farm', in Massingham, *England and the Farmer, op. cit.*, pp. 71–90, qu. pp. 87–8.

111 R. G. Stapledon, *Disraeli and the New Age* (London, 1943), p. 15.

112 R. Waller, *Prophet of the New Age: The Life and Thought of Sir George Stapledon* (London, 1962), p. 185.

113 Lymington, *Saturday Review*, 24 March 1934, quoted in R. Griffiths, *Fellow Travellers of the Right: British Enthusiasts for Nazi Germany, 1933–39* (Oxford, 1983), p. 319.

114 Lymington, *Ich Dien, op. cit.*, p. 11.

115 Stapledon, *Disraeli, op. cit.*, p. 169.

116 R. G. Stapledon, 'Imperialism', in Stapledon, *Way of the Land, op. cit.*, pp. 41–60, qu. p. 44.

117 *Ibid.*, p. 50; although Stapledon criticized imperialism's link to 'the capitalistic and patriarchal systems' with their suppression of youth: 'it is a parent-ridden and old-man-ridden system', p. 52. Stapledon's interest in psychoanalytic understanding is clear. In his contribution to the Collins *Britain in Pictures* series Lymington extended British human imperial urge to the animal: 'The animal blood of this small United Kingdom has been as outstanding as its human blood in its passage across high range, prairie, bush and forest'; Earl of Portsmouth, *British Farmstock* (London, 1950), p. 9. There is variation between those such as Lymington and Bell who propose white imperial agrarian settlement, and Gardiner and Stapledon who argue for the export of industry to the empire to leave Britain as a rural motherland. Lymington left Britain for his East African estates after the War.

118 H. J. Massingham, *The English Countryman* (London, 1942), p. 30.

119 Gardiner, *England Herself, op. cit.*, p. 85.

120 A. Bell, *The Open Air* (London, 1936), p. 13.

121 Craven, *op. cit.*; A. Roberts, *Eminent Churchillians* (London, 1994), pp. 287–322. Roberts presents Bryant's patriotic history, *English Saga, 1840–1940* (London, 1940), almost as a gesture of atonement to head off the threat of internment.

122 Blunden, 'Ourselves and Germany: A Minority Retrospect'; quoted in Griffiths, *op. cit.*, p. 362; though B. Webb, *Edmund Blunden: A Biography* (New Haven, 1990) asserts that Blunden had 'no sympathy for Nazism' (p. 215).

123 C. Turnor, *Yeoman Calling* (London, 1939), p. 163. Turnor died in 1940, and his work is praised in Kinship collections. The suggestion here is not that Turnor was a fascist, indeed he would seem another figure whose work cuts across the political spectrum. His earlier work for the Board of Education brought him into contact with Albert Mansbridge, founder of the Workers Educational Association, and he hosted the socialist Margaret McMillan's open-air schools at Stoke Rochford; see chapter 2 above. Mansbridge's autobiography *The Trodden Road* (London, 1940) is

dedicated to Turnor and his wife Sarah. Stoke Rochford Hall is now a National Union of Teachers training centre.

124 Turnor, *op. cit.*, p. 177; for plans, see pp. 274–8.

125 H. Williamson, *The Story of a Norfolk Farm* (London, 1942), pp. 154–6; and see the ecological agrarian vision of Williamson's 'Introduction' in Sir J. Russell, *English Farming* (London, 1942), pp. 7–10; also Keith, *op. cit.*, pp. 213–31. Gardiner, by contrast, put down Mosley's New Party as in essence suburban and middle class, R. Gardiner, *World Without End* (London, 1932), p. 34. Williamson's *Goodbye West Country* (London, 1937), telling in part of the move to Norfolk, also describes approvingly the new Germany, as Williamson attends a Nuremberg rally where he finds himself sitting next to Frank Buchman, leader of Moral Re-Armament, discussed in Chapter Four below, whose movement he compares unfavourably with Hitler's, pp. 234–8.

126 Jorian Jenks, 'Kommissars for Agriculture', *Action*, LI, 6 February 1937, p. 11; Jenks was BUF candidate for Horsham and Worthing in 1936, and interned in 1940; Craven, *op. cit.*, p. 153, p. 188, p. 212; Bramwell, *op. cit.*, pp. 166–8.

127 Massingham, in Jenks, *From the Ground Up, op. cit.*, p. v.

128 Lymington, *Famine, op. cit.*, p. 187; also Lymington, *Horn, op. cit.*, on Italy.

129 Portsmouth, *Knot, op. cit.*, p. 151.

130 Griffiths, *op. cit.*; Craven, *op. cit.*; Wright, *Village That Died, op. cit.*, pp. 171–5; Lymington's associates in these groups included William Joyce (later Lord Haw-Haw), A. K. Chesterton, Gardiner and Blunden.

131 Lymington, *Famine, op. cit.*, pp. 42–3; in 1943 in *Alternative to Death, op. cit.*, Lymington still suggested that the war might have been due to problems created in Germany by 'cosmopolitan lending', p. 35.

132 Lymington, *Famine, op. cit.*, pp. 20–21; Lymington met Mussolini in 1932 and Hitler in 1929 and 1939; they were 'linked in my mind by farming and constructive building', Portsmouth, *Knot, op. cit.*, p. 160.

133 On Gardiner, see M. Chase, 'Rolf Gardiner: An Inter-war, Cross-cultural Case Study', in *Adult Education Between Cultures*, ed., B. Hake and S. Marriott (Leeds, 1993), pp. 225–41; G. Boyes, *The Imagined Village: Culture, Ideology and the English Folk Revival* (Manchester, 1993), pp. 152–95; Wright, *Village That Died, op. cit.*, pp. 150–202.

134 Gardiner, in *Quarterly Gazette of the English Array*, April 1938, quoted in Griffiths, *op. cit.*, p. 146.

135 Gardiner, *England Herself, op. cit.*, p. 73; A. Bramwell, *Blood and Soil: Richard Walther Darre and Hitler's 'Green Party'* (Bourne End, 1985).

136 Rolf Gardiner, 'The Triple Function of Work Camps and Work Service in Europe' (1937), in Best, *Water, op. cit.*, pp. 109–25; also Lymington, *Famine, op. cit.*; Wright, *Village That Died, op. cit.*, pp. 188–9 discusses Gardiner's reservations regarding the Nazi Party, and his distinction of National Socialism and fascism in favour of the former as a religious rather than mass movement.

137 Public Record Office, IAB 23/48; my thanks to Denis Linehan for this reference.

138 Gardiner, *World, op. cit.*, pp. 48–51.

139 R. Gardiner and H. Rocholl, eds, *Britain and Germany: A Frank Discussion Instigated By Members of the Younger Generation* (London, 1928), p. 256, first published in Germany as *Ein Neuer Weg* (Potsdam, 1927); others in the volume proposed racial if not Nordic arguments; see also Gardiner's periodical *North Sea and Baltic*, published quarterly 1931–41. Gardiner, *World, op. cit.*, proposed re-orienting Britain from empire to Europe, hailing Hitler's idea of the Reich as a mystical European idea which 'concerns us all', p. 23.

140 Gardiner, *Britain and Germany, op. cit.*, frontispiece.

141 Gardiner, *England Herself, op. cit.*, p. 48; Chase, *Rolf Gardiner, op. cit.*, comments: 'He seems to have barely noticed those parts of the Bunde whose views he did not share', p. 234. See also *Paul, Angry Young Man, op. cit.*, p. 205, on the exchange between Paul and Gardiner, who in 1933 responded to Paul's criticism of Germany by stressing 'the intimate connections between the Youth Movement and National Socialism'.

142 Gardiner, *World, op. cit.*, p. 45.

143 Rolf Gardiner, 'The Kassel Festival' (1938), in Best, *Water, op. cit.*, pp. 131–6, qu. pp. 134–6.

144 Rolf Gardiner, 'Rural Reconstruction', in Massingham, *England and the Farmer, op. cit.*, pp. 91–107.

145 In 1951, Gardiner contacted Darre, in prison since 1945, in his attempt to rally the Kinship in Husbandry, Craven, *op. cit.*, pp. 194–5, p. 212.

146 Gardiner, *England Herself, op. cit.*, p. 146.

147 Massingham, *Natural Order, op. cit.*, pp. 3–4.

148 F. A. Hayek, *The Road to Serfdom* (London, 1944); for a contemporary critique, see H. Finer, *Road to Reaction* (London 1946).

149 Massingham, *Natural Order, op. cit.*, pp. 4–6; also Rolt, *High Horse, op. cit.*, chapter 9.

150 Balfour, *op. cit.*, p. 193.

151 *Ibid.*, pp. 200-1.

152 Gardiner, *England Herself, op. cit.*, p. 172; also Portsmouth, *Knot, op. cit.*, pp. 212–13.

153 Massingham, *Small Farmer, op. cit.*, p. 63.

154 Massingham, *Faith, op. cit.*, p. 11.

155 Sir W. Beach Thomas, *The Way of a Countryman* (London, 1944), p. 194.

156 Massingham, *England and the Farmer, op. cit.*, pp. 5–6; also Earl of Portsmouth, 'Remaking the Village Capitals of England', in Earl of Portsmouth and H. D. Walston, *Rural England: The Way Ahead, Three Broadcast Talks* (London, 1947), pp. 8–13.

157 H. J. Massingham, *Where Man Belongs* (London, 1946), p. 252.

158 Chase, 'This Is No Claptrap', *op. cit.*

159 H. J. Massingham, *Cotswold Country* (London, 1937), p. 28; Massingham anticipates the analysis of W. G. Hoskins after the War; see David Matless, 'One Man's England: W. G. Hoskins and the English Culture of Landscape', *Rural History*, IV (1993), pp. 187–207.

160 Portsmouth, *Alternative, op. cit.*, p. 55; Lymington, *Famine, op. cit.*, p. 171.

161 Lymington, *Ich Dien, op. cit.*, p. 20.

162 H. J. Massingham, 'Village Bedrock', in Blunden, *Return to Husbandry, op. cit.*, pp. 10–14, qu. p. 10.

163 H. J. Massingham, 'Introduction', in F. Thompson, *Lark Rise to Candleford* (London, 1945), pp. 7–15, qu. pp. 8–9.

164 Portsmouth and Walston, *op. cit.*, pp. 3–8.

165 Gardiner, *England Herself, op. cit.*, p. 171.

166 Jenks, *From the Ground Up, op. cit.*, p. 27.

167 Gardiner, *England Herself, op. cit.*, pp. 144–5, p. 154.

168 *Ibid.*, pp. 139–40; of his workcamps Gardiner wrote: 'to the palimpsest of the past was added a new and purposeful script of labour, song, and thought. Such things do not scratch the surface; they infect the soil and somehow add to its potency; for nothing is done without effect and the effect is registered in a subtle influence called genius loci', *ibid.*, p. 48.

169 Gardiner, *World, op. cit.*, p. 38, quoting John Buchan's 'Midwinter'.

170 Gardiner, *England Herself, op. cit.*, p. 75; in chapter 3 Gardiner describes his failure to get funding from the Special Areas Commission for workcamps, and marks himself out from other land settlement initiatives.

171 Massingham, *Remembrance, op. cit.*, pp. 140–2.

172 Gardiner, *England Herself, op. cit.*, pp. 58–60.

173 Gardiner, 'Rural Reconstruction', *op. cit.*, pp. 105–7.

174 Rolf Gardiner, 'Seven Years at Springhead' (1940–1), in Best, *Water, op. cit.*, pp. 143–52, qu. p. 148.

175 Gardiner, *England Herself, op. cit.*, p. 15; also Rolt, *High Horse, op. cit.*, p. 25.

176 Gardiner, 'Rural Reconstruction', *op. cit.*, pp. 100–1; also Gardiner, *England Herself, op. cit.*, p. 145.

177 *Balfour, op. cit.*, p. 199, p. 201.

178 Gardiner, *England Herself, op. cit.*, p. 171.

179 *Ibid.*, p. 14.

180 Massingham, *Faith, op. cit.*, p. 151, reviewing Bell's 'The Flower and the Wheel'.

181 Massingham, *Remembrance, op. cit.*, p. 50; also Massingham and Hyams, *op. cit.*, p. 97, p. 100 for proposals for Regional Land Wardens. Stapledon proposed a different 'centralized-decentralization', *The Land, op. cit.*, p. 315, and see Disraeli, *op. cit.*, pp. 48–52.

182 Massingham, *English Countryman, op. cit.*, p. 104.

183 Portsmouth, *Alternative, op. cit.*, p. 168; also Barlow, *op. cit.*, p. 207 on the 'natural region'.

184 Gardiner, *England Herself, op. cit.*, p. 166.

185 H. J. Massingham, *World Without End* (London, 1932), p. 16; Massingham, *Remembrance, op. cit.*, p. 84, p. 81; also Massingham, *Cotswold Country, op. cit.* The garden of stone metaphor is explored further in Catherine Brace, 'Finding England Everywhere: Representations of the Cotswolds 1880–1950', unpublished

PhD thesis, University of Bristol, 1997. Massingham followed *World Without End*, written as a diary of a Cotswold year, with *London Scene* (London, 1933), telling of a year in London, having been 'a Londoner all my life', p. ix. The book contains his fullest and not always negative discussion of contemporary building and the city, which he finds fails to present the unity and balance of the Cotswolds. Massingham moves towards a more straightforwardly anti-urban organicism through the 1930s, reflecting at the end of *London Scene* on his growing conviction of a 'spiritual necessity' to grow vegetables: 'I am going to leave London and become a quasi-countryman', p. 262. The 'quasi' self-billing would be less prominent in his later writing.

186 Rolf Gardiner, 'The Wessex Downland Ringed with Growing Towns' (1969), in Best, *Water, op. cit.*, pp. 283–8.

187 Massingham, *Cotswold Country, op. cit.*, p. 33; Massingham, *Remembrance, op. cit.*, p. 96.

188 Massingham, *Remembrance, op. cit.*, p. 119, p. 96; also Gardiner, *England Herself, op. cit.*, p. 25.

189 *Ibid.*, p. 86; Massingham, *English Downland, op. cit.*, *Cotswold Country, op. cit.*; H. J. Massingham, *Chiltern Country* (London, 1940); also see Massingham's three essays on 'English Earth and English Buildings' for the *Geographical Magazine*, 'Limestone', XIII (1941), pp. 295–307; 'Chalk', XIV (1941), pp. 12–25; 'The Lias', XIV (1941), pp. 122–33.

190 Massingham, *Remembrance, op. cit.*, p. 50.

191 Massingham, *English Downland, op. cit.*, p. 2.

192 *Ibid.*, p. 5.

193 Massingham, *Cotswold, op. cit.*, pp. 17–18.

194 Massingham, *English Countryman, op. cit.*, p. 57.

195 Massingham, *Plot, op. cit.*, p. 41.

196 Massingham, *Cotswold, op. cit.*, p. 61, p. 48.

197 *Ibid.*, p. 40; also see Massingham, *Chiltern, op. cit.*, chapter 6, 'Conquered Country'.

198 Rolf Gardiner, 'On the Functions of a Rural University', in Best, *Water, op. cit.*, pp. 88–94, qu. pp. 93–4.

199 Gardiner, 'Rural Reconstruction', *op. cit.*, p. 104; also Massingham, *English Countryman, op. cit.*, pp. 132–3.

200 H. J. Massingham, 'The Wiltshire Flax-Mill: An Example of True Husbandry', *Geographical Magazine*, XVI (1943–4), pp. 369–79, qu. pp. 371–2; also Massingham, *Where Man Belongs, op. cit.*, pp. 163–83 on judging flax with Hosking.

201 *Ibid.*, p. 173; Gardiner, *England Herself, op. cit.*, p. 122.

202 Gardiner, *England Herself, op. cit.*, p. 104, p. 74, pp. 163–4.

203 *Ibid.*, p. 119.

204 J.R.R. Tolkien, *The Fellowship of the Ring* (London, 1954), p. 19; see Veldman, *op. cit.*, on Tolkien's 'romantic interpretation of England's past and his comment on its present', p. 80. Like Gardiner Tolkien's vision was of a North European culture, and like the organicists he held that the War would be a victory for machine power whoever won.

205 T. S. Eliot, *Notes Towards the Definition of Culture* (London, 1948); Philip Mairet, 'Self-Sufficiency', in Massingham, *Natural Order, op. cit.*, pp. 53–65.

206 Eliot, *Notes, op. cit.*, p. 58, p. 52.

207 T. S. Eliot, *After Strange Gods* (London, 1934), p. 17; the passage is quoted in Stapledon, *The Way, op. cit.*, p. 74, and the book praised in Stapledon, *The Land, op. cit.*; see also S. Ellis, *The English Eliot* (London, 1991), pp. 80–1; Donald Davie, 'Anglican Eliot', in *Eliot in His Time*, ed. A. Walton Litz (Princeton, 1973), pp. 181–96. Stapledon's *The Hill Lands of Britain* (London, 1937) was reviewed in *The Criterion* by Mairet: 'I am sorry to have to tell him he is a revolutionary, attacking the financial structure of the real class system of his country'; *Criterion*, xvii (1938), pp. 338–43.

208 Eliot, *After Strange Gods, op. cit.*, p. 20; Bradshaw, *op. cit.*

209 T. S. Eliot, *The Idea of a Christian Society* (London, 1939), p. 31.

210 *Ibid.*, p. 61.

211 T. S. Eliot, 'The Dry Salvages', in *Four Quartets* (London, 1944), line 233.

212 T. S. Eliot, 'East Coker', in *Four Quartets, op. cit.*, lines 24–46, line 100.

213 Ellis, *English Eliot, op. cit.*, pp. 122–40.

214 T. S. Eliot, 'Little Gidding', in *Four Quartets, op. cit.*, line 38, line 5.

4 *The Organic English Body*

1 Bell, 'The Family Farm', *op. cit.*, p. 82.

2 Northbourne, *op. cit.*, p. 161.

3 Rolf Gardiner, 'Youth and Europe' (1923), in Best, *Water, op. cit.*, pp. 19–21, qu. p. 21.

4 For example, see Williamson, *Story, op. cit.;* Duncan, *Journal, op. cit.*; a female exception is Frances Donaldson, whose husband Jack funded the Peckham Health Centre (see below); see F. Donaldson, *Approach to Farming* (London, 1941); *Four Years Harvest* (London, 1945).

5 Duncan, *Journal, op. cit.*, cover blurb; Duncan's masque and anti-masque, *This Way to the Tomb* (London, 1946), with music by Benjamin Britten, was dedicated to Lymington.

6 Duncan, *Journal, op. cit.*, p. 137.

7 *Ibid.*, p. 90.

8 *Ibid.*, p. 118.

9 *Ibid.*, pp. 90–1, p. 89.

10 *Ibid.*, p. 124.

11 Peter Howard, 'Back to Earth', in R. Harman, ed., *Countryside Mood* (London, 1943), pp. 45–64; qu. p. 49; the essay is followed by a photo essay shot on Howard's farm by Richard Haile, 'The Call of the Land: The Spirit of the New Agricultural Pioneers', pp. 65–80. Howard was a Beaverbrook journalist who investigated MRA, sold 150,000 copies of his book *Innocent Men* (1941) which defended it against allegations of fascism, and resigned to join MRA and farm in Suffolk, where Buchman visited him in 1946, finding a 'wholesome place'; G. Lean, *Frank*

Buchman: A Life (London, 1985), p. 337; see P. Howard, *That Man Frank Buchman* (London, 1946). For more critical accounts, see T. Driberg, *The Mystery of Moral Re-Armament* (London, 1964); Neal Ascherson, 'Castle in the Air', *Independent on Sunday*, 30 June 1996, pp. 11–12, which records Howard forming a moral revivalist 'Up With People' MRA youth movement in America in the 1960s.

12   Howard, 'Back to Earth', *op. cit.*, pp. 62–3; for a discussion of parallel Catholic movements in Australia, influenced by Stapledon's ideas, see Martin Auster, 'Making the Earth Like Heaven: Christian and Secular-Professional Attitudes to Australian Land Settlement', *Journal of Religious History*, XVI (1991), pp. 304–14.

13   Kenneth Belden, 'The Spirit of Britain', in R. Harman, ed., *Countryside Character* (London, 1946), pp. 72–104. See also Howard's 'American Uncles' in the same collection, pp. 136–47.

14   Howard, 'Back to Earth', *op. cit.*, p. 61.

15   'Farmer Jarge (A Song of Moral Re-Armament)', by George Fraser, sung by Raymond Newell and Chorus with Orchestra (Columbia Records CA 17681).

16   S. Gibbons, *Cold Comfort Farm* (London, 1932).

17   G. Cavaliero, *The Rural Tradition in the English Novel, 1900–1939* (London, 1977); G. Cavaliero, *John Cowper Powys: Novelist* (Oxford, 1973); C. A. Coates, *John Cowper Powys in Search of a Landscape* (London, 1982); R. P. Graves, *The Brothers Powys* (London, 1983).

18   L. Powys, *Apples Be Ripe* (London, 1930).

19   J. C. Powys, *Wolf Solent* (Harmondsworth, 1964, first published London, 1929), p. 327; J. C. Powys, *A Glastonbury Romance* (London, 1933); J. C. Powys, *Weymouth Sands* (London, 1963; first published as *Jobber Skald*, London, 1935); J. C. Powys, *Maiden Castle* (London, 1937).

20   Powys, *Wolf Solent*, *op. cit.*, p. 67.

21   R. H. Ward, *The Powys Brothers* (London, 1935), p. 54.

22   Bell, 'Husbandry and Society', *op. cit.*, p. 6.

23   Bell, 'The Family Farm', *op. cit.*, p. 75.

24   *Ibid.*, pp. 89–90. Henry Williamson similarly declared: 'I want to see town children educated by bodywork in the country', in Russell, *English Farming*, *op. cit.*, p. 10.

25   H. J. Massingham, 'Rural Aesthetics', in Massingham, *Faith*, *op. cit.*, pp. 55–7.

26   D. Pepper, *Eco-Socialism: from Deep Ecology to Social Justice* (London, 1993); J. Marsh, *Back to the Land: the Pastoral Impulse in Victorian England from 1880 to 1914* (London, 1982).

27   Massingham, *English Countryman*, *op. cit.*, pp. 49–50.

28   F. MacCarthy, *Eric Gill* (London, 1989); MacCarthy brings out the complexity of Gill's medievalist engagement with modernist aesthetics. Gill's *Last Essays* were on the Kinship's recommended reading list.

29   Massingham, *Chiltern*, *op. cit.*, p. 108.

30   Rolt, *High Horse*, *op. cit.*, p. 98.

31   Massingham, *English Countryman*, *op. cit.*, p. 52.

32   Rolt, *High Horse*, *op. cit.*, pp. 62–3; 'George Bourne' (George Sturt), *Change*

in the Village (London, 1912). In this book Sturt is far less resistant to change than the organicist reading would make him out to be. Also see G. Bourne, *The Wheelwright's Shop* (London, 1923); Keith, *op. cit.*, pp. 149–70; Gervais, *op. cit.*, pp. 102–32. Sturt was promoted in similar fashion by F. R. Leavis, who also promoted Adrian Bell in his journal *Scrutiny*. Leavis mixes preservationist and organicist visions of the country. See Leavis and Thompson, *op. cit.*; Boyes, *op. cit.*, pp. 126–33 on Leavis and folk culture.

33 Massingham, *Chiltern, op. cit.*, p. 65.

34 *Ibid.*, p. 88.

35 Massingham, *Remembrance, op. cit.*, p. 132.

36 Massingham, *English Countryman, op. cit.*, p. 55.

37 *Ibid.*, p. 59.

38 Massingham, *Chiltern, op. cit.*, p. 58; also see H. J. Massingham, 'The Downs', in Massingham, ed., *The English Countryside, op. cit.*, pp. 86–93; Massingham, *English Countryman, op. cit.*; Massingham, *Plot, op. cit.*; Massingham, *Remembrance, op. cit.*; also Massingham, *Where Man Belongs, op. cit.*, pp. 130–41 on Chiltern chair-maker 'Goodchild of Naphill'.

39 Massingham, *Remembrance, op. cit.*, pp. 134–5.

40 Massingham, *Chiltern, op. cit.*, p. 87, on Edward Goodchild.

41 T. Hennell, *Change in the Farm* (London, 1934); T. Hennell, *British Craftsmen* (London, 1944). Hennell illustrated *Return to Husbandry*, *The Natural Order* and several Massingham books.

42 Massingham, *Chiltern, op. cit.*, p. 60; also see the photograph in Massingham, *English Countryman, op. cit.*, p. 59.

43 Hennell provides a parallel image of industrial labour in a drawing of Sheffield forgers in *British Craftsmen, op. cit.*, p. 34. For an organicist aesthetic of industry, see also P. Drabble, *Black Country* (London, 1952); Drabble went on to be a noted country commentator and presenter of the BBC sheepdog trial show 'One Man and His Dog'.

44 Massingham, 'Wiltshire Flax-Mill', *op. cit.*, p. 376.

45 Lymington, 'The Policy of Husbandry', *op. cit.*, p. 28; on the role of the Women's Land Army, see Chapter Five below.

46 L. Picton, *Thoughts on Feeding* (London, 1946), pp. 163–4.

47 Lymington, *Famine, op. cit.*, pp. 81–2; Massingham, *England and the Farmer, op. cit.*, plate 21.

48 Rolt, *High Horse, op. cit.*, pp. 129–30.

49 Portsmouth, *Alternative, op. cit.*, p. 18.

50 Bell, 'The Family Farm', *op. cit.*, p. 75, p. 84, p. 89.

51 Massingham, *English Countryman, op. cit.*, p. 65.

52 Balfour, *op. cit.*, p. 201.

53 Lymington, *Famine, op. cit.*, pp. 186–7.

54 Massingham, *Cotswold, op. cit.*, p. 100.

55 Massingham, *Chiltern, op. cit.*, pp. 94–6; also Rolt, *High Horse, op. cit.*, p. 34.

56 Massingham, *England and the Farmer*, *op. cit.*, plate 7.

57 Williamson, in Russell, *English Farming*, *op. cit.*, p. 10; also Portsmouth, *Alternative*, *op. cit.*, p. 22.

58 H. J. Massingham, 'The Emperor Jazz', in Massingham, *Faith*, *op. cit.*, pp. 53–5.

59 Massingham, *Where Man Belongs*, *op. cit.*, p. 9, p. 27.

60 *Ibid.*, p. 54.

61 Massingham, 'Rural Aesthetics', *op. cit.*, p. 57.

62 Massingham, *Faith*, *op. cit.*, pp. 30–1.

63 Portsmouth, *Alternative*, *op. cit.*, p. 37.

64 Boyes, *Imagined Village*, *op. cit.*, pp. 152–80; Wright, *Village That Died*, *op. cit.*, pp. 158–62; Trentmann, 'Civilization', *op. cit.* Douglas Kennedy, Director of the English Folk Dance and Song Society from 1925–61, was in the Kinship in Husbandry but organicist themes are not strong in his later writings, which do not discuss Gardiner, for example, D. Kennedy, *English Folk Dancing* (London, 1964).

65 Gardiner, *England Herself*, *op. cit.*, p. 126.

66 Rolt, *High Horse*, *op. cit.*, pp. 76–7; Rolt drew on the Upper Thames collections of Alfred Williams, p. 74, pp. 159–61; on Williams, see D. Harker, *Fakesong: the Manufacture of British 'Folksong' 1700 to the Present Day* (Milton Keynes, 1985).

67 Gardiner, *England Herself*, *op. cit.*, p. 129; Boyes, *op. cit.*, Wright, *Village That Died*, *op. cit.* When Gardiner does quote Sharp favourably it is to state: 'Modernity is the keynote of the folk-song', *England Herself*, *op. cit.*, p. 128. Gardiner's equivalent anti-picturesque folk culturist on the left was Conrad Noel, the communist vicar of Thaxted in Essex; see C. Noel, *An Autobiography* (London, 1945).

68 Rolf Gardiner, 'When Peace Breaks Out: Tasks of Youth in a Post-War World', in Blunden, ed., *Return*, *op. cit.*, pp. 20–25, qu. p. 23.

69 Gardiner, *England Herself*, *op. cit.*, pp. 131–2, p. 38.

70 *Ibid.*, p. 135.

71 Gardiner, 'When Peace Breaks Out', *op. cit.*, p. 24; Gardiner sought unsuccessfully to redirect the YHA towards an organic hiking through 'Wessex Hiker's Lodges', see Wright, *Village That Died*, *op. cit.*, pp. 153–4.

72 Gardiner, *England Herself*, *op. cit.*, p. 21.

73 *Ibid.*, p. 27.

74 *Ibid.*, p. 139; Gardiner's camps included the singing of polyphonic masses by William Byrd, *ibid.*, p. 42. Gardiner's is a very different sense of polyphony to that upheld in more recent discussions in cultural geography and cultural studies; see P. Crang, 'The Politics of Polyphony: Reconfigurations in Geographical Authority', *Environment and Planning D: Society and Space*, x (1992), pp. 527–49.

75 Duncan, *Journal*, *op. cit.*, p. 95.

76 Gardiner, 1936, quoted in Boyes, *op. cit.*, p. 169.

77 T. F. Powys, *Mr Weston's Good Wine* (London, 1927); Graves, *op. cit.*; Cavaliero, *op. cit.*, pp. 173–95; Wright, *Village That Died*, *op. cit.*, pp. 130–6. Wright notes how Gardiner's admiration for D. H. Lawrence led to him being suspected of extending his theories of dancing communion with the folk to other forms of intercourse, *ibid.*, p. 156.

78 L.T.C. Rolt, *Narrow Boat* (London, 1944); the book remains in print. See also L.T.C. Rolt, *Inland Waterways of England* (London, 1950); L.T.C. Rolt, *The Thames from Mouth to Source* (London, 1951). Rolt went on to produce many books on engineering on railway history and preservation. In the second volume of his autobiography Rolt recalls how he 'joined forces' with Massingham, Howard and Lymington in wartime; L.T.C. Rolt, *Landscape with Canals* (London, 1977), p. 70; also Rolt, *High Horse, op. cit.*; L.T.C. Rolt, 'Small Machines for Small Farmers', in Massingham, ed., *Small Farmer, op. cit.*, pp. 229–56; Veldman, *op. cit.*, p. 261 on Rolt and the Soil Association. There are two other volumes of autobiography, *Landscape with Machines* (London, 1971) and *Landscape with Figures* (Stroud, 1992). Rolt was an unacknowledged consultant for the Ealing film *Painted Boats*, a semi-documentary with commentary by Louis MacNiece, directed by Charles Crichton in 1945; Rolt, *Landscape with Canals*, pp. 79–84; C. Barr, *Ealing Studios* (London, 1993), p. 196.

79 Rolt, *Narrow Boat, op. cit.*, pp. 11–12.

80 *Ibid.*, p. 18.

81 Rolt, *High Horse, op. cit.*, pp. 82–3.

82 Rolt, *Narrow Boat, op. cit.*, p. 32.

83 *Ibid.*, p. 131.

84 Sibley, *op. cit.*, p. 102.

85 H. J. Massingham, 'Foreword', in Rolt, *Narrow Boat, op. cit.*, pp. vii–viii.

86 Rolt, *Narrow Boat, op. cit.*, p. 36.

87 For a parallel contemporary study, see Lady E. Smith, *British Circus Life* (London, 1948), with photographs by John Hinde, on 'the nomad creatures of the English road' (pp. 13–14), part of Collins's *British Ways of Life* series which also included a Mass-Observation study by W. J. Turner, *Exmoor Village* (London, 1947); see David Matless, 'Doing the English Village, 1945–90', in P. Cloke, M. Doel, D. Matless, M. Phillips and N. Thrift, *Writing the Rural: Five Cultural Geographies* (London, 1994), pp. 7–88.

88 Rolt, *Narrow Boat, op. cit.*, p. 26; Rolt's *Inland Waterways of England* had a frontispiece by Barbara Jones, then engaged in discovering canal art as one of *The Unsophisticated Arts* (London, 1951), 'at once English and exotic', p. 51. One suspects that Rolt might have regarded Jones's work as focusing on the style of decoration in a manner detached from its social production; see also M. Lambert and E. Marx, *English Popular Art* (London, 1951).

89 Rolt, *Narrow Boat, op. cit.*, p. 40.

90 *Ibid.*, pp. 79–80.

91 *Ibid.*, pp. 96–7.

92 *Ibid.*, p. 37.

93 *Ibid.*, p. 154; Rolt notes of the boatman, 'though I could not lose the company of books, I have often envied him his happy immunity from the howling bedlam of the hoarding and popular Press', p. 154. Richard Hoggart, *The Uses of Literacy* (London, 1957).

94 Rolt, *Narrow Boat*, *op. cit.*, pp. 194–5.

95 *Ibid.*, p. 110.

96 *Ibid.*, p. 125.

97 *Ibid.*, p. 119.

98 Massingham, 'Foreword', in *Narrow Boat*, *op. cit.*, p. viii; looking back Rolt would find the book 'too self-consciously arcadian and picturesque', Rolt, *Landscape with Canals*, *op. cit.*, p. 84.

99 L.T.C. Rolt, *Worcestershire* (London, 1949), p. 283, p. xiv.

100 Rolt, *Landscape with Canals*, *op. cit.*, p. 73. Angela Rolt's photographs illustrated later works such as *Inland Waterways of England*.

101 *Ibid.*, pp. 167–8, and chapter 5; also Samuel, *Theatres*, *op. cit.*, p. 185, p. 248.

102 Rolt, *Narrow Boat*, *op. cit.*, p. 75.

103 J. Wentworth Day, *Farming Adventure* (London, 1943), pp. 17–18; quoted in Massingham, *Plot*, *op. cit.*, p. 94.

104 Howard, *Testament*, *op. cit.*, p. 40.

105 L. J. Picton, 'Diet and Farming', in Massingham, *England and the Farmer*, *op. cit.*, pp. 108–30; Philip Oyler, 'Feeding Ourselves', in Massingham, *Natural Order*, *op. cit.*, pp. 66–79; the most substantive account is Jorian Jenks's 1959 review of organicist work, *'The Stuff Man's Made Of': The Positive Approach to Health through Nutrition* (London, 1959), which also discusses organic farming in general.

106 Northbourne, *op. cit.*, p. 46.

107 Balfour, *op. cit.*, p. 174.

108 Northbourne, *op. cit.*, p. 41.

109 *Ibid.*, p. 43; Picton, *Thoughts*, *op. cit.*, p. 86.

110 Northbourne, *op. cit.*, p. 39.

111 *Ibid.*, p. 46; G. T. Wrench, *The Wheel of Health* (London, 1938).

112 Picton, 'Diet and Farming', *op. cit.*, p. 111.

113 J. Wentworth Day, *Poison on the Land* (London, 1957); Day's concern is largely with the threat to game birds from pesticides; also see H. J. Massingham, *An Englishman's Year* (London, 1948), p. 183 on DDT. Pesticides did not become a matter of major public concern until the 1960s, see J. Sheail, *Pesticides and Nature Conservation: The British Experience, 1950–1975* (Oxford, 1985), especially chapter 3 on Government responses in the 1950s.

114 Northbourne, *op. cit.*, p. 64.

115 Massingham, *Plot*, *op. cit.*, p. 89.

116 *Ibid.*, p. 97, quoting letter from Laurence Easterbrook.

117 *Ibid.*, p. 97.

118 Albert Howard, 'Editorial', *Soil and Health*, 1 (1) (1946), p. 3; the Spring 1948 issue is a tribute to Howard following his death. The *News Letter on Compost* was issued three times a year from October 1941.

119 Portsmouth, *Alternative*, *op. cit.*, p. 11; Lymington, *Famine*, *op. cit.*, pp. 153–6; Wrench, *Wheel of Health*, *op. cit.*, pp. 23–38; Picton, 'Diet and Farming', *op. cit.*, pp. 121–4; Picton, *Thoughts*, *op. cit.*, pp. 176–83.

120 Northbourne, *op. cit.*, p. 53.

121 Sir Robert McCarrison, 'Nutrition and National Health', *Journal of the Royal Society of Arts*, LXXXIV (1936), pp. 1047–110, qu. p. 1102. McCarrison suggested a 'citizen army' of the unemployed should cultivate vegetables (p. 1103), and that wholewheat flour was crucial (p. 1059), but he addressed only briefly methods of farming (pp. 1049–50). The lectures were reproduced as R. McCarrison, *Nutrition and National Health* (London, 1944).

122 J. Ryan, *Picturing Empire: Photography and the Visualization of the British Empire* (London, 1997).

123 McCarrison, 'Nutrition', *op. cit.*, pp. 1061–3.

124 Massingham, *Englishman's Year*, *op. cit.*, p. 98; Picton, 'Diet and Farming', *op. cit.*, pp. 111–13.

125 Picton, *Thoughts*, *op. cit.*, p. 265.

126 Balfour, *op. cit.*, pp. 142–58; Wrench, *Wheel*, *op. cit.*; Picton, *Thoughts*, *op. cit.*, pp. 63–8; Northbourne, *op. cit.*, pp. 48–9; Conford, 'Alchemy', *op. cit.*

127 Howard, *Testament*, *op. cit.*, p. 74.

128 Wrench, *Reconstruction*, *op. cit.*, p. 15; Wrench, *Wheel*, *op. cit.*

129 Beach Thomas, *op. cit.*, p. 195.

130 Northbourne, *op. cit.*, p. 62, also pp. 56–7.

131 Duncan, *Journal*, *op. cit.*, p. 68.

132 *Ibid.*, p. 123.

133 Oyler, 'Feeding Ourselves', *op. cit.*, p. 66.

134 Lymington, *Famine*, *op. cit.*, p. 82; Oyler, *op. cit.*, p. 73.

135 Picton, *Thoughts*, *op. cit.*, p. 250.

136 Craven, *op. cit.*, p. 69.

137 Oyler, *op. cit.*, p. 76.

138 Oyler, *op. cit.*, p. 75; also Portsmouth, *Alternative*, *op. cit.*, pp. 158–9.

139 P. Oyler, *The Generous Earth* (London, 1950); David Mellor, 'The Body and the Land', in D. Mellor, ed., *A Paradise Lost: The Neo-Romantic Imagination in Britain 1935–55* (London, 1987), pp. 58–65.

140 Duncan, *Journal*, *op. cit.*, p. 87.

141 Lymington, 'The Policy of Husbandry', *op. cit.*, p. 19.

142 The rate rose from 70 per cent before the war to 85 per cent in March 1942, though wholemeal was not held to be popular with the general public. On this and issues of dietary improvement in wartime, see Ministry of Food, *How Britain Was Fed In Wartime* (London, 1946); A. Calder, *The People's War: Britain, 1939–1945* (London, 1969), pp. 404–5.

143 H. J. Massingham, 'Our Daily Starch', in Massingham, *Faith*, *op. cit.*, pp. 77–9; Massingham, *Plot*, *op. cit.*, pp. 228–9; Picton, *Thoughts*, *op. cit.*, pp. 126–8, pp. 165–9; Bishop, 'Constable Country', *op. cit.*

144 Picton, *Thoughts*, *op. cit.*, pp. 128–33, pp. 150–9.

145 *Ibid.*, p. 169; on pro-natalism in reconstruction debates, see Chapter Seven below.

146 'Our Murdered Bread', *Soil and Health*, 1 (1946), pp. 36–49; the journal reported

(p. 44) that Doris Grant's *Your Daily Bread* (London, 1944) had prompted two House of Lords debates.

147 John Maberly, 'The National Bread and its Effect upon Health', *Soil and Health*, 1 (1946), pp. 40–4.

148 Massingham, 'Our Daily Starch', *op. cit.*, p. 78.

149 Picton, *Thoughts, op. cit.*, pp. 20–21.

150 *Ibid.*, pp. 19–30; also Picton, 'Diet and Farming', *op. cit.*, pp. 115–17; Balfour, *op. cit.*, pp. 23–9; *British Medical Journal* (1939), Supplement, 15 April, pp. 157–9.

151 Picton, *Thoughts, op. cit.*, p. 23, p. 24, p. 29.

152 *British Medical Journal* (1939), 13 May, p. 1004; the journal had earlier published G. T. Wrench, 'Health and the Soil', *British Medical Journal* (1939), 11 February, pp. 276–7.

153 Picton, *Thoughts, op. cit.*, p. 29.

154 *Ibid.*, p. 77.

155 *Ibid.*, p. 96.

156 *Ibid.*, p. 179.

157 *Ibid.*, pp. 74–6; Balfour, *op. cit.*, pp. 139–40.

158 Picton, *Thoughts, op. cit.*, pp. 90–4; Balfour, *op. cit.*, pp. 137–9.

159 I. Pearse and L. Crocker, *The Peckham Experiment: A Study of the Living Structure of Society* (London, 1943); G. S. Williamson and I. Pearse, *Biologists in Search of Material* (London, 1938); G. S. Williamson, *Physician, Heal Thyself* (London, 1945); Jane Lewis and Barbara Brookes, 'A Reassessment of the Work of the Peckham Health Centre, 1926–1951', *Millbank Memorial Fund Quarterly*, LXI (1983), pp. 307–50; Jane Lewis and Barbara Brookes, 'The Peckham Health Centre, "PEP", and the Concept of General Practice During the 1930s and 1940s', *Medical History*, XXVII (1983), pp. 151–61; A. Stallibrass, *Being Me and Also Us: Lessons From the Peckham Experiment* (Edinburgh, 1989); A. Scott-Samuel, ed., *Total Participation, Total Health: Reinventing the Peckham Health Centre for the 1990s* (Guildford, 1990). For parallel studies, see Pyrs Gruffudd, '"A Crusade against Consumption": Environment, Health and Social Reform in Wales, 1909–1939', *Journal of Historical Geography*, XXI (1995), pp. 39–54; Elizabeth Lebas, '"When Every Street Became a Cinema": The Film Work of Bermondsey Borough Council's Public Health Department, 1923–1953', *History Workshop Journal*, XXXIX (1995), pp. 42–66.

160 Lewis and Brookes quickly pass over Peckham's connections to 'a related, dubiously scientific venture, called the Living Soil Society [sic], 'A Reassessment', *op. cit.*, p. 336. M.R.A. Chance, asking 'Where From Peckham?' (*The Lancet*, CCLVIII [1950], pp. 726–8) after the Centre's closure, ridiculed the linkage of health and soil: 'the importance of food grown on compost . . . after all is quite another matter, but in the minds of those running the centre they were inexplicably linked not to say confused', p. 727.

161 Stapledon, *Sunday Times*, 1938, quoted in Stallibrass, *op. cit.*, p. 110.

162 Balfour, *op. cit.*, p. 192.

163 Howard, *Testament, op. cit.*, p. 180; Howard, 'Soil Fertility', *op. cit.*, pp. 37–8.

164 Pearse and Crocker, *op. cit.*, pp. 24–5.

165 *Ibid.*, pp. 146–8.

166 Howard, *Testament*, *op. cit.*, p. 178. Members could camp at the farm and work the land; 29 families were evacuated there in wartime.

167 Pearse and Crocker, *op. cit.*, p. 123.

168 *Ibid.*, foreword.

169 *Ibid.*, p. 69.

170 *Ibid.*, p. 42.

171 *Ibid.*, p. 91. In 1948 Centre members set up a journal ironically entitled 'Guinea Pigs'.

172 *Ibid.*, pp. 164–5, p. 254, chapter 5 on the family consultation; also Williamson, *Physician*, *op. cit.*, pp. 116–17; Lewis and Brookes, 'A Reassessment', p. 332, note that such an attitude to birth control was 'an extremely progressive view for the inter war years'.

173 Pearse and Crocker, *op. cit.*, pp. 249–54.

174 *Ibid.*, p. 69.

175 *Ibid.*, p. 229.

176 *Ibid.*, p. 231.

177 *Ibid.*, pp. 131–4.

178 Williamson and Pearse, *op. cit.*, pp. 40–2; Pearse and Crocker, *op. cit.*, p. 130.

179 Quoted in Stallibrass, *op. cit.*, p. 53. Williamson was politically a conservative anarchist, opposing both medical orthodoxy and the National Health Service, and arguing for spontaneous communal order through a conservative model of family and community.

180 Pearse and Crocker, *op. cit.*, p. 192.

181 Balfour, *op. cit.*, p. 139.

182 Picton, 'Diet and Farming', *op. cit.*, pp. 117–18.

183 Picton, *Thoughts*, *op. cit.*, p. 154.

184 Picton, 'Diet and Farming', *op. cit.*, pp. 118–19.

185 Picton, *Thoughts*, *op. cit.*, pp. 193–209.

186 Oyler, 'Feeding Ourselves', *op. cit.*, p. 69.

187 *Soil and Health*, II (1947), p. 66.

188 McCarrison, quoted in Balfour, *op. cit.*, pp. 145–6.

189 Massingham, *Englishman's Year*, *op. cit.*, p. 141, quoting Day, *Harvest Adventure*, *op. cit.*

190 Picton, *Thoughts*, *op. cit.*, p. 242; Sibley, *op. cit.*; M. Douglas, *Purity and Danger* (London, 1966); for a wonderful parallel study of the Philippines see Warwick Anderson, 'Excremental Colonialism: Public Health and the Poetics of Pollution', *Critical Inquiry*, XXI (1995), pp. 640–69.

191 Gardiner, *England Herself*, *op. cit.*, p. 81.

192 Lymington, 'The Policy of Husbandry', *op. cit.*, p. 25; also Lymington, *Famine*, *op. cit.*, p. III.

193 Lymington, *Famine*, *op. cit.*, p. 138.

194 Lymington, 'The Policy of Husbandry', *op. cit.*, p. 30.

195 H. D. Walston, 'Agriculture in a Planned Economy', in Portsmouth and Walston, *Rural England*, pp. 13–18, qu. p. 13.

196 Picton, *Thoughts, op. cit.*, pp. 242–3.

197 Picton, 'Diet and Farming', p. 130; Picton, *Thoughts, op. cit.*, pp. 13–14.

198 Howard, *Testament, op. cit.*, p. 37; and pp. 104–15 on 'The Utilization of Town Wastes'. Howard addressed the Health Congress of the Royal Sanitary Institute in Portsmouth in July 1938 on 'The Manufacture of Humus from the Wastes of the Town and the Village', reprinted in Howard, *Testament*, pp. 235–43; and see Lionel Picton, 'The Economic Disposal of Excreta: Garden Sanitation', *British Medical Journal*, 9 February 1924.

199 Massingham, *Plot, op. cit.*, pp. 284–5, quoting Reginald Reynolds, *Cleanliness and Godliness* (New York, 1943), p. 274; also Northbourne, *op. cit.*, pp. 67–8. On health risks associated with human excrement on land see the review of Wrench's *Wheel of Health* in *The Lancet*, CCXXXVI (1939), p. 936, and a similar debate following the publication of the Cheshire *Medical Testament* in the *British Medical Journal*, including letters by Howard (15 July 1939, p. 142) and Wrench (29 July 1939, pp. 25 1–2).

200 *Reynolds, op. cit.*, pp. 267–8.

201 Picton, *Thoughts, op. cit.*, p. 16; it is not thought that Picton had metempsychosis via digestion in mind.

202 *Ibid.*, pp. 16–17.

203 Lymington, 'The Policy of Husbandry', *op. cit.*, p. 12.

204 Portsmouth, *Alternative, op. cit.*, p. 30.

205 *Ibid.*, p. 19.

206 Lymington, 'The Policy of Husbandry', *op. cit.*, p. 15.

207 Portsmouth, *Alternative, op. cit.*, p. 19.

208 Pearse and Crocker, *op. cit.*, p. 247.

209 Duncan, *Journal, op. cit.*, p. 92.

210 *Ibid.*, p. 91.

211 Northbourne, *op. cit.*, p. 58.

212 Stapledon, *Land, op. cit.*, p. 231.

213 C. Henry Warren, 'Corn', in *op. cit.*, p. 66; also Stapledon, *Disraeli, op. cit.*, p. 69.

214 Lymington, *Famine, op. cit.*, p. 11.

5 *Landscapes of War*

1 For varying accounts of the period, see P. Addison, *The Road to 1945: British Politics and the Second World War* (London, 1975); A. Aldgate and J. Richards, *Britain Can Take It: The British Cinema in the Second World War* (Oxford, 1986); C. Barnett, *The Audit of War: The Illusion and Reality of Britain as a Great Nation* (London, 1986); Calder, *People's War, op. cit.*; A. Calder, *The Myth of the Blitz* (London, 1991); S. Fielding, P. Thompson and N. Tiratsoo, *'England Arise!': The Labour Party and Popular Politics in 1940s Britain* (Manchester, 1995); P. Hennessy, *Never Again: Britain, 1945–1951*; G. Hurd, ed., *National Fictions: World War Two in British Films*

and Television (London, 1984); H. L. Smith, ed., *War and Social Change: British Society in the Second World War* (Manchester, 1986); R. Titmuss, *Problems of Social Policy* (London, 1950).

2 Ministry of Information, *Land at War* (London, 1945); K. Murray, *Agriculture* (London, 1955); S. Ward, *War in the Countryside, 1939–45* (Newton Abbot, 1988); L. Easterbrook, ed., *The Future of Agriculture* (London, *c.* 1943) (contributors included Stamp, F. G. Thomas, Stapledon and Russell).

3 Ministry, *Land at War, op. cit.*, p. 7, p. 8, p. 85, p. 30. Scotland and Ulster are given their own chapters; by implication the rest concerns England and Wales, and the language and imagery fixes the book as a whole firmly into rural Englishness.

4 *Ibid.*, p. 15.

5 A. G. Street, broadcasting in 1943, quoted in Waller, *op. cit.*, p. 261; R. G. Stapledon and W. Davies, *Ley Farming* (Harmondsworth, Penguin Special, 1941); Murray, *op. cit.*, pp. 250–3; Stapledon suggested that 9 million acres of seemingly 'permanent' grass should be ploughed up and put into rotational cropping.

6 Ministry, *Land at War, op. cit.*, pp. 40–45.

7 *Ibid.*, p. 28.

8 *Ibid.*, p. 29.

9 *Ibid.*, p. 60.

10 *Ibid.*, p. 12; Murray, *op. cit.*, pp. 300–3.

11 Ministry of Agriculture and Fisheries, *National Farm Survey of England and Wales: A Summary Report* (London, 1946), p. 13; Brian Short and Charles Watkins, 'The National Farm Survey of England and Wales 1941–3', *Area*, XXVI (1994), pp. 288–93. The latter forms part of a major research project into the workings and findings of the Survey, based in the Geography Departments of the Universities of Sussex and Nottingham.

12 Assessment form, reproduced in Ministry, *National Farm Survey, op. cit.*, p. 108; the Ministry regretted that 'there has been a tendency to identify the National Farm Survey largely in terms of this item', p. 51. By the end of 1943 the War Ags had taken over nearly 400,000 acres in England and Wales, although less than 10 per cent of cases involved eviction, Calder, *People's War, op. cit.*, pp. 426–7.

13 Calder, *People's War, op. cit.*, p. 427; A. G. Street, *Feather Bedding* (London, 1954), pp. 28–43.

14 Ministry, *Land at War, op. cit.*, pp. 11–12.

15 J. Wentworth Day, *History of the Fens* (London, 1954), p. 256. As noted in Chapter Three, Lymington and Northbourne served on War Ags; the political and cultural composition of these bodies demands further research.

16 Ministry, *Land at War, op. cit.*, p. 37.

17 *Ibid.*, p. 28.

18 *Ibid.*, p. 88; Murray, *op. cit.*, p. 272 gives a lower estimate; Easterbrook, *op. cit.*, p. 18, suggests that 700,000 pensioners returned to work on the land.

19 V. Sackville-West, *The Women's Land Army* (London, 1944); like the War Ags this was a new force which worked through established authority figures.

20 H. V. Morton, *I Saw Two Englands* (London, 1942), p. 275.

21 Sackville-West, *op. cit.*, p. 47; Sackville-West also highlighted regional and international migration into the Land Army, stressing the adaptability of women.

22 Ministry, *Land At War, op. cit.*, p. 89.

23 Sackville-West, *op. cit.*, p. 7.

24 *Ibid.*, pp. 25–6.

25 P. Summerfield, *Women Workers in the Second World War* (London, 1984).

26 Sackville-West, *op. cit.*, pp. 90–2.

27 *Ibid.*, p. 88.

28 Edith Olivier, 'The English Village in War-Time', *Geographical Magazine*, XIV (1942), pp. 282–90, qu. pp. 284–6; the same woman appears driving a tractor in C. Beaton, *Air of Glory: A Wartime Scrapbook* (London, 1941).

29 Calder, *People's War, op. cit.*, p. 428.

30 Sackville-West, *op. cit.*, p. 89.

31 *Ibid.*, p. III.

32 Ministry, *Land at War, op. cit.*, p. 92.

33 Ministry of Food, *op. cit.*, p. 45.

34 C. McCall, *Women's Institutes* (London, 1943), pp. 30–1; Maggie Morgan, 'Jam Making, Cuthbert Rabbit and Cakes: Redefining Domestic Labour in the Women's Institute, 1915–60', *Rural History*, VII (1996), pp. 207–19. In 1940, 1,631 tons were preserved; in 1941, 1,764 tons.

35 Calder, *People's War, op. cit.*, p. 430; D. Crouch and C. Ward, *The Allotment* (London, 1988; republished Nottingham, 1996); Murray, *op. cit.*, pp. 245–8; and see the Batsford *Home-Front Handbook* by Doreen Wallace, *How to Grow Food* (London, 1940).

36 Ministry, *Land at War, op. cit.*, pp. 93–4.

37 Winston Churchill, speaking in the House of Commons in 1934, quoted in Titmuss, *Problems, op. cit.*, p. 9.

38 *Ibid.*, p. 101. There were wide variations in the proportions of evacuees sent, reflecting levels of organization and perceptions of danger. All schools in evacuated areas were closed, despite many children not leaving. For general accounts, see Calder, *People's War, op. cit.*, pp. 35–49; C. Jackson, *Who Will Take Our Children?* (London, 1985); John Macnicol, 'The Evacuation of Schoolchildren', in Smith, ed., *War and Social Change, op. cit.*, pp. 3–31; C. Ward, *The Child in the Country* (London, 1988), pp. 47–56.

39 The return was ascribed to the diminished expectation of bombing, unhappiness in the reception areas, and general failures of the scheme due to the 'military, male and middle-class' outlook of organizers, emphasizing procedures for transport rather than reception; R. Padley and M. Cole, eds, *Evacuation Survey: A Report to the Fabian Society* (London, 1940), p. 4; Titmuss, *Problems, op. cit.*, p. 110. The scheme revived briefly during the Blitz, and later became more a welfare agency for mothers unable to look after children. There were also around 2 million private evacuees of all classes, with some resentment at well-off people relocating

themselves in safe remote hotels for the duration: 'About the 2,000,000 "private" evacuees, the historian knows nothing', Titmuss, *Problems, op. cit.*, p. 102. My focus here is on debates around the early operation of the public scheme.

40 Batsford, *How to See the Country, op. cit.*, p. 1.

41 Morton, *I Saw, op. cit.*, pp. 215–16.

42 See Padley and Cole, *op. cit.*, p. 59, on the House of Commons debate on evacuation, 14 September 1939.

43 R. Crompton, *William and the Evacuees* (London, 1940), p. 24.

44 National Federation of Women's Institutes, *Town Children Through Country Eyes* (Dorking, 1940); Padley and Cole, *op. cit.*; Women's Group on Public Welfare, *Our Towns: A Close-Up* (Oxford, 1943); S. Issacs, ed., *The Cambridge Evacuation Survey: A Wartime Study in Social Welfare and Education* (London, 1941); Barnett House Study Group, *London Children in War-Time Oxford* (Oxford, 1947); H. C. Dent, *Education in Transition* (London, 1944). In *Governing the Soul: The Shaping of the Private Self* (London, 1990) Nikolas Rose highlights evacuation surveys as part of a general argument on a shift in the Second World War in the social role of the human sciences, specifically psychology, in relation not only to childhood but adult labour and leisure. Rose's study provides a parallel investigation of the wartime and post-war shaping of the self to that of Part III of this book.

45 Women's Group, *op. cit.*, pp. 1–8.

46 *Ibid.*, p. xiv; Women's Institutes, *op. cit.*, p. 3.

47 Padley and Cole, *op. cit.*, p. 3, pp. 6–7.

48 *Ibid.*, p. 158, p. 75.

49 Titmuss, *Problems, op. cit.*, p. 111.

50 Padley and Cole, *op. cit.*, p. 73.

51 *Ibid.*, p. 28, p. 150; or might obtain medical certificates of exemption, Titmuss, *Problems, op. cit.*, p. 393.

52 J. M. Robinson, *The Country House At War* (London, 1989).

53 E. Waugh, *Put Out More Flags* (London, 1942), p. 79.

54 *Ibid.*, p. 80; Waugh also has the billeting officers running a racket with the children, selling them from family to family and splitting the proceeds, and rich arty-crafty couples trying to avoid evacuees by taking in paying guests.

55 Women's Institutes, *op. cit.*, p. 4.

56 *Ibid.*, p. 6, p. 11, p. 13.

57 Padley and Cole, *op. cit.*, p. 162.

58 *Ibid.*, p. 62; Titmuss, *Problems, op. cit.*, pp. 125–8; the rate was relatively high as evacuation took place at the end of the school holidays and so children had not been inspected for some months.

59 Women's Institutes, *op. cit.*, p. 6.

60 Padley and Cole, *op. cit*, p. 226.

61 *Ibid.*, p. 148.

62 Olivier, *op. cit.*, p. 286.

63 Women's Institutes, *op. cit.*, p. 15.

64 Padley and Cole, *op. cit.*, p. 226; also Olivier, *op. cit.*, p. 288.

65 Padley and Cole, *op. cit.*, p. 227, p. 230; and see Barnett House Group, *op. cit.*, pp. 65–8.

66 Padley and Cole, *op. cit.*, p. 5.

67 Titmuss, *Problems, op. cit.*, p. 182.

68 *Ibid.*, p. 168, quoting report from Inspector of Education in Devon.

69 Women's Institutes, *op. cit.*, p. 19.

70 *Ibid.*, p. 18.

71 *Ibid.*, pp. 21–2.

72 T. Harrisson, *Living Through the Blitz* (London, 1976), p. 100.

73 Calder, *Myth, op. cit.*; Calder, *People's War, op. cit.*, pp. 163–227; Harrisson, *Living, op. cit.*; J. Hasegawa, *Replanning the Blitzed City Centre* (Buckingham, 1992); Taylor, *Dream of England, op. cit.*, pp. 182–211; Titmuss, *Problems, op. cit.*

74 Calder, *People's War, op. cit.*, p. 164, p. 168; for the effects of bombing even on royalty, see Country Life's *Britain Under Fire* (London, 1941), with a foreword by Priestley and aimed in part at the USA, showing 'Britain Under Fire and Carrying On' with the King and Queen by their bombed palace as a frontispiece: 'Subject to Identical Trials and Chances'.

75 Calder, *People's War, op. cit.*, p. 186; Harrisson, *Living, op. cit.*, pp. 117–26.

76 N. Balchin, *Darkness Falls From The Air* (London, 1942), p. 96.

77 Titmuss, *Problems, op. cit.*, p. 271; even in September 1940 tube sheltering involved only 177,000 people, less than 5 per cent of the London population.

78 Ministry of Information, *Front Line, 1940–41: The Official Story of the Civil Defence of Britain* (London, 1942), p. 24; the book was edited by architectural writer J. M. Richards, and the text written by C. R. Leslie; see J. M. Richards, *Memoirs of an Unjust Fella: An Autobiography* (London, 1980), p. 160.

79 Calder, *Myth, op. cit.*, p. 125.

80 Balchin, *op. cit.*, p. 107.

81 J. B. Priestley, *'Postscripts'* (London, 1940), p. 7; Sian Nicholas suggests that Priestley was withdrawn in part due to arguments over whether 'personalities' should have the right to be on the air; S. Nicholas, '"Sly Demagogues" and Wartime Radio: J. B. Priestley and the BBC', *Twentieth Century British History*, VI (1995), pp. 247–66.

82 Ministry, *Front Line, op. cit.*, p. 159.

83 *Ibid.*, p. 5.

84 *Ibid.*, p. 37; the fireman was celebrated in Humphrey Jennings's 1942 film *Fires Were Started*, discussed in Aldgate and Richards, *Britain Can Take It, op. cit.*, pp. 218–45; also Robert Colis and Philip Dodd, 'Representing the Nation: British Documentary Film, 1930–45', *Screen*, XXVI (1985), pp. 21–33.

85 Taylor, *Dream, op. cit.*, pp. 205–6. A similar line of sight features in accounts of the role of the Home Guard as observers; see Morton, *I Saw, op. cit.*, pp. 283–6; Priestley, *Postscripts, op. cit.*, p. 9; C. Day Lewis, 'Watching Post' in R. Skelton, ed., *Poetry of the Forties* (Harmondsworth, 1968), pp. 41–2; S. P. Mackenzie, *The Home Guard: A Military and Political History* (Oxford, 1995).

86 Taylor, *Dream*, *op. cit.*, pp. 193–7; J. Pope-Hennessy, *History Under Fire* (London, 1941).

87 M. Harries and S. Harries, *The War Artists: British Official War Art of the Twentieth Century* (London, 1983), p. 189; on the WAAC, see Brian Foss, 'Message and Medium: Government Patronage, National Identity and National Culture in Britain 1939–45', *The Oxford Art Journal*, XIV (1991), pp. 52–72.

88 Quoted in Harries and Harries, *op. cit.*, p. 192.

89 Ministry, *Front Line*, *op. cit.*, p. 39.

90 *Ibid.*, pp. 57–9.

91 *Ibid.*, pp. 16–17, p. 73; Daniels, *Fields*, *op. cit.*, pp. 32–3.

92 Ministry, *Front Line*, *op. cit.*, p. 142, p. 144; and see pp. 78–81, 'A Borough in the Blitz', on 'Thamesborough'.

93 Titmuss, *Problems*, *op. cit.*, p. 280.

94 Ministry, *Front Line*, *op. cit.*, p. 65; and see Priestley, *Postscripts*, *op. cit.*, p. 72. Calder quotes an early September Mass-Observation report on 'unplanned hysteria . . . the press versions of life going on normally on Monday are grotesque', *Myth*, *op. cit.*, p. 133.

95 Stedman Jones, *op. cit.*, p. 313.

96 *Picture Post*, 9 March 1946; see I. Jeffrey, ed., *Bill Brandt: Photographs, 1928–1983* (London, 1993), pp. 82–5.

97 Quoted in Calder, *Myth*, *op. cit.*, p. 128.

98 Ministry, *Front Line*, *op. cit.*, p. 111, p. 118.

99 *Ibid.*, pp. 128–31.

100 *Ibid.*, p. 120, p. 123.

101 Harrisson, *Living*, *op. cit.*, p. 169; Titmuss, *Problems*, *op. cit.*, p. 309.

102 Society of Friends report quoted in Titmuss, *Problems*, *op. cit.*, p. 308; also Harrisson, *Living*, *op. cit.*, p. 230.

103 Gilbert McAllister, 'Introduction', in *Homes, Towns and Countryside: A Practical Plan for Britain*, ed. G. McAllister and E. McAllister (London, 1945), pp. xiii–xxx, qu. p. xiii.

104 Addison, *op. cit.*, p. 14, p. 18, also pp. 181–9; Fielding *et al.*, *op. cit.*, pp. 36–8; P. Ambrose, *Whatever Happened to Planning?* (London, 1986), pp. 31–64; Barnett, *op. cit.*, pp. 11–37, gives a more caustic view of the dreams of the '"enlightened" Establishment' and their 'Dream of New Jerusalem'.

105 *Picture Post* produced a famous New Year issue in January 1941 outlining 'A Plan for Britain', including Julian Huxley, J. B. Priestley and Maxwell Fry; see Ambrose, *op. cit*, p. 35; Barnett, *op. cit.*, pp. 21–2; T. Hopkinson, ed., *Picture Post, 1938–50* (Harmondsworth, 1970).

106 Hardy, *From Garden Cities to New Towns*, *op. cit.*, p. 205.

107 F. J. Osborn, 'Introduction', in *Replanning Britain*, ed. F. E. Towndrow (London, 1941), pp. 9–15; on parallel conferences in relation to social and economic policy, see Daniel Ritschel, 'The Making of Consensus: The Nuffield College Conferences During the Second World War', *Twentieth Century British History*, VI (1995), pp. 267–301. The Nuffield conferences also included Stamp and Osborn.

108 I. McCallum, ed., *Physical Planning: The Ground Work of a New Technique* (London, 1944); the book was made up of essays published in the journal from August 1943 to June 1944, including those by geographers Stamp, Taylor, Gutkind and Dickinson; in October 1943 the journal ran a special issue on 'Planning and Reconstruction', XCVIII (1943), pp. 301–28, setting out 'A Beveridge Plan for our Environment', p. 305.

109 Beveridge, opening the exhibition, quoted in *The Architects' Journal*, XCVIII (1943), p. xxxviii; Royal Institute of British Architects, *Rebuilding Britain* (London, 1943).

110 RIBA, *Rebuilding Britain*, *op. cit.*, p. 15, p. 56, p. 48.

111 *Ibid.*, p. 9.

112 *Ibid.*, p. 5.

113 *Ibid.*, p. 73.

114 *Ibid.*, p. 11.

115 *Ibid.*, pp. 66–7.

116 J. Betjeman, *English Cities and Small Towns* (London, 1943), p. 42.

117 D. Mellor, G. Saunders and P. Wright, *Recording Britain* (London, 1990); 76 out of 1,500 pictures were on Wales, none on Scotland; the scheme complemented the photographic National Buildings Record developed during the War, also on the prompting of Kenneth Clark. There are a few exceptions to the conventional aesthetic style of the images in the paintings of John Piper and Kenneth Rowntree, but the scheme of value is the same. The work was published in four volumes edited by Arnold Palmer and titled *Recording Britain* (Oxford, 1947); a fifth volume, *Recording Scotland*, edited by James R. Salmond, was issued in 1952. The CPRE were involved in the initiative, but the effect is to split senses of progress and preservation; see Matless, 'One Man's England', *op. cit.* Cornish reviewed a show of the work for *Nature* as 'The Record of Picturesque Britain', and suggested more should be done: 'Picture galleries are, of course, a help, but by no means sufficient. The most evident means at the command of the Government is a weekly broadcast allotted to the systematic teaching of the aesthetics of scenery', *Nature*, CL (1942), no. 3793, p. 63.

118 I. Christie, ed., *Powell and Pressburger: The Life and Death of Colonel Blimp* (London, 1994), p. x.

119 *Ibid.*, p. 306.

120 *Ibid.*, p. 289; see also the 1942 essay by Robert Graves, 'Colonel Blimp's Ancestors', in *Occupation: Writer* (London), pp. 192–6.

121 Christie, *op. cit.*; J. Richards and A. Aldgate, *Best of British: Cinema and Society, 1930–1970* (Oxford, 1983), pp. 61–74; K. MacDonald, *Emeric Pressburger: The Life and Death of a Screenwriter* (London, 1994).

122 Christie, *op. cit.*, p. xxi; M. Powell, A *Life in Movies: An Autobiography* (London, 1986), p. 403.

123 *A Canterbury Tale* is centred on the organicist visionary landowner and magistrate Colpepper, committed to archaeology, history and locality and defending his patch as his *alter ego* the 'Glue Man', daubing girls' hair with glue to stop them

fraternizing with soldiers stationed in the area. The other lead characters move from hostility to Colpepper to sympathy, and eventually decide not to give him away to the police. At one point the camera pans across the table in Colpepper's study to show a copy of Michael Graham's organicist summary of the humus-artificials debate, *Soil and Sense*, *op. cit*. On the film, see Richards and Aldgate, *Best of British*, *op. cit*., pp. 43–60; Nanette Aldred, 'A Canterbury Tale: Powell and Pressburger's Film Fantasies of Britain', in D. Mellor, ed., *A Paradise Lost: The Neo-Romantic Imagination in Britain, 1935–55* (London, 1987), pp. 117–24.

124 *Picture Post*, 21 September 1940; reproduced in Hopkinson, *op. cit*., pp. 79–87.

125 *Ibid.*, p. 79; Calder, *People's War*, *op. cit*., p. 138; Mackenzie, *op. cit*.; T. Wintringham, *Armies of Freemen* (London, 1940); David Fernbach, 'Tom Wintringham and Socialist Defence Strategy', *History Workshop Journal*, XIV (1982), pp. 63–91.

126 Christie, *op. cit*., p. 37.

127 McCallum, *op. cit*., pp. 16–17; RIBA, *Rebuilding Britain*, pp. 68–9; see also the opening sequences of Alexander Korda's 1939 film *The Lion Has Wings*, contrasting British modern order and German regimentation.

128 H. V. Morton, *I, James Blunt* (London, 1942), p. 12.

129 *Ibid.*, p. 57.

130 Taylor, *Dream*, *op. cit*., p. 202.

131 Aldgate and Richards, *op. cit*., pp. 115–37; C. Barr, *Eating Studios*, *op. cit*., pp. 30–3.

132 R. Warner, *The Aerodrome* (Harmondsworth, 1944, first published London, 1941); Maria Teresa Chialant, 'The Aerodrome: Proles, Pubs, and Power', in A. L. McLeod, ed., *A Garland for Rex Warner: Essays in Honour of his Eightieth Birthday* (Mysore, India, The Literary Half-Yearly Press, 1985), pp. 7–18; also see the introduction by Anthony Burgess to the 1982 edition of *The Aerodrome* (Oxford).

133 Cunningham, *British Writers*, *op. cit*., p. 234.

134 Warner, *Aerodrome*, *op. cit*., p. 188.

135 *Ibid.*, p. 10.

136 *Ibid.*, p. 47.

137 *Ibid.*, p. 61; though the rural mind is shifting already, with the first encounter of village and drome taking place at a local agricultural show where new machines are being demonstrated, p. 31.

138 *Ibid.*, p. 190. Chialant compares the novel to Orwell's 1984; Warner shared Orwell's brand of common sense Left politics (see below). On the far Right associations of Englishness and aviation, see D. Edgerton, *England and the Aeroplane* (London, 1991); on the air and the village, see also John Llewelyn Rhys, *England is My Village* (London, 1941), pp. 21–34.

139 Warner, *Aerodrome*, *op. cit*., p. 112.

140 *Ibid.*, p. 191.

141 Fielding *et al.*, *op. cit*.

142 Priestley, *Postscripts*, *op. cit*., pp. 36–7.

143 See especially Priestley's 'Postscript' on Dunkirk, *ibid.*, pp. 1–4.

144 G. Orwell, *The Lion and the Unicorn: Socialism and the English Genius* (London, 1941),

reprinted in S. Orwell and I. Angus, eds, *The Collected Essays, Journalism and Letters of George Orwell. Vol. II. My Country Right or Left, 1940–1943* (London, 1968), pp. 56–109; G. Orwell, *The English People* (London, 1947); the latter was written in 1943.

145 Orwell, *Lion, op. cit.*, p. 57. Orwell's citation by John Major has led to this work being labelled as an evocation of southern village-suburban Englishness, but this misses the social and geographical complexity of the full passage: 'The clatter of clogs in the Lancashire mill towns, the to-an-fro of the lorries on the Great North Road, the queues outside the Labour Exchanges, the rattle of pin-tables in the Soho pubs, the old maids biking to Holy Communion through the mists of the autumn mornings – all these are not only fragments, but characteristic fragments, of the English scene', p. 57. On Orwell, see R. Williams, *Orwell* (London, 1971), especially chapter 2; C. Norris, ed., *Inside the Myth. Orwell: Views from the Left* (London, 1984); Gerd Dose, '"England Your England": George Orwell on Socialism, Gentleness and the English Mission', in Diller *et al.*, *Englishness, op. cit.*, pp. 241–62.

146 Orwell, *Lion, op. cit.*, p. 59.

147 *Ibid.*, p. 109.

148 *Ibid.*, p. 68; Williams, *Orwell, op. cit.*, pp. 26–7; Beatrix Campbell, 'Orwell Paterfamilias or Big Brother?', in Norris, *op. cit.*, pp. 126–38.

149 Orwell, *English People, op. cit.*, p. 46.

150 *Ibid.*, p. 48; also R. Warner, 'May 1945', in Warner, *The Cult of Power* (London, 1946), pp. 135–45 on the relationship of expertise and everyday life.

151 Fielding *et al.*, *op. cit.*, pp. 27–30. ABCA was formed in June 1941, promoting an ideal of the citizen-soldier; Churchill and the Tory Right opposed ABCA and subsequently blamed it for swinging the voting intentions of servicemen in 1945; see also Directorate of Army Education, *British Way and Purpose* (London, 1944), a collected edition of booklets on reconstruction for the 'Soldier-Citizen', with sections on 'The Setting' by geographer C. B. Fawcett and 'The Home of the Citizen' by Elizabeth Halton working through planner-preservationist ideas on region, town, country and domesticity.

152 R. B. McCallum and A. Readman, *The British General Election of 1945* (London, 1964), pp. 142–3; Calder, *People's War, op. cit.*, pp. 577–8.

153 McCallum and Readman, *op. cit.*, p. 59.

154 Labour Party, *Let Us Face The Future* (London, 1945), p. 2.

155 *Ibid.*, pp. 3–4.

156 Quoted in Hennessy, *op. cit.*, p. 67.

157 Raphael Samuel, 'Introduction: Exciting to be English', in R. Samuel, ed., *Patriotism*, vol. I (London, 1989), pp. xviii–lxvii; Hennessy, *op. cit.*, pp. 435–6; J. Fyrth, ed., *Labour's High Noon: The Government and the Economy, 1945–51* (London, 1993), pp. xx–xxii.

158 Addison, *op. cit.*, p. 248.

6 *Geographies of the Reconstruction*

1 Eva Taylor, 'Britain after the War', *Geographical Magazine*, v (1941), pp. 240–51, qu. p. 240.

2 T. Sharp, *Exeter Phoenix* (London, 1946), p. 146, discussing 'Conformities' in building frontages.

3 G. Cherry, *Town Planning in Britain since 1900* (Oxford, 1996), pp. 113–32; A. Cox, *Adversary Politics and Land: The Conflict over Land and Property Policy in Post-war Britain* (Cambridge, 1984); J. B. Cullingworth, *Environmental Planning vol. 1, Reconstruction and Land Use Planning* (London, 1975); S. V. Ward, *Planning and Urban Change* (London, 1994), pp. 80–115; for more general social histories, see Hennessy, *op. cit.*; Fielding *et al.*, *op. cit.*; Fyrth, *op. cit.*; P. Addison, *Now the War is Over* (London, 1985); R. Hewison, *In Anger: Culture in the Cold War, 1945–60* (London, 1981); M. Sissons and P. French, eds, *Age of Austerity, 1945–1951* (London, 1963).

4 See, for example, chapter 2 of Robert Hewison's general survey *Culture and Consensus: England, Art and Politics since 1940* (London, 1995), in which 'Britain in the 1940s' is gathered under the general title 'Deep England'. Both Hewison and Simon Schama in *Landscape and Memory* reproduce Frank Newbould's wartime poster for the Army Bureau of Current Affairs showing a downland scene with the caption 'your Britain – fight for it now' as an example of general rural Englishness, but they do not mention the three other posters in the ABCA series which gave the same caption to images of modern flats or new schools. It is the conjunction of such imagery that preoccupies this chapter.

5 S. Badmin, *Village and Town* (Harmondsworth, 1943), p. 31. Puffin Books were edited by Noel Carrington, co-editor of *The Face of the Land*; see S. Hare, ed., *Penguin Portrait: Allen Lane and the Penguin Editors, 1935–1970*, pp. 133–9.

6 Royal Commission on the Distribution of the Industrial Population, *Report* (London, Cmd. 6153, 1940); the Commission went beyond the earlier work of the Special Areas Commission in seeking a solution for 'depressed' areas through national planning; on the rhetoric of industrial survey, see Denis Linehan, 'Commercial Geographies: A Cultural Geography of Industrial Landscapes in Interwar Britain', PhD thesis, University of Nottingham, 1997.

7 Taylor, *Britain, op. cit.*, and see Taylor's evidence to the Barlow Commission for the Royal Geographical Society, Royal Commission, *op. cit.*, p. 152.

8 Royal Commission, *op. cit.*, p. 186, also pp. 98–103; ironically George Pepler of the Ministry of Health and CPRE upheld Germany as a possible model in his attached memorandum on 'Planning in Some Other Countries', stating that its National Office for Space Distribution was responsible for 'the planning and arrangement of German living space in accordance with the population of the Reich', p. 300. There is a tension within moves for regional planning as to whether it was to bolster or undercut central national authority. Geographer and planner E. A. Gutkind argued for the latter: 'The modern conception of the universe as an unlimited and yet

systematic space, and the dethronement of absolute values and their replacement by relative valuations, are leading us away from a world where the balancing power of a centre was dominant', E. A. Gutkind, *Creative Demobilisation vol. 1: Principles of National Planning* (London, 1943), p. 224.

9 Royal Commission, *op. cit.*, p. 220, minority report.

10 Expert Committee on Compensation and Betterment, *Final Report* (London, Cmd. 6386, 1942); Committee on Land Utilization in Rural Areas, *Report* (London, Cmd. 6378, 1942); G. M. Young, *Country and Town: A Summary of the Scott and Uthwatt Reports* (Harmondsworth, 1943).

11 L. Mumford, *The Culture of Cities* (London, 1938); M. Luccarelli, *Lewis Mumford and the Ecological Region* (London, 1995); D. Lillenthal, *TVA: Democracy on the March* (Harmondsworth, Penguin Special, 1944); J. Huxley, *TVA: Adventure in Planning* (London, 1943); Geddes, *Cities, op. cit.*; E.G.R. Taylor, *Planning Prospect* (London, 1945); P. Hall, *Cities of Tomorrow* (Oxford, 1988), pp. 136–73; West Midland Group, *English Country: A Planning Survey of Herefordshire* (London 1946); West Midland Group, *Conurbation: A Survey of Birmingham and the Black Country* (London 1948). The Group included Stamp, Sharp and landscape architect Geoffrey Jellicoe. Mumford wrote the Foreword for *Conurbation*.

12 P. Abercrombie, *Greater London Plan 1944* (London, 1945); J. H. Forshaw and P. Abercrombie, *County of London Plan* (London, 1943); the latter had been criticized by decentralization enthusiasts such as Osborn and Mumford, but the former was seen to rectify its deficiencies; see L. Mumford, 'The Plan of London', in Mumford, *City Development* (London, 1946) pp. 165–99; Hardy, *From Garden Cities, op. cit.*; see also Chapter Seven below on Mumford and domesticity.

13 Abercrombie, *Greater London, op. cit.*, p. 20.

14 *Ibid.*, p. 11; also West Midland Group, *Conurbation, op. cit.*, pp. 199–222 on the 'Green Setting'.

15 Abercrombie, *Greater London, op. cit.*, p. 13.

16 *Ibid.*

17 *Ibid.*, p. 20.

18 H. Orlans, *Stevenage: A Sociological Study of a New Town* (London, 1952), pp. 50–70; the phrases are chapter headings.

19 N. Pevsner, *The Englishness of English Art* (London, 1956), p. 189; N. Pevsner, *The Reith Lectures 1955: The Englishness of English Art. An Illustrated Guide* (London, 1955).

20 Orlans, *op. cit.*; also B. Mullan, *Stevenage Ltd: Aspects of the Planning and Politics of Stevenage New Town, 1945–78* (London, 1980); J. Balchin, *First New Town* (Stevenage, 1980).

21 Orlans, *op. cit.*, p. 3.

22 Stamp, letter to *The Times*, 3 May 1949, quoted *ibid.*, p. 34.

23 *Ibid.*, pp. 137–8, pp. 162–3.

24 *Ibid.*, p. 70.

25 Letter to the *Hertfordshire Express*, 2 March 1946, quoted *ibid.*, pp. 139–40.

26 *Hertfordshire Express*, 19 May 1945, quoted *ibid.*, p. 48.

27 Abercrombie, *Greater London, op. cit.*, p. 8, p. 7.

28 Local farmer, quoted in Orlans, *op. cit.*, p. 176.

29 *Ibid.*, p. 67.

30 Quoted *ibid.*, p. 138.

31 *Ibid.*, p. 101.

32 Hardy, *From New Towns, op. cit.*, p. 31.

33 New Towns Commitee, *Final Report* (London, Cmd. 6876, 1946), p. 4; Orlans, *op. cit.*, p. 23.

34 Orlans, *op. cit.*, p. 66.

35 *Ibid.*, p. 175, p. 63.

36 *Ibid.*, p. 69.

37 *Ibid.*, p. 65.

38 *Ibid.*, pp. 141–2; also see E. M. Forster, 'Havoc', in Williams-Ellis, *Britain and the Beast, op. cit.*, pp. 44–7.

39 Sharp, *Exeter, op. cit.*, p. 10; also R. Tubbs, *Living in Cities* (Harmondsworth, 1942), pp. 20–21.

40 Sharp, *Exeter, op. cit.*, p. 134; *cf* B. Spence, *Phoenix at Coventry: The Building of a Cathedral* (London, 1962).

41 Abercrombie's projects included London, Glasgow, Hull, and Plymouth, Sharp's Oxford, Durham, Exeter, Salisbury; see the essays on Sharp and Abercrombie in G. Cherry, ed., *Pioneers in British Planning* (London, 1981); G. Dix, 'Patrick Abercrombie 1879–1957', pp. 103–30, and K. Stansfield, 'Thomas Sharp 1901–1978', pp. 150–76.

42 Sharp, *Exeter, op. cit.*, p. 9.

43 *Ibid.*, p. 29.

44 *Ibid.*, p. 87.

45 J. Paton Watson and P. Abercrombie, *A Plan for Plymouth* (Plymouth, 1943), p. 66.

46 Sharp, *Exeter, op. cit.*, p. 96.

47 J. M. Richards, ed., *The Bombed Buildings of Britain, 1940–45* (London, 1947, first edition 1942), p. 7; Richards also suggested they might be preserved 'frankly for their beauty', p. 7.

48 Tubbs, *op. cit.*; the book was a sequel to the 1940 'Living in Cities' exhibition. Tubbs was Secretary of the Modern Architectural Research Group, and would go on to design the Dome of Discovery at the 1951 Festival of Britain.

49 The film was commissioned by Cadbury Brothers, and part written and narrated by Dylan Thomas; see John R. Gold and Stephen V. Ward. '"We're Going to Do it Right this Time": Cinematic Representations of Urban Planning and the British New Towns, 1939–1951', in *Place, Power, Situation and Spectacle: A Geography of Film*, eds. S. Aitken and L. Zonn (Lanham, MD, 1994), pp. 229–58; John Gold and Stephen Ward, 'Of Plans and Planners: Documentary Film and the Challenge of the Urban Future, 1935–52', in *The Cinematic City*, ed. D. Clarke (London, 1997), pp. 59–82; Gold and Ward also consider *Proud City* (1945) on the County of London

Plan and featuring Abercrombie, and *The Way We Live* (1946) on the Plan for Plymouth, directed by Jill Craigie.

50 C. B. Purdom, *How Should We Rebuild London?* (London, 1945).

51 Gold and Ward, 'We're Going', *op. cit.*, pp. 237–9; Bressey's transport plan for London with Edwin Lutyens, *Highway Development Survey* (London, 1937) was criticized by Abercrombie in the County of London Plan as not addressing the source of the problem.

52 T. Sharp, *Oxford Replanned* (London, 1948), pp. 18–19.

53 Nigel Whiteley, 'Modern Architecture, Heritage and Englishness', *Architectural History*, XXXVII (1995), pp. 220–37; A. Saint, *A Change of Heart: English Architecture Since the War. A Policy for Protection* (London, English Heritage, 1992); A. Saint, *Towards A Social Architecture: The Role of School-Building in Post-War England* (New Haven, 1987); for an early review which while not seeking to define an architectural Englishness highlights a new architecture in England/Britain in reconstruction and beyond see T. Dannatt, *Modern Architecture in Britain* (London, 1959), with an introduction by John Summerson.

54 T. Sharp, *English Panorama* (London, 1950, first edition 1936), p. 112; the exclusive social mores of this aesthetic are captured in Gordon Cullen's comparison in *Townscape* (London, 1961), p. 14, of good town planning and a successful dinner party: 'Conformity gives way to the agreement to differ within a recognized tolerance of behaviour.'

55 'The Second Half Century', *Architectural Review*, CI, pp. 21–36, qu. p. 36; for a critical view, see Reyner Banham, 'Revenge of the Picturesque: English Architectural Polemics, 1945–1965', in *Concerning Architecture*, ed. J. Summerson (Harmondsworth, 1968), pp. 265–73; on the *Architectural Review's* critique of New Town housing, see Chapter Seven below. A key source for Pevsner, who published a series of pieces on the picturesque in the journal between 1944 and 1948, was Christopher Hussey's *The Picturesque* (London, 1927).

56 Pevsner, *Englishness, op. cit.*, p. 183.

57 *Ibid.*, p. 80.

58 Colin MacInnes, 'The Englishness of Dr Pevsner', in C. MacInnes, *England, Half English* (London, 1961), pp. 119–29.

59 Pevsner, *Englishness, op. cit.*, p. 183.

60 *Ibid.*, p. 185, p. 183, p. 188; see 'A Programme for the City of London', *Architectural Review*, XCVII (1945), pp. 157–96; 'Plan for the St Paul's Area', *Architectural Review*, C (1946), pp. 123–50; on Holford's plan, see G. E. Cherry and L. Penny, *Holford: A Study in Architecture, Planning and Civic Design* (London, 1986), pp. 160–74.

61 Sharp, *Oxford, op. cit.*, p. 36; on townscape see also T. Sharp, *Oxford Observed* (London, 1952); Cullen, *op. cit.*

62 Ministry of Housing and Local Government, *Design in Town and Village* (London, 1953); Holford was President of the Town Planning Institute for 1953; Gibberd was the Architect Planner of Harlow New Town. Throughout the book the argument is for a mix of flats and houses.

63 T. Sharp, *The Anatomy of the Village* (Harmondsworth, 1946), p. 51. The book sold 50,000 copies, and was originally prepared in conjunction with the Scott Report, for which Sharp had been Secretary. Elements of the book echo the Report almost word for word, for example, pp. 73–5 of the Report, but the Ministry of Works and Buildings refused the book's publication, and only after eighteen months of pressure was Sharp able to publish it in a form not associated with the Ministry; Stansfield, *op. cit.*; Matless, 'Doing the English Village', *op. cit.*

64 Sharp, in *Design in Town and Village, op. cit.*, p. 7.

65 Sharp, *Anatomy, op. cit.*, pp. 5–6.

66 Committee on Land Utilization, *op. cit.*, p. 73.

67 P. Mauger, *Buildings in the Country* (London, 1959), pp. 127–8; also Sharp, in *Design in Town and Village, op. cit.*, p. 15. Mauger is presented as a more-than-metropolitan man, 'whose firm practises not only from Central London but from a village in Hertfordshire' (dust-jacket).

68 N. Pevsner, *North-East Norfolk and Norwich* (Harmondsworth, 1962), p. 19. Pevsner suggests that if modernism is to be equated with the Brutalism of Alison and Peter Smithson's Hunstanton school then 'Tayler and Green's rural housing on the other hand can almost be called post-modern'.

69 Mauger, *op. cit.*, p. 31; also S. Crowe, *The Landscape of Power* (London, 1958).

70 Mauger, *op. cit.*, p. 29.

71 *Ibid.*, p. 226.

72 Issues of community and leisure in the country will be addressed in Chapter Seven.

73 C. S. Orwin, *Problems of the Countryside* (Cambridge, 1945), pp. 1–4. Orwin was Director of the University of Oxford's Agricultural Economics Research Institute; see their book *Country Planning: A Study of Rural Problems* (Oxford, 1944).

74 *Ibid.*, pp. 105–9.

75 K. Jeremiah, *A Full Life in the Country: The Sudbury & District Survey & Plan* (London, 1949), p. 13. Jeremiah was Planning Officer for the Sudbury and District Planning Association, formed in spring 1944, and lived in Sudbury from November 1944, based in a new Planning Centre in the centre of town, where information was displayed and meetings held. Students from the Bartlett School of Architecture and local schoolchildren helped with the survey. A model of the replanned urban area formed the centre of the exhibition; Mumford was a guest at the exhibition and conference held in the town hall in June 1946.

76 *Ibid.*, pp. 11–12.

77 *Ibid.*, p. 32.

78 Sir Charles Bressey, 'Transport', in McAllister and McAllister, *Homes, Towns and Countryside, op. cit.*, pp. 60–6, qu. p. 64.

79 Jeremiah, *op. cit.*, p. 38.

80 *Ibid.*, p. 52; Jeremiah anticipates the later policy of 'Category D' villages in County Durham, which were deemed no longer viable and to be allowed to die.

81 Mumford, *ibid.*, p. 12; see also S. Baron, ed., *Country Towns in the Future England* (London, 1944).

82 Robert E. Dickinson, 'The Social Basis of Physical Planning', *Sociological Review*, XXXIV (1942), pp. 51–67, pp. 165–81, qu. p. 52, pp. 103–4; Dickinson argued for Frank Pick's idea of the 'Social Unit' as the basis of physical planning. See also Robert Dickinson, 'The Distribution and Functions of the Smaller Urban Settlements in East Anglia', *Geography*, XVII (1932), pp. 19–31.

83 W. Christaller, *Central Places in Southern Germany* (London, 1966, first German ed. 1933); see Dickinson, 'Social Basis', *op. cit.*, pp. 61–4; McCallum, *op. cit.*, p. 107; Arthur Smailes, 'The Urban Mesh of England and Wales', *Transactions of the Institute of British Geographers*, XII (1946), pp. 87–101; Smailes was involved in the village survey co-ordinated by Cecil Stewart discussed in Chapter Seven below.

84 It is unlikely that Dickinson, who knew Germany well and wrote against Nazi political philosophy and for a regional federalist political structure in Germany after the War, was aware of Christaller's role; see R. E. Dickinson, *The German Lebensraum* (Harmondsworth, Penguin Special, 1943); R. E. Dickinson, *The Regions of Germany* (London, 1945). On Christaller's role in plans which foresaw the settlement of German peasants through the creation of groups of villages centred around a larger village or Hauptdorf, see Mechtild Rossler, 'Applied Geography and Area Research in Nazi Society: Central Place Theory and Planning, 1933 to 1945', *Environment and Planning D: Society and Space*, VII (1989), pp. 419–31.

85 Orwin, *Problems, op. cit.*, pp. 89–90.

86 Lord Addison, *A Policy for British Agriculture* (London, 1939), p. 273; Addison was Labour Minister of Agriculture 1930–31; on Labour and agriculture, see Malcolm Chase, '"Nothing Less Than a Revolution"?: Labour's Agricultural Policy', in Fyrth, *Labour's High Noon, op. cit.*, pp. 78–95.

87 A. D. Hall, *Reconstruction and the Land* (London, 1942), pp. 260–2, p. 275.

88 See the collection of essays from *The Field, Programme for Agriculture*, ed. B. Vesey-Fitzgerald (London, 1941), including Addison, Hall, and Street. Of nine generally far from socialist contributors only Lymington dissented from some form of public ownership.

89 F. W. Bateson, ed., *Towards a Socialist Agriculture* (London, 1946), p. viii.

90 F. W. Bateson, 'The Problem Stated', *ibid.*, pp. 1–2 7, qu. p. 3.

91 F. W. Bateson, 'The Democratization of Control', *ibid.*, pp. 151–67, qu. p. 157.

92 R.S.G. Rutherford and F. W. Bateson, 'Co-operation in Agriculture', *ibid.*, pp. 124–35, qu. p. 130.

93 *Ibid.*, frontispiece; these are the final two verses of a ten-verse poem, first published in the *New Statesman and Nation*.

94 Chase, 'Labour's Agricultural Policy', *op. cit.*

95 Stuart Laing, 'Images of the Rural in Popular Culture, 1750–1990', in Short, *English Rural Community, op. cit.*, pp. 133–51.

96 D. H. Robinson, *The New Farming* (London, 1951, first ed. 1938), p. 17.

97 *Ibid.*, facing p. 113.

98 Scott was known for rural interests, having been involved in Hampshire CPRE and in rural reconstruction debates after 1918; he was a Conservative MP from 1910

to 1929, and had been involved in the eugenics movement from before the First World War; Jones, *Social Hygiene*, *op. cit.*, p. 45; he also provided a Foreword to Lymington and Walston, *op. cit.*, expressing sympathy with Lymington's views.

99 'A New Stamp', *The Economist*, 3 October 1942, p. 413.

100 L. D. Stamp, 'The Scott Report: A New Charter for the Countryside', *Geographical Magazine*, XV (1942–3), pp. 391–404; L. D. Stamp, 'The Scott Report', *Geographical Journal*, CI (1943), pp. 16–30; L. D. Stamp, 'Agriculture', in McCallum, *Physical Planning*, *op. cit.*, pp. 150–5; also see Stamp's two volumes for the British Council, *The Face of Britain* (London, 1940) and *The Land of Britain and How It Is Used* (London, 1946).

101 Committee on Land Utilization, *op. cit.*, p. vi, p. 1, pp. 88–9.

102 *Ibid.*, p. 33.

103 *Ibid.*, p. v; also Stamp, 'A New Charter', *op. cit.*, p. 397.

104 Committee on Land Utilization, *op. cit.*, p. 46; Stamp, 'Agriculture', *op. cit.*, pp. 153–4.

105 Stamp, 'Scott Report', *Geographical Journal*, *op. cit.*, p. 29.

106 Orwin, *Problems*, *op. cit.*, pp. 67–8.

107 Committee on Land Utilization, *op. cit.*, p. 121.

108 Stamp, 'Scott Report', *Geographical Journal*, *op. cit.*, p. 16.

109 Stamp, 'A New Charter', *op. cit.*, p. 394.

110 *Economist*, *ibid.*; the piece was a commentary on Stamp's appointment in 1942 as chief adviser to the Ministry of Agriculture and Fisheries on rural land use.

111 Committee on Land Utilization, *op. cit.*, p. 47, also p. 4.

112 Stamp, 'A New Charter', *op. cit.*, p. 396.

113 Joad, *Untutored*, *op. cit.*, p. 199; Mandler, *Fall and Rise of the Stately Home*, *op. cit.*, pp. 311–44.

114 E. Waugh, *Brideshead Revisited* (London, 1945).

115 Quoted in P. *Wright, Journey Through Ruins*, *op. cit.*, p. 76.

116 *Ibid.*, pp. 67–97; J. Gaze, *Figures in a Landscape: A History of the National Trust* (London, 1988); J. Lees-Milne, *People and Places: Country House Donors and the National Trust* (London, 1992).

117 J. Lees-Milne, *Caves of Ice* (London, 1983), p. 172; quoted in Hewison, *Heritage Industry*, *op. cit.*, p. 61; see also V. Sackville-West, *English Country Houses* (London, 1942), p. 47: 'The system was, and is, a curious mixture of the feudal and the communal, and survives in England to-day. One wonders for how long?' On the revival of country houses through the 1950s and beyond, see Mandler, *op. cit.*, pp. 355–400.

118 Wright, *Journey*, *op. cit.*, p. 87.

119 Sharp, *Town Planning*, *op. cit.*, pp. 121–2; a similar design by *Britain and the Beast* contributor W. A. Eden for 'Country dwellings that do not pimple the countryside' can be found in Bertram, *Design*, *op. cit.*

120 L. D. Stamp, *Man and the Land* (London, 1955), facing p. 251; also S. Crowe, *Tomorrow's Landscape* (London, 1956), pp. 58–9; G. Jellicoe, replying to Stamp at

the Royal Geographical Society, Stamp, 'Scott Report', *Geographical Journal, op. cit.*, p. 25. Key landscape design works also include S. Crowe, *The Landscape of Roads* (London, 1960); Crowe, *Power, op. cit.*; Crowe became landscape architect to the Forestry Commission; G. Jellicoe, *Studies in Landscape Design* (London, 3 vols, 1960, 1966, 1970); B. Colvin, *Land and Landscape* (London, 1947); N. Fairbrother, *New Lives, New Landscapes* (London, 1970); also see the landscaping schemes by Jellicoe and Thomas Sharp in West Midland Group, *Conurbation, op. cit.*, pp. 227–49.

121 Crowe, *Tomorrow, op. cit.*, p. 55.

122 Crowe, *Power, op. cit.*, p. 108.

123 Crowe, *Tomorrow, op. cit.*, p. 197.

124 Crowe, *Power, op. cit.*, p. 30, pp. 39–55.

125 Crowe, *Roads, op. cit.*, p. 13.

126 Jellicoe, *Studies*, vol. II, pp. 12–16; also Crowe, *Tomorrow*, p. 153, on 'the Silbury Hill of the future'.

127 J. Betjeman and J. Piper, *Murray's Berkshire Architectural Guide* (London, 1949), p. 148.

128 *Tawny Pipit* (1944), directed by Bernard Miles. The socialist Miles played the eccentric local Colonel, and included in the story a visit from a female Soviet sniper, for whom the village children sing the Internationale and to whom the Colonel gives his old telescopic rifle.

129 P. Marren, *The New Naturalists* (London, 1995); the advisory role included locating and supervising sites for close-up filming on the Norfolk Broads; see E. Hosking, *An Eye for a Bird: The Autobiography of a Bird Photographer* (London, 1970), pp. 36–8.

130 Geoffrey Grigson, 'Preface', in *Nature in Britain*, ed. W. J. Turner (London, 1946), pp. 5–9; the volume brought together six books from Collins's *Britain in Pictures* series, including Fisher's *The Birds of Britain*.

131 Nicholson had been involved in the formation of Political and Economic Planning in the early 1930s; on Tansley, see Chapter Two above. There are some connections to a conservative ruralist engagement with nature, for example in Vesey-Fitzgerald's 1946 *British Game* volume in the New Naturalist series, and in the stress placed on the need for 'cordial relations' between shooting interests and naturalists, Wild Life Conservation Special Committee, *Conservation of Nature in England and Wales* (London, Cmd. 7122, 1947), pp. 38–44.

132 Tansley was a leading figure in the Society for Freedom in Science, formed in 1940 to counter the Social Relations of Science Movement which sought to determine the utility of science in terms of direct social benefit; see the excellent study by Stephen Bocking, 'Conserving Nature and Building a Science: British Ecologists and the Origins of the Nature Conservancy', in Shortland, ed., *Science and Nature, op. cit.*, pp. 89–114.

133 *Ibid.*; also J. Sheail, *Nature in Trust: The History of Nature Conservation in Britain* (London, 1976), pp. 89–121; Wild Life Conservation Special Committee, *op. cit.*; all the Committee members were associated with the New Naturalist series, and

most will crop up in this chapter and Chapter Seven. Huxley and E. N. Buxton
moved from the Hobhouse Committee, other members were Captain C. Diver,
C. S. Elton, E. B. Ford, John Gilmour, Nicholson, Tansley, J. A. Steers and Arthur
Trueman. Richard Fitter was initial Secretary. On the National Parks Committee,
see Chapter Seven below. See also Sheail's study *Seventy Five Years in Ecology: The
British Ecological Society* (Oxford, 1987).

134 Bocking, *op. cit.*; also Bocking's *Ecologists and Environmental Politics: A History
of Contemporary Ecology* (New Haven, 1997); John Sheail, 'From Aspiration to
Implementation: The Establishment of the First National Nature Reserves in
Britain', *Landscape Research*, XXI (1996), pp. 37–54; Sheail, *Nature in Trust, op. cit.*,
notes the continuing key role of local trusts, especially as regional sub-committees
of the Conservancy generally failed to function.

135 Wild Life Conservation Special Committee, *op. cit.*, p. 40; Sheail, *Pesticides,
op. cit.*

136 A. Tansley, *Our Heritage of Wild Nature* (Cambridge, 1945), p. 63.

137 Wild Life Conservation Special Committee, *op. cit.*, p. 3; connections can be made
between this expert-managerial outlook and the recasting of the management of
nature through reserves and national parks in colonial territories after the War,
especially in Africa. Many new naturalist figures would be involved with the World
Wildlife Fund, which it could be argued extended a colonial philosophy and
politics of land and nature into the post-colonial era, in terms of the treatment of
both animals and people. For a fascinating post-war study, see Roderick Neumann,
'Ways of Seeing Africa: Colonial Recasting of African Society and Landscape in
Serengeti National Park', *Ecumene*, II (1995), pp. 149–71.

138 D. Worster, *Nature's Economy: A History of Ecological Ideas* (Cambridge, 1985),
pp. 239–40.

139 E. M. Nicholson, *Britain's Nature Reserves* (London, 1957), p. 64.

140 Wild Life Conservation Special Committee, *op. cit.*, p. 101; on sewage farms see
also R. Fitter, *London's Natural History* (London, 1945), p. 4.

141 Tansley, *Wild Nature, op. cit.*, p. 35.

142 Wild Life Conservation Special Committee, *op. cit.*, p. 20.

143 *Ibid.*, p. 12, p. 14.

144 *Ibid.*, pp. 29–30.

145 *Ibid.*, p. 24.

146 Marren, *op. cit.*; L. D. Stamp, *Britain's Structure and Scenery* (London, 1946); E. B.
Ford, *Butterflies* (London, 1945). Stamp's was the biggest selling *New Naturalist*
volume, eventually selling 62,000 hardback copies.

147 Marren, *op. cit.*, pp. 50–2.

148 In editorial statement at the front of each *New Naturalist* volume; Marren, *op. cit.*,
pp. 46–63. There were parallel developments in sound at the time, in the sound
recordings pioneered by Ludwig Koch, who produced disc 'sound books' with
texts by Huxley and Nicholson and contributed to the development of nature
programmes on radio, and in the mimicry of nature noises on radio by such figures

as Percy Edwards; see L. Koch, *Memoirs of a Birdman* (London, 1954); P. Edwards, *Call Me At Dawn* (Ipswich, 1948).

149 J. Fisher, *The Birds of Britain* (London, 1942); J. Gilmour, *British Botanists* (London, 1944); Fisher's book sold 100,000 copies. 132 titles were published in the series from 1941–50. See also the series of gardening texts by T. C. Mansfield, for example, '*Of Cabbages and Kings*' (London, 1945), illustrated by colour photography by John Hinde, who would also illustrate Turner, *Exmoor Village, op. cit.*, and Smith, *British Circus Life, op. cit.*, and go on to set up a leading postcard-manufacturing company, seeing colour photography as a mass medium of beauty; see J. Hinde, *Hindesight* (Dublin, Irish Museum of Modern Art, 1993); Matless, 'Doing the English Village', *op. cit.*

150 *Marren, op. cit.*, pp. 64–91; the Ellis's taught at Bath Academy of Art and were known for their poster design, including those for Pick's London Passenger Transport Board and Shell.

151 Ivy Davison, review of W. H. Pearsall, *Mountains and Moorlands* (London, 1950), *Geographical Magazine*, XXIII (1950), p. xvi.

152 Cyril Connolly, quoted in Marren, *op. cit.*, p. 62; Marren describes the photographs as 'early, nicely engraved milestones on the freeway of modern colour photography', p. 63.

153 E. G. Neal, *Exploring Nature With a Camera* (London, 1946), p. 99.

154 E. Hosking and C. Newberry, *Birds in Action* (London, 1949), p. 19; also E. Hosking and C. Newberry, *Intimate Sketches From Bird Life* (London, 1940); E. Hosking and C. Newberry, *The Art of Bird Photography* (London, 1944).

155 Ryan, *Picturing Empire, op. cit.*, chapter 5.

156 Neal, *op. cit.*, pp. 100–1.

157 Hosking and Newberry, *Birds in Action, op. cit.*, p. 9.

158 *Ibid.*, pp. 76–85.

159 Mary Field, 'Nature Films in Geography', *Geographical Magazine*, XXXI (1958), pp. 72–81; Wilson, *Culture of Nature, op. cit.*, pp. 118–55. The BBC Natural History Unit was formed in July 1957.

160 J. Fisher, *Watching Birds* (Harmondsworth, 1940), p. 121.

161 'Editors' Preface', in H. J. Fleure, *A Natural History of Man in Britain* (London, 1951), p. xv; also Stamp, *Man and the Land, op. cit.*; J. A. Steers, *The Sea Coast* (London, 1953); G. Manley, *Climate and the British Scene* (London, 1952); K. C. Edwards, *The Peak District* (London, 1962); on geography and evolutionary theory, see Livingstone, *Geographical Tradition, op. cit.*

162 Fleure, *op. cit.*, facing p. 91, facing p. 179; on Fleure, see J. A. Campbell, *Some Sources of the Humanism of H. J. Fleure* (Oxford, 1972, University of Oxford School of Geography Research paper no. 2).

163 Fleure, *op. cit.*, p. 331.

164 E. M. Nicholson, *Birds and Men* (London, 1951), p. 229. The book is organized by habitat rather than species. Also E. M. Nicholson, 'Birds and Men', *Geographical Magazine*, XXIII (1950), pp. 227–32.

165 Nicholson, *Birds and Men, op. cit.*, p. 222.

166 *Ibid.*, pp. 228–32.

167 Fitter, *London's Natural History, op. cit.*; the book sold 40,000 copies; R. Fitter, *London's Birds* (London, 1949); R. Fitter, *Birds of Town and Village* (London, 1953), in the Collins *County Naturalist* series, see Marren, *op. cit.*, pp. 220–1; R. Fitter, *Home Counties* (London, 1951), one of the Collins *About Britain* guides for the Festival of Britain. Like Nicholson, Fitter was involved with Political and Economic Planning.

168 Fitter, *London's Birds, op. cit.*, p. 15.

169 Fitter, *London's Natural History, op. cit.*, p. 104; the series editors are more gloomy than Fitter, presenting the book as showing a 'progressive biological sterilisation', p. xii.

170 *Ibid.*, p. 160, quoting Jefferies's *Nature Near London* concerning a railway embankment between Clapham and Balham.

171 Fitter, *London's Birds, op. cit.*, p. 24.

172 *Ibid.*, frontispiece.

173 Fitter, *London's Natural History, op. cit.*, p. 208.

174 Fitter, *Home Counties, op. cit.*, p. 34.

175 *Ibid.*, pp. 55–6.

176 Fitter, *London's Natural History, op. cit.*, pp. 265–8; the list is by E. J. Salisbury, Director of Kew Gardens.

177 *Ibid.*, p. 230; see also Nicholson, *Birds and Men, op. cit.*, p. 221 on 'the favourable effects upon bird life of the bombardment of our cities from the air'.

178 Fitter, *London's Natural History, op. cit.*, p. 236.

179 Mellor, ed., *A Paradise Lost, op. cit.*, pp. 62–5.

180 R. Macaulay, *The World My Wilderness* (London, 1950), p. 53; Macaulay's book *Pleasure of Ruins* (London, 1953) ends with 'A Note on New Ruins', pp. 453–6, and features drawings of bomb damage by Piper.

181 Macaulay, *World, op. cit.*, p. 25.

7 *Citizens in Reconstruction*

1 Sharp, *English Panorama, op. cit.*, p. 142.

2 Abercrombie, *Greater London, op. cit.*, p. 14.

3 Patrick Abercrombie, 'Towns in the National Pattern', in McAllister and McAllister, *op. cit.*, pp. 1–23, qu. p. 21.

4 Quoted in Orlans, *op. cit.*, p. 82, from the *Architect's Journal*, 8 July 1948, p. 45; Orlans gives a similar quote from the Chair of Stevenage Development Corporation.

5 June 1948, quoted in Fielding *et al.*, *op. cit.*, p. 104, along with a similar speech in the House of Commons, 17 October 1945; see also Hennessy, *op. cit.*, p. 163.

6 Orlans, *op. cit.*, pp. 94–5.

7 Frederick Gibberd, 'The Design of Residential Areas', in *Design in Town and Village, op. cit.*, pp. 20–70, qu. p. 26.

8 Forshaw and Abercrombie, *op. cit.*, p. 21.

9 Paton Watson and Abercrombie, *op. cit.*, p. 78.

10 Committee on Land Utilization, *op. cit.*, p. 53.

11 Agricultural Economics Research Institute, *op. cit.*, p. 267; also National Council for Social Service, *Village Halls and Social Centres in the Countryside* (London, 1945, first edition 1930).

12 Mauger, *op. cit.*, p. 181, quoting Gropius, *The Scope of Total Architecture*. See also W. Gropius, *Rebuilding Our Communities* (Chicago, 1945), which cited Peckham in proposing the 'Cultivation of the "Social Soil"', p. 54.

13 C. Stewart, *The Village Surveyed* (London, 1948). Stewart marked his work out from the picturesque, describing Sutton as 'normal to the point of dullness', and suggesting that: 'The confirmed town-dweller will recite dreamily a long string of nostalgic associations – thatched cottages, old grey church, elms, lichen and ducks-on-a-pond . . . The first thing to be done is to sweep away all these romantic notions', pp. 17–18; Matless, 'Doing', *op. cit.* The survey worked through Geddes's categories of place, work and folk, and the team included landscape architect Brenda Colvin and geographer Arthur Smailes.

14 Stewart, *op. cit.*, p. 154; survey sociologist Dennis Chapman commented: 'There must be "no diagnosis without therapy"', p. 149; see also Sir Stephen Tallents, 'We Planned Ourselves', *Geographical Magazine*, XXI (1948), pp. 313–20.

15 Stewart, *op. cit.*, p. 62.

16 *Ibid.*, p. 65.

17 F. Gibberd, *Harlow New Town* (Harlow, 1952, first edition 1947), p. 22.

18 Paton Watson and Abercrombie, *op. cit.*, p. 85.

19 Orlans, *op. cit.*, pp. 95–6; C. Reilly and N. J. Asian, *Outline Plan for the County Borough of Birkenhead* (Birkenhead, 1947); see also the Labour Party pamphlet by Cicely McCall, author of *Women's Institutes*, on *Village Life and the Labour Party today* (London, 1947).

20 Paton Watson and Abercrombie, *op. cit.*, p. 86.

21 Sharp, *Anatomy*, *op. cit.*, pp. 60–5.

22 *Ibid.*, p. 28.

23 *Ibid.*, p. 65; Sharp exercised his principles in designs for new Forestry Commission villages in Kielder Forest, see *Design in Town and Village*, *op. cit.*, p. 19. Eight villages were proposed but only three had been partially built when the scheme was curtailed in 1952.

24 Christaller, *op. cit.*, p. 14, discussing 'Centralization as a Principle of Order'.

25 Committee on Land Utilization, *op. cit.*, p. 54; the Committee's only meeting outside London was at Impington Village College.

26 H. Rée, *Educator Extraordinary: The Life and Achievement of Henry Morris, 1889–1961* (London, 1973); H. Morris, *The Village College* (Cambridge, 1925), reproduced in Rée, *op. cit.*, pp. 142–56; Robertson-Scott, *England's Green and Pleasant Land*, *op. cit.*, pp. 182–4. Morris first proposed the colleges in 1924; four were established before the War, at Sawston (1927–30), Bottisham (1937), Linton (1938) and

Impington (1938–40). After the War, at the request of Lewis Silkin, Morris became involved in New Town community and arts centre projects at Hatfield and Welwyn, see Rée, *op. cit.*, pp. 112–24. Morris represented the Association of Directors and Secretaries for Education on the Council for Visual Education, see below.

27 Rée, *op. cit.*, p. ix.

28 Morris, 1926, quoted *ibid.*, p. 19.

29 H. C. Dent, *The Countryman's College* (London, 1943), p. 3, p. 6; also Orwin, *Problems*, *op. cit.*, pp. 62–4.

30 Morris, 'Village College', in Rée, *op. cit.*, p. 152.

31 Dent, *Countryman's College*, *op. cit.*, p. 31.

32 McAllister and McAllister, *op. cit.*, facing p. 43.

33 Dent, *Countryman's College*, *op. cit.*, p. 14.

34 *Ibid.*, p. 18; N. Pevsner, *Cambridgeshire* (Harmondsworth, 1954), describes Impington as 'one of the best buildings of its date in England, if not the best', quoted in Rée, *op. cit.*, p. 75; also E. M. Fry, *Fine Building* (London, 1944), pp. 77–9. Sharp reproduces Impington in *English Panorama*, *op. cit.*, p. 147, and Linton in *Town Planning*, *op. cit.*, facing p. 65.

35 Jack Pritchard, quoted in Rée, *op. cit.*, p. 71 .

36 Dent, *Countryman's College*, *op. cit.*, pp. 21–2.

37 Henry Moore, quoted in Rée, *op. cit.*, p. 72.

38 M. Roberts, *Living in a Man-Made World: Gender Assumptions in Modern Housing Design* (London, 1991); Davidoff *et al.*, *op. cit.*; Meryl Aldridge, 'Only Demi-Paradise? Women in Garden Cities and New Towns', *Planning Perspectives*, 11 (1996), pp. 23–39; Denise Riley, '"The Free Mothers": Pronatalism and Working Women in Industry at the End of the Last War in Britain', *History Workshop Journal*, 11 (1981), pp. 58–118; Rose, *Governing the Soul*, *op. cit.*; Summerfield, *op. cit.*; on parallels after the First World War, see Caroline Rowan, 'For the Duration Only: Motherhood and Nation in the First World War', in *Formations of Nation and People*, *op. cit.*, pp. 152–70. Housing was a key issue in the 1945 election campaign, but the five million homes promised by Labour were slow to materialize, and there was widespread squatting in empty property and disused military camps in the summer of 1946.

39 John Gloag sat with Gordon Russell and others on the committee approving designs for the Board of Trade's 'Utility' furniture range from 1942 to 1952; the Council for Industrial Design was set up in 1944 out of the former Council for Art and Industry, which Pick had chaired from 1934. Russell was Director between 1947–59, seeking like Gloag to rework an Arts and Crafts ethos for a machine age. See John Heskett, 'Industrial Design', in *Modern Britain*, ed. B. Ford (Cambridge, 1992), pp. 288–318; Roberts, *Living*, *op. cit.*, pp. 81–9 on the Dudley Commitee's 1944 Report on the 'Design of Dwellings'.

40 G. McAllister, 'Introduction', *op. cit.*, pp. xxix–xxx.

41 Leopold Friedman, 'The Culture of Living', in McAllister and McAllister, *op. cit.*,

pp. 120–32, qu. p. 122; Gropius, *Rebuilding, op. cit.*, p. 27, considered '"Wife-Saving" Devices'.

42 Friedman, *op. cit.*, p. 129.

43 McAllister and McAllister, *op. cit.*, facing p. 17.

44 Riley, *op. cit.*, p. 97.

45 *Ibid.*, p. 107.

46 *Ibid.*, p. 89.

47 Orwell, *English People, op. cit.*, pp. 41–2.

48 Quoted in Roberts, *Living, op. cit.*, p. 45.

49 Labour Party, *op. cit.*, p. 80.

50 Friedman, *op. cit.*, p. 123.

51 Editor of *Town and Country Planning*, quoted in Orlans, *op. cit.*, p. 105. From Hardy, *From New Towns, op. cit.*, pp. 34–5 it would seem that the editor was Elizabeth McAllister.

52 G. McAllister, 'Introduction', *op. cit.*, p. xxix; also Royal Commission, *op. cit.*, p. 225 (minority report).

53 Mumford, 'The Plan of London', *op. cit.*, pp. 192–3; for a reading of Mumford as a social radical, see Ramachandra Guha, 'Lewis Mumford: The Forgotten Environmentalist: An Essay in Rehabilitation', *Capitalism, Nature, Socialism*, 11 (1991), pp. 67–91.

54 Mumford's critique was first published in the *Architectural Review*, and reprinted by Faber in their *Re-Building Britain* series, to which he had contributed in 1942 with 'The Social Foundations of Post-War Building'. This was also reprinted in Mumford, *City Development, op. cit.*, pp. 239–64, and parts appeared in amended form in L. Mumford, *The Condition of Man* (London, 1944), pp. 394–413, 'The Basis of Renewal'.

55 Mumford, 'Plan for London', *op. cit.*, p. 188.

56 Mumford, 'Social Foundations', *op. cit.*, p. 157; Mumford echoed Stapledon in upholding the countryside as 'not only a producer of food but a breeder of men', *ibid.*, p. 162, and cautioned against immigration and a decline in the global white population: 'It is only by a fresh mobilization of vitality that the Western peoples will be able to hold their own', *ibid.*, p. 146.

57 *Ibid.*, p. 164.

58 Abercrombie, *Greater London, op. cit.*, p. 49.

59 Film shown in Peter Hennessy's Channel 4 series *What Has Become of Us?*

60 Abercrombie, *Greater London, op. cit.*, between pp. 170 and 171.

61 J. M. Richards, 'Failure of the New Towns', *Architectural Review*, CXIV (1953), pp. 29–32; Hardy, *From New Towns, op. cit.*, pp. 46–8.

62 Richards, 'Failure', *op. cit.*, p. 32.

63 Gordon Cullen, 'Prairie Planning in the New Towns', *Architectural Review*, CXIV (1953), pp. 33–6; on the use of photography in such commentary, see John R. Gold and Margaret Gold, '*Outrage* and Righteous Indignation: Ideology and Imagery of Suburbia', in *The Behavioural Environment*, ed. F. W. Boal and D. N. Livingstone (London, 1989), pp. 163–81.

64 *Architectural Review*, CXIV (1953), p. 28; the image is reproduced in Cullen, *Townscape*, *op. cit.*, pp. 132–3; Richards and Cullen's articles brought a friendly reply from Lionel Brett, architect-planner of Hatfield, saying that residents rarely wanted "'urbanity" as you and I define it', *Architectural Review*, CXIV (1953), pp. 119–20.

65 I. Nairn, *Outrage* (London, 1956), p. 365, first published as a special issue of the *Architectural Review*, CXVII (1955), pp. 361–460; also I. Nairn, *Counter-Attack against Subtopia* (London, 1956), first published as a special issue of the *Architectural Review*, CXX (1956), pp. 353–440; Gold and Gold, *op. cit.*

66 Nairn, *Outrage*, *op. cit.*, p. 363.

67 I. Nairn, *Your England Revisited* (London, 1964), p. 77.

68 J. M. Richards, *The Castles on the Ground: The Anatomy of Suburbia* (London, 1973, first edition 1946), p. 85.

69 *Ibid.*, p. 91.

70 *Ibid.*, p. 93.

71 *Ibid.*, pp. 84–5.

72 Richards, 'Failure', *op. cit.*, p. 32.

73 F. J. Osborn, *Green-Belt Cities* (London, 1946), p. 102; quoted in Orlans, *op. cit.*, p. 164.

74 F. J. Osborn, *Can Man Plan? And Other Verses* (London, 1959), p. 127.

75 Sharp, *Town Planning*, *op. cit.*, p. 111.

76 Stamp, 'Scott Report', *Geographical Journal*, *op. cit.*, p. 18; also Committee on Land Utilization, *op. cit.*, p. 14.

77 Coburn, *op. cit.*

78 Youth Hostels Association, *Handbook 1940* (Welwyn Garden City, 1940), p. 101.

79 Prof J. R. Hicks, quoted on advertisement, *ibid.*, inside front cover.

80 Jack Cox, *Camping for All* (London, 1953), p. viii.

81 National Parks Commission, *The Country Code* (London, 1951).

82 *Ibid.*, p. 20.

83 J. Dower, *National Parks in England and Wales* (London, Cmd. 6628, 1945); J. Sheail, 'John Dower, National Parks and Town and Country Planning in Britain', *Planning Perspectives*, II (1995), pp. 1–16.

84 Dower, quoted in the discussion following J. A. Steers, 'Coastal Preservation and Planning', *Geographical Journal*, CIV (1944), pp. 7–27, qu. p. 25.

85 Hobhouse Committee, *Report of the National Parks Committee* (England and Wales), (London, Cmd. 7121, 1947); H. Abrahams, ed., *Britain's National Parks* (London, 1959). National Parks worked through parallel principles of 'educated access' to the National Forest Parks run by the Forestry Commission from the late 1930s; see George Revill and Charles Watkins, 'Educated Access: Interpreting Forestry Commission Forest Park Guides', in *Rights of Way*, ed. C. Watkins (London, 1996), pp. 100–28.

86 For a proposal for the latter, see Arrow, 'Broads as a National Park', *op. cit.*, pp. 86–100; for an alternative form of park, see the special number of the same journal

by Eric de Mare, 'The Thames as a Linear National Park', *Architectural Review*, CVIII (1950), pp. 1–78.

87 Hobhouse Committee, *op. cit.*, p. 9.

88 Hugh Dalton, 9 April 1946, quoted in Coburn, *op. cit.*, p. 120.

89 Quoted in Coburn, *op. cit.*, p. 141, from the parliamentary debate on the National Parks Bill.

90 The following information is taken from Stephenson, *Forbidden Land*, *op. cit.*

91 *Footpaths and Access to the Countryside* (London, Cmd. 7207, 1947).

92 Richard Weight, *Pale Stood Albion: The Promotion of National Culture in Britain, 1939–56*, PhD thesis, University of London, 1995; Chase, 'Labour's Agricultural Policy', *op. cit.*

93 National Parks Commission, *op. cit.*, p. 3; there was also tension over access to land acquired by the military in wartime and retained after the 1945 Requisitioned Land and War Works Act: 'Total war does not favour the survival of organizations which stand for the freedom of the individual; and it was an ominous symbol of this fact when Service Departments retained for their own use, even after the War, large areas of beautiful countryside', Coburn, *op. cit.*, p. 100; see also Joad, *Untutored*, *op. cit.*, p. 159; Wright, *Village That Died*.

94 Quoted in Stephenson, *Forbidden Land*, *op. cit.*, p. 208. On Labour and popular leisure in general, see Fielding *et al.*, *op. cit.*, chapter 6.

95 Joad, *Untutored*, *op. cit.*, p. 218; see also the introduction to C.E.M. Joad, ed., *The English Counties* (London, 1948), pp. 7–16.

96 John Dower, 'The Landscape and Planning', *Journal of the Town Planning Institute*, XXX (1944), pp. 92–102, qu. p. 95.

97 Dower, *National Parks*, *op. cit.*, p. 23.

98 *Ibid.*, p. 19; also Cornish, *National Parks*, *op. cit.*, p. 30; Williams-Ellis, 'Our Physical Environment', *op. cit.*, p. 227.

99 Dower, *National Parks*, *op. cit.*, p. 23.

100 *Ibid.*, p. 31.

101 Dower, 'Landscape', *op. cit.*, p. 92.

102 *Ibid.*, p. 96.

103 *Ibid.*, p. 94.

104 *Ibid.*, pp. 95–6.

105 *Ibid.*, p. 97.

106 *Ibid.*, p. 98.

107 Dower, *National Parks*, *op. cit.*, p. 23; on the holiday camp as cultural landscape see C. Ward and D. Hardy, *Goodnight Campers! The History of the British Holiday Camp* (London, 1986).

108 Stamp, quoted in discussion in Steers, 'Coastal Preservation', *op. cit.*, p. 23.

109 Political and Economic Planning, 'Planning for Holidays', *Planning*, IX (1942), no. 194, pp. 1–15, qu. p. 6.

110 *Ibid.*, p. 12.

111 *Ibid.*, p. 6.

112 Joad, *Untutored, op. cit.*, pp. 229–31.

113 Political and Economic Planning, 'Holidays', *op. cit.*, p. 8.

114 R. Shields, *Places on the Margin* (London, 1991).

115 Fielding *et al.*, *op. cit.*, p. 152.

116 Hilde Marchant, 'Life in a Holiday Camp', *Picture Post*, 13 July 1946, in Hopkinson, *op. cit.*, pp. 192–6.

117 Wild Life Conservation Special Committee, *op. cit.*, p. 19.

118 Steers, 'Coastal Preservation', *op. cit.*, p. 15.

119 Stoddart's obituary of Steers suggests the epitome of a particular culture of geography: outdoor, organized, committed to conservation and planning via state action, happy in the field. David Stoddart, 'Obituary: James Alfred Steers', *Transactions of the Institute of British Geographers*, n. s., XIII (1988), pp. 109–15.

120 Steers, 'Coastal Preservation', *op. cit.*, p. 17, my emphasis.

121 *Ibid.*, p. 8.

122 *Ibid.*, pp. 11–12.

123 *Ibid.*, pp. 13–14.

124 *Ibid.*, p. 19.

125 *Ibid.*, pp. 20–21.

126 J. A. Steers, *A Picture Book of the Whole Coast of England and Wales* (Cambridge, 1948), preface; J. A. Steers, *The Coastline of England and Wales* (Cambridge, 1948).

127 Stamp, in Steers, *The Coastline, op. cit.*, p. xiii.

128 Abercrombie, *ibid.*, p. xv.

129 Steers, *ibid.*, p. xviii.

130 Fraser Darling, in Steers, *A Picture Book, op. cit.*, p. 10.

131 *Ibid.*

132 A. E. Trueman, *Geology and Scenery in England and Wales* (Harmondsworth, 1949), p. 10. The book was first published in 1938 as *The Scenery of England and Wales* by socialist publisher, Victor Gollancz. Trueman was knighted in 1951, when chair of the University Grants Committee. For popular geology, see also Stamp, *Britain's Structure, op. cit.*

133 Trueman, *op. cit.*, p. 12.

134 *Ibid.*, p. 9.

135 *Ibid.*, p. 193.

136 S. W. Wooldridge, 'The Status of Geography and the Role of Fieldwork', 1954 Presidential Address to the Geographical Association, in S. W. Wooldridge, *The Geographer as Scientist* (London, 1956), p. 73. On the Council, see John H. Barrett, 'The Field Studies Council: How it All Began', *Biological Journal of the Linnean Society*, XXXII (1987), pp. 31–41.

137 Wooldridge, *op. cit.*, p. 74.

138 *Ibid.*, p. 78.

139 Fagg and Hutchings, *op. cit.*; see also Hutchings's 1961 Presidential Address to the Geographical Association, 'Geographical Field Teaching', *Geography*, XLVII (1962), pp. 1–14; G. E. Hutchings, *Landscape Drawing* (London, 1960), based on an earlier

Field Studies Council Guide; Geoffrey Hutchings, 'The River Mole', *The New Naturalist*, 1 (1948), p. 184.

140 S. W. Wooldridge and G. E. Hutchings, *London's Countryside* (London, 1957).

141 James Fisher, 'The New Naturalist: A Journal of British Natural History', *The New Naturalist*, 1 (1948), pp. 3–5, qu. p. 3.

142 'Uncle Mac', 'Introduction', in James Fisher, ed., *Nature Parliament: A Book of the Broadcasts* (London, 1952), pp. xi–xvii; also L. C. Lloyd, 'Naturalists On the Air', *The New Naturalist*, 1 (1948), pp. 214–16.

143 Fisher, *Watching Birds*, *op. cit.*, preface; see also Fisher's four volumes for Penguin on *Bird Recognition*, from 1951; also B. Campbell, *Bird Watching for Beginners* (Harmondsworth, 1952).

144 Fisher, *Watching Birds*, *op. cit.*, p. 11.

145 *Ibid.*, p. 64.

146 *Ibid.*, p. 12.

147 *Ibid.*, p. 39.

148 Brian Vesey-Fitzgerald, 'On Being a Local Naturalist', *The New Naturalist*, 1 (1948), pp. 181–5, qu. p. 183; a *Directory of Natural History Societies*, with a foreword by Huxley and Fitter, gave a point of entry into the local network, see *The New Naturalist*, 1 (1948), pp. 186–206.

149 Fisher, *Birds of Britain*, *op. cit.*, reprinted in Grigson, *Nature in Britain*, *op. cit.*, pp. 161–206, qu. p. 205.

150 T. H. Harrisson and P.A.D. Hallam, 'The Great Crested Grebe Enquiry, 1931', *British Birds*, XXVI (1932), pp. 62–92, 102–31, 142–55, 174–95; Fisher, *Watching Birds*, *op. cit.*, p. 174; David Chaney and Michael Pickering, 'Authorship in Documentary: Sociology as an Art Form in Mass Observation', in *Documentary and the Mass Media*, ed. J. Corner (London, 1986), pp. 29–44.

151 James Fisher, 'Evolution and Bird Sociality', in *Evolution as a Process*, eds J. Huxley, A. C. Hardy and E. B. Ford (London, 1954), pp. 71–83.

152 G. White, *The Natural History of Selbourne* (Harmondsworth, 1941); G. White, *The Natural History of Selbourne* (London, 1947); both edited by James Fisher. The 1947 Cresset Press edition is illustrated with wood engravings by Clare Oldham, cut to suggest a strikingly sharp observational light, very different to those by Clare Leighton in the 1941 Penguin edition.

153 H. J. Massingham, ed., *The Writings of Gilbert White of Selbourne* (London, 1938); Worster, *op. cit.*, pp. 19–20.

154 James Fisher, 'Introduction', in White, *Natural History* (1947), *op. cit.*, pp. ix–xxi, qu. p. xiv–xv; the introduction is based in part on a 1945 radio broadcast.

155 *Ibid.*, p. xviii.

156 *Ibid.*, p. xv.

157 *Journal of the Town Planning Institute*, XXX (1944), pp. 74–7, pp. 154–6; also CPRE Archive, University of Reading, file 398.

158 *Ibid.*, p. 75, p. 154.

159 *Ibid.*, p. 74.

160 *Ibid.*, p. 154.

161 Information from CVE Annual Reports, held in Bodleian Library.

162 It is unclear whether the pamphlet by Dower on *Planning and the Countryside*
     listed in the CVE 1946 Book List as soon to be published was ever issued, or one by
     Elizabeth McAllister listed as in preparation in the *Journal of the Town Planning
     Insititute.*

163 W. F. Morris, *The Future Citizen and his Surroundings* (London, 1946; first published
     1942), pp. 5–6.

164 F. J. Osborn, 'Introduction', in Cornish, *Beauties, op. cit.*, p. 9.

165 Morris, *Future Citizen, op. cit.*, p. 6.

166 *Ibid.*, p. 8.

167 *Ibid.*, p. 13.

168 *Ibid.*, p. 3.

169 *Ibid.*

170 Williams-Ellis, in H. Adams, *Art and Everyman* (London, 1946, first ed. 1944), p. 2;
     see also H. Adams, *The Adventure of Looking* (London, 1949); H. Adams, *Approach
     to Landscape Painting* (London, 1938, reprinted 1947).

171 Adams, *Art and Everyman, op. cit.*, p. 10.

172 *Ibid.*, p. 12.

173 Sir C. Reilly, *Architecture as a Communal Art* (London, 1946), p. 6.

174 *Ibid.*, p. 17; the pamphlet's foreword by Giles Gilbert Scott is more guarded in its
     enthusiasm for modernism.

175 N. Pevsner, *Visual Pleasures from Everyday Things* (London, 1946), p. 4; on visual
     education, see also 'Second Half Century', *Architectural Review*, CI (1947) pp. 21–6.

176 Pevsner, *Visual Pleasures, op. cit.*, p. 4.

177 A. Jarvis, *The Things We See: Indoors and Out* (Harmondsworth, 1946), pp. 26–7;
     many of Jarvis's examples are drawn from the kinds of reconstruction literature
     considered in Chapter Six above.

178 *Ibid.*, p. 46.

179 *Ibid.*, p. 4.

8 *Landscape and Englishness in an Altered State*

 1 I. Cox, *The South Bank Exhibition: A Guide to the Story it Tells* (London, 1951).

 2 'South Bank Exhibition', *Architectural Review*, CX (1951) pp. 71–140, see pp. 80–106
    on 'The Exhibition as Landscape'; the landscape architect of the 'Downstream'
    section was Peter Shepheard, who had pictured Ongar for the *Greater London Plan*
    and worked in Stevenage.

 3 'A Survey of Lansbury's "Live" Architecture', *Architects' Journal*, CXIV (1951),
    pp. 276–301; M. Gaskell, *Model Housing: From the Great Exhibition to the Festival
    of Britain* (London, 1986); Lansbury included work by Gibberd and Jellicoe.

 4 M. Banham and B. Hillier, eds., *A Tonic to the Nation: The Festival of Britain, 1951*
    (London, 1976); Barry Curtis, 'One Continuous Interwoven Story (The Festival

of Britain)', *Block*, II (1985/6), pp. 48–52; Owen Gavin and Andy Lowe, 'Designing Desire: Planning, Power and the Festival of Britain', *Block*, II (1985/6), pp. 53–69; Michael Frayn, 'Festival', in Sissons and French, *Age of Austerity*, *op. cit.*, pp. 330–52; Hewison, *Culture and Consensus*, *op. cit.*; A. Seago, *Burning the Box of Beautiful Things: The Development of a Postmodern Sensibility* (Oxford, 1995). The Festival is evidently concerned with Britishness as much as Englishness, but many of these texts reflect the extent to which English Festival events saw a discourse of Britishness being subsumed *within* that of Englishness.

5 Gavin and Lowe, *op. cit.*, p. 65.

6 C. H. James, S. R. Pierce and H. C. Rowley, *City of Norwich Plan* (Norwich, 1945).

7 B. Taylor, *The Festival of Britain* (London, 1951).

8 *Geographical Magazine*, XXIV (1) (1951), 'Festival Number'.

9 Geoffrey Grigson, 'Using This Book', pp. 5–6 in each of twelve *About Britain* Guides, published by Collins (London 1951). The series included Fitter's Guide to the Home Counties, *op. cit.*

10 *The Story of the Festival of Britain* (London, 1952), pp. 28–9.

11 Taylor, *Festival*, *op. cit.*, p. 67.

12 *Story of the Festival*, *op. cit.*, p. 28.

13 *Didcot Celebrations: Official Handbook* (Didcot, 1951), p. 3; the message is dated 22 February 1951.

14 J. B. Priestley, *Festival at Farbridge* (London, 1951), p. 391.

15 *Didcot*, *op. cit.*, p. 55.

16 Dylan Thomas, 'The Festival Exhibition, 1951', in D. Thomas, *Quite Early One Morning* (London, 1954), pp. 50–7; Thomas also comments: 'In "Homes and Gardens," blink at the grevious furniture, ugly as sin and less comfy', p. 56. See also the variety of memories of the Festival in Banham and Hillier, *Tonic*, *op. cit.*, and Seago's reading of the Festival as an exercise in Victoriana, Seago, *op. cit.*; Seago tends to conflate the Festival and Coronation as reassertions of heritage Englishness.

17 Banham and Hillier, *Tonic*, *op. cit.*, pp. 125–7.

18 'The Festival of Punch', *Punch*, 30 April 1951, pp. 1–114.

19 *Ibid.*, pp. 22–3, 16–17, 10–11.

20 *Ibid.*, pp. 96–7; see also Daniel Pettiward's 'Exhortation To All Parish and Rural District Councils', p. 89, and P. M. Hubbard's 'Local Body Makes Good', p. 109, on the efforts of Farthingham Borough Council; also 'Pomp For All Circumstances. Circular Letter to Local Festival Councils', pp. 110–11.

21 *Didcot*, *op. cit.*, p. 5.

22 Stamp, *Man and the Land*, *op. cit.*, pp. 249–56; Weight, *Pale Stood Albion*, *op. cit.*; Hewison, *Culture and Consensus*, *op. cit.*, pp. 66–9.

23 W. G. Hoskins, *Chilterns to Black Country* (London, 1951); W. G. Hoskins, *East Midlands and The Peak* (London, 1951); on Hoskins, see Matless, 'One Man's England', *op. cit.*; Roy Millward, 'William George Hoskins, Landscape Historian (1908–1992)', *Landscape History*, XIV (1992), pp. 65–70.

24 W. G. Hoskins, *The Making of the English Landscape* (London, 1955), p. 14.

25 W. G. Hoskins, *Rutland: A Shell Guide* (London, 1963), p. 7; also W. G. Hoskins, *Leicestershire: A Shell Guide* (London, 1970); W. G. Hoskins, *Midland England* (London, 1949); on Rutland, see Simon Rycroft, 'Access and Alignment: A Passport to Rutlandshire', in Watkins, ed., *Rights of Way, op. cit.*, pp. 129–41; Cosgrove *et al.*, 'Landscape and Identity', *op. cit.*

26 W. G. Hoskins, *Local History in England* (London, 1959), p. 6.

27 Hoskins, *Making, op. cit.*, p. 231.

28 *Ibid.*, p. 232.

29 On Hoskins's narrative of landscape history which, unlike the planner-preservationists, looked to a sixteenth- and seventeenth-century 'peasant civilization' rather than an eighteenth-century spirit of design, see Matless, 'One Man's England', *op. cit.*, pp. 192–5. On 'peasant civilization', see Hoskins, *Midland England, op. cit.*, pp. 61–79, 'The Old Midland Village'.

30 *Ibid.*, p. 206.

31 Barr, *Ealing Studios, op. cit.*, pp. 159–65. Hoskins was not averse to campaigning to stop environmental change, notably in Exeter where he became a Liberal councillor in 1963.

32 Samuel, *Theatres, op. cit.*; Rolt combined this with works extolling the virtues of engineering, both Victorian and contemporary, as in his volumes commemorating motorway construction, published by construction companies. Rolt is a complex figure whose work deserves more attention.

33 J. Betjeman, ed., *Collins Guide to English Parish Churches* (London, 1958); Hoskins provided the entries for Devonshire and Rutland.

34 Hoskins, *Rutland, op. cit.*, p. 16.

35 Many photographs in Hoskins's early publications, for example, the Batsford publication *Midland England, op. cit.*, were by F. L. Attenborough, Principal of University College Leicester where Hoskins was employed, fellow enthusiast for landscape history and father of the more famous David and Richard Attenborough.

36 Philip Larkin, 'Going, Going', in *Collected Poems* (London, 1988), pp. 189–90; previously published in complete form in *High Windows* (London, 1974). Much of Larkin's work could be read in terms of a melancholy dwelling on a vernacular Englishness, though in a far more complex fashion than Hoskins or Betjeman. The celebrated photograph of Larkin perched on the 'England' sign on the Scottish border was taken only after Larkin had urinated behind it. One of the best summaries of this brand of landscaped Englishness 'from the inside' is Larkin's 1971 introduction to the American edition of Betjeman's *Collected Poems*, 'It Could Only Happen in England', reprinted in P. Larkin, *Required Writing: Miscellaneous Pieces, 1955–1982* (London, 1983), pp. 204–18. The theme of Englishness and race addressed at various points in this book recurs here, given the debates over Larkin's racism following the publication of A. Thwaite, ed., *Philip Larkin: Selected Letters* (London, 1993), and A. Motion, *Philip Larkin: A Writer's Life* (London, 1993). Larkin's sense

of an essential Englishness eroded aligns with a reaction against supposedly alien black presences (as well as against trade unionists and revolting students). I have not encountered a similar alignment in Hoskins's work. A good discussion of these debates, resisting the options of either disqualifying Larkin from poetry due to racism or asserting that racism was a private matter detached from the public published poetry, is by Christopher Hitchens, 'Something About the Poems: Larkin and "Sensitivity"', *New Left Review*, CC (1993), pp. 161–72.

37 Department of the Environment, *How Do You Want to Live? A Report on the Human Habitat* (London, 1972), pp. x–xi. Larkin's poem is reproduced over a photograph of the ICI chemical works on Teesside.

38 Wright, *Journey Through Ruins, op. cit.*, pp. 67–97.

39 Mandler, *Stately Home, op. cit.*, pp. 355–88.

40 See, for example, P. Cormack, *Heritage in Danger* (London, 1976); for an analysis of debates in the 1970s, see Wright, *On Living, op. cit.*, pp. 33–56; Mandler, *Stately Home, op. cit.*, pp. 401–18.

41 On Lees-Milne, see Patrick Wright, 'James Lees-Milne: A Superannuated Man?', *Modern Painters*, II (1989) pp. 34–41; on the 'Revivalist Fable' of supposed post-war philistinism and later resurgent heritage associated with Prince Charles and others, see Wright, *Journey Through Ruins, op. cit.*, pp. 349–91; Daniels, *Fields of Vision, op. cit.*, pp. 11–42.

42 J. Wyndham, *The Midwich Cuckoos* (Harmondsworth, 1960), p. 11.

43 Hoskins, *Making, op. cit.*, p. 232; the book was written in Steeple Barton, close to the U.S. Air Force base at Upper Heyford.

44 Veldman, *Fantasy, op. cit.*; Veldman shows, however, that opposition to nuclear weapons did not always imply opposition to nuclear power. CND campaigner J. B. Priestley's play *A Summer Day's Dream* (London, 1949) envisaged an England after the atom bomb choosing to return to a craft-based civilization, cited in Wiener, *English Culture, op. cit.*, p. 79.

45 E. P. Thompson, 'The Peculiarities of the English', in E. P. Thompson, *The Poverty of Theory* (London, 1978), pp. 35–91, qu. p. 35.

46 Samuel, *Theatres, op. cit.*, pp. 51–118.

47 M. Bracewell, *England is Mine: Pop Life in Albion* (London, 1997); D. Hebdige, *Subculture: The Meaning of Style* (London, 1979); D. Hebdige, *Hiding in the Light* (London, 1988), section 2; J. Savage, *England's Dreaming: Sex Pistols and Punk Rock* (London, 1991).

48 A. Sillitoe, *Saturday Night and Sunday Morning* (London, 1958); S. Daniels and S. Rycroft, 'Mapping the Modern City: Alan Sillitoe's Nottingham Novels', *Transactions of the Institute of British Geographers*, XVIII (1993), pp. 460–80.

49 Lowerson, 'Mystical Geography of the English', *op. cit.*; G. McKay, *Senseless Acts of Beauty: Cultures of Resistance since the Sixties* (London, 1996); for early versions of alternative prehistoric landscape, see J. Bord and C. Bord, *Mysterious Britain* (London, 1972); Michell, *The View Over Atlantis* (London, 1969).

50 R. Carson, *Silent Spring* (London, 1963).

51 M. Shoard, *The Theft of the Countryside* (London, 1980), p. 9.

52 R. Mabey, *The Common Ground* (London, 1980), p. 24. Mabey's book represents an important attempt to think through the cultural nature of arguments over conservation, as does the work of the charity Common Ground, formed in 1983; see Matless, 'Doing the English Village', *op. cit.*; D. Crouch and D. Matless, 'Refiguring Geography: Parish Maps of Common Ground', *Transactions of the Institute of British Geographers*, n. s. XXI (1996), pp. 236–55; D. Matless and G. Revill, 'A Solo Ecology: The Erratic Art of Andy Goldsworthy', *Ecumene*, II (1995), pp. 423–48.

53 Conford, *Organic Tradition*, *op. cit.*; Abelson, *Mirror of England*, *op. cit.*

54 Rolf Gardiner, 'Harvest Thanksgiving: Cerne Abbas', in Best, *Water*, *op. cit.*, p. 294; also Wright, *Village That Died*, *op. cit.*, pp. 288–9.

55 G. Roberston, M. Mash, L. Tickner, J. Bird, B. Curtis and T. Putnam, eds., *Futurenatural: Nature, Science, Culture* (London, 1996).

56 R. Williams, *Keywords: A Vocabulary of Culture and Society* (London, 1976), p. 184.

57 Richard White, 'Environmental History, Ecology, and Meaning', *Journal of American History*, LXXVI (1990), pp. 11–16; see also White's elaboration of such a revisioning of nature–culture relations in *The Organic Machine: The Remaking of the Columbia River* (New York, 1996). For a related critique of foundationalism, see David Demeritt, 'Ecology, Objectivity and Critique in Writings on Nature and Human Societies', *Journal of Historical Geography*, XX (1994), pp. 22–37. Schama's *Landscape and Memory*, *op. cit.*, also uses landscape as a category through which to question the sense of nature as a victim of culture, arguing against deep ecological formulations of wilderness.

58 Regional policy and its possibilities provides another reference point from the earlier period. For an analysis of the linked cultural and political geographies of England, see Peter J. Taylor, 'The English and their Englishness: "A Curiously Mysterious, Elusive and Little Understood People"', *Scottish Geographical Magazine*, CVII (1991), pp. 146–61; Peter J. Taylor, 'The Meaning of the North: England's "Foreign Country" Within?', *Political Geography*, XII (1993), pp. 136–55.

SELECT BIBLIOGRAPHY

Abelson, Edward, *A Mirror of England: An Anthology of the Writings of H. J. Massingham* (Hartland, 1988)

Abercrombie, Patrick, *The Preservation of Rural England* (London, 1926)

—, *Town and Country Planning* (London, 1933)

—, *Greater London Plan* (London, 1945)

Addison, Paul, *The Road to 1945: British Politics and the Second World War* (London, 1975)

Aldgate, A., and J. Richards, *Britain Can Take It: The British Cinema in the Second World War* (Oxford, 1986)

Balfour, Eve, *The Living Soil* (London, 1943)

Banham, Mary, and Bevis Hillier, eds, *A Tonic to the Nation: The Festival of Britain, 1951* (London, 1976)

Banham, Reyner, 'Revenge of the Picturesque: English Architectural Polemics, 1945–1965', in *Concerning Architecture*, ed. John Summerson (Harmondsworth, 1968), pp. 265–73

Barnett, Corelli, *The Collapse of British Power* (London, 1972)

—, *The Lost Victory* (London, 1995)

Barr, Charles, *Ealing Studios* (London, 1993)

Bender, Barbara, ed., *Landscape: Politics and Perspectives* (Oxford, 1993)

Benewick, Robert, *The Fascist Movement in Britain* (London, 1972)

Bertram, Anthony, *Design* (London, 1938)

Best, Andrew, ed., *Water Springing from the Ground: An Anthology of the Writings of Rolf Gardiner* (Fontmell Magna, 1972)

Bhabha, Homi, ed., *Nation and Narration* (London, 1990)

Bishop, Peter, *An Archetypal Constable: National Identity and the Geography of Nostalgia* (London, 1995)

Blunden, Edmund, ed., *Return to Husbandry* (London, 1943)

Bocking, Stephen, 'Conserving Nature and Building a Science: British Ecologists and the Origins of the Nature Conservancy', in *Science and Nature*, ed. M. Shortland (London, 1993), pp. 89–114

—, *Ecologists and Environmental Politics* (New Haven, 1997)

Boumphrey, Geoffrey, *British Roads* (London, 1939)

Boyes, Georgina, *The Imagined Village: Culture, Ideology and the English Folk Revival* (Manchester, 1993)

Bracewell, Michael, *England is Mine: Pop Life in Albion* (London, 1997)

Bradshaw, David, 'T. S. Eliot and the Major: Sources of Literary Anti-Semitism in the 1930s', *Times Literary Supplement* (5 July 1996), pp. 14–16

Bramwell, Anna, *Blood and Soil: Richard Walther Darré and Hitler's 'Green Party'* (Bourne End, 1985)

—, *Ecology in the Twentieth Century* (London, 1989)

Brookes, Rod, '"Everything in the Garden is Lovely": The Representation of National Identity in Sidney Strube's Daily Express Cartoons in the 1930s', *Oxford Art Journal*, XIII (1990), pp. 31–43

Calder, Angus, *The People's War: Britain, 1939–1945* (London, 1969)

—, *The Myth of the Blitz* (London, 1991)

Carey, John, *The Intellectuals and the Masses* (London, 1992)

Carrington, Noel, *The Shape of Things* (London, 1939)

Cavaliero, Glen, *The Rural Tradition in the English Novel, 1900–1939* (London, 1977)

Chase, Malcolm, 'This Is No Claptrap, This Is Our Heritage', in *The Imagined Past*, eds M. Chase and G. Shaw (Manchester, 1989), pp. 128–46

—, '"Nothing Less than a Revolution"? Labour's Agricultural Policy', in *Labour's High Noon*, ed. J. Fyrth (London, 1993), pp. 78–95

—, 'Rolf Gardiner: An Inter-war, Cross-cultural Case Study', in *Adult Education Between Cultures*, eds B. Hake and S. Marriott (Leeds, 1993)

Cherry, Gordon, ed., *Pioneers in British Planning* (London, 1981)

Coburn, Oliver, *Youth Hostel Story* (London, 1951)

Colls, Robert, and Philip Dodd, eds, *Englishness: Politics and Culture, 1880–1920* (London, 1986)

Conford, Philip, *The Organic Tradition* (Hartland, 1988)

—, 'The Alchemy of Waste: The Impact of Asian Farming on the British Organic Movement', *Rural History*, VI (1995), pp. 103–14

Cornish, Vaughan, *National Parks, and the Heritage of Scenery* (London, 1930)

—, *The Scenery of England* (London, 1932)

—, *Scenery and the Sense of Sight* (Cambridge, 1935)

Cosgrove, Denis, and Stephen Daniels, eds, *The Iconography of Landscape* (Cambridge, 1988)

Cosgrove, Denis, Barbara Roscoe, and Simon Rycroft, 'Landscape and Identity at Ladybower Reservoir and Rutland Water', *Transactions of the Institute of British Geographers*, XXI (1996), pp. 534–51

Craven, Josef, '"Health, Wholeness, Holiness": Radical Right and Fascist Attitudes to the British Countryside, 1918–1939', M. Phil thesis, University of Birmingham, 1993

Crawford, O.G.S., and Alexander Keiller, *Wessex from the Air* (Oxford, 1928)

—, *Said and Done: The Autobiography of an Archaeologist* (London, 1955)

Crouch, David, and David Matless, 'Refiguring Geography: Parish Maps of Common Ground', *Transactions of the Institute of British Geographers*, XXI (1996), pp. 236–55

Cullingworth, J. B., *Environmental Planning Vol. 1, Reconstruction and Land Use Planning* (London, 1975)

Cunningham, Valentine, *British Writers of the Thirties* (Oxford, 1988)

Daniels, Stephen, 'Marxism, Culture and the Duplicity of Landscape', in *New Models in Geography*, vol. II, eds R. Peet and N. Thrift (London, 1989), pp. 196–220

—, *Fields of Vision: Landscape Imagery and National Identity in England and the United States* (Cambridge, 1993)

Diemendberg, Edward, 'The Will to Motorization: Cinema, Highways and Modernity', *October*, LXXIII (1995), pp. 91–137

Diller, H. J., ed, *Englishness* (Heidelberg, 1992)

Dower, John, 'The Landscape and Planning', *Journal of the Town Planning Institute*, XXX (1944), pp. 92–102

Driver, Felix, 'Moral Geographies: Social Science and the Urban Environment in Mid-Nineteenth Century England', *Transactions of the Institute of British Geographers*, XIII (1988), pp. 275–87

Eagleton, Terry, *The Ideology of the Aesthetic* (Oxford, 1990)

Edgerton, David, *England and the Aeroplane: An Essay on a Militant and Technological Nation* (London, 1991)

Ellis, Steve, *The English Eliot* (London, 1991)

Fielding, Steven, Peter Thompson, and Nick Tiratsoo, *'England Arise!': The Labour Party and Popular Politics in 1940s Britain* (Manchester, 1995)

Fisher, James, *Watching Birds* (Harmondsworth, 1940)

Fitter, Richard, *London's Natural History* (London, 1945)

Foss, Brian, 'Message and Medium: Government Patronage, National Identity and National Culture in Britain 1939–45', *Oxford Art Journal*, XIV (1991), pp. 52–72

Foucault, Michel, 'Nietzsche, Genealogy, History', in *The Foucault Reader*, ed. Paul Rabinow (Harmondsworth, 1986), pp. 76–100

Fussell, Paul, *The Great War and Modern Memory* (Oxford, 1975)

Fyrth, Jim, ed., *Labour's High Noon: The Government and the Economy, 1945–51* (London, 1993)

Gardiner, Rolf, *England Herself* (London, 1943)

Gavin, Owen, and Andy Lowe, 'Designing Desire: Planning, Power and the Festival of Britain', *Block*, XI (1985/6), pp. 53–69

Gervais, David, *Literary Englands* (Cambridge, 1993)

Gikandi, Simon, *Maps of Englishness: Writing Identity in the Culture of Colonialism* (New York, 1996)

Gilroy, Paul, *'There Ain't No Black in the Union Jack': The Cultural Politics of Race and Nation* (London, 1987)

—, *Small Acts* (London, 1993)

Golan, Remy, *Modernity and Nostalgia: Art and Politics in France Between the Wars* (London, 1995)

Gold, John, *The Experience of Modernism: Modern Architects and the Future City, 1928–1953* (London, 1997)

—, and Margaret Gold, *'Outrage* and Righteous Indignation: Ideology and Imagery of Suburbia', in *The Behavioural Environment*, eds F. W. Boal and D. Livingstone (London, 1989), pp. 163–81

—, and Stephen Ward, 'Of Plans and Planners: Documentary Film and the Challenge of the Urban Future, 1935–52', in *The Cinematic City*, ed. D. Clarke (London, 1997), pp. 59–82

Green, Martin, *Children of the Sun: A Narrative of 'Decadence' in England after 1918* (London, 1977)

—, *Mountain of Truth: The Counterculture Begins* (London, 1986)

Griffiths, Richard, *Fellow Travellers of the Right: British Enthusiasts for Nazi Germany, 1933–39* (Oxford, 1983)

Groning, G., and J. Wolschke-Bulmahn, 'Politics, Planning and the Abuse of Early Ecological Ideas in Germany, 1933–45', *Planning Perspectives*, II (1987), pp. 127–48

Gruffudd, Pyrs, 'Selling the Countryside: Representations of Rural Britain', in *Place Promotion*, eds J. Gold and S. Ward (Chichester, 1994), pp. 247–63

—, '"A Crusade against Consumption": Environment, Health and Social Reform in Wales, 1900–1939', *Journal of Historical Geography*, XXI (1995), pp. 39–54

Hall, Peter, *Cities of Tomorrow* (Oxford, 1988)

Hansen, Peter, 'The Dancing Lamas of Everest: Cinema, Orientalism and Anglo-Tibetan Relations in the 1920s', *American Historical Review*, CI (1996), pp. 712–47

Hardy, Denis, *From Garden Cities to New Towns* (London, 1991)

—, *From New Towns to Green Politics* (London, 1991)

—, and Colin Ward, *Arcadia for All* (London, 1984)

Harrisson, Tom, *Living Through the Blitz* (London, 1976)

Hennessy, Peter, *Never Again: Britain, 1945–1951* (London, 1992)

Herf, Jeffrey, *Reactionary Modernism: Technology, Culture and Politics in Weimar and the Third Reich* (Cambridge, 1984)

Hewison, Robert, *The Heritage Industry* (London, 1987)

—, *Culture and Consensus: England, Art and Politics since 1940* (London, 1995)

Hill, Howard, *Freedom to Roam* (Ashbourne, 1980)

Hirsch, Eric, and Michael O'Hanlon, *The Anthropology of Landscape* (Oxford, 1995)

Hitchens, Christopher, 'Something about the Poems: Larkin and "Sensitivity"', *New Left Review*, CC (1993), pp. 161–72

Hoskins, W. G., *The Making of the English Landscape* (London, 1955)

Howkins, Alun, 'The Discovery of Rural England', in *Englishness*, eds R. Colls and P. Dodd (London, 1986), pp. 62–88

Hurd, G., ed., *National Fictions: World War Two in British Films and Television* (London, 1984)

Jenks, Jorian, *The Stuff Man's Made Of: The Positive Approach to Health through Nutrition* (London, 1959)

Joad, Cyril, *A Charter for Ramblers* (London, 1934)

—, *The Untutored Townsman's Invasion of the Country* (London, 1946)

Jones, Greta, *Social Hygiene in Twentieth Century Britain* (London, 1986)

Keith, W., *The Rural Tradition* (Brighton, 1975)

King, Anthony, *The Bungalow* (London, 1984)

Kirkham, Pat, *Harry Peach, Dryad and the DIA* (London, 1986)

Latour, Bruno, *We Have Never Been Modern* (London, 1993)

Lewis, Jane, and Barbara Brookes, 'A Reassessment of the Work of the Peckham Health Centre, 1926–1951', *Millbank Memorial Fund Quarterly*, LXI (1983), pp. 307–50

Light, Alison, *Forever England: Femininity, Literature and Conservatism Between the Wars* (London, 1991)

Linehan, Denis, 'Commercial Geographies: A Cultural Geography of Industrial Landscapes in Interwar Britain', PhD thesis, University of Nottingham, 1997

Lowerson, John, 'Battles for the Countryside', in *Class, Culture and Social Change*, ed. Frank Gloversmith (Brighton, 1980), pp. 258–80

—, 'The Mystical Geography of the English', in *The English Rural Community*, ed. Brian Short (Cambridge, 1992), pp. 152–74

Luckin, Bill, *Questions of Power: Electricity and Environment in Inter-war Britain* (Manchester, 1990)

Lymington, Viscount, *Famine in England* (London, 1938)

MacInnes, Colin, 'The Englishness of Dr Pevsner', in *England, Half English* (London, 1961), pp. 119–29

Mandler, Peter, '"Against 'Englishness'": English Culture and the Limits to Rural Nostalgia, 1850–1940', *Transactions of the Royal Historical Society*, XII (1997), pp. 155–75

—, *The Fall and Rise of the Stately Home* (London, 1997)

Marren, Peter, *The New Naturalists* (London, 1995)

Marsh, Jan, *Back to the Land: The Pastoral Impulse in Victorian England from 1880 to 1914* (London, 1982)

Massingham, H. J., *Downland Man* (London, 1926)

—, *Remembrance: An Autobiography* (London, 1941)

—, ed., *England and the Farmer* (London, 1941)

—, ed., *The Natural Order* (London, 1945)

Matless, David, 'Ages of English Design: Preservation, Modernism and Tales of Their History, 1926–39', *Journal of Design History*, III (1990) pp. 203–12

—, 'Definitions of England', *Built Environment*, XVI (1990), pp. 179–91

—, 'Nature, the Modern and the Mystic: Tales from Early Twentieth Century Geography', *Transactions of the Institute of British Geographers*, XVI (1991), pp. 272–86

—, 'An Occasion for Geography: Landscape, Representation and Foucault's Corpus', *Environment and Planning D: Society and Space*, X (1992), pp. 41–56

—, 'Regional Surveys and Local Knowledges: The Geographical Imagination in Britain, 1918–39', *Transactions of the Institute of British Geographers*, XVII (1992), pp. 464–80

—, 'Appropriate Geography: Patrick Abercrombie and the Energy of the World', *Journal of Design History*, VI (1993), pp. 167–78

—, 'One Man's England: W. G. Hoskins and the English Culture of Landscape', *Rural History*, IV (1993), pp. 187–207

—, 'Doing the English Village, 1945–90', in P. Cloke *et al.*, *Writing the Rural* (London, 1994), pp. 7–88

—, 'Moral Geography in Broadland', *Ecumene*, I (1994), pp. 127–56

—, '"The Art of Right Living": Landscape and Citizenship 1918–39', in *Mapping the Subject*, eds S. Pile and N. Thrift (London, 1995), pp. 93–122

—, 'Visual Culture and Geographical Citizenship: England in the 1940s', *Journal of Historical Geography*, XXII (1996), pp. 424–39

—, 'The Geographical Self, the Nature of the Social, and Geoaesthetics', *Progress in Human Geography*, XXI (1997), pp. 393–405

—, 'Moral Geographies of English Landscape', *Landscape Research*, XXII (1997), pp. 141–56

—, and George Revill, 'A Solo Ecology: The Erratic Art of Andy Goldsworthy', *Ecumene*, II (1995), pp. 423–48

Matthews, Jill Julius, '"They Had Such a Lot of Fun": The Women's League of Health and Beauty between the Wars', *History Workshop Journal*, XXX (1990), pp. 22–54

McAllister, Gilbert, and Elizabeth McAllister, eds, *Homes, Towns and Countryside* (London, 1945)

McKay, George, *Senseless Acts of Beauty: Cultures of Resistance Since the Sixties* (London, 1996)

Mellor, David, ed., *A Paradise Lost: The Neo-Romantic Imagination in Britain, 1935–55* (London, 1987)

—, Gill Saunders, and Patrick Wright, *Recording Britain* (London, 1990)

Merricks, Linda, *The World Made New: Frederick Soddy, Science, Politics and Environment* (Oxford, 1996)

Mitchell, Don, *The Lie of the Land: Migrant Workers and the California Landscape* (Minneapolis, 1997)

Mitchell, W.J.T., ed., *Landscape and Power* (Chicago, 1994)

Morden, Terry, 'The Pastoral and the Pictorial', *Ten: 8*, XII (1983), pp. 18–25

Morton, H. V., *In Search of England* (London, 1927)

Nash, Catherine, 'Reclaiming Vision: Looking at Landscape and the Body', *Gender, Place and Culture*, III (1996), pp. 149–69

Naylor, Gillian, 'Design and Industry', in *Early 20th Century Britain*, ed. Boris Ford (Cambridge, 1992), pp. 254–93

Northbourne, Lord, *Look to the Land* (London, 1940)

Oliver, Paul, Ian Davis, and Ian Bentley, *Dunroamin: The Suburban Semi and Its Enemies* (London, 1981)

Orlans, Harold, *Stevenage: A Sociological Study of a New Town* (London, 1952)

Orwell, George, *The Lion and the Unicorn: Socialism and the English Genius* (London, 1941)

—, *The English People* (London, 1947)

Peach, Harry, and Noel Carrington, *The Face of the Land* (London, 1930)

Pearse, Innes, and Lucy Crocker, *The Peckham Experiment* (London, 1943)

Pepper, David, *Eco-Socialism: From Deep Ecology to Social Justice* (London, 1993)

Pevsner, Nikolaus, *The Englishness of English Art* (London, 1955)

—, *Studies in Art, Architecture and Design Volume Two: Victorian and After* (London, 1968)

Picton, Lionel, *Thoughts on Feeding* (London, 1946)

Plowden, William, *The Motor Car and Politics, 1896–1970* (London, 1971)

Portsmouth, Earl of, *Alternative to Death* (London, 1943)

Potts, Alex, 'Constable Country between the Wars', in *Patriotism*, vol. I, ed. R. Samuel (London, 1989), pp. 160–86

Priestley, J. B., *English Journey* (London, 1934)

Rée, Harry, *Educator Extraordinary: The Life and Achievement of Henry Morris, 1889–1961* (London, 1973)

Revill, George, and Charles Watkins, 'Educated Access: Interpreting Forestry Commission Park Guides', in *Rights of Way*, ed. C. Watkins (London, 1996), pp. 100–28

Richards, J., and A. Aldgate, *Best of British: Cinema and Society, 1930–1970* (Oxford, 1983)

Riley, Denise, '"The Free Mothers": Pronatalism and Working Women in Industry at the End of the Last War in Britain', *History Workshop Journal*, XI (1981), pp. 58–118

Robbins, D., 'Sport, Hegemony and the Middle Classes: The Victorian Mountaineers', *Theory, Culture and Society*, IV (1987), pp. 579–601

Roberts, Marion, *Living in a Man-Made World: Gender Assumptions in Modern Housing Design* (London, 1991)

Rollins, W. H., 'Whose Landscape? Technology, Fascism and Environmentalism on the National Socialist Autobahn', *Annals of the Association of American Geographers*, LXXXV (1995), pp. 494–520

Rolt, L.T.C., *Narrow Boat* (London, 1944)

Rose, Nikolas, *Governing the Soul: The Shaping of the Private Self* (London, 1990)

—, 'Identity, Genealogy, History', in *Questions of Cultural Identity*, eds Stuart Hall and Paul Du Gay (London, 1996), pp. 128–50

Rosenthal, Michael, *The Character Factory: Baden-Powell and the Origins of the Boy Scout Movement* (London, 1986)

Ryan, Deborah, *The Ideal Home Through the 20th Century* (London, 1997)

Ryan, James, *Picturing Empire* (London, 1997)

Rycroft, Simon, and Denis Cosgrove, 'Mapping the Modern Nation: Dudley Stamp and the Land Utilisation Survey', *History Workshop Journal*, XL (1995), pp. 91–105

Saint, Andrew, *Towards a Social Architecture: The Role of School-building in Post-war England* (New Haven, 1987)

Samuel, Raphael, *Theatres of Memory* (London, 1994)

—, ed., *Patriotism*, 3 vols (London, 1989)

Schama, Simon, *Landscape and Memory* (London, 1995)

Schwarz, Bill, 'The Language of Constitutionalism: Baldwinite Conservatism', in *Formations of Nation and People* (London, 1984), pp. 1–18

Seago, Alex, *Burning the Box of Beautiful Things* (Oxford, 1995)

Searle, G. R., 'Eugenics and Politics in Britain in the 1930s', *Annals of Science*, XXXVI (1979), pp. 159–69

Shand, J. D., 'The Reichsautobahn: Symbol for the Third Reich', *Journal of Contemporary History*, XIX (1984), pp. 189–200

Sharp, Thomas, *Town and Countryside* (London, 1932)

—, *Town Planning* (Harmondsworth, 1940)

—, *The Anatomy of the Village* (Harmondsworth, 1946)

Sheail, John, *Nature in Trust: The History of Nature Conservation in Britain* (London, 1976)

—, *Rural Conservation in Interwar Britain* (Oxford, 1981)

—, *Pesticides and Nature Conservation: The British Experience, 1950–1975* (Oxford, 1985)

—, *Seventy Five Years in Ecology: The British Ecological Society* (Oxford, 1987)

—, 'John Dower, National Parks and Town and Country Planning in Britain', *Planning Perspectives*, X (1995), pp. 1–16

Shortland, M., ed., *Science and Nature: Essays in the History of the Environmental Sciences* (Oxford, 1993)

Smith, H. L., ed., *War and Social Change: British Society in the Second World War* (Manchester, 1986)

Stallybrass, P., and A. White, *The Politics and Poetics of Transgression* (London, 1986)

Stapledon, R. G., *The Land: Now and To-Morrow* (London, 1935)

Stephenson, Tom, ed., *The Countryside Companion* (London, 1939)

—, *Forbidden Land* (Manchester, 1989)

Summerfield, Penny, *Women Workers in the Second World War* (London, 1984)

Tansley, Arthur, *Our Heritage of Wild Nature* (Cambridge, 1945)

Taylor, Harvey, *A Claim on the Countryside: A History of the British Outdoor Movement* (Keele, 1997)

Taylor, John, *A Dream of England: Landscape, Photography and the Tourist's Imagination* (Manchester, 1995)

Taylor, Peter, 'The English and Their Englishness', *Scottish Geographical Magazine*, CVII (1991), pp. 146–61

Titmuss, Richard, *Problems of Social Policy* (London, 1950)

Trentmann, Frank, 'Civilization and Its Discontents: English Neo-romanticism and the Transformation of Anti-modernism in Twentieth-century Western Culture', *Journal of Contemporary History*, XXIX (1994), pp. 583–625

Veldman, Meredith, *Fantasy, the Bomb and the Greening of Britain: Romantic Protest, 1945–1980* (Cambridge, 1994)

Wallace, Anne, *Walking, Literature and English Culture* (Oxford, 1993)

Waller, Robert, *Prophet of the New Age: The Life and Thought of Sir George Stapledon* (London, 1962)

Ward, Colin, and Denis Hardy, *Goodnight Campers! The History of the British Holiday Camp* (London, 1986)

Ward, Sadie, *War in the Countryside, 1939–45* (Newton Abbot, 1988)

Ward, Stephen, *Planning and Urban Change* (London, 1994)

Warren, A., 'Popular Manliness: Baden-Powell, Scouting and the Development of Manly Character', in *Manliness and Morality*, eds J. A. Mangan and J. Walvin (Manchester, 1987), pp. 199–219

Watkins, Alfred, *The Old Straight Track* (London, 1925)

Weight, Richard, 'Pale Stood Albion: The Promotion of National Culture in Britain 1939–56', PhD thesis, University of London, 1995

Whiteley, Nigel, 'Modern Architecture, Heritage and Englishness', *Architectural History*, XXXVIII (1995), pp. 220–37

Wiener, Martin, *English Culture and the Decline of the Industrial Spirit, 1850–1980* (Cambridge, 1981)

Williams-Ellis, Clough, *England and the Octopus* (London, 1928)

—, ed., *Britain and the Beast* (London, 1937)

Williamson, Tom, and Liz Bellamy, *Ley Lines in Question* (Kingswood, 1983)

Wright, Patrick, *On Living in an Old Country* (London, 1985)

—, *A Journey Through Ruins* (London, 1991)

—, *The Village that Died for England: The Strange Story of Tyneham* (London, 1995)

—, and Tim Putnam, 'Sneering at the Theme Parks', *Block*, XV (1989), pp. 45–55

ACKNOWLEDGEMENTS
FOR THE 1998 EDITION

Many have contributed to this book, although some may not have realized it at the time, and may now regret having done so. Academic colleagues in Nottingham, and previously in Oxford, Hull and Bristol, have helped to shape the ideas presented here. Stephen Daniels has provided insight and inspiration over a number of years. Charles Watkins has helped to explore byways of twentieth-century history and local landscape. George Revill has consistently been a source of intellectual curiosity. Denis Linehan, Pyrs Gruffudd, Peter Bishop, Denis Cosgrove, David Crouch, Nigel Thrift, Marcus Doel, David Harvey, John Cole, Felix Driver, David Sibley and Andrew Leyshon have contributed in important ways. I also thank colleagues in the Social and Cultural Geography Research Group of the Institute of British Geographers, which has played a significant role in reshaping cultural geography over recent years, always in a spirit of generous discussion and support. Doctoral students in Nottingham and Oxford, Master's students on Nottingham's 'Landscape and Culture' course and undergraduates on the course which shares this book's title, if not all its contents, have also made important contributions as I chewed over ideas. Staff in the Hallward Library at the University of Nottingham and at the CPRE Archive in Reading were always helpful. The editors and referees of the *Journal of Historical Geography*, *Transactions of the Institute of British Geographers*, *Journal of Design History*, *Built Environment*, *Ecumene*, *Rural History* and *Mapping the Subject* have made valuable comments on earlier versions of some of the material included here.

The book is not only a product of academic sites, however. Second-hand bookshops have offered space for exploration between work and non-work. Likewise, general wanderings by car, bike or foot have prompted things; a number of friends have shared/ suffered such trips, and I hope some will have pleasant memories of them. The initial credit for an interest in these matters must, however, go to my parents, Brian and Audrey Matless, who have given continual support and love throughout, and whom I can't thank enough.

ACKNOWLEDGEMENTS FOR THE 2016 EDITION

Since the first edition of this book, colleagues in the School of Geography at the University of Nottingham have continued to provide valuable support, notably those in the Cultural and Historical Geography research group. The response of undergraduate, masters and doctoral students to the material in the book has indicated the ways in which debates over landscape and Englishness might continue to evolve. David Gilbert and Brian Short were genial co-editors for a 2003 collection on the *Geographies of British Modernity*, whose introduction and afterword developed themes from the first edition. The preface for the 2016 edition notes others whose work has shaped lines of thought.

The new edition has also been informed by the comment, insight and love of my wife Jo and our son Edwyn; aspects of the new preface echo our common experience.

PHOTOGRAPHIC ACKNOWLEDGEMENTS

The author and publishers wish to express their thanks to the following authors or sources of illustrative material and/or permission to reproduce it. Every effort has been made to trace copyright holders, but the publishers would be interested in hearing from anyone not here acknowledged.

Colin Allan: 60; *Architectural Review*: 8; the author: 1–3; Barnaby's Picture Library: 31; B. T. Batsford Ltd: 35, 36, 38, 58, 59, 75; 'Batt' (Oswald Barrett): 57; Stuart Black: 8; Bodleian Library (Conservative Party Archives): 52; M. de Bunsen: 34; Brian Clayton: 36 (top photo); CPRE Archive, Rural History Centre, University of Reading: 5; J. M. Dent: 22, 57; Department of English Local History, University of Leicester/F. L. Attenborough: 80; Roy Foyster: 77–9; Eyre & Spottiswoode/D. J. Watkins-Pitchford ('BB'): 41; George Greenwell: 48; Thomas Hennell: 38; Eric Hosking Trust: 61, 62; G. E. Hutchings: 74; the Trustees of Barbara Jones' estate: 64; Dorien Leigh: 45 (top photo); Conroy Maddox: 73; Methuen & Co.: 74; Peters, Fraser & Dunlop Group Ltd: 9; Royal Society for the Encouragement of Arts, Manufactures & Commerce: 43, 44; Peter Shepheard: 72; R. Tilbrook: 59; E. Warne-Browne: 75; and Alfred Watkins: 23.

INDEX

Illustration numbers are in *italic*